Polish-Jewish Relations 1939-1945

BEYOND THE LIMITS OF SOLIDARITY

Polish-Jewish Relations 1939-1945

BEYOND THE LIMITS OF SOLIDARITY

EWA KUREK

iUniverse, Inc.
Bloomington

Polish-Jewish Relations 1939-1945
Beyond the limits of solidarity

First published in Poland in 2006 by:
Wydawnictwo
Wyższej Szkoły Umiejętności - Kielce

Second publishing in Poland in 2008 by:
Wydawnictwo CLIO - Lublin

Cover design: Karolina Matjunin

Translated by:
Katarzyna Bednarska
David Dastych

iUniverse books may be ordered through booksellers or by contacting:

iUniverse
1663 Liberty Drive
Bloomington, IN 47403
www.iuniverse.com
1-800-Authors (1-800-288-4677)

ISBN: 978-1-4759-3831-9 (sc)
ISBN: 978-1-4759-3832-6 (e)

Library of Congress Control Number: 2012912874

Printed in the United States of America

iUniverse rev. date: 05/01/2013

There exists a solidarity among men
as human beings that makes each co-responsible
for every wrong and every injustice
in the world

Karl Jaspers

Acknowledgements

This book could not have been written without
the help of
SOCIETE HISTORIQUE et LITTERAIRE in Paris
THE BARBARA PIASECKA-JOHNSON
FOUNDATION
Grants by these Institutions enabled
me to conduct research on Polish-Jewish
relations during WW II

With special thanks for their generous contribution to the
translation of this book to the Polish Army Veterans
Association of America District No. 2, Inc. New York City, N. Y.
Commander Antoni Chroscielewski

My thanks also to
Bozenna Urbanowicz Gilbride
for raising the funds and assistance
in seeing this book come to fruition.

Ewa Kurek

CONTENTS

PREFACE

By the Author

For more than twenty years, with short breaks, I have been doing research on Polish-Jewish relations, trying to resolve the puzzles of the reality of the Second World War and the Holocaust in Poland. It's not an easy task. As time goes by I discover, every now and again, new aspects of the problem and new realms of Polish-Jewish terra incognita, and the endeavor becomes ever more difficult.

Research on Polish-Jewish relations in post-war Poland was difficult because political conditions in a communist-ruled state were not favorable for normal development of this type of historiography. For the most of the forty four years of the communist government in Poland neither Jews nor Poles were free to conduct historical research or even to contact each other. Szewach Weiss, Israeli ambassador to Poland, said: *We have lost almost two generations of our dialogue. In the 1970s, if anybody wanted to come over here [to Poland], just to visit a graveyard where his family members lay, he had no such possibility. And here [in Poland] remained our friends and family members, living and dead.*[1] For the reason that Polish communist government attempted to efface the fact that Jews once lived in Poland, my first article about

---

[1] See: *Burzył mury milczenia* [*He destroyed the walls of silence*], Szewach Weiss, Israeli ambassador to Poland, in an interview with Dorota Kosierkiewicz, in: 'Echo dnia', December 22, 2003.

Jewish children saved in Polish priories was published by underground press.[2]

A separate question is a problem of myths and distortions, sometimes purposeful manipulations of the truth, charging the Poles with responsibility for the Holocaust, originating not so much from the side of the Germans, what could be even somehow justifiable, but from Jewish sources. About one of the reason of manipulation of the truth by the Jews, Marek Edelman said: *When at the beginning of the 1950s, Antek [Cukierman] went to the United States for the first time to collect funds for a Memory Museum he wanted to build in a kibbutz, he attacked American Jews for not having sent money to Poland during the war, for not putting pressure on President Roosevelt to act against the mass-murder of Jews in Europe. They got angry with him and said they wouldn't give a dime. And Antek understood – continued Edelman – he shouldn't have said what was on his mind. At the next meeting he didn't shout [...] but perhaps it should be like that: if one wants money from someone, better not provoke him?*[3]

Among other reasons, the problem of Polish-Jewish relations during the Second World War is a subject where particular facts are not unequivocally assessed and defined, provoking many disputes and emotionally engaging both Poles and Jews. It's a subject wherein every Jew and every Pole seems to become an expert. For these reasons, some results of my research probably will arouse the indignation of a Jewish reader, and other results will outrage a Polish reader. Some Jews probably will accuse me of anti-Semitism, and some Poles will say I slander my own nation. I just can't help it. It's always been so.

Over forty years ago, Hannah Arendt wrote to one of her opponents "...very often people who are just relating some unpleasant facts are being accused of lack of spirit or of lack of that thing you call *Herzenstakt*. In

2 E. Kurek, *Udział Żeńskich Zgromadzeń zakonnych w akcji ratowania dzieci żydowskich w Polsce 1939-1945* [*Polish Convents and their contribution to the saving of Jewish children in Poland 1939-1945*], in: Spotkania, 29, 1985; see also: *Your Life is Worth Mine: How Polish Nuns Saved Hundreds of Jewish Children in German-Occupied Poland, 1939-1945* by Ewa Kurek, Hippocrene Books, N.Y. 1997.
3 J. Szczęsna, *Ostatni Mohikanie i nowy naród* (*The last of the Mohikans and the new nation*), in: 'Gazeta Wyborcza' June 28-29, 2002

other words, [...] these emotions are being often used to hide the real truth."[4]

In my book I, too, *only relate some unpleasant facts,* in order to discover *the real truth.* Facts always will remain facts. Once they come into being, facts are not to be changed. Therefore, as one can't change them, Poles and Jews should strive to finally reconstruct these facts and to explain them, also to familiarize themselves with them and to accept their existence for the sake of almost a thousand years of Polish and Jewish cohabitation on Poland's soil. Even if the two nations had no perspective of a common future, the *real truth* should become the foundation of common Polish-Jewish reconciliation and of mutual support. Ambassador Szewach Weiss once said: *...we lived in peace side by side for 900 years. I say side by side, because our Polish-Jewish life ran on separate tracks. You were following your course, and we were following our own. We were not thwarting your designs and we lived more or less peacefully for centuries. Poles never built ghettos for Jews. In Poland only Germans built them. And they also built the concentration camps, where they murdered Poles and Jews.*[5]

Because the Polish-Jewish past, marked by living side by side, preconditioned the behaviour and the mutual relationships of the two

---

[4] H. Arendt, *Eichmann w Jerozolimie,* Kraków1987, p. 394. [see also: *Eichmann In Jerusalem: A Report on the Banality of Evil,* New York 1963.]

[5] The world's historiography was inconceivably distorting the truth. The German-built death camps and concentration camps on Polish territory were often called "Polish camps"; and in a multitude of publications on Polish anti-Semitism and in accusations of Polish complicity in the murder of the Polish Jews on Poland's soil the truth was slowly lost. However, it was not true that the Poles had begun the Second World War, and that the Poles as a nation murdered their Jewish fellow citizens. The real perpetrators were the occupiers of Poland, the Germans. Władysław Bartoszewski told the TVN Fakty news, on September 16, 2003: *Soon it will become evident that the only victims of the war were Germans and Jews.* The truth about the annihilation of the European Jews by the Germans, not by the Poles, about the fact that a popular slogan *Polish death camps,* repeated almost everywhere in the West, was a horrible historical lie, that truth was to be revealed to the world – after many diplomatic and political efforts – only in January 2005 on the 60th anniversary of the liberation of Auschwitz by a Resolution of the European Parliament, where one can read about Auschwitz, as *death camp Auschwitz-Birkenau, created by Nazi Germany.* [See: European Parliament Resolution on Remembrance of the Holocaust, anti-Semitism and racism," January 27, 2005.]

nations during the Second World War, I dedicate the two initial chapters of my book to the problem of cohabitation, trying to find answers to the many questions pertaining to living conditions and mutual relations between Poles and Jews in the time before the Holocaust. The next chapters are dedicated to the most *unpleasant facts* of Polish-Jewish relations during the Second World War. For the last sixty years, since the end of WW II, these facts have been burdened with most of the controversy arising between Poles and Jews. Therefore, these chapters deal with the attitudes of Poles and Jews toward the mass murder of Jews, the Holocaust, carried out by the Germans in the years 1942-1945. To use more precise language, the particularly *unpleasant fact* for both nations is the participation of Poles and Jews in the execution of the "Final Solution of the Jewish Question" (*Endlösung der Judenfrage)*, the participation of some members of both nations in the crime of the annihilation of the Jews by the Germans. The scope of this participation, though not yet finally recognized and known, may be more or less precisely defined from the existing and credible historical sources. It may yet be cleared up who among the Poles and the Jews, collaborated with the Germans and why, and what were the political, religious and national reasons for this collaboration.

There is also a problem of judgment. In Polish historiography and tradition any collaboration with occupiers, no matter who -- German, Soviet, Swedish, Russian or Austrian has always been called treason, and is still regarded as such. Any collaboration of Poles with the Germans during the Second World War has been treated as treason, including any cases of the participation of Poles in the annihilation of Polish Jews. In the Jewish tradition and historiography we can find certain relativism, because Jewish opinions on the collaboration of Jews with Germans, also their participation in the mass murder of their own nation, are not unequivocal. Hannah Arendt, who was the first to turn attention to the problem of the collaboration of Jews in the Holocaust, wrote: "...The problem I had chosen to examine was the collaboration of Jewish officials and functionaries with the executors of the "Final Solution", and this matter was so awkward because one could not say that they were traitors. (There were some traitors, too, but this was insignificant)."[6]

This opinion suggested by Hannah Arendt has not been fully explained to this day. So far, nobody has answered the question why *a collaboration of Jewish functionaries with the executors of the "Final Solution"* couldn't be defined as treason, while other forms of Jewish collaboration with the Germans had been called such. Nobody has answered still another question, why, in view of Jewish relativism in the judging of Jews collaborating with Germans, this relativism was not applied equally to the Poles. Without proper understanding of the reasons for relativism in the judgment of the complicity of Jews in the German-executed mass murder of the Polish Jews, and the reasons for the lack of relativist judgments in the complicity of Poles, there is no way to explain and understand Polish-Jewish relations in that period. I focus attention on these particular problems in the last part of my research, presented in this book.

The unequivocal Polish judgments and the relativist Jewish judgments can not change the fact that both the Poles and the Jews collaborating with the Germans in the annihilation of the Jewish nation share personal guilt for causing death of a certain part of the murdered Jewish nation. These judgments don't change the fact that the witnesses of the genocide, which is always a crime against the very essence of the human being, survived the experience of the mass murder deeply wounded at heart. To this day, all surviving Jews who witnessed the annihilation of their own nation remain injured. And surviving Poles, who witnessed the mass murder, remain injured same as the Jews. Nothing can change the fact that the Jewish nation had been murdered before the very eyes of the Poles and that the great majority of the European Jewry had been killed on Polish soil so our fatherland became the mass grave of the Jews.

Soon after the end of the Second World War, Karl Jaspers (1883-

---

6 H. Arendt, *Eichmann w Jerozolimie*, Kraków1987, p. 394. [see also: *Eichmann In Jerusalem: A Report on the Banality of Evil*, New York 1963.]

1969)[7], one of the greatest German philosophers, and one of the very few who could not be accused of collaboration with Hitler's regime, attempted to typologize the notion of guilt.

Based on the premise that *understanding and clarifying the problem of guilt is the vocation of philosophy and theology*, Karl Jaspers singled out four types of guilt:

Criminal guilt: These are "acts capable of objective proof and violate unequivocal laws." Only individuals, not groups, can be criminally guilty (although in some circumstances it can also be a crime to belong to a criminal organization). Charges of criminal guilt come from outside of the accused and guilt is judged by a court of law.

Political guilt: This is guilt that citizens bear for the deeds of statesmen and citizens, and means that all citizens face the consequences for the deeds

---

7 About Karl Jaspers: Born in Oldenburg, Germany on February 23, 1883, died in Basel, Switzerland on February 26, 1969, a German philosopher and psychologist; studied medicine, worked in a psychiatric clinic ; 1916-1948 Professor of the Heidelberg University, Germany, first Professor of Psychology, from 1921 Professor of Philosophy; 1933-1945 deprived of his right to teach, and from 1938 of the right to publish; 1948-1961 Professor of the University in Basel, Switzerland [...] In philosophy he was one of the main representatives of existentialism, exploring specially threats to the authenticity of the human existence in the contemporary civilization and possibilities to counter them by becoming conscious of the human freedom; Jaspers explored the being in extreme situations of the human existence; such exploration always reaches to the limits of cognition, which is the *Encompassing* (in German: *Umgreifende)* – in ourselves or beyond, as the world and the transcendental; the reason (in opposition to the contemplating intellect) turns towards the transcendental; reading the symbols of the transcendental (in German: *Chiffeschrift*) is the quintessence of Jasper's philosophy (Philosophie, vol. 1-3 1932, Von der Wahrheit 1947); Jaspers is also the author of several historical-philosophical studies (among other: Grossen Philosophen 1957). He also has published political and social dissertations, among other Situation der Zeit (1913), Die Schuldfrage (1946, Polish edition, Problem winy, 1982), Wohin treibt die Bundesrepublik? (1966); autobiographical works Schicksal und Wille (1967), Philosophical Autobiography (1963, Polish edition Autobiografia filozoficzna, 1993).Other publications: Philosophy of Existence (in German 1938, Filozofia egzystencji, in Polish 1990), Reason and Existenz. Nietsche and Christianity (1960, Polish edition Rozum i egzystencja. Nietsche a chrześcijaństwo, 1991), Philosophical Faith and revelation (1962, Polish edition, Wiara filozoficzna wobec objawienia, 1999), Ciphers of Transcendence (1970, Polish edition, Szyfry transcendencji, 1995). Authorities: Sokrates,Confucius,Jesus: From the Great Philosophers (1966, Polish edition, Sokrates, Budda, Konfucjusz, Jezus, 2000). The Karl Jaspers' biographical note from: Encyklopedia Gazety Wyborczej,Warszawa 2005, volume VII, pages 347-348.

of their nation. Political guilt falls on people who oppose the régime in power as well as those who support it. Charges of political guilt come from outside of the accused, and guilt is successfully judged by the victorious party in a war or capitulation, at any rate as a function of political power, although even these charges, may be "mitigated' by appeal to "natural and international law";

Moral guilt: "I, who cannot act otherwise than as an individual, am morally responsible for all my deeds, including the execution of political and military orders (...) The principle "an order is an order" is never valid. As a crime always remains a crime, even if committed by order, every crime is subject to moral punishment. The court is my own conscience and my bonds to friends and fellow creatures, companions, who care about my soul;

Metaphysical guilt: There exists a solidarity among men as human beings that makes each co-responsible for every wrong and every injustice in the world, especially for crimes committed in his presence or with his knowledge. If I fail to do whatever I can to prevent them, I too am guilty. If I was present at the murder of others without risking my life to prevent it, I feel guilty in a way not adequately conceivable either legally, politically or morally. That I live after such a thing had happened weighs upon me as indelible guilt. As human beings, unless good fortune spares us such situations, we come to a point where we must choose: either to risk our lives unconditionally, without chance of success and therefore to no purpose – or to prefer staying alive, because success is impossible. That somewhere among men the unconditioned prevails – the capacity to live only together or not at all, if crimes are committed against the one or the other, or if physical living requirements have to be shared – therein consists the substance of their being. But that this does not extend to the solidarity of all men, or to that of fellow citizens or even smaller groups, but remains confined to the closest human ties – therein lays this guilt in all of us. Jurisdiction rests with God alone.

Karl Jasper's typology of guilt is important not only as a philosophical concept but also as a source of information about a definite epoch and a definite generation. This concept, formulated in the atmosphere of the beginning of the Nuremberg Trial, is at the same time one of the first attempts by Germans to account for the destruction of Europe caused by their nation. Karl Jaspers stated: *The war was unleashed by Hitler Germany.*

Every German is made to share the blame for the crimes committed in the name of the Reich, which chose to begin that war. We are collectively liable. Not every German, but only a very small minority of Germans should be punished for the crime. Probably every German has a reason for moral self-examination. Probably each thinking German participated in that metaphysical experience.[8]

Karl Jaspers thinking became an inspiration for the title and principal thesis of my book. Coming across in reliable historical sources the particularly *unpleasant fact* of Poles and Jews cooperating with the perpetrators of the "Final Solution", i.e., the problem of collaboration of certain groups of both nations in the German-inflicted genocide of the Jewish nation, I have decided – by rejecting both Jewish relativism and Polish unequivocal judgment – to subject Poles and Jews to precisely the same judgment that Karl Jaspers applied to Germans after the Second World War. That is, to answer the question, what guilt burdens Poles responsible for helping the Germans in the mass murder of Jews, and what guilt burdens Jews helping the Germans. In this way only, by unequivocal assessment of *unpleasant facts*, and by measuring equally the guilt of each nation, can we reach the truth and understand the drama of those Poles and Jews, who have been exposed, by the indifference of the world and the barbarity of Hitler empowered by the Germans, to the dilemmas of their life, perhaps the most difficult in the history of the human race.

About twenty years ago, the Polish literary critic and essayist Jan Błoński said: *Instead of haggling and exculpating, we should first think of ourselves, of our sins or weakness.*[9] And Hannah Arendt, attacked by Jewish circles for writing her book *Eichmann in Jerusalem*, in which she unveiled some truths about the behavior of Jews toward the annihilation of their own nation, responded to one of her critics: *Evil caused by my own nation saddens me more than the evil caused by other nations.*[10]

Evil caused by my own nation saddens me more than the evil caused by other nations. I also don't try to haggle and to exculpate the crimes

---

[8] K. Jaspers, „Problem winy", Warszawa 1982; [see also: Karl Jaspers, „The Question of German Guilt" (paperback), Fordham University Press; 2Rev Ed edition, January, 2001].

[9] J. Błoński, *Biedni Polacy patrzą na getto* [„Poor Poles Look at Ghetto"], Kraków, 1994, p. 21.

[10] H. Arendt, op. cit. p. 393-394.

perpetrated by the Poles. In the first place, I think about Polish sins and weaknesses – quoting Hannah Arendt and Jan Błoński. But I don't hesitate to treat the Jews with the same severity as I treat my own nation, and I don't hesitate to call a spade a spade.

Jewish evil cannot be hidden; only by comparing Polish evil to Jewish evil can we really learn about the Polish-Jewish reality. It's high time to unveil these facts, more or less unpleasant for both Poles and Jews. Only then can these facts become a basis for honest historical discussion about their assessment and interpretation.

Some of the theses presented in my book probably also will not withstand the test of time. But I avoided formulating them as unshakable truths about Polish-Jewish relations during the last world war. I am breaking a wall of silence, surrounding subjects inconvenient for both Poles and Jews, hoping that my work will initiate open discussion and cooperation in historical research on these aspects of our common history, that until this day have remained unclear or about which we, Jews and Poles, had no prior idea. There is no other way to the truth. After dozens of years of disputes about the Holocaust, after torrents of mutual accusations, only the truth, even the most painful truth, can cause our nations to find a way to final reconciliation.

The basic sources for my research are predominantly Jewish. For one reason, when examining only Polish sources I was unable to achieve final clarity of the subjects examined. I had a continuous feeling that touching such fragments of the Polish-Jewish reality of the last war, as had not been covered by Polish sources, I would never be able to fully understand them and to classify them; I understood that if I ever wanted to find answers to the questions rankling my heart, I should seek instruction in the works of Jewish authors; that it was necessary to look for Jewish light; only it could reveal clear details of matters concealed from non-Jewish eyes. Only Jewish authors could shed light on the matter and facilitate my understanding. That's why I based my research for this book, sources and literature alike, almost exclusively on the works of Jewish authors.

My reading of Jewish authors -- historians and authors of memoirs, chronicles and personal accounts -- suggested to me that the first error in researching Polish-Jewish relations during the Second World War is to treat Polish Jews as a typical nation, to apply to them the same historical standards as to other European nations, or to perceive them as one of the many ethnic minorities living on Polish soil.

Comparing Polish Jews and the magnitude of their tragedy to the tragedies of other nations in the Second World War, using for this purpose historical and national stereotypes, universal for this part of Europe, one cannot grasp anything. Jews as a nation don't fit any European pattern. They are subject to some different rules, and for that reason the key to understanding them is to be found elsewhere. The history textbooks of European nations, save for ancient Greece and Rome, reach back only to the first millennium of our era, when from a tribal nebula emerged, during several centuries, particular tribes – the protoplasts of the future nations. The textbooks of Jewish history reach back to thousands of years before Christ. From this history comes a basic truth, which the Poles – and not only they in Europe – never remembered or did not want to remember. The truth about a fully developed nation, with its own language and culture, own religion and tradition, its own patriotic feelings and understanding of political matters, which came to settle on the Polish lands about a thousand years ago. The nation, which – as opposed to other national minorities or to other tribes in ancient times – never had submitted, because it could not, to normal assimilation processes, typical for other national minorities; the nation, which for the reasons mentioned above could not meet local expectations for fear of loosing its identity. It could only enrich its own tradition, or, as others define this process, it could create a separate culture of the Polish Jews, in the framework of the Jewry.

In order to understand the circumstances and conditions of the annihilation of the Polish Jews in the first half of the twentieth century, and also to grasp the pattern of the Polish-Jewish relations in that period, one has to understand that in the early Middle Ages (about one thousand years ago), the one when the Polish state was being formed, and the criteria of the Polish nation, patriotism and culture, were worked out several centuries later, on our territory a fully developed Jewish nation settled, whose culture, social structures and intellectual development were much higher than those of the host nation. This distant moment of history, generally not perceived by Polish historians and not exposed sufficiently by Jewish historians, was of utmost significance for the co-habitation of the Poles and Jews on the Polish land, and also outweighed all the other considerations of the Holocaust of the Polish Jews.

Only when I understood the national, religious and cultural exceptionality of Polish Jews, could I begin to reread and rediscover the substance of basic Jewish historical sources that originated in the years of the last world war. Asking new questions of these Jewish sources, I received from them the answers which determined the final scope and form of this book.

Apart from lesser ones, the most important Jewish sources, fundamental to the results of my research presented in this book, are the following: "Notes from the Warsaw Ghetto" by Emanuel Ringelblum[11]; "Warsaw Diary of Adam Czerniakow – Prelude to Doom"[12]; "The Lodz Ghetto Diary";[13] "Still Round the Circle: Talks with the Soldiers of the Warsaw Ghetto".[14] The common feature of all these sources is their unshakeable authenticity, their verifiable information and the fact that they have been created by the inhabitants of the ghettos.

In a Preface to Emanuel *Ringelblum's "Notes from the Warsaw Ghetto"* Artur Eisenbach [a known Jewish historian] wrote: *Personal, handwritten notes, sketches and essays by Rigelblum make up an integral part of the secret Ghetto Archives. They embrace almost the whole period of the war and occupation, from October 1939, until his tragic death in March 1944. Notes from the first year of the war were written ad hoc, during a conversation with*

---

[11] Emanuel Ringelblum *"Kronika getta warszawskiego wrzesień 1939 – styczeń 1943"*, Warszawa 1983 [See also: "Notes from the Warsaw Ghetto" by Emanuel Ringelblum, paperback, Ibooks Inc., 2006].

[12] Adam Czerniakow *"Dziennik getta warszawskiego 6.IX.1939 – 23. VII 1942"*, Warszawa, 1983 [See also: Hilberg *"Warsaw Diary of Adam Czerniakow – Prelude to Doom"*, Ivan R. Dee Publisher,1998].

[13] *"Kronika getta łódzkiego"* ["The Lodz Ghetto Diary"], preface and notes by D.Dąbrowska and L. Dobroszycki, Łódź 1965.

[14] A. Grupińska *"Ciągle po kole"* ["Still Round the Circle: Talks with the Soldiers of the Warsaw Ghetto"], Warszawa 2005.

someone, seldom ex post, sometimes on paper napkins, at a meal, in the office. Only in a free moment, or at night, he rewrote them in a more complete form. At the beginning he noted current, more important news every day, later he passed to weekly reports, then to monthly reports, finally to sporadic notes. A keen observer, he could catch a glimpse of essential facts and phenomena [...] The Notes, apart from being a valuable source for the history of Hitler's occupation of Poland, seem to be a matchless, unique historical document, enabling one to grasp the social consciousness of the Warsaw ghetto.[15] Therefore, "*The Notes from the Warsaw Ghetto*" is undoubtedly an authentic, unshakeable as to the authorship and timing, historical source. In absence of this source one could hardly imagine how to reconstruct the history and the atmosphere of the Jews of Warsaw and of several other centers of Jewish population during the Second World War.

"*The Warsaw Diary of Adam Czerniakow*", embracing the period from the 6th of September 1939 until the 23rd of July 1942, represents a slightly different character. Adam Czerniakow, a Senator of the Polish Republic, the Chairman of the Jewish Religious Community in Warsaw, and later the Mayor of the Jewish Autonomy, took notes on war-time reality from a different perspective. In his official positions, he was both a participant and a creator of the reality he described. In his Preface to the Polish edition of this highly valuable historical source, Marian Fuks [a Jewish historian] wrote that Czerniakow's "*Diary*" enables us to observe "how the tragedy" of the Warsaw Jews "increased".[16]

In his Preface to "*The Diary of the Ghetto of Lodz*", Professor Lucjan Dobroszycki [a Jewish historian] wrote that this source: ...*is a document of great significance. As to the wealth of information, it is an unprecedented source in the whole literature about the Lodz ghetto. In this "Diary", as in no other source document of this type, the majority of the facts and events described was based either on the first hand information, or on documents unknown to the general public. This circumstance mainly results from the fact that the*

---

15 A. Eisenbach, *Preface* to: "*Kronika getta warszawskiego wrzesień 1939 – styczeń 1943*" ["Notes from the Warsaw Ghetto"], Warszawa 1983.

16 M. Fuks, *Preface* to: "*Dziennik getta warszawskiego 6.IX.1939 – 23. VII 1942*", ["*Warsaw Diary of Adam Czerniakow – Prelude to Doom*"], Warszawa, 1983.

"Diary" was compiled in an institution, which had the access to almost full documentation of the Lodz ghetto: the Archive Department of the Superior of the Elders of the Jews in Litzmannstadt-Getto.[17]

The interviews made by Anka Grupińska are different in character from the sources described above.[18] Dozens of years after the end of WW II, the author collected accounts of some soldiers of the resistance movement in the Warsaw ghetto. The participants of these events talk about facts, but also about their own reflections developed in the past decades. Just as in other sources of similar type, these relations are particularly valuable for understanding the motivations of the participants of these war-time events that made them take part.

---

[17] L. Dobroszycki, *Preface* to: *"Kronika getta łódzkiego"* ["The Lodz Ghetto Diary"], Łódź 1965. A totally different picture of the Lodz ghetto is demonstrated by the memoirs written dozens of years after the end of WW II (in the 1990s) by a secretary to the Chief of the Judenrat in Litzmannstadt-Getto. See: E. Cherezińska, *Byłam sekretarką Rumkowskiego – Dzienniki Etki Daum [I was Rumkowski's secretary. The diaries of Etka Daum]*, Warszawa 2008.
[18] A. Grupińska *"Ciągle po kole"* ["Still Round the Circle: Talks with the Soldiers of the Warsaw Ghetto"], Warszawa 2005.

CHAPTER I

THE MULTINATIONAL POLISH STATE
1918-1939

I t is not possible to understand the various aspects or events of the Second World War in Poland, while at the same time trying to grasp the breadth of Polish-Jewish relations, the realities of the genocide and of the rescue of Jews without a fundamental knowledge of the complex ethnic composition of the Polish State. The multinational ethnic character of the residents of pre-war Poland, especially pronounced to the east of the Wisła (Vistula) River, influenced the multifaceted postures with regard to the military-political campaigns of the occupying forces, as well as with regard to the implementation of repressions that had been imposed on specific national groups in a very direct manner. In other words, it is not possible to apply the historical templates that had been drawn upon in other European countries occupied by the Germans. For in these other countries, there was a clear and unequivocal distinction between the chronology and the course, as well as the political and social-national extent of the Holocaust, which simply are not relevant with regard to Poland. The reason for the afore mentioned state of affairs lays both in the geopolitical conditions of the Polish State 1918-1939, as well as in the complex national structure of the population residing within its territory.

The genesis of the multinational character of Poland can be traced back to some remote events, especially to those dating as far back as the reign of Polish King Casimir the Great (1333-1370). He is commonly referred to as the one who "inherited a Poland made of wood, and left behind a Poland constructed of brick." To this day he is credited with, above all, being the great builder of Poland, as well as being a reformer of law and administration; as being the one who also placed peace and the internal development of his own country above conflict. Nothing can be further from the truth. For it was during this alleged peaceful monarchy of King Casimir the Great that ten offensive wars were prepared and ignited outside of Poland's borders, the result of which was an expansion of territory from 106.000 km² to more than 270.000 km² during the course of his thirty-seven-year reign, while his number of subjects increased from 600,000 to 1,300,000.[19] Since a great portion of King Casimir the Great's acquired territories included the Ukrainian lands of the Red Ruthenia, his conquests inaugurated the process of transforming the Kingdom of Poland into a multinational state which, in the centuries that followed, brought with it all the consequences connected to such an undertaking.[20] The construction of this multinational state was further espoused by King Casimir with the passing of legal decrees, among which the most expansive were the ones passed in 1334 and later confirmed in 1364 and in 1367, which pertained to privileges granted to Jews enabling them to establish Jewish settlements on land belonging to Poland.

A multinational Poland, which had already existed toward the end of the XIV century, and which remained in various forms of unification

---

[19] R. Heck, *Polska w dziejach politycznych Europy* [*Poland in the political history of Europe*], in: 'Polska dzielnicowa i zjednoczona' [Poland fragmented and united], Warszawa 1972, p. 323-324. See also: J. Wyrozumski, *Kaziemierz Wielki* [*Casimir the Great*], Wrocław 1986.

[20] The wars over Red Ruthenia (Ruś Czerwona) lasted from 1340 to 1366. Red Ruthenia, which had been won with such great effort, passed for ten years under Hungarian dominance (1377-1387). It was taken back in the military expedition led personally by Queen Jadwiga. See: R. Heck, op. cit., p. 329-340 and J. Wyrozumski, op. cit., p. 71-101.

with the Grand Duchy of Lithuania between the years of 1385 to 1795[21] – not including the Tartars, the Dutch, the Gypsies, and the Germans in addition to the representatives of other greater or lesser exotic peoples – was inhabited by Poles, Lithuanians, Rusyns (Ukrainians and Belarusians), as well as Jews. For Poles and Lithuanians, the Polish State[22] was their own state in which the King of Poland and the Great Duke of Lithuania ruled equally, and in 1569, a mutually elected single sovereign. Between the Ukrainians and Belarusians, who for centuries had been referred to as the Rusyns, although contemporary Ukrainian and Belarusian historians may not agree with this statement, some gravitated toward Lithuania in the political and national sense, as well with regard to outlook, while others toward the Crown. However, all of them did consider the territory of the Polish State to be their own country and their own state.

While the political regime and the laws of the Polish State had, over the centuries, laid the foundation for future nationalistic awakenings on the one hand, it also cultivated a sense of separateness with regard to Moscow among the inhabitants on the other. In addition, it provided a dossier of indelible traditions of sorts, one rooted in a citizenship mentality. The remnants of this mentality are still redolent among Ukrainian society to this day. Leszek Moczulski recalls the following: *At the end of the nineties, I was discussing the results of yet another election with the leader of the Ukrainian liberation movement and former prisoner of Soviet concentration camps, Mychajl Horyn. He slammed his fist into the map and said, "We will*

---

21 The Krev Union, which was signed in 1385 between Poland and the Great Kingdom of Lithuania, empowered the Lithuanian prince Władysław Jagiełło to assume the Polish throne. The Union of Vilnius and Radom (1401) connected the two countries with military alignment and supreme royal power. The Union of Horodło (1413) regulated the king appointment process and tightened relationships between Polish and Lithuanian elites. The Union of Lublin (1569) established 'one, common, and indivisible Republic'.

22 Writing about the Polish State, for the years 1385-1795 I have in mind The Republic of Both Nations: Poles and Lithuanians or The Polish-Lithuanian Commonwealth (Rzeczpospolita Obojga Narodow).

Ewa Kurek

only succeed as far as the former [Polish] pre-partition border".[23] This theory was later proven by the Orange Revolution in the Ukraine.

In 1795, the Polish-Lithuanian Commonwealth, referred to as the Polish-Lithuanian State that had been formed as a result of the Union of Lublin in 1569, was wiped off from the map of Europe by Russia, Prussia and Austria. The drama of the partitions of the multinational Polish-Lithuanian Commonwealth converged with the XVIII- century process of social and economic transformations that were still in progress, and which blossomed into a rapid expansion of national consciousness throughout almost all of Europe during the XIX century.

It is difficult to depict the character this process could have taken in Poland under the conditions of a sovereign state. Under the partitions, however, it culminated in the complete breakdown of a mutual identity of the state. In other words, to the extent that Poles and Lithuanians, or Jews and Rusyns, had considered the Polish-Lithuanian Commonwealth to be their own state before 1795, the Polish State that was reborn in 1918 was considered a state belonging only to Poles. The Lithuanians, Ukrainians and Belarusians chose separate paths to independence, while Polish Jews undertook to fight for achieving their own autonomies.[24]

---

[23] L. Moczulski, *Żywot z koszmarem w tle* [*The life with a nightmare in the background*], 'Gazeta Wyborcza', July 26-27, 2003.

[24] In the most coherent and best documented book *Państwo w państwie? Autonomia narodowo-kulturalna w Europie Środkowo-Wschodniej w XX wieku* [*A State within a State? National and cultural autonomy in East Central Europe in the 20th century*], Jolanta Żyndul presents the process of crystallization of the autonomy ideas among Polish Jews. *Państwo w państwie? Autonomia narodowo-kulturalna w Europie Środkowo-Wschodniej w XX wieku*, Warszawa 2000; See also: F. Brzeziński, *Prawa mniejszości. Komentarz do traktatu z dn. 28 czerwca 1919 r. pomiędzy Polską a Głównemi Mocarstwami* [*The rights of minorities. A commentary on the treaty between Poland and Major Powers (June 28, 1919)*], in: 'Przegląd Dyplomatyczny', No. 5 (1920), p. 160-188; J. Dawidsohn, *Gminy żydowskie* [*Jewish communities*], Warszawa 1931; J. Katz, *A State within a State, the History of Anti-Semitic Slogan*, in: 'Emancipation and Assimilation. Studies in Modern Jewish History', New York 1972; A. Chojnowski, *Koncepcje polityki narodowościowej rządów polskich w latach 1921-1939* [*Ethnic Policy Concepts of Polish Governments 1921-1939*], Wrocław-Warszawa-Kraków 1979; J. Marcus, *Social and Political History of the Jews in Poland 1919-1939*, Berlin-New York-Amsterdam 1983; *A history of Polish Jewry during the Revival of Poland*, New York 1991; W. Paruch, *Od konsolidacji państwowej do konsolidacji narodowej. Mniejszości narodowe w myśli politycznej obozu piłsudczykowskiego*

We can disagree and discuss the degree to which the Polish State that was reborn after 123 years of captivity was the product of Poles' struggles for independence, or merely the precise exploitation of advantageous political conjuncture, or even just a fortuitous coincidence or a miracle. There is no doubt that it came into existence despite the will of the outside world[25], and for all the years that it did exist, from 1918 to 1939, it was accompanied by not only a rather understandable chagrin of the nations that formerly occupied it (Germany, Austria and Soviet Russia), but also to the chagrin of practically all of the remaining countries of Western Europe.[26]

In the course of the six centuries that had passed from the time of the reign of King Casimir the Great (1333-1370) up until the installation of an independent statehood in 1918, Poland had won and lost wars, had lost and regained its independence, and it had amended its laws and borders. One of the few constants of character which have survived throughout the centuries has been that which was brought about by the last of the Piast kings, its multinational make-up. However, by this time the Polish State of 1918-1939, its multinational character had already taken on a new quality,

---

(1926-1939) [From state consolidation to national consolidation. Ethnic minorities in the thought of Piłsudski's followers' political camp (1926-1939)], Lublin 1997.

[25] A commendable though forgotten exception in this regard is The States. In Norman Davies's *God's playground*, the author says: "During the meeting with Paderewski in November 1916, the president-elect Woodrow Wilson uttered one of his first recorded observations, expressing friendliness towards the concept of independent Poland. On January 21, 1917, in his first official speech in US Senate Wilson mentioned 'independent Poland' and her right of 'access to the sea'. A year later, on January 8, 1918, the thirteenth of the Wilson's 'Fourteen Points' referred to 'united, independent and autonomic Poland with free, unlimited access to the sea'. This generous expression of American views regarding Poland was the only declaration of this kind uttered by a leader of a world power and, at the same time, unaffected by any particular course of events" (Norman Davies, *Boże igrzysko* [*God's playground*], Kraków 2003). See also: L. Gerson, *Woodrow Wilson and the rebirth of Poland 1914-1920*, New Haven 1953; V. Mamatey, *The United States and East Central Europe 1914-1920: a study in Wilsonian Diplomacy and Propaganda*, Princeton 1959.

[26] While Hitler called Poland 'a laughable country', or 'a so called country, devoid of any national, historical, cultural, or moral basis', and Molotov addressed the country as 'a hideous bastard of the Versailles Treaty', J. M. Keynes, a theoretician of modern capitalism, characterised it as 'an economic impossibility with no industry but Jew-baiting'; Lloyd George, in turn, deemed Poland's independence 'a defect of history'. Moreover, in 1939 he did not hesitate to say that 'Poland deserves what she got.' See: N. Davies, op. cit., s. 861.

different from that of the defunct Polish-Lithuanian Commonwealth of 1795. One hundred twenty three years of partitions had effectively destroyed the concord of administrative structures of the state, as well as the sense of mutual state identity that had been shared by Poles, Lithuanians, and Rusyns. With irreversible effects, the rules of coexistence between Polish Jews and Polish authorities, as well as with the Polish population, that had been established over the course of centuries gone by, were now lost. As a result, on the verge of the XX century, the descendants of the inhabitants of the Polish-Lithuanian Commonwealth – the Poles, Lithuanians and Rusyns, who were now referred to as Ukrainians and Belarusians – were not engaged in a common struggle to rebuild their lost common unified state, but rather for sovereign national states: Poland, Lithuania, Belarus, and the Ukraine. From among the peoples of the Polish-Lithuanian Commonwealth, only the fights of the Poles and Lithuanians were crowned victorious: an independent Poland and Lithuania were restored to the map of Europe in 1918. The nationalist struggles of Ukrainians that had been undertaken with the hope of building a sovereign national state, and the efforts of the Belarusians both ended in a calamity which condemned them to an existence as ethnic minorities within the Polish State. For obvious reasons, Polish Jews were the only group not to undertake to create their own independent state in 1918, but rather concentrated their efforts on trying to gain the most expansive possible autonomy for themselves: *...No doubt it was difficult for most Poles to understand why Jews had been enjoying citizenship rights in the West, while in Poland they had to demand additional minority rights.*[27]

As for the ethnic make-up of the Polish State that was reborn in 1918, it did not differ much from the Polish-Lithuanian Commonwealth which capitulated in 1795. Based on the census report of 1931, Poles constituted 64% of the inhabitants of Poland. More than a third of the population of the country were representatives of other nationalities: Ukrainians, 16%; Jews, 10%; Belarusians, 6%; including the 4% of combined Germans, Lithuanians, Russians, Gypsies, Czechs, Slovenians, Karaites and Tartars. Poland in 1939, not including the negligible four percent of other minority

---

[27] M. C. Steinlauf, *Pamięć nieprzyswojona [Unassimilated memory]*, Warszawa 2001, p. 32.

groups scattered throughout the entire country, was inhabited by Jews as well as three Christian nations: Poles, Ukrainians, and Belarusians.

The peoples residing within the borders of Poland in 1939 were dispersed unevenly throughout the country. This state of affairs was the result of political traditions of the Polish State, especially of the provisions agreed to in Union of Lublin of 1569. It was also the result of one hundred twenty three years of ethnic policies imposed during the period of the partitions. The largest ethnic and religious mosaic that existed during the twenty-year period between the wars was represented by the inhabitants of the Ukrainian lands that had been incorporated into the Rzeczpospolita (Commonwealth). In trying to visualize how this state of affairs did exist, it is worth reaching for the description of the modestly sized Wołyń locale called Powursko: *With Poles – it was clear, Catholics. With Ukrainians – Eastern Orthodox and "Sztunda's". Sztunda is some sort of religion. There are a few Sztundas in the village* [Jehovah's Witnesses – note E.K.]. *They do not attend Orthodox church, or synagogue, or church. They gather at private homes and they pray in their own way. They don't drink vodka, they keep house well, they don't bother anybody, and nobody bothers them. Jews are Jews – they go to synagogue. There were still others, a little bit strange – Greek Catholics, and it was difficult to assign them to any particular group: Kuracz, Sykuta, Smyk and Stepanko from Cegielnia, and even our church keeper, Serednicki – every Sunday they went to church, spoke Russian or Polish at home, they prayed from some little book written in the Cyrillic alphabet. And before Easter, their priest would come around for Easter Retreat, and their priest had a wife, like Orthodox priests do. There was also Mr. Klauze and our Karol, the Germans, the Evangelicals. Aside from that, Szurka Wołkow, the metal worker, a Kacap, a real Russian.* [28]

The criteria used to identify nationalitites in Poland was faith, although that too often escaped established stereotypes. Poles were the easiest to identify (they were generally Catholic, although in the southern regions there were also Evangelicals), and Jews going to synagogue. This process

---

28 J. Zięba, *Znad Stochodu* [*From the Stochod River*], Lublin 2001, p. 60. The term *sztunda*, which is used by the author, was probably known only in the east of Poland and concerned Jehovah's Witnesses.

was somewhat more difficult in the case of Ukrainians and Belarusians, for there were members of the Eastern Orthodox Church and Greco-Catholics as well, and, especially among Belarusians, there were Catholics. Regardless of nationality, among the non-Jewish inhabitants of pre-war Poland, it was possible to encounter moderately sized groups of members practically of all the religions in the world. Undisputable is the fact that in certain regions of the country, national minorities, especially Ukrainians and Belarusians, in certain northern municipalities Lithuanians as well, constituted a majority among the inhabitants. Despite a twenty-year campaign of enacted policies to shift these proportions (settlements in the East, among others), this state of affairs remained unchanged up until the outbreak of the Second World War.

The co-existence between the nationalities of the multinational Poland was regulated by law. Article 109 of the Constitution of the Polish State, ratified in 1921, proclaimed that: *Every citizen has the right to preserve their nationality and cultivate their language and national values.*[29] Of course it is possible to debate the extent to which nationalistic policies of the Polish State were in accordance with the binding Constitution. It is possible to present a slew of infractions against it, but generally speaking, all the nationalities residing within the borders of Poland lived under conditions that were more than tolerable in their day with regard to the cultivation of one's native tongue and nationality at the very least.[30]

The largest ethnic minority group in pre-war Poland was the Ukrainians. They resided mostly in the voivodships (provinces) located

---

[29] *Powstanie II Rzeczpospolitej – Wybór dokumentów 1866-1925* [*The Rise of the Polish State. The Selection of Documents 1866-1925*], ed. H. Janowska, T. Jędruszczak, Warszawa 1984, p. 631.

[30] J. Tomaszewski, *Mniejszości narodowe w Polsce XX wieku* [*Ethnic minorities in the 20th century Poland*], Warszawa 1991, p. 19. See also: L. Zieleniewski, *Zagadnienie mniejszości narodowych w Konstytucji Rzeczpospolitej* [*The question of ethnic minorities in the Constitution of the Republic of Poland*], Warszawa 1935; W. Paruch, *Od konsolidacji państwowej do konsolidacji narodowej. Mniejszości narodowe w myśli politycznej obozu piłsudczykowskiego (1926-1939)* [*From state consolidation to national consolidation. Ethnic minorities in the thought of Piłsudski's followers' political camp (1926-1939)*], Lublin 1997; M. Waldenberg, *Kwestie narodowe w Europie Środkowo-Wschodniej. Dzieje. Idee.* [*Ethnic questions in East Central Europe. A history and ideas.*], Warszawa 1992.

in the south-east regions as well as Wołyń and Polesie.[31] There were three voivodships in which Ukrainians constituted the majority of inhabitants: Stanisławow, 72.9%; Wołyn, 69.3%; Tarnopol, 54.5%; and in the fourth, Lwow, 44.6%, almost half; while in the Polesie region and in the city of Lwów, 19.3% and 16.0% respectively.[32] If we are to add the fact that the towns located within these (voivodships) were mostly inhabited by a vast Jewish population, it is not difficult to understand the truth about Poles representing the de facto ethnic minority in the area surrounding the fourth territory of the pre-war Poland.

Ukrainian lands had been incorporated into the Polish State as early as the XIV century. It would be no exaggeration to say that from the beginning of time, the underlying bane of contention between Poles, the Polish State, and the Ukrainians residing on its territories, had been the matter of land. The stormy events that affected this part of Europe from the XV to the XX century did very little to alter the state of affairs. Despite the passage of time, at the onset of the XX century, the Ukrainians still remained a nation of peasants, while the landowners of a great portion of Ukrainian lands were the Poles. In the twenty-year period between the wars, the social structure of the Ukrainians presented itself as follows: peasants, 82%; manual laborers, 13%; while the intelligentsia made up barely 1%. Meanwhile, among landowners of large agricultural farms with over 500 hectares of land (over 1200 acres), the Ukrainians constituted barely 1.3%.[33] The owners of a substantial majority of land assets, not including the negligible group of Russians and Jews, were the Poles. The result of the parceling out of abandoned granges and the distribution of parceled land among Polish soldiers, as well as peasants from central Poland, the 1920's saw the conflict over land expand to throngs of Polish peasant-settlers and their families whom the Ukrainian considered to be thieves of their land, right along with the Polish nobility. In this way,

---

[31] From 1944 almost all these lands had been incorporated into the Ukrainian Soviet Socialist Republic and from 1991 into Ukraine.

[32] J. Tomaszewski, *Ojczyzna nie tylko Polaków* [*Not only Poles' Motherland*], Warszawa 1985, p. 52.

[33] Ibidem, p. 56 and 68.

on the eve of the outbreak of WWII, the Ukrainian-Polish multifaceted nationalist conflict already had a highly relevant and expansive economic underpinning in the form of the conflict over land which had been ongoing between Poles and Ukrainians for centuries.

The development of the Ukrainian nationalist movement within cultural, political and economic fields, did not take on significant dimensions until the cusp of the XIX and XX centuries. As for its form and geographical scope, that was very much dependent upon the partition powers. After the partition of Poland, Ukrainian lands found themselves under Russian and Austrian rule. Russian rule severely suppressed any signs of national distinction that surfaced: from 1905, the concept of a Ukrainian state did not exist in Russia, and all Ukrainians were expected to become Russians, or at the very least Malorussians (Small Russia). In the Austrian partition, and since both Poles and Ukrainians took advantage of the autonomy, the opportunities to form a Ukrainian nation were far greater. From the middle of the XX century, the Austrian rulers afforded the Ukrainian nationalist communities with obvious care, recognizing them as an outstanding counterweight to Polish communities. During this time, the Greek Catholic Church, which was considered to be Ukrainian, gained more confidence.[34] In 1900, the honor of Bishophood was bestowed upon Count Andrzej Szeptycki (1865-1944), a man of great character and expansive perspectives who turned out not only to be a religious leader, but also a Ukrainian statesman. At the beginning of the XX century, the Ukrainians were in fact a nation which possessed not only its own cultural elite and economic structures, but also an institutionally well-functioning Church which enjoyed an immensely powerful and influential political elite. All of these factors became very apparent when Poland began her quest for independence.

---

[34] Greek Catholics, also known as Uniates, are the followers of the Uniate Church created by the Union of Brest. The Union was negotiated between the representatives of the episcopate of the Orthodox Church on the Polish lands and the Holy See; it was approved by a papal bull *Magnus Dominus et laudabilis nimi* (December 23, 1595). The Bull was proclaimed at the Synod of Brześć Litewski on October 19, 1596. The Uniate Church observes the Orthodox liturgy and recognizes supremacy of Rome.

The armed conflicts that took place between the years of 1918-1920 revealed that rebirth and freedom had very different meanings for Ukrainians inhabiting the eastern territories of the Polish-Lithuanian Commonwealth that capitulated at the end of the XVIII century than they did for other inhabitants of Poland. The Ukrainians lost their first battle of the XX century for an independent Ukrainian State. As for the extent to which the calamity of the Western Ukrainian National Republic was perceived by Poles as being a not entirely understood duplicity perpetrated by the Ukrainian Cossacks, for Ukrainians, during the entire duration of the twenty-year period between the wars, the capitulation of their nation was a point of reference and source of consciousness that, as a nation, it found itself within the borders of Poland against its will as a direct result of their own calamity. Poles, both the political elite as well as the population at large, lived with the impression that the Ukrainian lands along with their inhabitants, the Rusyns as they had been called from the earliest of times, belonged to Poland because that is the way it had always been, and that is the way it must be. Meanwhile, in the Ukrainian consciousness, Poles along with their reborn state functioned as a partition power for the entire duration of the twenty-year period between the wars.[35] It seems that this very dramatic political cognitive dissonance in the consciousness of Poles and Ukrainians most notably impacted Polish-Ukrainian relations in the years leading up to the Second World War, as well as for its duration. Wasyl Mundryj, Vice-Marshal of the Sejm of the Polish State [Sejm: the Lower Chamber of the Polish Parliament – translator note], said this in an interview with the press in 1935: *The entire Ukrainian populace stood firmly on the foundation of not recognizing Polish statehood. This was natural, after all. The recollections of the war that ended not so long ago were quite vivid, and things could have been different.*[36]

---

[35] J. Tomaszewski, *Ojczyzna nie tylko Polaków* [*Not only Poles' Motherland*], Warszawa 1985, p. 58.

[36] Quotation after: J. Tomaszewski, *Ojczyzna nie tylko Polaków* [*Not only Poles' Motherland*], Warszawa 1985, p. 60. The only element which united various Ukrainian political organizations was the objection to Polish statehood. The left, which had been influencing Ukrainian society from the 1930s, was mainly represented by the Communist Party of Western Ukraine (CPWU) [Komunistyczna Partia Zachodniej Ukrainy] and Ukrainian

The military disaster that occurred between the years of 1918-1920 did not mean that Ukrainians had given up on the idea of an independent Ukraine. Because the reborn Poland, which was considered by Ukrainians to be a partition power and as such they were not obliged to be loyal to the occupier, presented an obstacle to their achieving this dream, the Ukrainian political elite wasted no time in turning to Poland's neighbors to the west, Germany and Austria, in search of support for their cause toward achieving independence. And here we come upon the most crucial element regarding Polish-Ukrainian relations which impacted these relations during WWII with equal gravity as did the afore mentioned matter of perceiving the reborn Poland as being a partition power, and thus leading to the association of Ukrainian political and military organizations with Germany and Austria – the future occupying forces of Poland, as well as the authors and executors of the plan to annihilate European Jewry.

The tradition of linking the Ukrainian struggles for independence with Vienna and Berlin can be dated at least as far back as the years preceding the First World War. On the threshold of the XX century, the Revolutionary Ukrainian Party (Ukraińska Partia Revolucyjna – UPR), in a pamphlet published in Lwów bearing the title Samostijna Ukraina (Independent Ukraine), discussed how it was natural for nations to aspire to ambitions

Farmers and Workers Socialist Union (Sel-Rob) [Ukraińskie Włościańsko-Robotnicze Zjednoczenie Socjalistyczne] that was created in 1926 by the merger of the Ukrainian Socialist Farmers Union (Sel-Sojuz) [Ukraińskie Zjednoczenie Socjalistyczne – Związek Włościański] and the Free People Party [Partia Wolności Ludu]. The left demanded full ethnic equality and supported USSR. The latter, however, obviously opposed to the independence of Poland. Similarly, although Ukrainian National-Democratic Union (UNDO), which dated back to the 19th century and which enjoyed considerable support in the Ukrainian society, was only moderately nationalistic and rejected radical left as well as radical nationalism, it treated Polish administration of the Ukrainian lands as temporary occupation. In the 1930s, UNDO abandoned absolute opposition, agreed with Polish government and entered the Seym. In the face of the threat of German aggression in July 1939 UNDO expressed an opinion that 'in case of the war between Poland and Germany Ukrainians should openly support Poland in the interest of Ukraine herself' [Quotation after: J. Tomaszewski, *Ojczyzna nie tylko Polaków* [*Not only Poles' Motherland*], Warszawa 1985, p. 75.]. On the first days of September 1939 UNDO publicly declared loyalty. On the other hand, an illegal terrorist party – Ukrainian Military Party (UWO) and its political representation Organization of Ukrainian Nationalists (OUN) - considered Poland and USSR as main enemies of independent Ukraine.

of their own statehood and of the political liberation of the Ukrainian people. In 1902, the Ukrainian National Party made its appearance in the Ukrainian political arena which put forth the slogan, "Ukraine for Ukrainians". Ukrainian politicians did look to Russia for the most part. However, certain documents were uncovered in 1913 which indicated that they had also established Ukrainian-German contacts, which in turn resulted in them being labeled as tools in the hands of Berlin politicians.[37]

The goals standing before the Ukrainian populace had already been outlined by the Ukrainian National Council on August 3, 1914. In a manifesto signed, among others, by Levycki and Pavlyk, the Ukraianians were already discussing the approaching hour of liberation and they identified their victory with the victory of Austro-Hungary. The Association of Ukrainian Riflemen went into action in September and although they later suffered severe losses, their military efforts made quite an impression on Vienna. The Austrian government issued its support to the Association for the Liberation of Ukraine. The Association, which promoted an independent and democratic Ukrainian state, also tried to entice Berlin, which is where they moved their headquarters to in 1915. Despite the fact that it did not achieve great success, it was hardly ignored by the German government which subsidized its activities.

In the twenty-year period between the wars, in planning to gain the support of Germany and Austria to further their cause of an independent Ukraine, the Association for the Liberation of Ukraine had reinvented itself within the environs of the illegally functioning terrorist group, the Ukrainian Military Organization. Their political representation, which had its roots in the Organization of Ukrainian Nationalists (OUN) that had been created in 1929, was founded no place other than in Vienna itself. From its inception, the OUN aimed to reclaim, build, defend and expand the independent, united Ukrainian state. It promoted the concept of an armed struggle and led terrorist campaigns that had been modeled on examples of Italian Fascism. Its activities within the Polish State were

---

37 P. Wandycz, *Pod zaborami: Ziemie Rzeczypospolitej w latach 1795-1918* [*Under partitions: Polish lands 1795-1918*], Warszawa 1994, p. 425.

illegal, and on more than one occasion, it resorted to using terrorist tactics: between the years of 1929-1930, resulting from the activities of OUN guerillas, farm buildings of Polish landowners and Polish settlers perished in conflagrations. At the hands of the OUN, the Vice-Chairman of the BBWR[38], Tadeusz Hołówko, was killed in 1931; in 1934, the Minister of Internal Affairs, Bronisław Piernacki, along with many other renowned representative from the ruling camp were killed. From the 1930's on, the OUN's hopes of gaining independence for Ukraine had been tied with Nazi Germany.

The third largest national minority group of the Polish State 1918-1939, with close to two million members (6.1% of the general population), were the Belarusians. They resided mostly in rather closely-knit areas throughout four voivodships (provinces): Polesie, Nowogród, Wilno and Białystok. According to the census report of 1931, Belarusians constituted the majority of inhabitants in the Polesie and Nowogród voivodships, 57.8% and 58.3% respectively; while the Wilno and Białystok voivodships presented percentages that were adequately lower, 32.1% and 16.4% respectively. The social structures of Belarusians were most similar to those of Ukrainians: approximately 92% of the Belarusian populace supported itself by working in the fields, while the percentage of manual laborers stood at roughly 7%; the percentage of Belarusian intelligentsia or small business owners was rather negligible. As for the matter of faith, Belarusians, in an overwhelming majority, practiced Eastern Orthodoxy, although there were quite a few Catholics among them.

On the cusp of the XIX and XX centuries, the Belarusian movement to rekindle its national culture started to show some signs of progress. In 1906, the Belarusian newspaper made its debut, and the first representative of their native written dramatic arts, Jan Kupała (1882-1942), appeared. The national movement in Belarus, on the other hand, was so weak that it was barely discernible beneath the layers of Polish and Russian influences that had been so prevalent and dominant throughout Belarussian community.

---

38 BBWR: Bezpatryjny Bloc Współpracy z Rządem-Nonpartysan Bloc for the Cooperation with the Government [translator note M.B.]

Belarusian activities in 1905 were quite limited in scope; Belarusians had suddenly found themselves on the threshold of the early stages of national political movements.

Paradoxically, the years between 1915-1917 had a tremendous impact on the awakening of Belarusian consciousness. For it was during this period that Belarus found itself under German occupation of the First World War. Belarusian lands had been incorporated into the military administration of Ober-Ost[39], which had been created in the fall of 1915, and whose belt of operations ran along the Russian-German front line. At first, the German authorities paid attention only to the Polish upper classes. They were quick to recognize, however, that since local Poles were engaged in an independent policy aiming to revitalize the historical Polish-Lithuanian Commonwealth, they needed to lend Belarusians and Jews their support while attempting to put them in direct opposition to the Poles. At the end of 1915, the Germans forbade the study of the Russian language and introduced the usage of the Belarusian language in schools. As of 1916, the Belarusian language had been elevated to equal status with all other languages. Belarusian elementary schools had been created, and since there was a shortage of Belarusian teachers, appropriate pedagogical courses were organized. The Germans also allowed for the publication of a Belarusian newspaper called "Homan" ("the Voice"). With the appearance of this newspaper along with the activities promoted by the Confederation of the Grand Duchy of Lithuania, anti-Polish sentiments began to surface. Belarusian historians have assessed the German occupation of 1915-1917 and its impact on the development of Belarusian consciousness in this way: *Such a wide range of rights* [as existed during the German occupation – E.K.] *had never been granted to Belarusians before. [...] Belarusian cultural-educational initiatives could only have developed so successfully through the support that had been granted by the occupying forces. After all, many Belarusian activists had put a great deal of effort into proving to Ober-Ost management that the Belarusian nation possesses a rich history and culture,*

---

39 Ober-Ost – short for Oberbehefehlshaber der gesamten Deutschen Streitkräfte im Osten, which is German for "Supreme Commander of All German Forces in the East"; it was in command of the Eastern front [translator note].

and that because of that, it has just as much right to be independent as any other nation. The recognition of a Belarusian national identity by the Germans had finally been achieved, and the national Belarusian movement was injected with a new dynamic energy as a result.[40]

On February 21, 1918, the Germans invaded Minsk. Encouraged by the policies that had been promoted by the Germans in recent years, Belarusian activists took advantage of the German presence and its favorable attitude toward them, and on March 9, 1918, the Executive Committee of the Council of the All-Belarus Congress issued its constitution, Ustawna Hramota, in which there is mention of the Belarusian People's Republic (Białoruska Republika Ludowa – BRL). On March 25, 1918, the Belarusian People's Republic announced its independence: *April 25, 1918, at the initiative of R. Skirmuntt and his group, the Council of the Belarusian People's Republic dispatched a telegram to the Emperor of Germany, Wilhelm II, expressing gratitude for 'liberating Belarus from under foreign oppression', and at the same time requesting help in strengthening their national independence and territorial indivisibility through this alliance with the German Reich.*[41]

Belarusian historians have this to add: *Despite this sounding paradoxical, it was only under the protection of the German Tenth Army of the occupying forces that the Belarusians were able to prove their ability to construct a nation. [...] On August 27, 1918, Germany began its gradual evacuation of troops from Belarusian lands between the Dnieper and Beresina Rivers. [...] The delegation representing the Council of the People's Republic was fruitless in their bids to beseech Berlin to hand over control of Belarus after the German withdrawal. [...] The only country which agreed to maintain relations with the rulers of the Belarusian People's Republic was Lithuania. It is interesting to note that the idea of a national alliance with Lithuania was at first supported by clerical-landowner circles from the Minsk territories. Within the leadership of the Belarusian People's Republic, Roman Skirmuntt was the representative. At the onset of the German withdrawal (in October, 1918) a delegation was created with Jerzy Czapski at its head and it issued a memorandum to the chief*

---

[40] Z. Szybieka, *Historia Białorusi 1795-2000 [A History of Belarus 1795-2000]*, Lublin 2002, p. 187-188.

[41] Ibidem, p. 217.

of staff of the Tenth Army, in which they petitioned Emperor Wilhelm II for the creation of the Grand Duchy of Lithuania-Belarus under the protectorate of the German state. [...] Why was the Belarusian People's Republic unable to defend itself? [...] They simply did not possess a strong enough backing on the part of the Belarusian populace who remained indifferent to the Belarusian campaign. [...] They also did not have enough money. The landowners were certainly in a position to lend financial backing to the cause, but they were placing their hopes on the rebirth of the Polish State. Jewish small business owners were also in a position to lend financial backing to the cause, but they remained indifferent to the Belarusian campaign, and, like the Belarusian peasants, they too were counting more on Russian Bolshevism.[42]

This epic quote from Zachary Szybieki's *History of Belarus*, brings home the notion that, as far as the Belarusian national minority is concerned, this was a nation which, in a sense, sprouted during the years of the 1795-1918 partitions, during the period when Poland did not exist on European political maps, and whose leaders were not able to identify with the rebirth of the Polish nation. The positive experiences they had taken away with them after years of German occupation, in addition to their historically justified aims, both captured the attention of those Belarusians who possessed a sense of national distinction and directed it toward Germany and a reborn Lithuania. Thanks to the support from these two nations in 1921, within the borders of the Polish State, the Central Committee of Belarusian Uprising was created, whereas within Lithuanian territories, the Union of Free Belarusian Riflemen was created, directing its activities against Poland. Another organization in the uprising was led by a former officer to the Tsar, Wiaczesław Razumowicz, also known as Ataman Chmara. The anti-Poland crusades that had been perpetrated by Belarusian partisans during the years of 1921-1922 encompassed the Grodno and Białystock regions, and there were approximately ten thousand active participants involved.[43]

At the same time, the communizing Belarusian environments represented by the Communist Party of Western Belarus, that was being

---

42 Ibidem, p. 222-226.
43 Ibidem, p. 280.

directed by Moscow, having gained support of the ever more relevant ranks
of Belarusian peasantry, were preparing for an anti-Poland uprising: *In
the summer of 1924, partisan divisions of the BSRR* [the Belarusian Soviet
Socialist Republic – translator note] *crossed the border and began campaigns
in Western Belarus, having a constant retreat within Soviet territories. The
partisans attacked the homes of landowners, policemen, and office clerks by
night, and killed hundreds of people. Local Belarusians had joined the Soviet
partisans.*[44]

Although the Belarusian uprisings were ultimately subdued, that did
not mean that during the twenty-year period between the wars Poland had
managed to convince Belarusians to lend their loyalty towards a mutual
state. The seemingly advantageous changes that had occurred within the
territories of Soviet Belarus, in addition to the reassuring propaganda coming
out of Moscow, only widened the circle of Belarusian devotees sympathetic
to the cause of incorporating the land they lived on into the USSR.

It is estimated that at the time of the outbreak of WWII, there were
3,474,000 Jews residing in Poland. Every tenth citizen of the Polish State
1918-1939 was a Jew. One would be hard put to find such statistics in any
other European country. For the sake of comparison: Jews constituted
barely 1.6% of the inhabitants of the USRR; 4.6% in Czechoslovakia; 4.5%
in Romania; 4.5% in Hungary; 0.8% in Bulgaria; 0.5% in Yugoslavia;
0.8% in France; 1.2% in Belgium; 1.7% in Holland; 0.2% in Denmark;
and 0.1% in Norway.[45] The XIX century process of awakening national
consciousness that was ongoing throughout the nations of Europe was not
lost on the nation of Jewish people. The process involved in developing a
Jewish national consciousness within Poland was contingent upon many
factors: the character and specific nature of Polish Jewry; the prevailing
political conditions resulting from the non-existence of the Polish State;
and the fact that, since Jews, like Poles, resided throughout its entire area,
it was dependent on the policies of the partition powers: Austria, Prussia,
and Russia.

---

[44] Ibidem, p. 286.
[45] W. Bartoszewski, Z. Lewinówna, *Ten jest z ojczyzny mojej* [*How Poles Helped the Jews, 1939-1945*], Kraków 1969, p.7.

At the time the first partition of Poland took place in 1772, on the lands that had been taken by Austria, the Jewish population consisted of approximately half a million people, who, despite their previous attachment to the Polish crown, welcomed their new rulers joyfully.[46] It shortly thereafter became apparent that their joy was, if nothing else, a bit premature. As Majer Bałaban writes: [The Empress] *Maria Theresa had never acquired such a mass of Jews in any of the lands she had inherited as she had when she acquired Galicia. Above all [...] considering Galicia to be a momentary acquisition, she decided to capitalize on the taxation power the Jews represented in order to repair the constant ill state of financial affairs of the country.*[47] Already as early as 1773, utilizing the license prescribed by the *Betteljuden* statute, Maria Theresa ordered that all Jewish beggars be expelled to the border of Poland. In the years that followed, *family books* were introduced for the purpose of recording births, deaths, and the amount of taxation due. The age limit on newlyweds was raised and high marriage taxes were imposed. In this way, the Jewish population was subject to absolute administrative control. This also helped curb the population growth. The legal restrictions as they pertained to Jews were continued under Emperor Josef II, the result of which was a reduction in the Jewish population by half over the course of a few dozen years of the Austrian partition. Around 1830, the Jewish population residing mainly in the eastern territories of Galicia stood at roughly 250,000.

After the third partition of Poland, in 1795, within the borders of Russia, there were more than a million Jews who were bound by restrictions on resettlement outside of the settlement zone which in 1791 stretched as far as the lands of Poland and areas which lay on the Black Sea that had been gained during the war with Turkey. In the quarter century that followed, the settlement zone was reduced in size considerably. The Statute for Management of Jews, which was issued in 1804, incorporated the Jewish population into one of four states and granted them rights equal to those of the Christians population, although instituting a ban on leasing

---

[46] M. Bałaban, *Dzieje Żydów w Galicji i w Rzeczypospolitej Krakowskiej 1772-1868* [*A history of Jews of Galicia and the Republic of Kraków 1772-1868*], Warszawa 1912, p. 18-20.
[47] Ibidem, p. 20-21.

33

out of taverns, the production of alcohol and running for public office in the self-government of larger cities.

The relatively small population of Polish Jews that lived within the Prussian partition found itself in the most advantageous of circumstances in the legal sense. The General Statute of 1797 recognized all Jews, residents of Prussia, as separate guilds and sanctioned their division into groups of those who were favored and those who were tolerated. In 1833, the new Judenordung (Jewish Order) granted rights to all Polish Jews inhabiting the lands of the Prussian partition equal to those of the remaining Jews who resided on Prussian territory. In 1848, the Prussian constitution made exercising one's citizens' and political rights available to all, regardless of their faith. All of this served to facilitate a fairly speedy process of assimilation. However, Polish Jews within the Prussian partition, in 1849 this consisted of roughly 77,000 people who made up about 5% of the general population and 25% of the male population, assimilated not into Polish culture, but rather into German culture.

Berlin, the center of the Haskalah movement (the Jewish Enlightenment) that had been initiated at the end of the XIII century by the group centered around Moses Mendelssohn, for obvious reasons, had made its strongest impact on the territories of western Poland. By 1860, Haskalah had spread to the territories of both the Russian and Austrian partitions, as well as to Ukrainian territories reaching as far as Odessa, and by the end of the XIX century, that also included the remaining Russian territories. The main premise of Haskalah was the emancipation of Jews, which could be achieved by following the path of getting closer to the population of the countries in which they resided. A condition of emancipation was reforming the Jewish religion and customs, which could only be achieved by enrolling Jewish youth in public schools. The XIX century on Polish lands was indeed characterized by an unprecedented rise in the number of Jewish schools, which also taught the Polish language. In the Kingdom of Poland, which had been carved out of the lands within the Russian partition, aside from the Polish-language Rabbinical School in Warsaw and trade schools, during the years of 1825-1840, there were five elementary schools in operation, whereas in the sixties of the XIX century, that number rose to twenty nine.

The elementary school for Jews in Kazimierz in Kraków was opened in 1830. During the 1860's, secular schools for Jews existed in 14 cities of the Austrian partition. Within the Prussian partition, compulsory education was instituted in the XIX century, and this included Jewish youth, of which as much as 80% did attend private schools. In the decades that followed during the XIX century, the expansion of Jewish education continued, and it was quite impressive in terms of numbers and results.

1. The Jewish quarter in Poryck, 1916.

All of this, however, was just a drop in the bucket as far as realizing the main premises of Haskalah, which is why Jewish historian Majer Bałaban concluded the following at the beginning of the XX century: *... **one who, based on these numbers, would infer that Hasidism was slowly disappearing would be mistaken; these numbers are merely a one-sided measure of the culture of a country; for just beyond these numbers there exists an enormous, condensed mass of Orthodoxy [Hasidism] which is very far removed from public schools or any new way of thinking.***[48]

---

[48] Ibidem, p.211.

From the earliest of settlements in Poland, in every generation of Jews, there have always been instances of solitary families or individuals who for any variety of reasons chose to separate themselves from Jewry: they accepted Baptism, they became members of aristocratic families, and the second or third generation would become Poles. These were mainly doctors, wealthy merchants and representatives of freelance professions. The spread of Haskalah over the course of the entire span of the XIX century created a phenomenon which was much more vast in scope in terms of Polonization than had been hitherto observed. This was understood to mean converting to Christianity and completely cutting one's self off from one's Jewish roots.

Of course the matter can be debated as to whether converting and melding into the Polish community was an easy decision for Jews to make, or whether it was the right decision, and whether it brought about the desired results as far as the attitudes of Poles in the XIX century were concerned. On the one hand, the social-political circumstances that existed as a consequence of Polish lands being torn asunder by the partitions resulted in change in attitude towards those who only a few dozen years earlier had been welcomed into Polish circles without any obvious signs of antagonism, and whose Jewish roots were of very little significance, and were very soon disregarded. Now, there was finger-pointing and an aberrant sense of extreme distrust permeated throughout. Over the course of generations that followed, the once-upon-a-time national-religious associations were not soon to be forgotten. On the other hand, undisputed evidence does indeed exist which indicates that, during the XIX century, there had in fact been instances of irrefutable conversions taking place whose end result was absolute acceptance on the part of the Polish populace.[49]

---

[49] Taking into consideration the fact that nobody among the Jews accepted by the Poles brandished their origin, we are not able to say what the exact scale of the phenomenon was. It seems that the success of the Jews' assimilation to Polish culture and nation depended equally on the attitude of the Poles and on the personal attitude of the Jews who made such a decision. On no account, however, should we demonize this phenomenon and say that full assimilation to Polish society in the 19th century was impossible. The truth, as is usual in such cases, lies somewhere in between; precise numbers and character of the phenomenon is not certain. For example, recently I have discovered quite a surprising fact: one of the prominent Polish convents in 19th century was founded by a Jew. Her parents Christianized when she was in

Haskalah, the development of schooling, the changing social-political circumstances, as well as the prevalent trend of awakening of national identity of European peoples all contributed to the laying down of the foundation for the elemental emancipation of Polish Jews, especially when compared to previous centuries, which was understood to signify an abandonment of religious Orthodoxy in exchange for obtaining an education while at the same time remaining within Jewish national circles. Within a relatively short period of time, educated Jews, which included doctors, lawyers, and especially journalists and men-of-letters, created an intelligentsia community which was rapidly expanding in absolute numbers and significance, and despite having an excellent command of the Polish language, it still remained limited to Jewish circles in the nationalist sense, and in terms of unavoidable religious and cultural orientation as well. From the mid-XIX century, it was this community which took the lead as far as the social-political scene of Polish Jewry was concerned.[50] Hosts of enlightened Jews, precursors and propagators of Haskalah, swelled like a tidal wave as a result of the aforementioned development of education in general, and Jewish education specifically. This was also strengthened through the enforcement of favorable policies granting Jews the same rights as other inhabitants of Polish lands (in the Prussian partition in 1848; and in the Russian and Austrian partitions in the 1860's). Compulsory military

---

her teens. (I am not entitled to give the name of that convent since the founder herself did not flaunt her origin). To originate a convent and to attract young people one must have enjoyed authentic trust and admiration. If that was possible in the first generation of baptized Jews, it means that neither rejection nor Polish anti-Semitism could have been as huge as some like to describe it. Modern psychology and sociology accurately explain the phenomena of acceptance or rejection of individual people and social groups. It is attested that such occurrences arise not because of the people's nationality or religion, but rather because of particular traits of these people's personalities.

[50] The role of the Jewish intelligentsia in forming of socio-political life of Polish Jews in the 19th and 20th centuries has been reflected in abundant literature: J. Tomaszewski, *Najnowsze dzieje Żydów w Polsce* [*Modern history of Jews in Poland*], Warszawa 1993; E. Mendelsohn, *Zionism in Poland. The Formative Years, 1915-1926*, New Haven – London 1981; E. Mendelsohn, *On modern Jewish Politics*, New York – Oxford 1993; E. Mendelsohn, *Żydzi Europy Środkowo-Wschodniej w okresie międzywojennym* [*Jews of East Central Europe in the period between the two World Wars*], Warszawa 1992.

service, which had been instituted in the XIX century, also played a role in the emancipation of Polish Jews, which was understood to mean a departure from the ghetto. Polish Jews who were subject to Austrian rule served in the military as of 1804; in the Russian partition, all Polish Jews were forced into military duty in 1843; for Polish Jews in the Prussian partition, military service was obligatory as of 1845.

It is possible to divide Polish Jews at the threshold of the XX century into at least three groups without fear of being too far off the mark: Polonized, emancipated, and those who were described by Majer Bałaban as being ***an enormous, condensed mass of Orthodoxy.***

In 1918, Poles had finally won independence for Poland. In the reborn Poland, Polonized Jews were simply Poles. Emancipated Jews undertook to fight for obtaining autonomies within the framework of a democratic nation, and when that turned out to be unrealistic, they wanted to create the most comfortable living conditions which would be most conducive to fostering the development of their culture and language; or formed ties with the Communist movement and declared outright war against the reborn Polish State. As for the masses of Orthodox Polish Jews [Hasidism], the emergence of a Polish State was of very little significance.

It is necessary to keep in mind, however, that the aforementioned distinct Jewish groups were not quite so rigid or unambiguous as they have been described. In almost every Jewish family in Poland between the years of 1918 and 1939, it was indeed possible to encounter both Polonized and emancipated Jews, as well as those who remained loyal to the *condensed mass of Orthodoxy.*[51]

It is possible to engage in endless discussions over whether emancipated Jews were able to find dignified living conditions within the Polish State of 1918-1939, or whether Polish pre-war anti-Semitism was the worst of all possible types that existed and that could be encountered in the world, as well as whether emancipated Polish Jews were loyal citizens of a

---

[51] Polish Jews' diaries are an excellent example of the divisions among Polish Jews in the 19th and 20th centuries as well as in the times of the II Polish Republic. See: J. Olczak-Ronikier, *W ogrodzie pamięci* [*In the garden of memory*], Kraków 2002; I. Kowalska, I. Merżan, *Rottenbergowie znad Buga* [*The Rottenbergs of the Bug River*], Warszawa 1989, and many others.

mutual nation. However, in debating the problem of emancipated Jewish environments, we are dealing with a mere circle of no more than 10-20% of Polish Jewry. The rest, the environments of Orthodox Jews, lived in their own world to which Poles had no access, nor did Poles, Polonized or emancipated Jews particularly wanted to gain access. It is indeed the Polish Hasidim, and not the Polonized or emancipated Jews, that we have in mind when speaking of Polish Jews.

The first and fundamental matter, which in a way dictates how to understand everything that happened with Polish Jews during WWII, is the understanding of the unique nature of this portion of the Jewish population which chose Poland as the place in which to settle, and which, as a result of the programmed campaigns of the Germans, fell victim to the Holocaust. For Polish Jewry, as a sociological-historical phenomenon, is an extraordinary instance not only within the scope of the history of Jewish people, but also of the world. A vital matter seems to be, above all, an attempt to identify a people, who up until the time of their complete annihilation, did live on our lands. Perhaps it is difficult to admit, but the truth of the matter is that, in the cultural and religious sense, as well as in the sense of possessing a consciousness of national identity, at the moment that the first Jews set foot on Polish lands, we Poles were still sitting up in the proverbial tree. In order to better understand the sense and significance of this very fact, let us use the year 1000 as the basis for this comparison, as that is a year most contemporary historians are apt to consider a turning point in the development of Europe.

Poland converted to Christianity in the year 966, but in the X century, a considerable group of countries spanning from the Baltic to the Adriatic also adopted Christianity: Croatia, the Czechs, Hungarians, as well as Scandinavia, starting with Denmark. In 999, the congregation of Freemen took a vote to decide to adopt Christianity as the official religion of Iceland. A year later, in the afore mentioned year 1000, the Holy Roman Emperor, Otto III, came in pilgrimage to the tomb of Saint Adalbert, a martyr from our newly Christianized part of Europe, and presented Polish King Bolesław Chrobry (Boleslaw the Brave) with the lance of St. Maurice, a gesture which became the foundation of Polish statehood.

It was at roughly the same time that Jewish settlers had first set foot on Polish lands.[52] They did not possess a country of their own, and they had abandoned any such ideas close to a thousand years earlier, along with the fall of Bar Kokhba revolt.[53] But what they did have was a collective historical memory that had been perfectly preserved and cultivated through great pietism, and which held recollections of their own distant nation and Jewish kings from which a sense of nationalistic separateness and national pride flowed. They possessed their own religion, language, written word, traditions and culture. This state of affairs automatically precluded any chance of assimilation for those Jewish settlers arriving in Poland, which itself was just getting its bearings in terms of statehood and culture. On principle alone, it was impossible for the Polish population to assimilate to the foreign culture that the settlers had brought with them. Since both Jews and Poles already had a great deal to lose in the epochal year of 1000, from that point forward they never stood as a unified whole, and over the

---

[52] The presence of Jews in Poland from the X century is confirmed by historical sources. Ibrahim ibn Jakub, for example, the author of the first description of the Polish State of Mieszko I, mentions Jewish merchants visiting Poland. From the end of the XI century the flow of Western European Jews intensified, which was caused mainly by their persecution in the times of the Crusades. The increase lasted, with variable intensity, until the first half of the XVII century. As a result, the Polish Republic became the largest concentration of Jews in Europe.

[53] 'Bar Kokhba revolt (132-135 A.D.), the last in antiquity Jewish national effort against Rome; the direct reason of the rising was emperor Hadrian's order concerning the construction of the town of Aelia Capitolina on the ruins of Jerusalem (after the Jewish-Roman war 66-70 A.D.) and the Temple of Capitoline Jupiter in the place of the ancient Jerusalem Temple, as well as the forbiddance of circumcision (which was punished with death). Both orders raised huge indignation among the Jewish people. Simon bar (ben) Kosiba (Kozeba) took the lead of the rebels. [...] After Jerusalem had been taken by the partisans, Simon bar Kokhba ordered to mint new coin commemorating this event and which would determine the beginning of the new era. Perhaps even the reconstruction of the Temple had been undertaken. Nevertheless, Romans, supported by reinforcements, soon took control of the city. The rebels' desperate fight ended with failure. In 135 A.D., after the fall of the last fortress of Betar, Romans began heavy repressions towards Jews. It is estimated that the Romans took over and destroyed 50 fortresses and 985 inhabited centers; around 580 thousand Jews died in the fights and many were taken prisoners. Jewish people were forbidden to enter the city now called Colonia Aelia Capitolina. In the end, the times of Diaspora began.' See: *Słownik Judaistyczny* [*The Judaic Lexicon*], Warszawa 2003, Vol. I, p. 142-143.

course of the next millennium, both resided on Polish lands, but lived alongside each other.

Therefore, the key to understanding what came to pass between Poles and Polish Jews in Poland during the Second World War, is recognizing that there was a thousand-year-long parallel co-existence of sorts: the events of Poland and of Poles progressed across Polish lands along a corridor which was positioned parallel to another corridor that ran across the same Polish lands along which the events of Polish Jews progressed as well. These two worlds, both Polish and Jewish, over the course of one thousand years, existed alongside each other but never actually came into contact with one another. Each one revolved around its own self-sustaining life, barely even catching a glimpse of or tolerating the other, or even feeling any particular need to unite. The truth regarding the specific nature of the millennium during which Poles and Jews merely existed alongside each other on Polish lands does not carve an obvious path for itself into the consciousness of either nation. Perhaps the essence of this situation was captured in a most straightforward manner by Jewish journalist David Warszawski, who recently wrote the following: *Only the descendant of an assimilator was qualified [...] to write about the 'Polish-Jewish marriage' which had seen both its good and bad days. Both Poles and Jews are aware that no marriage ever existed. What did exist was a forced cohabitation under one roof, which had been imposed by history, with children conceived on the sly.*[54]

In this case, I find David Warszawski's description to be highly valid and exceptionally apt. The greatest mistake in Polish, Jewish and all other historiographies regarding the Holocaust seems to be this: a lack of awareness with regard to the specificity of Polish Jewry. The author quoted above also draws attention to yet another vital quandary, or rather puts forth a theory I can agree with, which explains the sixty-year-long misunderstanding that has existed between Poles and Jews.

First of all, almost all of the Polish Jews who survived the Holocaust came from communities of assimilated Jews, which means groups that, to

---

[54] D. Warszawski, *Siła odrzuconych* [*The strenght of the rejected*], in: 'Wprost', October 20, 2002.

a greater or lesser degree, had had some sort of ties with the Polish state as well as with Poles. Therefore, among other things, the fundamental condition to surviving the Holocaust for Jews was knowledge of the Polish language and knowing the Poles who would have to assist them in hiding. Second of all, the few from among those who, despite not having knowledge of the Polish language and not having any social contacts within Polish circles did survive the hell of the Holocaust [i.e., members of the Hasidic Jewish Orthodox communities], almost never voiced their opinions with regard to the Second World War because they were not in the habit of engaging in any non-religious disputes, nor did anyone even really ask them to do so. Hence the monopoly on writing memoirs and historical works from the moment the Second World War ended has always belonged to assimilated Jews. It is their voices that can be heard in every corner of the world, it is they who set the tone in published works on the topic of Polish-Jewish relations, and it is they who coined the stereotype of the *Polish-Jewish marriage* which had seen both its good days and bad days. There could be nothing more misleading. After years of conducting research on Polish-Jewish relations, I do give David Warszawski credit and do subscribe to his theory that Polish-Jewish relations, at the very least were: *a forced cohabitation under one roof, which had been imposed by history, with children conceived on the sly.* As for the Polish-Jewish marriage, it can be broached prudently in Poland only with regard to assimilators. Therefore, we stand here today faced with the task of writing the history of Polish-Jewish relations from square one, and of reevaluating that which had transpired on Polish lands.

The primary example of falsified pictures from the time of the Holocaust in Poland arose mainly as a result of being constructed on the faulty foundation of events as relayed by assimilators and their descendants, the concept of the Jewish ghetto during the Second World War. The Jewish ghettos in Poland are perceived by most historians to be the creation of the Germans who concentrated the Jewish population within separately designated neighborhoods in Polish cities for the purpose of making the annihilation of Jews easier to execute. Because Jewish witnesses to the Holocaust come from circles of assimilated Jews, and since assimilated

Jews never lived inside the ghettos before the war, their accounts generally refer to the moment when they suddenly found themselves inside the ghettos, as they did in fact only find themselves inside the ghettos once the clear command by the Germans had been issued. If nearly all Jewish accounts discuss the moment at which Jews entered the ghettos, if this can be verified by historians based on other reliable sources, including German sources which contain the specific dates of the specific ghettos being established, if within all the remaining European countries with the Jewish Diaspora the concept of the ghetto before the war was an unknown structure, then the picture of the ghetto that is presented as a structure that had been drawn up by Germans and only for the duration of the war is certainly deserving of the right to be an obligatory historical truth.

Meanwhile, the truth about Jewish ghettos in Poland is somewhat more complex and does not necessarily correspond to the realities that existed in any other country in the world. A significant majority of Polish Jews, those who were so brutally murdered that there is no one even left who might attest to their existence, which constitutes roughly 85% of Polish Jewry, did live inside the ghettos before the Second World War. They had lived inside ghettos in Poland for centuries. For them the ghettos were home and a part of daily life. Władysław Bartoszewski writes: *There were several thousand freelance Jews in Warsaw: lawyers, doctors, engineers, men-of-letters, and actors. But there were only about three hundred thousand of the more conservative ones, all of whom lived only within their own communities, inside a ghetto of sorts. Inside this neighborhood, there was not a single Jew, a homeowner, who would have even considered renting an apartment to a Christian, be that a Pole, a German, or a Czech. This was an impossibility for a very basic reason: it was a sin for a devout Jew to have an outsider living amongst their own, within their community. Their homes belong to the community. An outsider is not to be permitted to enter. In the sense of volitional isolation, Jews built their own ghettos themselves. And that could have continued had it not been for what Hitlerism brought. Those Jews who had been cultivated in isolation, not knowing Polish customs, or even the language, were the most difficult to rescue from the Holocaust, even to the extent to which it had been attempted. If anything, under German occupation, the area of the so-called "Jewish residential neighborhood" was expanded, and Jews from other neighborhoods, Polonized or not, were locked up inside of them. The place where the "Heroes of the Ghetto" statue stands today was the place where "average Jews" once lived.*[55]

It is worth mentioning that the Jewish ghettos were not a Polish invention and that it was not the 'inherent anti-Semitism' of the Poles that led to shutting the Jews in the ghettos, which is a suggestion that has been voiced by many 'experts'. Krzysztof Burnetko presents the origin of the Jewish ghettos as follows: *On the 29th of March 1516, the Senate of the Republic of Venice proclaims a decree saying that the local Jews 'should all live together near San Gerolamo, in the Ghetto. To make sure that they do not go around from the side of the Old Ghetto, where there is a little bridge, two gates are going to be built.' (i.e. the Ghetto Nuovo island – the New Foundry; The Old Ghetto was known as Ghetto Vecchio, i.e. The Old Foundry.).*

It is also true that before the formation of the Venetian ghetto Jews had been living in isolation. The streets and districts inhabited by the Jews existed throughout the Middle Ages. The fact is, however, that those districts were never purely Jewish. [...] This was the case with the street of St. Anne in Kraków (today near the Jagiellonian University's Collegium Maius): even in the fifteenth century its right side was inhabited by Jews, while the left side (where there's a church today) by Christians. What is more, such separation of Jews stemmed not only from external pressures. [...] Because of the wave of persecutions [in Western Europe XIII-XV century. – E.K.], Jews were more and more likely to settle in close proximity to other Jews. Not only did they feel safer, but also it was easier to defend themselves from the pogroms (on the other hand, however, a purely Jewish settlement was an easy target for the other side).

Still, the fear of being assimilated was not the sole reason for the isolation of the Jews. The free choice of the Jews themselves was equally important: by tightening the national and religious bonds they tried to save their cultural and religious identity. Regarding themselves as monotheists, the Jews reckoned that they should not come into contact with any other religion, and particularly with

---

55 W. Bartoszewski, *Warto być przyzwoitym* [*It is worthwhile being decent*], Editions Spotkania, Paris 1986, p.25.

its sacrum. For example, in the XIII century orthodox Jews suggested that when Christians walked the streets during the Corpus Christi procession, a religious Jew could not leave his house. A similarly motivated advice said that pious Jews should not live in a house whose windows overlooked a church [...].

2. The Jewish quarter in Warsaw, Mostowa Street corner of Freta Street, 1937.

From today's perspective it may seem astounding that the Jews did not escape from these ghettos. The reason was a simple one: for Jews in those times a life beyond the community was unimaginable. Judaism meant being a member of the community, and there were no Jews who could be religiously indifferent. Separatism is the basis of religion and culture as well as the way of defending them. [...]. Fernand Braudel, a French medievalist whom even his opponents called 'the prince of world history', considered the ghettos of those times both as prisons where the Jews had been shut off and a citadel where 'the Jews themselves had retreated to defend their beliefs and the continuity of the Talmud.'"[56]

In the middle of the XX century Poland was the only country in the world where 85% of Jews functioned in a social form that did not differ from the forms of the Middle Ages.

However, the problem may be very simple. It happens very often that historical phenomena are explained with logical wise theories that seek to clarify what really happened. Doing so we forget that dealing with history means reconstructing the lives of ordinary people - mortals who did not always behave logically and were seldom free from natural human weaknesses, including lying.

We forget that in the case of the war-time lives of the Polish Jews we are reconstructing their history on the basis of the accounts of witnesses, many of whom still live here today. Many of them – mainly because of their present social position and their place of residence – are reluctant to admit that their fathers, grandfathers and uncles wore gabardines (were Hasidim). The 'gabardine' image of the ancestors differs so much from the modern reality which surrounds the contemporary Jews that it is best to throw insults at the person who exposes the inconvenient truth and shatters the idealized picture of the Polish Jews as civilized and enlightened people. It does not matter whether this truth is discovered by a Pole or by a Jew. In the confabulators' opinion the truth about the Polish 'gabardine' Jews should die with them.

Of course, presenting the past in colors brighter than what they really were is not a Jewish characteristic. Many legends about the borderland gentry of 1920s and 1930s Poland circulated among the older generation of Poles. Every borderland family was thought to be fabulously rich. In their narratives, the lands taken by the Bolsheviks increased to the rank of latifundia. In fact, they were nothing more than little manor houses with

---

[56] K. Burnetko, *Getto: od azylu do Zagłady* [The Ghetto: from asylum to Extermination], in: „Historia Żydów: trzy tysiąclecia samotności", Wydanie specjalne „Polityki", Nr 1/2008, s. 47.

a few dozen acres of land. It is probable that the case with the Polish Jews looks similar. It appears that behind the diligently concealed truth about the Polish Jews is the desire to idealize one's own past and to give it a more civilized form and content.

The Jews who survived the Extermination were almost solely the assimilated ones and their accounts are the basis of the reconstructed picture of the disappeared Polish Jewry. The dead cannot speak. Above all, it is the Jews themselves who do not want to own up to the murdered Polish Hasidim. That is why the image of the pre-war ghettos, poverty, ignorance and negligence is disappearing from the Jews' accounts. Polish Hasidim are disappearing.[57]

What did the largest residential neighborhood of Polish Jews looked like before the outbreak of WWII? Stefan Żeromski, who died in 1925, described the Warsaw ghetto in this way in his story entitled *Early Spring* ["Przedwiośnie"]:

Leaving to attend lectures or to go to the anatomy laboratory, returning from classes or from town, Baryka had to tread through the neighborhood inhabited by Jews. Although they were dispersed throughout the entire vicinity of Warsaw, they settled in this one like a uniform mass, creating a closed organism of a couple-hundred-thousand individuals. At first, the sight of Jewish houses, apartments and stores were disgusting to look at for this newcomer because of their specific brand of ghastliness, but later it started to intrigue him, and finally it accosted him in an overwhelming manner in the form of a conundrum. Cezary resolved to spend his free time wandering through the adjacent streets: Franciszkańska, Świętojerska, Gęsia, Miła, Nalewek and others. The Jews residing or working in this locality created what is known as a ghetto. But this settlement of theirs was not a product of the past, it had no history. Just the names of the streets alone are an indicator that it hadn't always

---

57 It is probable that this is the reason why independent historical research on the Holocaust of Polish Jews meets with serious objections - a fact I have mentioned in the Introduction. It is further confirmed by the vitriol flung at Marek Edelman when he said that before the war had started, Anielewicz – a Ghetto Rising hero – painted fish scales so that they looked fresh. The image of the national hero who would 'refresh' spoiled fish in a little Jewish shop was impossible to accommodate with the image of enlightened and rich Polish Jews, which has long been proffered by Jewish diarists and some historians.

been this way. Nobody settled them here separately, like, let's say, Pope Paul IV in Rome, so that they wouldn't interact with Christians. Nobody forced them to live exactly here and not someplace else. They flowed into this neighborhood on their own, they were drawn one to another, and growing constantly, they created a ghetto of their own free will. On these streets the Polish signs in shops, warehouses and workshops had already started to disappear. They have been replaced by Jewish signs. You didn't really see Poles around here much anymore. Every once in a while you could come upon a Pole who happened to be the guard in an apartment building, or on a street where the only Pole happened to be a policeman.

3. The Jewish quarter in Warsaw, the backyard of Nalewki Street 15, 1937.
Fot. R. Wiszniak

These streets have an awfully unattractive look about them. The apartment buildings constructed by the Jews and owned by them have a shoddy urban look of shameless vulgarity and ugliness about them. The war had stripped them of the oil or clay paint. The oil paint has twisted into pipettes and coils, and on the surface of these houses it resembles the filthy peyos (side curls) on a grimy Israelite. The interiors and courtyards of these houses are not only stripped of their oil or clay top layer, but also of plaster which in some place has peeled off in pieces, and in some places entire section of wall have peeled off.

Bare brick walls shine through, but they are covered in sticky layers of filth, they are full of cracks, stains, discolorations, smears and revolting splatters which seem not to bother any of the residents. How awful must the cesspools, garbage dumps, drains, sinks, gutters and pavements themselves be! Most of the courtyards are dark, divided up, blocked, full of crates, scraps, debris and junk, shreds and rags. The melancholy of these courtyards cannot be put into words. The sadness of these windows is deaf, constantly looking out onto the rancid and disgusting alleys, the stripped walls covered in streams of filth, the hallways and cellars reeking of decay.

4. The Jewish quarter in Lublin, Lubartowska Street, 1916.
Fot. Stefan Kielsznia

They play here, in these diseased corridors, throngs of Jewish children, dirty, sickly, skinny, ashen, and greenish. If only a ray of sunshine would break through these winter clouds and peer into this lamentable scene. When the winter wind howls and the frost is biting, these children are thrown into hiding spots where the old ones jabber on about business, profits and making a quick buck. Cezary did once manage see two teenage kids huddling together and walking up the long Franciszkańska Street heading somewhere. Their little legs were drenched in the sticky, black, watery mud of the sidewalks and gutters, and their clothes were soaking wet and filthy. This pair was wretched beyond description. Their legs were poking-stick skinny, and their arms looked like bird bones. Their faces did not look human either, more like a vulture's or a hawk's, and their eyes were grim and crazed. This pair was waving their translucent palms, shaking their heads that sat upon their spindly necks and they were bitterly and rabidly discussing something. What can these two have been talking about? Was it also about profits and making a quick buck? Cezary followed them for quite a while as they bounced off walls and lampposts dragging themselves to some unknown destination which, quite frankly, was not even worth their effort. [...]

On the days before Sabbath, he would sneak over to the long "hospitable manor" stands (market stalls) where they sold kosher food stuffs, vegetables, meat and other culinary tidbits. There he saw a show full of the strangest absurdities, uncontrollable laughter, but deeply pathetic at the same time. These places were overrun with grunting, squalling, and grumbling generated by an exchange of goods that could only be fashioned by Jews. Buyers and sellers of offal bits, snippets of geese, legs, heads, necks, beaks, wings, herring, potatoes, orange scraps, candies and fruit – they were at each other's throats, ripping it out of each other's hands, hurling packs of insults at one another, ripping money out of clenched fists. Everybody had dawn in their hair, they were splattered with the blood of innocent ducks and roosters. Wandering through the crowd were types which defy description, unknown anywhere on the planet, in rags so battered and shiny, it looked as though the only thing holding them together was a crusty layer of glistening grease – there were half naked hucksters meandering about, half naked beggars in this sea of people stood off to the side bowing their heads in a monotonous gesture, like powerless stalks in the middle of a field – begging for a morsel in the Name of God. This entire shindig was reminiscent of the council of the damned possessed by the devil, going eyeball-to-eyeball over something.

What strikes me as being the most amazing of all are the stores in this neighborhood, or rather the tiny shops, wedged into the ground floors of apartment buildings. Main streets and side streets are literally crammed full with these tiny cells. On the outer-door of these hole-in-the-wall locales, there hang metal shingles with signs in the Jewish language. Therefore, the goods being sold in these booth establishments are meant only for the Orthodox Jewish population. How paltry, how unimaginative, how pitiable are the goods of these magazines! The share capital of each one of them can't possibly exceed twenty zlotys. A bit of scrap iron, some animal skins, a few bundles or bushels of foodstuffs, a few rolls of threads or shoelaces and some boot polish are sources of income for people who laze about freezing and dozing for days on end into the evening hemmed into these narrow, low-ceilinged, little cages constructed of planks.

5. The Jewish quarter in Lublin, Krawiecka Street, 1930.
Fot. W. Ziolkowski

One time, Baryka waded into a large courtyard whose revolting interior no pen can describe, for whose unprecedented level of disorder, filth, and disgusting mindlessness of articles being strewn about there are no words. These were the remnants of an iron depository, or rather old scrap iron. And there were scores of ironmonger shops carrying damaged, old, or lousy iron. One could say that this entire courtyard had been eaten away by rust, and that the rust was all that remained as evidence of that former state which had withered away. And the Jews who herded in droves to this place, shouting, swarmed atop the heap and were locked in hand-to hand combat over something or other, were themselves rusty, eaten through to their deaths by rust.

Suddenly, a freight truck drove into the courtyard carrying some sort of huge load wrapped in tarp. Soon, with their combined efforts, the load was removed from the truck and the tarp was discarded onto the frozen mud. Under the tarp there was a mass eaten away by rust: sawed-off pieces of pipes, twisted gridiron gates, screws, hooks, fragments of pokers, halves of forceps, bolts, warped nails, the bases of food storage containers whose use was unknown, pointy and zigzag bits of iron fencing, keys, iron heaters, braziers, fragments of windowpanes, doorknobs without fasteners, and tons of unsorted scraps of iron of various genus. Upon revealing the contents of the tarp, throngs of Jews, men and women alike, materialized out of nowhere, as though they were emerging from beneath the earth, mostly old, lopsided, all twisted and deformed, rusted, and covered with unruly hairy overgrowths all over. This entire brood, amidst wild screams and wrangling, started grasping for selected bits, pieces and slivers of iron, obtaining them amidst indescribable rows and haggling. It was not possible to grasp who these people were. Byers? Merchants? Middle-men? Collectors?

Cezary was under the impression that this was a group of old idlers who specialized in gathering up old pokers. He couldn't be bothered respecting their indigence or understanding the sense in their occupation. In their pursuits of tremendous gains they had evidently fallen from grace and were now seeking even the most negligible gains, not pausing for one moment from dreaming of the big ones. Not unlike the ones from the shops, the dungeons and caves, they're just lurking about waiting to pounce on the opportunity to make a quick buck by literally doing nothing. What kind of reform would it possibly take to elevate them to a higher social standing? What could be done to possibly help these people, in order to make them equal to others in terms of rights, possessing some of the prosperity in the world, in employment, customs, and way of life?

There was a surfeit of wretches-ragamuffins who were wasting the innate mobility of the Jewish race on cheating each other, expending energy on quarreling over offal bits, herring, scraps of meat, and doing nothing, literally doing nothing to earn an honest wage, obtain permanent gainful employment in factories or workshops. Many, of course, did overwork themselves in those streets as porters, drivers, assistants, salesmen, and they even had a different outward expression, normal, human. Hunched over, lopsided and deformed, hairy, bearded, filthy, sources of endless entertainment in their shallow little caps and long, dirty smock-frocks that hung down to their heels, gadding about and flooding the streets, floundering about, entering and exiting, cackling, arguing, not accomplishing much of anything really. Cezary arrived at the general conclusions that the Jews who live in this neighborhood which he has been forced to spend time in are a bunch of active and talkative slackers.[58]

The picture of the Warsaw ghetto up until the outbreak of WWII, which means in a period of barely fourteen years, probably did not change. Of course we can accuse Stefan Żeromski of being an anti-Semite and cast doubt on the description presented by him, as well as debate the matter of fairness with regard to the judgements of Polish Jews expressed in his novel. But to negate the fact that Jewish ghettos existed long before the outbreak of the Second World War is not possible. Just as it is not possible to negate the fact that Polish Jews had lived inside ghettos in Poland for centuries because complete isolation was their own chosen way of survival.

The Warsaw ghetto before the outbreak of WWII was not the only centre of Jewish life in Poland. Such centres existed in most large cities and in practically all Polish towns east of the Wisła (Vistula River). This is how one of them describes their old town:

In our day, Dubienka was a settlement endowed with urban rights. In Skryhiczyn, Dubienka was referred to as "in town". One would walk or drive" into town" to do some shopping, "in town" people would attend church or Orthodox church, or even the cemetery. And everyone was clear in the fact that Dubienka was "in town", a settlement of five thousand inhabitants, of which there were about, if not more than, four thousand Jews. [...] When

---

[58] S. Żeromski, *Przedwiośnie* [*Early Spring*], Warszawa 1978, p. 294-298.

holidays would arrive, everyone would take a break from their daily cares and obligations. At that time, one would have arrived at the conclusion that [Jews – E.K.] transported themselves in their memories to a life that had existed five thousand years earlier, to matters which had taken place on distant lands thousands of kilometers away, among people who have long since disappeared from the face of the earth. This symbolic-historical character was not only present on holidays, but also every Saturday when Jewish families would festively celebrate. [...] In the 1930's, Chanina Blass built her home on the hillside next to the little chapel, and that's why we called the figure in the chapel "the saint next door to Chanina". This fusion of a [Catholic – E.K.] "saint" with that of a person who wore the customary apparel required by Polish Chasidim, with her long skirt and the fringes of her ritual shawl hanging out from beneath her long overcoat, always sounded a bit funny to us.

On Saturday afternoons, the students of Chedera, [the religious Jewish school – E.K.] would occasionally be tested on their progress by their fathers or grandfathers. My brothers, as well as the other grandchildren, would usually be tested by Grandfather. He enjoyed bragging about and showing off the talents his grandkids possessed, and so he would invite other members of the family to participate in the testing: his son, sons-in-law, and even nephews. He would select the rather difficult texts for these occasions, and instruct the candidates to recite them by heart, comment, and justify. He cared that the form of the recited words expressed be interesting, so that those in attendance could enjoy it all the more. My eldest brother was often the grandson whose abilities Grandfather liked to show off in front of the rest of the family. [...] Grandfather was curious about Warsaw. When he stayed with us in Warsaw, I remember that he wanted to visit Łazienki Gardens, but he could not bring himself to shed his ritual attire. My mother, who wanted to please Grandfather, would hire a coach and they would ride around the park so that he could get his fill of greenery which he missed so much while in the city.[59]

Poles, Ukrainians Belarusians and all the other national minorities residing within the Polish State 1918-1939 were not identified based on their appearance or where they chose to live. If they did not openly declare

---

[59] I. Kowalska, I. Merżan, op. cit., p. 67.

their nationality, if they did not in some way intimate this, there was no possible way to assert who they were, in terms of their nationality that is. Ukrainians and Belarusians often spoke Polish equally as well as Poles, and among the latter, fluent knowledge of the Belarusian or Ukrainian languages was hardly a rarity. From the multitude of inhabitants of Poland, only the Jews stood out at first glance. In large cities they lived within the areas of their own neighborhoods, they constituted the majority of inhabitants in small towns and they stood out from among all the other inhabitants of Poland as a result of their attire, i.e., *by wearing the customary apparel required by Polish Chasidim, such as the long skirt and the fringes of their ritual shawl hanging out from beneath their long overcoat.* Today, it is difficult to imagine what Polish cities and towns even looked like before the war. A certain image can be gained by paying a visit to either Israeli or New York Orthodox neighborhoods whose inhabitants are descendents of Polish Chasidim.

As far as Polish laws and the Polish outlook on reality, Polish Jews were in fact a national minority in Poland. They were also the national majority of the Jewish population, a people without a country whose populace stretched out across a vast area beyond the Polish borders. The national dualism of Polish Jews, who constituted both a national minority and majority, resulted in Polish Jews not fitting into any other European country's national or sociological template. This truth, although sometimes difficult to bear, more and more frequently stirs the consciousness of historians, and in turn the consciousness of Jewish historians.

A sign of the times of sorts with this regard is the voice of Pierre Vidal-Naquet, who published an article with a rather telling title called, "I collect insults from all sides", in which he wrote: *The extraordinary circumstances of Jews from Eastern Europe allowed them to understand that* **it is not possible to consider Polish Jews as being Poles of the Mosaic faith.** *This is where the problem lays. [...] In 1967, I realized what Jewish communes in the East were all about. It was then that it dawned on me, that before the war, there had been nine million people living in the Diaspora, all of whom spoke the same language, the international language from Moscow to Kraków, from Prague to Strassburg, and even as far as New York. I started* *to read Yiddish literature in translation, quite extraordinary, and I suddenly understood what had been irreversibly destroyed by the war: it was an entire civilization, a distinct culture.*[60]

It is not possible to consider Polish Jews as being Poles of the Mosaic faith – the discovery of this fundamental truth about Polish Jews seems to be the key to understanding the Holocaust. Without it, there is no possible way of understanding anything. Nor is it possible to understand why Pierre Vidal-Naquet, as a result of publishing this very basic of truths, should collect insults from all sides.

It seems that Polish Jews from the period between 1918 and 1939 ought to be regarded in three ways: as a national minority residing within the borders of the Polish State; as the largest Jewish Diaspora in the world; but above all as an ethnic group which, as a result of its social, national, and cultural character, was identified by Jewish historian Alexander Hertz in the following way: *Throughout all the centuries of being in Poland, up until the moment of their own annihilation, Jews created a caste. A caste is something much larger in scale than a ghetto. The latter is an isolated territorial entity. A caste encompasses a whole wider group within a certain territory, irregardless of being localized here or there, or its factions or its individual members. Polish Jews, usually living within local ghettos, as a whole constituted a caste. [...] Jews signified a cultural group par excellence. They were a distinct religious and linguistic group. They possessed specific historical traditions. They had created their own literature, philosophy and art. They had their own justice and common-law system. All of these elements contributed to the lifestyle ideal and to its execution in the context of a caste. It is only in very few caste systems that we can encounter so complete and multifaceted a cultural organization as we do among Jews. [...] Within Poland's civil state, the character of the caste system of certain social groups was supported in the rules of law. [...] Nonetheless, the caste system can also exist and develop when there is no legalized sanction backing it up. In Poland, during the period between the wars, this system did exist despite the fact that it was not imposed by law,*

---

[60] P. Vidal-Naquet, *Zbieram obelgi z różnych stron [I receive insults from different sides]*, in: 'Gazeta Wyborcza', 12-13 October, 2002.

nor were there any formal laws in place which would have stood to protect it, as it were. The caste system fell more under the jurisdiction of common-law. These social rules, although devoid of any legal sanctions, can have no lesser implications than do the most severe of legal verdicts.[61]

On the eve of the outbreak of the Second World War, Poland was a multi-national state bearing all the same consequences that accompany being such a state during peacetime. This means that, not only was it colored by the national emotions that resulted from the social, political and economic difficulties, but also with the hues that the wealth of multiculturalism and a multicolored daily life can offer. It was a state in which, aside from Poles, and not counting the smallest of ethnic groups, Ukrainians and Belarusians, lived as well the caste population of Polish Jews.

On September 1, 1939, Germany invaded Poland. Seventeen days later, the Soviets did the same from the East. The war verified the value of the multi-national structure of the Polish State by putting the solidarity of all the inhabitants of the various nations living there to a very cruel test.

---

[61] A. Hertz, *Żydzi w kulturze polskiej* [*Jews in Polish Culture*], Warszawa 1988, p. 83-87.

CHAPTER II

POLISH JEWS:
FOREIGNERS OR FELLOW-CITIZENS?

At the hands of the Germans, the hecatomb of the Jews played itself out on Polish lands during the Second World War. This has brought about an examination of Polish-Jewish events through the prism of the Holocaust by Polish and Jewish historians alike, whether they like it or not. For this reason, in many instances, in wanting to gain an understanding of the mutual relations of both nations during the times before the outbreak of WWII, we must reach out to Jewish authors for whom the experience of the Holocaust was a lot that fate had not handed them. The Jewish historian, Majer Bałaban, at the threshold of the XX century, summed up the centuries-long presence of Jews on Polish lands in this way: *The fates of Israel were the same all over the world. The same impulses, which influenced their direction, existed everywhere. Over the centuries, religious and economic envy had tossed Jews from the borders of Lorraine in France, through Germany to Poland for the purpose of concentrating them into a relatively small area, in turn creating the conundrum which is yet to be unraveled. And so the question arises as to whether this human rage was checked at the border of the Rzeczpospolita (the Commonwealth), or did it accompany Jews further during their stay on this land? The answer is simple! In Poland, as far as Jews were concerned, there was indeed an enemy population among the bourgeois whose aims included eliminating Jews from their cities, but Jews did come upon a source of constant support in the nobles and magnates. The ones who best looked after Jews, however, were the kings. These Polish kings, with few exceptions, allowed for the valid demands of the Jews to be heard. Much to Poland's praise, it must be said that in a long chain of monarchs, not one could be found who, like Emperor Charles IV, would sell the Jews out to urban hordes for a substantial profit, or like Albrecht V who, based on the accusation of a single woman, burned all the Jews of Vienna at the stake (1421). As a matter of fact, still as late as in the second half of the XVII century, Leopold I expelled all the Jews from Vienna (1670), and in so doing, threw a few thousand families into the clutches of starvation and forced exile. I will not mention the expulsion of Jews from nearly all German cities in the XV century, or the en masse expulsion from England (1290), from France (1306), from Spain (1492), or from Portugal (1498).*

It is only from this angle that the history of Jews in Poland should be examined, for only then shall we come to understand why, despite the same human rage, and despite persecution at the hands of the clergy and the bourgeois, such a large number of Jews did gather here. Jews were not being expelled from Poland, and in the dark Middle Ages this was a sign of progress, a tolerance unknown to any other European country at the time. The fair-minded nature of the Polish crown and the support of the nobility were the mainstay of Jews. Based on that, they were able to settle on Polish lands in comfort and abundance within the limits of possibility.[62]

In light of the words of this Jewish historian, the sentiments expressed by Marek Edelman in an interview in 1985 seem somewhat dubious, to say the least: *Because the Polish nation, as you very well know, is tolerant. There has never been anything bad done against minorities here, against religion, this is an extraordinary nation. Kazimierz Wielki (Casimir the Great) welcomed Jews and cherished them, and to this day loves them. And that's where it ends. And why should we discuss this? This is unnecessary. [...] ...Narutowicz was*

---

[62] M. Bałaban, *Dzieje Żydów w Krakowie i na Kazimierzu 1304-186 [A History of Jews in Kraków and in the Kazimierz District 1304-1868]*, Kraków 1912, p. XVIII-XIX.

not assassinated because he was Narutowicz, but because he was elected with Jewish votes. After all, those Jewish members of Parliament who were supposed to vote for him in the Sejm, they were not assaulted. The nation assaulted them. Come on, it was no accident that Narutowicz had been assassinated. After all, Niewiadomski [who murdered Narutowicz – EK] was not an idiot. He was the emanation of a certain portion of this country. At the time, a very great portion. Assaulting Jews was commonplace. Because the Church teaches that a Jew killed Christ. [...] ... all the anti-Jewish pogroms flowed out of the Church.[63]

It makes no difference whether it is Majer Bałaban's assessment, or the truth heralded by Marek Edelman that is used as a point of departure. What must be underscored is that relations between the nations of multi-national Poland, only in part, were dictated by faith. In any case, it was neither the type of faith espoused, nor the degree of religious tolerance that served as the deciding factor with regard to mutual relations. It was cultural, economic and political factors that played the critical role. In other words, the degree and type of contact between the various groups, economic collisions as well the degree to which national consciousness had been developed. During the years of 1795 to 1939, the attitudes that had been fostered with regard to the loss and rebuilding of the Polish State also played a significant role. As far as Polish-Jewish relations were concerned, that which played the most vital role was the relationship between the two nations during the period of the fallen Polish statehood. In other words, the period which started with the first partition of Poland in 1772 and ended with the reconstruction of the Polish State in 1918, the period when Poland had found herself under Prussian, Austrian and Russian occupation.

It was during the time of the Polish State 966-1795 that, within the social structures that had existed in the civil state, Polish Jews, though not formally designated a state, were treated as a de facto state, and were not obligated to engage in matters pertaining to politics or the military. The most important aspect in this, however, was not the will of Jews themselves per se, but rather the strict laws and obligations that were

---

[63] A. Grupińska, *Ciągle po kole* ["Still Round the Circle: Talks with the Soldiers of the Warsaw Ghetto"], Warszawa 2005, p. 30.

applicable within each state. In accordance with these laws and obligations, a member of the nobility was obliged to defend and politic, a peasant to plow, a priest to pray, a bourgeois to perform his trade and look after the city, a Jew to conduct business and issue loans. Since matters of politics and armed military defense were the responsibility of the nobility state, Jews were generally relieved of the obligation of politicking and serving in the army. As a result, they were not required to declare any political or patriotic positions. It sufficed that they behaved like loyal citizens of Poland, paid their taxes, and performed their designated roles within their state structure fairly well. Over the course of centuries, the relations between the Jewish states and the remaining states in Poland were also quite basic and straightforward: the bourgeois were at odds with Jews over economic domains and, in modern-day discourse, the job market; the Church labeled them as faithless and, as a result of that, outside of banking or trade related contact, persecuted them to a certain degree as compared to other countries; the Kings always defended and protected them; as for the magnates, aristocracy and peasants, depending on their needs and the epoch in question, sometimes they supported Jews, at other times persecuted them, but always looked upon them in disdain. These sentiments had no bearing on conducting a wide range of business ventures with Jews, the scale of which usually depended on the material resources of both parties involved. Jacek Jezierski, a castellan, wrote this in 1791: *I consider Jews to be Polish citizens and useful merchants, as there exists no other kinds of Jewish merchants in Poland as far as I know, for I regard only those merchants who export a country's product from that country.*[64]

It is clear that Jews fulfilled a specific role within the economic structures of the civil state. They resided in Polish cities, towns and villages, but in Poland they had their own Jewish Parliament[65], Jewish court system, Jewish religion, and their rhythm of life was dictated by their religion. Up until the time of the partitions, because there had not existed such a need

---

[64] A. Żbikowski, *Żydzi [The Jews]*, Wroclaw 1997, p. 53.
[65] *The Jewish Parliament of Four Lands;Four Lands Vaad* – the central government authority of the Jews in Poland in the years 1580-1764, which consisted of seventy kahal delegates representing the four Polish lands.

prior to that, no one from among Poles or Jews even pondered over what Poland might signify to Polish Jews: a homeland, or simply land on which to reside; do Polish Jews identify with the Polish State, or do they simply identify with the tiny ersatz homelands installed into enclaves which are embodied by specific cities or villages, as well as with the possibility of attaining suitable living conditions. This arrangement was convenient for both Polish Jews and Poles. It allowed the first group to lead a relatively peaceful and safe existence in accordance with their religion. The latter, because Jews did not interfere with politics and did pay the taxes that had been imposed on them fairly regularly, Poles carried on conducting business deals with Jews and did not give the notions of Jewish lifestyles or Jewish patriotism a second thought. It will not be too much of a stretch to claim that, at the threshold of Poland losing her independence, in the second half of the XVIII century, the political aspect of the Polish population, which constituted roughly 10% of the noble class, knew only this about their fellow-inhabitants: Polish Jews resided in their country, they met all of the required economic demands, they followed a different faith, they had their own language and style of dress, and they were governed by their own laws. Based on that, they did constitute a de facto fifth state along with the Polish kings, noble class, peasants and clergy, whose existence for centuries had been dependent upon privileges granted by the Polish kings.[66]

The tradition that had been fostered in Poland over the course of centuries was to leave Polish Jews to their own devices: they were subject to their own courts, Jewish self-governmental as well as religious structures. It must be admitted that this notion of "being left to one's own devices" was very appealing to Jews, if for no reason other than it did create a sort of ersatz little Jewish state they could call their own. Majer Bałaban writes the following: *Jews in the Poland of the XVIII century constituted a coherent*

---

[66] In the historical literature the Jews were rarely referred to as a separate class. Nevertheless, this view is gaining more and more supporters and it appears that this is the way they should be treated. See: A. Eisenbach, *Emancypacja Żydów na ziemiach polskich 1785-1870* [*Emancipation of Jews on Polish lands 1785-1870*], Warszawa 1988, p. 40; S. Grodziski, *W królestwie Galicji i Lodomerii* [*In the kingdom of Galicia and Lodomeria*], Kraków 1976, p. 110.

mass, disconnected completely from the rest of the nation. They had a very expansive self-government, which was based on 'Kahals' (Jewish communities), and concluded with the Parliament of Four Lands, which held deliberations twice a year, in spring and autumn. [...] The Marshals (Speakers) of the Jewish Parliament in Poland, they were called by the Polish Kings in Latin: 'Judeanus qui in nostra aula residet' [the Jew who officiates in our court."[67]

The order of things which had been solidified over the course of centuries started to break down in the second half of the XVIII century. The administrative reform which was supposed to lead to the creation of a centralized government apparatus, instead resulted in the electoral diet of the last King of Poland, King Stanisław August Poniatowski (1764-1795), ratifying the act to abolish the national representation of Jewish land-ownership and communal organs within Poland and Lithuania. This left only the leadership of the Jewish communities as the lowest rung of self-government in tact, which was supposed to represent the interests of the Jewish community with regard to local authorities: sub-prefects, treasury authorities, city offices and owners of private cities. At the source of the parliamentary decision regarding the abolishment of higher structures of Jewish self-government lay in the economic claims of the aristocracy (collecting debts "from the synagogues") on the one hand, and on the other the attempt to curtail the kahal's plutocratic extortion tactics being imposed on the plebs.[68]

Regardless of the cause, the electoral diet of 1764 demolished the hitherto existing structure of relations between the Polish and the Jewish communities. In addition, Jewish matters, which up until that point, to a greater or lesser degree, had existed outside the margins of the political arena, were now transferred under the jurisdiction of the deliberations of the Parliament of the Polish-Lituanian Commonwealth. With that said, Polish Jews now found themselves at the central focal point of the politically oriented portion of the Polish population, at least for the time-being. A significant point is that it was during this very period, close to the above mentioned electoral parliament, that the statement that the Jewish

---

[67] M. Bałaban, *Dzieje Żydów w Galicyi* [*A History of Jews in Galicia*], Lwów 1914, p. 3.

[68] A. Eisenbach, *Emancypacja żydowska na ziemiach polskich 1785-1870* [*Emancipation of Jews on Polish lands 1785-1870*], Warszawa 1988, p. 42.

population exists as a "nation within a nation" and "a state within a state" was coined.[69]

Up until the time of the partitions, and let us not fear negative associations in connection with this rather apt statement, Polish Jews constituted a state within a Polish State of sorts, and the sole link between the legal-administrative structures, the religious population among Polish Jews and the Polish State was the contemporaneous Judeanus in residence at the Royal Court. The partitions caused the social-political centuries-old accord that had settled into existence over the course of generations to shatter suddenly and irreversibly, and placed both nations in situations previously unknown to them. Another consequence of the 1772 first partition, but especially of the 1795 third partition, was that everything previously deemed insignificant suddenly became of utmost importance. For the greater majority of the Polish population, substituting their white eagle for the foreign eagles of the occupiers was quite traumatic. Although it is true that there had been Poles who disgraced themselves by engaging in treason or collaboration with the enemy, in general, however, especially among the bourgeois, and with the passing of time the peasants as well, Poles did undertake to fight a relentless life-and-death battle for their independence which would continue for many generations to come.[70]

---

[69] Ibidem, p. 42.

[70] In the review of the first edition of my book, professor Marek Jan Chodakiewicz wrote: 'In fact, Polish peasants did not fight for Poland. [...] It can be stated that a certain number of Polish peasants remained indifferent to Poland's independence even in the first days of World War II.' [See: M. J. Chodakiewicz, *Recenzje* [*Reviews*], in: „Glaukopis", No 7/8, Warszawa 2007, p. 361-362.]. Indeed, in the First Republic of Poland peasants did not fight for freedom; the fact is, however, that in state society the defense of borders lay within the competence of the gentry, not the peasantry or, if we treat Jews as a state, the Jewry. In this respect, at the moment Poland lost independence, Polish peasants and Polish Jews were on a similar, or rather on the same level of national consciousness: the fight for freedom, which had never before belonged to the competencies of these two classes, was for them an absolute novelty. The Poles' first liberation effort – the Kosciuszko Insurrection in 1794 – attracted similar, though minimal, number of the two states' representatives, i.e. the peasant military units armed with scythes (*kosynierzy*) and the Berek Joselewicz's regiment.

As for Polish peasantry's and Jewry's attitude towards the struggle for freedom in later periods, the difference between these two classes consists in the numbers of men actively fighting for independence. The number of Jews did not change significantly in the period

Someone once described Jews as having lived in a dark shadow until the time of the partitions. This depiction seems to be highly accurate. One thing is for certain, Jews did undoubtedly live in the shadow of the throne of the Majestic Polish Kings, although it was somewhere more on its peripheries, to be more precise, beyond the general current of Polish social-political goings-on. But at the end of the XVIII century, the multi-national Poland had ceased to exist as a state. The royal throne was no longer casting a shadow. From the twilight into the light of day, a naked reality emerged with the charm of obscurity stripped away, accompanied by the reality of Jewish life on Polish lands.

From among the peoples inhabiting the lands of the Polish-Lithuanian Commonwealth, the first to stand in line to defend their country were the title holders of the state: Poles and Lithuanians. Alongside them, the absence of a shadow revealed a void. Neither Belarusians nor Ukrainians identified with the Polish-Lithuanian Commonwealth enough to sacrifice either their lives or their fortunes. From among Polish Jews, on the other hand, according to Majer Bałaban's words: ...*nobody really noticed the sudden shift in attitude, no one understood the gravity of the occupation, and no one was overly concerned that a treaty among the three partition powers had been signed.* [71]

The imagination of every generation reaches only as far back as its own experience, perhaps even as far back as a few preceding generations. Therefore, Polish Jews imagined that the partitions of Poland had very little bearing on the seemingly smooth flow of Jewish life that had gone on for centuries. For how could the fact that, as of tomorrow, the Jewish Speaker representing Jewish interests, instead of residing at the Polish royal court,

---

preceding World War II and remained at the level of 1-2 %. For Polish peasants, on the other hand, XIX and XX centuries was the time of dynamic development of national consciousness as well as of a quick course of patriotism and citizenship. In the successive bids for independence peasants took more and more active part. In the Home Army's ranks of the Lublin region peasantry constituted almost 80% of soldiers and over 80% of those who fell in the struggle for a free Poland. [Compare: N. Getter, J. Schalla, Z. Schipper, *Żydzi bojownicy o niepodległość Polski* (*Jewish fighters for Poland's independence*), Lwów 1939; E. Kurek, *Zaporczycy w fotografii 1943-1963* (*Zapora's soldiers in photography 1943-1963*), Lublin 2001, p. 13].

[71] M. Bałaban, *Dzieje Żydów w Galicyi* [*A History of Jews of Galicia*], Kraków 1914, p. 19.

shall reside at the Russian Tsar's or the Austrian Emperor's court have any impact on anything? Jews from the town of Brody near Lwów accepted the first partition of Poland in the following way:

Austrian armies, under the command of General Hadik, surged towards Lwów and shortly thereafter, Count Pergen took authority over the newly fashioned province. Everyone everywhere was required to take the oath of homage to 'Her Majesty the Empress', and in Lwów this ceremony took place at the cathedral. [...] Lwów Jews paid their homage in the square in front of the cathedral. The homage of the Jews from Brody town was far more ceremonious as it took place in the synagogue. Obviously, Brody Jews were already far closer to European culture at that time. 'Wienner Diarium' (known as 'Wienner Zeitung' as of 1780), in its issue nr. 9 describes the following: 'Disguised in masks as Turks, (Jews) with postal trumpets at their mouths, started to surround the main streets and outskirts of Brody in the afternoon of December 29, 1773, luring fellow-worshipers to the synagogue. Inside the huge divine edifice decorated with tapestries, rugs, silver platters and chandeliers, a silver crown was placed on display. Below that, a lavish buffet with tables covered with a variety of beverages, confections and an assortment of dried fruit and nuts, etc. At six in the evening, among gasps of awe, the brilliant illumination of all four sides of the synagogue, using 6,000 oil lamps, 600 wax and 400 tallow candles, was underway. There was a gilded two-headed eagle, six elbows tall, ablaze inside the synagogue. There were 60 torches and 4 barrels of tar alighted in the streets leading to the synagogue.

At seven o'clock, everyone came to the glowing structure: those commanding the army, Major-General von Graeven, the Commandant of the square, the Margrave de Torres, Imperial and Royal Directors from the district office under Count Strassoldo, and many other public officials, officers and dignitaries. Upon the arrival of the above mentioned individuals, such a tumult and gridlock started to stir in the street, that the soldiers were barely able to maintain order enough to secure a safe passageway to the entrance of the synagogue. The music, which complemented the event very well, greeted the arriving guests, and when everything had calmed down, the Jewish syndic, Abraham Usiel, Doctor of Medicine, gave his thank-you speech which was dedicated to the government representatives. This was followed by the Elder Cantor (Oberschulsinger), accompanied by the entire instrumental and choir sections, saying prayer, whose final word "Amen" was repeated over and over by the entire gathering with great exuberance and jubilation. Afterwards, everyone was regaled with choices of wine, Turkish fruits and sweets, and the most distinguished of Jews drank to the good health of the Empress with great esteem. Money was thrown at the street crowd, and the insolvent were offered alms. At nine o'clock, all the invited guests returned to their homes feeling very satisfied, while the locals, upon singing Psalm 72 accompanied by the orchestra, continued to enjoy the evening until eleven o'clock. The Jewish syndic (Judenpromotor), Samuel Rabinowicz, hosted a fabulous party with music at his home, and celebrations continued in other homes as well, well into the night. Joyful cheers in honor of the Empress and the new order resonated all around.[72]

The gravity of the current situation and the suddenly different circumstances that Poland had found herself in, as well as the circumstances of Jews, were certainly not lost on Berek Joselewicz, a Jew, who wrote the following in an appeal to his brethren on October 1, 1794:

Attention children of the Tribe of Israel! Who among you has The Eternal and Almighty carved into their heart, and who wishes to assist in the fight for our homeland, as all of us should. Now the time is upon us to put all our strength into doing so. [...] Our protector, Tadeausz Kościuszko, who is indeed a messenger sent by The Eternal Almighty, undertook to place all his efforts to accomplish putting forth a Jewish regiment. He is in possession of exceptional abilities, a superior intellect and a merciful heart. He is the chosen leader. Let us take this, fellow brethren, as an example to follow! [...] Rise to your feet! Open up your eyes! [...] We need nothing more than to be honorable and possess the valiant heart of a hero. Almighty God is with you, and I shall serve as your guide! [...] Help restore the hitherto oppressed Poland. Loyal brethren! We should be fighting for our homeland, for as long as we still possess even a drop of blood flowing through our veins. Even if we shall never see the day,

---

[72] Ibidem, p. 19-20. It is significant that 14 years after the described event Majer Bałaban does not see in the behaviour of the Brody Jews the tragedy of betrayal of motherland, of Polish king and of the Polish State; instead, he draws conclusions that are surprising even today, after one century. Namely, he states that the Jews of Brody bowed down before the invader - and in a synagogue - because *already in those days they were closer to the European culture...*

then our descendants shall experience a safe and carefree existence, and shall never have to wander like wild animals. Dearest brethren! Awaken yourselves like lions and leopards...[73]

6. Colonel Berek Joselewicz in the battle of Kock, 1809.

Juliusz Kossak

Tadeusz Kościuszko expressed a similar sentiment in his appeal to Polish Jews dated September 17, 1794:

Nothing can be more convincing, even to the most distant of nations, concerning the sacred nature of the task before us or of the justice that our present-day revolution holds, than the sacrifice of those who are separated from us through religion and customs, and who, in an effort to support our own, of their own free will, are ready to sacrifice their lives. [...]In our current year of 1794, on the days of the 17th and 18th of April, when Warsaw suffered

---

[73] Ibidem, p. 115-116.

bloodshed in battle with Moskal invaders, Jews residing in the city threw themselves at arms, fought valiantly at close range with the enemy and showed the world that where humanity has the most to gain, sparing one's life is of little significance. The following permit issued by the Commander-in-Chief reveals that they had always undertook to matters of liberty. There exists no inhabitant of Polish lands who would not harness whatever efforts necessary to participate in an uprising of a nation, or in securing liberty whilst envisioning the happiness of that nation. Out of concern over these appeals, Berek Joselewicz and Józef Aronowicz, both of whom are Jews, both of whom are mindful of the land from which they were born, mindful that in liberating her, they along with all others shall inherit all the benefits she has to offer, have presented their demand and willingness to create a Jewish regiment of light cavalrymen. Upon commending their eagerness, I passed on my blessing for them to recruit into the aforesaid corps, and to provide them with all military armors and necessities in order that they might join the ranks of the Polish State as swiftly as they are able, and fight off the enemy to the best of their capabilities.[74]

After the fall of the Kościuszko Uprising, the Jewish Colonel joined the legions, and Polish General Dąbrowski greeted *the citizen colonel with unaffected joy.* Colonel Berek Joselewicz perished on May 5, 1809 in the battle of Kock. He was the first Jew who, when the moment of mutual need arose, stood up to fight for the freedom and independence of Poland. Not only that, he was the first Jew who, as described by one Jewish historian: *...wanted to, and knew how to, break through the tyranny of the Kahals and the omnipotence of the Zadiks (Hasidim religious leaders) for whom the notion of Jews serving in the military at that time, and even later on, was comparable to abandoning Judaism.*[75]

Colonel Berek Joselewicz was successful in recruiting close to one hundred Polish Jews into his regiment. If we are to factor in the handful of intrepid Warsaw Jews referred to in Tadeusz Kościuszko's afore mentioned appeal, then we are talking about a few hundred Polish Jews who took the warranted stance of proprietors of this land. Is that considered to be a

---

[74] Z. Hoffman, *Berek Joselewicz*, w: Kalendarz żydowski 1984-1985 [*Berek Joselewicz*, in: The Jewish Calendar 1984-1985], Warszawa 1984, p. 116.
[75] Ibidem, p. 120.

big number or a small one for the end of the XVIII century? In absolute numbers, that total is tragically low. However, if we were to balance that with the fact that the battle waged by Berek Joselewicz and the handful of Jews close to him was elevated to the status of being symbolic or exemplary, worthy of being followed by other Jews, then the number was exceptionally high. However, it is important to note that the remaining Jews did not follow Berek Joselewicz in his example, and that the Jewish Colonel along with Commander Tadeusz Kościuszko turned out to be incurable romantics who were completely out of touch of reality, and who had ignited an unrealistic hope that Polish Jews would join the fight for an Independent Poland en masse. It was this hope that accompanied Poles and Lithuanian for the entire duration of the XIX century.

7. Tadeusz Kościuszko in the battle of Racławice, 1794.
Jan Styka and Juliusz Kossak

For Poles, the 123-year-period of captivity was a significant segment of time in their history. Upon being deprived of their independence and their own nation, they never truly came to terms with the fact that the Polish State had disappeared from the map of Europe. Their life-and-death strife with their partition powers was undertaken by nearly every generation that had been touched by captivity. The years 1794, 1812, 1830, 1846, 1863 – every single one of those was linked to hope, uprising, and yet another calamity. Adam Mickiewicz wrote *Mister Thaddeus, or the Last Foray in Lithuania: a History of the Nobility in the Years 1811 and 1812 in Twelve Books of Verse* between the years 1832-1834. Poles and Lithuanians had already had the devastation of the Kościuszko Uprising, of being at Napoleon's side, and of the November Uprising behind them. Yet another generation was coming of age in captivity, a generation on whom the solicitude over the freedom of their homeland had left so indelible a stigma that it remains to this day. Here is the portrait of a Pole-Lithuanian as drawn by our poet:

> *The Poles, although renowned they among nations stand*
> *That they more than their life love their own native land,*
> *Each is ready to leave it, run to earth's frontiers,*
> *In misery and wanderings to spend many years,*
> *Fighting mankind and fate, if, while tempest wild blows,*
> *The hope shines that he serves yet his Fatherland's cause.*[76]

During the time of the partitions, Poles needed human solidarity in a way that they had never needed it before, or since. They went in search of it to all corners of the world. Above all, they had counted on the solidarity of their fellow-inhabitants, the Polish Jews. Berek Joselewicz, and a handful of likeminded Jews, ignited a hope that other Jews would follow in their footsteps, for they had all grown up on the same land, and therefore must share the same feelings and thoughts. An expression of this hope is Mickiewicz's idealized Jew, Jankiel, who is smart, honest, useful, speaks Polish, and in addition, conspires and is the first to bring the Polish hymn *Dąbrowski's Mazurian* [Mazurek Dąbrowskiego] to Lithuania. This is how the poet imagined the ideal Polish Jew to be:

---

[76] A. Mickiewicz, *Pan Tadeusz*, [The full title in English: *Mister Thaddeus, or the Last Foray in Lithuania: a History of the Nobility in the Years 1811 and 1812 in Twelve Books of Verse.*] Wrocław 1973, p. 325.

...From afar the whole tavern, tottering, and off-square,
Most resembled a Jew who is nodding at prayer [...]
In the middle stood Jankiel in full-length capote
To the ground, with silk loops and with silver clasps caught.
One hand gravely inside his black silken sash placed,
With the other his beard stroked, grey, reaching his waist [...]

8. The concert of the Jew Jankiel.
Michal Elwiro Androlli

The old Jew, wide reputed to be a good man,
Long the lease held. No peasant, nor yet gentleman
At the manor his service would ever run down;
Why complain? Here the best choice of drink could be found,
He kept careful accounts, but gave no one short weight,
Good cheer encouraged, drunks though would not tolerate, [...]
In all music versed, he had a great reputation;
On the cembalo, greatly beloved by his nation,

He performed at the manors: his playing amazed,
And his singing, for skill and musicianship praised.
Though a Jew, quite correctly pronounced he our tongue,
He especially favored the national song; [...]
Rumor, true or not, had it that to him we owed
That, in fact, he the first was to bring from abroad
And to soon make familiar throughout the whole shire
That song that through the world now is famed and admired,
And which for the first time, in the Ausonian regions
To Italian ears sounded the trumps of our legions. [...]
It made Jankiel rich; sated with profit and fame,
His cembalo sweet-voiced he hung up and became
An inn-keeper; with children and wife settled down.,
He was, too, under-rabbi in neighboring town,
In all homes a guest welcome, one never afraid
To give sound advice; knew much about the grain trade,
And its transport by water: a much-needed role
In this country. - Known also to be a good Pole.[77]

Enjoying his fame of being *known to be a good Pole*, the idealized Jew, Jankiel, had won a place in the hearts of Poles and Lithuanians, the protagonists of the Mickiewicz poem, having earned their respect and recognition. They had accepted his distinctive religious aspect and style of dress, and they respected his profession because he loved his homeland and he was right there with them in battle. Meanwhile, reality could not have been any further from the ideal that Mickiewicz had created. As for the year 1812, a very significant year in Poland's history, the year in which Poles had been counting on breaking through to independence at Napoleon's side, the Jewish historian Majer Bałaban wrote this:

[The Tsar] Alexander I had his own Chasidic leader, and that was the Lithuanian Rebbe[78] *Zelman Sznejor from Lad. His faithful had been following*

---

[77] Ibidem, p. 159-162.
[78] A Yiddish word meaning master, teacher or mentor.

the movements of the French army, and he alone, after having been pursued by
the armies of Prince Józef of Poland, found refuge in Alexander's camp and it
was here that he died in 1913. [...] The more dire Napoleon's situation became,
the more dark spirits emerged to the surface of the earth. In Lwów, the zenith
of these reactions was achieved on June 29, 1814, when an announcement by
the mayor, Mr. Lorenz, instructed all citizens of the Tsar's city to rejoice in
the victory over Napoleon's defeat. [...] From illustrations, we are familiar
with triumphal arc that had been erected in the main square, and we also
know the names of the Jews who, along with the others, participated in the
festivities celebrating Napoleon's defeat. A true irony of fate! And so, Isaak
Wolf Rapoport illuminated his own windows and composed loyal slogans;
Salomon Goldberg expressed his joy in sixteen poems; Menachem Schneier the
restaurateur, the Pinkas Wolf et Sohn company, Gabriel Reizes, and Isaak
Silberstein all illuminated their windows; in addition, a poem in twenty verses
in Lemberg' appeared in print. [...] Almost the entire gmina (municipality)
had gathered at the synagogue where Rabbi Jakób Ornstein gave a sermon
whose content and form were most apt to the prevailing tastes of the times.
[...] After the sermon, which was later submitted for print in Hebrew, the
synagogue choir sang eleven stanzas of the customary hymn and a few psalms.
The hymn was also submitted for print along with Ornstein's sermon, and this
rare publication of combined texts has been preserved to commemorate the
loyalty the current Jewish gmina had celebrated...[79]

During the 123 years of captivity, although Poland had been divided
by the borders of the partition powers, the Polish populace never lost
contact with each other between the neighborhoods that had fallen under
the separate Prussian, Austrian and Russian reigns. This is why the various
reports, especially those that were political in nature, were able to spread
throughout the country relatively quickly. This included reports of the
stance taken by Polish Jews with regard to the captors. It is even safe to
assume that the last one, although in a probably somewhat exaggerated
form, had spread at lightening speed. The reaction to these reports was
quite uniform throughout all three partitions, and resulted in ever more

---

[79] M. Bałaban, *Dzieje Żydów w Galicyi* [*A History of Jews of Galicia*], Kraków 1914, p. 86-88.

stringent political postures being taken with regard to the Jewish co-inhabitants. This is why in 1815, by the decree of the Congress of Vienna, the Polish Kingdom that had been created from the land under the Russian partition, a special Committee to the Matters of the Peasantry and Jews was called. The presiding head arbiter, Prince Adam Czartoryski, wrote this in 1816: *Jews are not indigenous inhabitants of our lands. They are nonresidents, foreigners, outsiders.*[80] Contained within the disquisition of the Committee was an outline of negative characteristics of Jews, including slovenliness and an unwillingness to perform physical labor. At roughly the same time, the allegation of Jews having no real established ties to the country had also surfaced.

In an effort to understand the rapidly expanding and ever deepening chasm between the Poles and Jews residing on lands that had arisen out

---

[80] A. Eisenbach, *Emancypacja żydowska na ziemiach polskich 1785-1870* [*Emancipation of Jews on Polish lands 1785-1870*], Warszawa 1988, p. 176. The author presents the Council's opinion in the following way: 'The introduction to this document emphasizes the fact that among current social questions with which the government was faced, the issue of the Jewish population should occupy one of the topmost positions. Because „humanity, righfulness, the words and the spirit of the constitution, and prudence, recommend that the current state of humilitation of this populous and capable nation should be changed; the causes of the Reaction, which harms both sides, should be averted." Accordingly, one should reform the customs of the Jewish population, improve their situation, kindle the spirit of citizenship and the devotion to their country. Only then will it become their homeland. After this liberal declaration it is stated that the Jews, however long they had lived in Poland, „are not natural inhabitants of our land; rather, they are migrants, foreigners, strangers" since they have preserved the customs and the character of a separate nation. Although at different times they did acquire priviledges and liberties, it was not due to their contributions to the country but rather by the rulers' sufferance. This is why "as a foreign nation, the Jews have no right to citizenship and every case of granting them privileges is a favor and beneficence." The granted privileges had been "overused and they cannot be considered neither the source nor the foundation of their rights or claims." [...] thereby having evaluated the situation, it is declared that "the only reason for granting them these liberties is the rightfulness, humanity, prudence, the spirit of the age and the general interest." "Accepting these principles, it seems that we cannot refuse the people that had been living with us for such a long time any of these rights." Above all, it is necessary to change their customs because "the flaws are probably not the result of the inborn inclination...", but the effect of these people's oppression, contempt and bias against them. "Oppression, violence, limited possibilities of sustenance would introduce greed, deceit and disgrace in any nation."'

of the circumstances following the partition due to a variety of political stances, in an effort to grasp the thought processes which led Jews to be devoid of any sense of solidarity with those who were fighting for the homeland they shared with their fellow-inhabitants, the Poles, let us refer to a Jewish legend from Napoleonic times which was recalled by a Jewish historian:

In the 'hauses' and at the 'courts' of Zadiks [leaders of the Hasidim communitys - EK], *there were loud discussions on events that were taking place all over the world, and the pious were searching for advice on how to cure all the ills of life. It is no wonder that word of the Napoleonic armies marching in and the echoes of bloody warfare being waged on battlefields all across Europe had penetrated the walls of the ghettos and had become the primary topic of conversation among the Zadiks and their faithful.*

The legend goes as follows: Mendel, the Zadik from Rymanów, summoned his faithful in order that they might pray together for the success of the Napoleonic battles. Naftali Horowitz, the Zadik from Ropczyce, was somewhat taken aback by the request of his master and asked for the reason why. "That Napoleon is the greatest of nonbelievers ever to occupy a throne, and you would have us pray for his success?" Rabi Mendel contemplated long over his response, and finally jumped from his chair and yelled, "And even if that's true, God forbid, what if Napoleon were to fail?!" Naftali from Ropczyce was not satisfied with this response and inquired further, "Why should this Napoleon succeed?" "The world depends on Napoleon's victory," the Rebbe from Rymanow replied, "He has his own defender, his own angel up in heaven! And you say that he is a nonbeliever! And who among them is not a nonbeliever? They all have their own inclinations 'in their schools' and they'd like to stuff all our Jewish children inside them. The one thing you should be clear on is that if Napoleon is victorious, then all the princes in the land shall recognize that you do not oppress the nation of Israel. They have oppressed all the lands everywhere, and now it's time for them to be oppressed. They have been handing down sentences, and now it's time for them to learn that there is a judge and jury, a sentence hanging over their heads!"

Naftali from Ropczyce did not allow himself to be thrown off track, and he tried to explain to the master from Rymanow that no leader had until that time ever mixed nations with each other, just like Napoleon, no other leader had ever been so eager not to aim to eliminate the differences between Jews and other nations as he. "But we have been a separate nation for eons, different from these that he would have us mingle with!" Mendel from Rymanów did not know how to respond to this. So he headed to Lublin to see the master Jakob Izaak for the purpose of seeking enlightenment from him. He presented him with all the bits of wisdom that the Zadik from Ropczyce had put forth and awaited a reply. The Lublin Zadik listened very carefully to the deductions of his friend, looked out the window, looked around in all directions, thought long, but did not utter a single word. The impatient Zadik from Rymanów traveled further to Kozienice to meet with the local Maggid [A Jewish advisor- E.K.].

The Kozienice Maggid was a frail man, and on top of that, the Zadik from Rymanów had come on Friday, the day on which the Rebbe Izrael liked to take a rest in bed after his bath. The Rebbe Mendel, however, did not allow him to settle down serenely in bed. Instead, he unloaded the entire matter in a single breath. The Maggid, who had just been reclining peacefully, suddenly jumped to his feet and shouted in a mighty voice, "They say that Napoleon has a great protector in heaven, but this is what we say: You, Sir, are the haughtiest of them all! You, Sir, are higher than all the angels in heaven... He, Napoleon, drafted Jews into the army and forced them to mutilate their Saturdays and blight other sacred commandments! Let all those who trespass into temptation and sin perish!" The Kozienice Maggid despised Napoleon with every fiber of his being because he saw in him the perpetrator of destruction of the Jewish religion.[81]

Flowing from incompatible practices of recognizing and interpreting the same historical events, the Jewish parables indicate how divergent the values within the political spheres that dictated the worlds of both Polish Jews and Poles really were. They further prove how, although Polish and Jewish worlds did exist alongside each other on the same Polish lands, they were in fact perfectly separated by an impassable weatherproof curtain. Were there any realistic possibilities which would have allowed Polish Prince Adam Czartoryski to find a common tongue with the Jewish Maggid from Kozienice or any other Rabbi? We are not even talking about

[81] M. Bałaban, *Dzieje Żydów w Galicyi* [*A History of Jews of Galicia*], Kraków 1914, p. 86-88.

reaching a mutual agreement with regard to a political stance, but rather about a congruent way of thinking, behaving and reacting to the external surrounding reality.

For the Polish minds that had been burning to engage in a fight for freedom, even if they had really wanted to, at the threshold of the XIX century, it was not possible to grasp what it was exactly that Jews had issues with as far as their perception of Napoleon, or the soldier, or the emperor who had promised Poland her freedom. Just as the Jews, who had been running from one Rabbi to the next, for whom Napoleon represented the *greatest of nonbelievers*, were not capable of grasping why Poles were so very excited over the French nonbeliever. Nor were they able to understand why Poles were expecting Jews to defend Polish matters that were entirely incomprehensible to them, and in addition mutilate their age-old commandments, blight the good name of the Jewish nation and stand up to fight alongside the current captives of the land they inhabit.

With regard to the period of the Polish State 966-1795, Majer Bałaban wrote that *Jews continued to come upon a source of support from the nobles and magnates*. It seems that, in fact, the first half of the XIX century, in the years following the Napoleonic calamity and that of the November Uprising, the period during which Poles' hopes of rapidly recovering their independence had been buried, was the period during which the hitherto supportive nobles and magnates had begun to systematically withdraw their support of Polish Jews as a result of the stance taken by Jews with regard to the fight for freedom. For it was the nobles and magnates, a "political state" as it was commonly referred to, who, from the beginning of Polish history, had always been obliged to defend the Polish State. In this way, the very same Jews who in 1791 had been considered to be *useful Polish citizens*, and who, despite being classified by Father Gintyłło as *local natives with the knowledge of written Hebrew*, were now, in the aftermath of the Napoleonic calamity, in the political opinion of the Polish nation, being more prevalently perceived as *not being indigenous inhabitants of our lands; nonresidents, foreigners, outsiders*.

In the face of having had such negative experiences, during almost the entire XIX century, Poles did not lose hope of successfully awakening the mass of Polish Jews to join in their mutual fight for a free and independent Poland. In 1832, Joahim Lelewel composed an appeal to Polish Jews in Polish, German and French:

Sons of Israel! If there are any among you who harbor ill will towards us, ask yourself the reason why, and try to recall the words of the Rabbis: "The sins of man against God are forgiven on the 'Day of Atonement', but the sins of man against another are not forgiven on this day if man himself does not find a solution to the problem". If we have sinned against you, then we shall face God on Judgment Day. On victory day, however, we would like to have an accurate reckoning with you. Every Polish son, Jew or Catholic, shall stand right here to present their account of what they had done to contribute to the good of the whole, and how much effort they had put into the rebuilding of our homeland. Every effort and every service shall be weighed at the moment when this native land can be called our own, at which time we shall divide this freedom amongst ourselves together, or each for themselves according to a mutual agreement. If you should demand a complete separation from us and a return to the land of Jacob, very well! Whatever you shall request shall be granted in the name of equity with regard to your wishes. Rise with us for this reason and unite with us in prayer so that God may grant us victory. The hour of freedom shall ring very soon. This matter cannot be delayed. Work with us, and do so immediately, for "one who looks into the wind, does not sow; one who looks into the clouds, does not reap".[82]

Poles who fought in the November Uprising in 1831 were supported through active battle by 43 Jewish doctors and a few hundred Jewish volunteers. Three Jews were awarded the Virtuti Militari medal for bravery.[83] In 1848, when the Springtime of Nations (Wiosna Ludów) surges broke out, and yet another faint ember of hope glimmered for Poland and her freedom, Bohdan Rzędzianowski from Staisławowo wrote an apt poem addressed to his Polish Jewish brothers:

---

[82] M. Bałaban, *Dzieje Żydów w Galicyi* [*A History of Jews of Galicia*], Kraków 1914, p. 121. The leaflet, hidden deeply in the kahal archives of Kraków and other Galician cities, was preserved to the author's times; the content of the leaflet is quoted after him.
[83] A. Żbikowski, op. cit., p. 77.

Oh, Israel, why do you look upon Polish movements from afar?
What do you possess inside that prevents you from welding with us
your spirit?
A difference in faith will not stand in the way of you being a brother
to a Pole
A brotherly equality will help sweeten the bitterness of years already
gone by.
For it is the same God who rules over us, who over Palestine ruled,
He imposes the same sacred law on us that had been imposed on you
in Sinai [...]
And so together, and in harmony for our nation and God so dear
United in the slogan in the Polish land, as before her a common enemy
shall flee![84]

Jews from Kazimierz in Kraków became actively involved in the events
of 1848. Upon hearing the news of the Pillersdorf Constitution that had
been announced in Vienna in April, they proceeded to demolish the houses-
of-ill-repute that had been maintained in their city for centuries, as well as
practically lynching the kosher leaseholder, Leibl Torbeg. The character of
these events, which were linked to Jewish communal life in general, was
significant only locally. It did, however, serve to spur the Jewish intelligentsia
of Kraków, with Jonatan Warschauer and Krzepicki at its head, to create
perhaps the first ever patriotic postulates since the time of Berek Joselewicz.
On May 22, 1848, in the German-language periodical, "Orient", Kraków
Jews published an appeal calling upon their fellow-faithful to actively support
the cause of Poland's independence, in which they wrote the following:

Brothers in Israel! The noble Polish nation, to which European civilization
is deeply indebted, and to which over two million of our brethren owe everything,
this Polish nation which took in our fathers when the sons of Germania and Galia
had shamefully expelled them and pushed them into misfortune, this nation
which was stripped of its land 80 years earlier, and which has demonstrated

---

84 M. Bałaban, *Dzieje Żydów w Galicyi* [*A History of Jews of Galicia*], Kraków 1914, p. 154-
155.

*unprecedented fortitude and courage in its fight for freedom ever since, this nation is close to seeing its dreams come true, is close to achieving its goals... We, Jews, come from this country, we belong to this Polish land, we were born here, we share a common homeland with Poles. There are countless other links which connect us with this noble nation. Why, we have had to endure the same suffering and oppression, exile and shame as they now do... Brothers! After all that, am I really supposed to hesitate over whether or not to get involved in the sacred matter of **supporting this noble nation through fortune and blood**? Are we, for even one second, going to hesitate over whether to support the Germans or the Poles?...The noble Polish nation, which went before the emperor to petition for our political equality, deserves that we suffer at least one human casualty, deserves that we suffer the labor pains for a better tomorrow. Therefore, Brothers, let us not skimp on casualties or hardship, and let us show the world that we still have Maccabean blood flowing through our veins, and that our hearts pound for everything that is beautiful and noble. Oh, may the mercy of God flow down upon us and may our prayers be answered. Amen.*[85]

In response to the appeal of Kraków Jews, Poznań Jews wrote the following in the next issue of "Orient":

If your culture and customs have become so Polonized, and you wish to include yourselves in the liberation of a subjugated Poland, then at least have the ability to justly judge our love for the German nation. For only he who truly loves his country is capable of understanding the love of a country.[86]

Exceptionally patriotic and deeply heartfelt in its expression, the appeal of the Kraków Jewish intelligentsia was the result of the stance that the Poles, who had been fighting for freedom, had been clamoring and dreaming of it. It was then, and still remains to this day, a valuable bridge between the two nations. In 1848, the Jewish population of Kraków consisted of 13,000 living in Kazimierz. The only Jews who were permitted to live outside of Kazimierz were those who had at least finished secondary school, were professors or doctors at an academy, artists, merchants or manufacturers, were able to read and write in Polish or German, and

---

[85] Ibidem, p. 162-163.
[86] A. Zbikowski, op. cit., p. 83.

whose style of dress did not differ from that of Christian residents of the city. There were barely 196 Jews who fell into that category. The drama of the situation of 1848 lay in the fact that the authors of the appeal were speaking on behalf of a very narrow segment of a social group which constituted a mere 1.5-2% of the general Jewish population of Kraków. It was this very narrow segment of the Jewish population which sustained the stance that had been demonstrated by Berek Joselewicz, which was perceived by Poles as the only appropriate stance. Over the course of the years between 1795 and 1848, this group consistently remained at the same percentage level, and as the future would demonstrate, they were never able to rely on the desired support that had been expressed in the appeal addressed to the throngs of their fellow-faithful. The response, however, which was issued by the Poznań Jews, did signal the arrival of yet another phenomenon which was potentially dangerous to Poles, and with the passing of the next few decades of captivity, it did come to take on an ever greater significance among Polish Jews. Word of the expansion of assimilation of Polish Jews that was taking place within the cultures and communities of Russia, Prussia and Austria, was perceived by Poles to be outright high treason, and it also became one of the primary driving forces behind Polish anti-Semitism.

The Jewish historian, Majer Bałaban, at the threshold of the XX century, wrote this about the Polish Jews from Poznan with mockery and a hint of derision: ...*they go around clearly declaring themselves as Germans and they openly express their German patriotism [as well as] spin their declarations of love for the Germans.*[87] At the end of the XX century, Andrzej Żbikowski defends the reply issued by Poznań Jews in 1848 by stating the following: *The gravity of the matter at hand in itself excuses the lofty tone. The Wielkopolska Jews had made a choice and they remained faithful to it.*[88] In understanding the epoch in question, the assessment offered by the Jewish historian does seem to be more readily accessible. However, it is only possible to imagine how Poles may have reacted to the

---

[87] M. Bałaban, *Dzieje Żydów w Krakowie i na Kazimierzu 1304-186 [A History of Jews in Kraków and in the Kazimierz District 1304-1868]*, Kraków 1912, p. 162-163.
[88] A. Zbikowski, op. cit., p. 83.

current *declarations of love for the Germans...* The fact of the matter is that in 1848, in Poznan, anti-Jewish insurrections did occur. The correlation between the pro-German declarations of the Jews from Poznan and the Polish anti-Jewish insurrections in the same geographical area does not warrant a great deal of research.

The echoes of calamity following the Springtime of Nations had not yet settled when Poles under Russian captivity started to prepare their next uprising. In manifestations that heralded the uprising, especially during the manifestation of February 27, 1861, Warsaw Jews did in fact support Polish national aspirations. However, in the tragic two years of struggles that occurred during the January Uprising, which broke out on January 22, 1863 and lasted well into the autumn of 1864, there was a mere handful of Polish Jews who actively participated, and that number did not exceed two hundred persons.[89]

Despite clear signals that the hopes expressed by Poles with regard to Polish Jews including themselves in the struggles for freedom were utterly lacking in foundation, Poles' appeals for solidarity did not subside for the remaining decades of the XIX century that followed. In the twenty years from the time the letters had been exchanged between the Jews of Krakow and Poznan, and a few years following the calamity of the January Uprising, Franciszek Smolka, during the Austrian Parliament, rebutted in this way to the opponents of granting all Jews constitutional freedoms:

The esteemed Member of Parliament declares that we can grant equal rights to Jews only when they become Poles. [...] This same esteemed Member of Parliament has also stated that twenty years have passed since Jews were granted equal rights, and that they still have not become Poles. I, on the other hand, state this: this is true, but this is true because they are equal only in theory and not in practice. The fact that they are equal in theory only causes their sense of bitterness towards us, which has been festering in their hearts, to increase. For they are aware that they had been granted these privileges in Vienna and that we are refusing them in practice... They will not be Poles,

---

[89] N. Getter, J. Schall, Z. Schipper, *Żydzi bojownicy o niepodległość Polski* [*Jewish fighters for Poland's independence*], Lwów 1939, p. 70-73.

nor can they first become Poles unless we are ready to surrender to them all
that they are entitled to [...] it is necessary to start with justice with regard to
them, un-curtailed justice. And only then, I declare before you, Gentlemen, if
not they, then certainly their children shall be Poles.[90]

With his fiery speech, Franciszek Smolka had won equal rights for all
Polish Jews residing within the territories of the Austrian partition. Polish
Jews, in their general mass, did not become Poles during that generation or
during any other generation that followed. Concurrently, it is necessary to
specify here, that the Polish clamor for Polish Jews to become Poles was in
no way missionary in tint or hue. This was not about converting to another
faith, for as Adam Mickiewicz had written: *Though a Jew, quite correctly*
pronounced he our tongue and *known also to be a good Pole.* His sentiment
was made complete by the words of the rhymester from Stanisławowo: *A*
difference in faith will not stand in the way of you being a brother to a Pole!

According to the nineteenth-century understanding of the matter
at hand, Poles never questioned the right of Jews to practice their own
religion (Jews could easily have been Poles whilst maintaining their faith,
style of dress and traditions), but rather they were demanding that Jews
became Poles through a brotherhood of bloodshed for their common
homeland, Poland. Poles considered Polish Jews to be the sons of Polish
land, and they were only demanding that which, according to the Polish
way of thinking, a son owes his motherland, nothing less than a fight
for her freedom. Despite the passing of several decades, the idea of a
Polish-Jewish blood-brotherhood that had been proposed to Jews was
understood and undertaken only by a very small number of Polish Jews.
Every partition generation had roughly the same percentage of Polish Jews
as were represented by the underlings of Colonel Berek Joselewicz and the
defender of Warsaw in the ranks of Kościuszko's rebels.

As for what created the vacuum that existed, into which the Polish
clamor for Jewish solidarity and the appeals of future "Berek Joselewicz's"
fell on deaf ears, that is further explained by a reading of the *Judaic Guide*
written by Hilary Nussbaum in 1893, in which he writes that the most

---

[90] M. Bałaban, *Dzieje Żydów w Galicyi* [*A History of Jews of Galicia*], Kraków 1914, p. 207-208.

important Jewish holiday, which commemorates the Jewish exodus from Egypt, is Pesach (Passover). The most important aspect of this holiday is the celebratory dinner called Seder, which Jewish families sit down to on the eve of the holiday: *The Pesach 'Seder' ceremony begins with the father of the family saying the 'Kiddush' blessing over the wine, after which everyone at the table says 'Amen' and tips their glass of wine. The tipping of wine glasses during the specific prayers throughout the entire course of the evening meal takes place four times. Hence the name of this ceremony, 'Arba Kosos', which means 'four cups'. This is followed by everyone placing their hands on the platter containing the matzo, which is raised in the air, and the following passage from the Haggadah is recited: 'This is the bread of poverty which was consumed by our predecessors on Egyptian lands. Any who are hungry, let them join us for this meal, any who are in need, let them participate in Pesach together with us.* **Presently we are here, next year we shall be in the lands of Israel.** *Presently we are slaves, next year we shall be free'.*

After Pesach, the next Jewish holiday is the spring festival of Lag Ba'Omer which recalls to memory the persecution of Jews during Roman times. Hilary Nussbaum describes the traditions associated with this holiday in this way: *The custom of Jewish youth playing soldiers by donning wooden swords and bows and arrows on Lag Ba'Omer has survived to this day. This is intended to serve as a tribute to honor the students of R. Akiba, known from the history of the Bar Kokhba Revolt as the brave rebels who served on the field of war against the Romans, and who demonstrated unprecedented valor up until its last stand at Betar.*

There are also other Jewish holidays and festivals (Sukkot, the feast of booths, Chanukah and Purim) associated with rich liturgical binds and folkloric customs. They evoke events connected with Jewish history reaching as far back as hundreds or thousands of years prior to their setting foot on Polish soil. As for Jewish prayer, however, and the behaviors, customs and stances associated with it, I will take the liberty here to invoke the following fragment from Nussbaum's "Guide": *The development of prayer spanned nine centuries. From the public campaigns of the Great Synagogue (Knesset Hagdola) founded by Ezra in Jerusalem (430 B.C.), to the closing of the Talmud (500 A.D), this process of development underwent four main stages during this period: 1) From the return of the exiles to Jerusalem and the reinstitution of Divine Service at the rebuilt Temple to the banning of Israeli religious practices by the Syrians; 2) From the victory of the Maccabees to the destruction of the nation by Titus; 3) From that moment forward until uprising of the Israelites under Bar Kokhba; 4) From the suppression of the rebellion to the closing of the Talmud. The last of these stages is what prompted the Israelites to recognize that the time had come to abandon any and all violent means associated with attaining political status, to lay down their arms and step back from any political ambitions, and to rather make a concerted effort to focus on strengthening the spirit of Israel through performing religious practices and sustaining spiritual devotion.*[91]

Now, a mere fragmentary glance at Jewish traditions and religion will suffice in stating that Polish Jews, although they had resided on Polish lands for nearly one thousand years, never identified with Poland as a homeland in the contemporary meaning of the word, that is with the country for whose freedom one sacrifices one's life. However, it is certain that they did identify with Poland as the country in which they were born. First of all, they had a very keen awareness of being members of a nation that had been chosen by God. Secondly, they possessed their own history, and Israel never ceased to be their true sole homeland, for a return to which they prayed at least once a year. Within that context, the fight for freedom that Poles had been enthralled in was not a matter for which Polish Jews were able to fight. Most salient is the question that was posed at the end of the XX century by the Jewish historian describing the chronicles of Berek Joselewicz's regiment: *What was it that was so inherent in this person that [...] he was not willing to shed his uniform, he wanted to serve a homeland, despite the fact that for him, and for many others, this service to this homeland* **was objectively a service to a foreign cause on foreign land.**[92]

Polish Jews, although they had resided on Polish lands for nearly one

---

91 H. Nussbaum, *Przewodnik Judaistyczny obejmujący kurs literatury i religii* [*A Judaic guide including the course of literature and religion*], Warszawa 1893, p. 227-228, 243, 248 and 266-267.

92 Z. Hoffman, *Berek* Joselewicz, in: „Kalendarz Zydowski 1984/85" [The Jewish Calendar 1984/85], Warsaw 1984, p. 118.

thousand years, the majority of them always considered Poland to be a *foreign land,* and service to Poland was considered a *foreign matter.* Aside from the negligible percentage of the generational few like Berek Joselewicz, Polish Jews never recognized Poland as their homeland in the objective and prevalent meaning of the word. They lived within the historical traditions of their own nation, but in a world of "virtual" tradition, mysticism, religion and legend for Poles. What did Poland constitute for them? In their own language they referred to her as *Polin,* which phonetically does sound like the word "Poland". But *Polin,* in the language of Jews is, above all: an ancient term designated for a resting place, safe night lodging, a settlement, and a life in peace for persons leaving Judea.[93] So it seems that Poland, for all those generations of Polish Jews, served as nothing more that a mere place to rest, a place for a tranquil temporary existence, a place to settle. It was not a homeland in whose defense blood should be spilled.

From that perspective, the most important matter for Jewish settlers was finding a place in which they could settle, live in peace and practice their own religion. As to whether that place was ruled by a Polish king, an Austrian emperor, or a Russian tsar, that was secondary. For Polish Jews, the reign of the partition monarchies was equally as legitimate as that of the Polish crown. They would welcome these rulers with all due honors, they would pray for them, and they would subjugate themselves to them with almost no resistance at all. In the end, during their Seder feast, they would claim that *presently we are slaves.* And isn't it true that, to a slave, it makes no difference whose captivity they are under: Polish, Russian, Prussian or Austrian? Even if it is not all together irrelevant whose captivity they are under, then at least for the purpose of changing masters, the slave never puts their own life at risk.

In their anticipation for Jewish patriotism with regard to Poland, in their expectation of shedding blood for the freedom of their shared homeland, Poles of the nineteenth century were extremely naive. They were demanding the impossible from Jews. If we had, however, taken a closer look at Jewish history, tradition, liturgy, as well as the binding principles Jews must uphold,

[93] I. Stemplowska, R. Stemplowski, *Laicy czytają „Polin",* w: „Śladami Polin – Studia z dziejów Żydów w Polsce [*Laymen read „Polin",* in: On the track of Polin – Studies in the Jewish history in Poland], Warszawa 2002, s. 168.

then it would become apparent that even if they had wanted to, Jews –
followers of the Jewish religion – would not have been able to reconcile the
historical-religious burdens of their own nation with the burdens of Polish
history and the Polish concept of patriotism and freedom. Therefore, Polish
Jews, on principle alone, were not able to become Poles, at least not based on
the nineteenth-century-Poland understanding of that concept.

During the XIX century, it was difficult for Poles to comprehend
the stance taken by Polish Jews. It is difficult even today. It is, however,
necessary to accept the fact that this stance had been dictated by thousands
of years of living in the Diaspora, and it was commanded in the Bible: *As
a result of the nation of Judea having been beaten up and dismantled, as well
as the Judeans being exiled to Babylonia, the prophet Jeremiah was the first to
explain to the Judeans themselves the attitude they should express in their new
homeland with regard to the non-Jewish nation and its superior authority.
He then told them this: 'Wake up all the houses and start living there, plant
gardens and use their fruit. Take wives and give birth to sons and daughters,
give your sons wives, and your daughters husbands, so that they can give birth
to sons and daughters. Multiply there and do not let your numbers recede. Look
for what is good in the country to which I have relocated you, and pray for its
good, as you too shall prosper from its goodness.* From the same Babylonia,
from the times of Sassanid rule, one of the most renowned Amorites
expressed the following sentiment: *The laws of a country have the same power
with regard to Jews as to their own'. After rebuilding their second nation, the
Jews in Palestine, under the dominion of Persian and Syrian kings, made daily
offerings for the success and prosperity of their foreign kings. This custom was
later passed into law among Jews settled in various countries to ensure that they
demonstrate their loyalty and love for said domain and country, and pray for
the good of said countries, a practice which continues to this day.*[94]

With the above aspect in mind, for religious Polish Jews, despite their
great affection for Polish kings, the king of Poland was no different from
any other monarch of any partition power in that he was a *foreign king*.
Loyalty to the emperor or tsar, and acquiescence to the laws imposed on

---

[94] H. Nussbaum, op.cit., p. 314-315.

Polish lands, was, in the Jewish sense of understanding, a norm with the same binding obligations as the norms that had been established by Polish kings and Polish Parliament in centuries past.

The XIX century was a time during which Poles could have recognized Jews, their fellow-inhabitants, as brothers. Since owing to the brotherhood that could have been forged through mutual blood spilled in defending the freedom of their shared homeland, both nations could have fused together into one indivisible family, and fortified in this way, could have weathered the storms that awaited them together, all the while retaining the distinctive aspects of their respective faiths, customs and languages. Things happened very differently, however. Despite the constantly increasing, although still negligible percentage of Jewish patriots (in the Polish sense of the word), Polish Jew did not undertake to fight side by side with Poles for the freedom of their common Polish State. The dreams of Berek Joselewicz, Adam Mickiewicz, Joachim Lelewel, the Kraków Jewish intelligentsia and Franciszek Smolka never came to fruition. Above all because of what Poles couldn't have known due to the language barrier, and because the greater majority of Polish Jewry felt that *service* [to Poland] *to the homeland was* [for Polish Jews] *objectively a service to a foreign cause on foreign land,* and some continue to feel this way to the present day.[95]

The stance of Polish Jews with regard to the matter of independence, in addition to economic conditions being in the hands of the partition powers ruling over the Polish State, were the most crucial factors that played

---

[95] A. Cala, *Wizerunek Żyda w polskiej kulturze ludowej* [*The image of a Jew in Polish popular history*], Warszawa 1992, p. 29-29. The author says: 'Medieval ecclesiastical and state legislation forbade the Jews, as well as the women, to bear arms and be engaged in soldiering. Our turbulent history did not let this law be strictly observed, however. Jews took active part in the defense of cities; moreover, they were obliged to do it, especially in the borderland regions. They became defenceless only when anti-Semitic, specially trained troops started to step forward against them.' In her work embracing centuries of Jews' existence in Poland, the author tries to answer the question why the numbers of Jews participating in wars was so scant. Her vision is rather typical and widespread in the post-war times. The absurdity of the thesis that Jews became defenceless only when anti-Semitic, specially trained troops started to step forward against them is proved in the aforementioned Hilary Nussbaum's *Judaic guide...,* which had been written well before 'Polish anti-Semitic troops' – so exposed in Cała's book – ever appeared.

a role in the best of Polish traditions, those of tolerance and protection with regard to the national Jewish minority during the XIX century, being buried once and for all. This also contributed to the shape of the new brand of stance Poles would take with regard to their Jewish fellow-inhabitants. Lasting over the course of a few generations, a direct threat to Polish national survival was, on the one hand, due to the absence of Jewish solidarity, the gradual fading away of the sense of positive protectionism among Poles with regard to their Jewish guests which, during centuries past, had allowed the latter to live a relatively peaceful life. On the other hand, this created a brand of protectionism which was structured around the idea that only those who fight for her freedom are entitled to citizenship with equal rights on Polish land.

Today, with the vast knowledge pertaining to the mechanisms that dictated the stance taken by Polish Jews being greater than it was two centuries ago, and with having the perspective of the events that occurred during the cruel XX century behind us, we can attempt to understand the Brody Jews, as well as Jews from all other locales throughout Poland, who, during all the years of captivity, without reservations, displayed foreign eagles on their synagogues, and refused to undertake to fight for a Polish, that is for a *foreign matter,* in order to preserve the hitherto Jewish lifestyle and the structures of the ersatz self-government that had been constructed through hardship on Polish lands. Today, we can attempt to understand and fully accept the fact that the stance taken by Polish Jews was dictated by, above all, their concern over persevering and preserving the shape and form of the Jewish lifestyle they had managed to build on Polish lands because it guaranteed survival for the Jewish community.

We do not demand too much from our predecessors. For the hope of regaining freedom, all the generations of Poles who had come to live between 1795 and 1918 paid a cruel toll in blood and fortune. For the freedom of the Polish State, countless ranks of the best of sons and daughters of this land sacrificed their lives. None of the Polish partition generations expected their Jewish fellow-inhabitants to change their religion, in the same way that a change of religion was not expected from Polish Tatars, for instance, who, as orthodox Muslims, did die in defense of the homeland they shared with Poles. From their fellow-inhabitants, the Polish Jews, the partition generations of Poles expected nothing more than common solidarity in their fight for freedom and in rebuilding their once existent state. Having never seen it come to fruition during 123 years of captivity, the stance of Polish Jews with regard to the partition powers and the absence of expected Jewish solidarity in battle were ultimately called by their proper name: limitless ingratitude and outright betrayal by foreigners.

Polish historian and politician, Joachim Lelewel, in 1832, very close to one hundred years before Poland had regained her independence, wrote this to the Jews: *On victory day, we would like to have an accurate reckoning with you. Every Polish son, Jew or Catholic, shall stand right here to present their account of what they had done to contribute to the good of the whole, and how much effort they had put into the rebuilding of our homeland.*

Because Polish Jews, aside from some honorable exceptions, refused their mutual homeland blood and fortune, when victory day did arrive, and the time for reckoning had come, they stood before Poles empty-handed. No explanations would suffice. Poles, in accordance with the logic imposed by these basic facts, claimed that the Jewish nation, which had been residing on Polish lands for nearly one thousand years, was not deserving of trust, equal rights, respect or the solidarity of the reconstructed Polish State. They further claimed that Polish Jews, in general, are merely foreigners on Polish lands.

The attitude of Polish Jews regarding the matter of Poland's independence dictates the answer to the question posed in the title of this chapter: foreigners or fellow-citizens? The concept of citizenship, in the most prevalent understanding of the meaning of the word, presupposes the existence of clear and intelligible citizens' rights, as well as equally clear and intelligible responsibilities of the citizen with regard to their country. One of the fundamental principles in the field of laws and obligations when it comes to the fine line of citizen-state matters is the right of the citizen to defend his person and to protect his own interests, as well as the obligation of said citizen to stand in defense of the state in a situation when the existence of either is threatened.

Poles, along with Lithuanians, were the titular property owners of the multi-national Polish-Lithuanian Commonwelth which fell in 1795, and they had a right to expect solidarity from Jews in the fight for rebuilding the state which had for centuries guaranteed protection to Jews and their interests. 123 years of captivity was an exercise and test in citizenship for all the nations that had been living within the borders of Poland at the time. Needless to say, Jews did not pass the test in citizenship. In characterizing the fight for regaining freedom of their once mutual state as not being a Jewish matter, Polish Jews behaved not like citizens of the Polish State, but rather like foreigners. They had, therefore, been designated as foreigners during the twenty-year-period between the wars, and they were treated as foreigners during the Second World War.

In order to understand the alien aspect of Polish Jews and the harsh criticism of this very facet by the generations of pre-war Poles, it is worth making reference to modern times. It seems, in this case, the most apt comparison of the multi-national nature of Poland would be that of the United States. Since the misfortune of terrorism had befallen the United States, as of September 11, 2001, American Catholics and Jews, Greek Orthodox and Protestants, the descendents of the once newly arrived Poles, Chinese, British and Blacks all participate in the fight to defend their mutual home. The place where their ancestors were born or the religions they follow today are not important, nor are the color of their skin or their facial characteristics. A citizenship stance requires the citizens of the United States to stand arm-in-arm to fight for the peace and prosperity of their mutual American home. In this situation, if ten million Americans of Polish descent were suddenly to declare that the fight being waged by the United States was not a matter for their concern because their loyalty obligates them only to the Polish nation, Polish historical traditions and the Polish State, then the rest of American citizens would have the right to brand them as foreigners and require them to return to the home of their ancestors immediately. If, in that case, we were to apply a uniform measure to appraise all the nations in the world, if we were to apply a uniform measure to appraise the citizen aspect of attitudes, then we must admit that Poles in 1918, due to the absence of solidarity on the part of Jews in the fight to regain Polish independence, had every legitimate basis and right to designate Jews living in Poland not as fellow-citizens, but as foreigners.

This conviction was further enhanced by the stance taken by Polish Jews with regard to the newly reborn Polish State, and it had emerged even before Poland had regained her independence for the final time.[96] The Zionist Conference that had been in session in Warsaw on October 21 and 22 in 1918, in its resolution pertaining to *The matters of politics of the country*, came forth with the demand for granting Jews a constitutional guarantee of a national autonomy within the reconstructed Polish State.[97]

9. The first Regional Zionist Conference, November 12, 1919 in Chelm, Poland.

[96] On entering the areas of the Russian partition, already during World War I did the Germans announce that Polish Jews shall be granted the rights of ethnical minority. The experiences gained in the Russian territory encouraged Polish Jews to implement the ideas of Jewish autonomy in Poland. First actions were taken already in September 1918 (Izaak Grünbam's return of from Russia), i.e. before the declaration of Poland's independence. See also: P. Wróbel, *Przed odzyskaniem niepodległości*, w: „Najnowsze dzieje Żydów w Polsce" [*Before regaining independence*], ed. J. Tomaszewski, Warszawa 1993, p. 122; J. Żyndul, *Państwo w państwie?* [*A state within a state?*], Warszawa 2000, p. 85; „Hajnt", no. 177, October 4, 1918, p. 3; *Zasady naszego programu politycznego* [*The principles of our political program*], Warszawa 1917; *Organizacja Syjonistyczna w Królestwie Polskim w sprawie narodowego i politycznego uprawnienia Żydów* [*The Zionist Organisation in the Kingdom of Poland regarding national and political rights of Jews*], Warszawa 1918.

[97] *Materiały w sprawie żydowskiej w Polsce* [*Materials regarding the Jewish issue in Poland*], ed. I. Grünbaum, vol. I, Warszawa 1919, p. 6-7; „Hajnt", no. 198, October 27, 1918, p. 3.

As to the shape the autonomy that Polish Jews were expecting to obtain in Poland was to take, that had already been submitted by Jewish parliamentarians in May of 1919, when the Polish Parliamentary forum was discussing the future Polish constitution for the very first time. Izaak Grünbaum said this at the time:

We are demanding one thing, that Polish Jewry be granted the ability to organize itself for the sake of meeting our own specific needs that no one else could possibly meet. We are not saying that no one else would want to meet these needs, only that no one other than Jews are capable of achieving this. [...] We are demanding that we be able to create an organization, based on constitutional principles, that would be obligated to meet the specified needs of Polish Jewry.[98]

Izaak Grünbaum's thoughts were further enhanced by Samuel Hirszhorn:

The constitution should guarantee all national minorities, and Jews qualify as such, their own self-government to oversee the areas of culture, schooling in one's native tongue, social services and charity, in other words, a national-cultural autonomy. This should be a union that is both public-legal in nature, envisioning a person of law, and having an ethnic commune serve as its local organ. Its reach should correspond to the limits of the political commune, with the Chief National Council at its head, who should be elected by all members of this union based on the five-tier adjectival electoral law system irregardless of sex.[99]

A year later, Izaak Grünbaum went before the Polish Constitutional Committee on behalf of the Association of Jewish National Members of Polish Parliament with a proposal for a Jewish autonomy, which was contained within a dossier of proposed minority articles, among which proposed article 113 read as follows:

*The lands of the Polish State, which are inhabited mostly by a majority of non-Polish nationalities, **shall constitute autonomous provinces** [highlighted by E.K.] which shall receive separate legislative representation, selected on*

---

[98] Sprawozdania stenograficzne Sejmu Ustawodawczego [Stenographic reports from the Legislative Polish Parliament], pos. 37, May 13, 1919, l. 5-6.

[99] Sprawozdania stenograficzne Sejmu Ustawodawczego [Stenographic reports from the Legislative Polish Parliament], pos. 37, May 13, 1919, l. 66.

the basis of general, direct, equal, secret and proportional representational elections. A separate set of guidelines shall determine the competence of these legislative bodies as well as delineate the relation of the autonomous province with regard to the Polish State.[100]

On the Sejm floor forum, during session on November 16 and 17, 1920, in the middle of discussions regarding the proposed minority articles, as well as the propositions made by Izaak Grünbaum, Mieczysław Niedziałkowski of the Polish Socialist Party (PPS) interjected:

We are prepared to grant extensive rights to further the cause of the cultural development of every minority group residing within our State. However, there exists an enormous chasm between that and the position occupied by certain aspects of Jewish opinions with regard to Zionist partisanship and Jewish labor partisanship, for instance, which are present in Poland at this time. Therefore, we **absolutely, categorically, as well as with complete composure and clear social conscience, reject all the concepts which would attempt to turn the Polish State into the communal property of both Poles and Jews.** *[...] We are prepared to grant extensive rights to foster the cultural and political growth of national minority fractions which are dispersed throughout the Polish State, but we* **absolutely must abide by the general rule which states that the Polish State is a state which is Polish only.** *[highlighted by E.K.]*[101]

The resentment among Socialists was shared by the Polish right-wing which was represented by Father Kazimierz Lutosławski, who conceded that Jewish demands for autonomy would ultimately lead to this:

...in order for the (Polish – E.K.) territory to be the communal property of several nations, and for the state organism not to be the product of one nation's mindset, but rather a cooperation with limited guarantees in which the combined efforts of several nations create a government for the sake of satisfying their material interests. (...) The proposed solution (by Polish Jews – E.K) would reduce the Polish population to nothing more than pariahs in this country. And how would that appear? Citizens of Jewish, Ruthenian, or

---

[100] Druki sejmowe: Sejm Ustawodawczy [The Polish Parliament Prints: The Legislative Parliament], print No. 1883.
[101] Sprawozdania stenograficzne Sejmu Ustawodawczego [Stenographic reports from the Legislative Polish Parliament], pos. 185, November 16, 1920, l. 37.

German nationality would share all the same rights as citizens of the Polish population, they would sit down alongside us at all large assemblies in equality, and aside from that, they would have their own bodies in which they would prepare their united fronts for the collective actions of the entire Polish State? (....) If we were to take this route, we would have to promote the right to national self-government for the unfortunate Polish population as well.[102]

Despite the fact that Polish Jews, paraphrasing the words of Joachim Lelewel from 1832, had very little to say for themselves as far as what *they had done to contribute to the good of the whole, and how much effort they had put into the rebuilding of our homeland,* because during the 123 years of captivity, apart from the symbolic exceptions estimated at 1-2%, they never demonstrated their solidarity to Poles, nor did they ever involve themselves in the fight towards the rebuilding of their mutual state. They were, however, the first in line to attempt to seize the profits that flowed from gaining independence, which included their demand for co-ownership of the Polish State. In the inference of the generation of Poles who lived during the twenty-year period between the wars, this was in no way a stance of citizenship, for only foreigners could behave in this manner with regard to the reconstructed Polish State.

As foreigners and an ethnic minority inhabiting Poland, the community of Polish Jews was denied the right to autonomy. However, from the moment of regaining independence in 1918 to the outbreak of the Second World War every Jew living in Poland had just the same civil rights as the Poles. Therefore, Polish Parliament's decision to reject the Jewish Deputy Assembly's demand for the Jewish autonomy echoes the catchphrase coined during the French Revolution: *Nothing for the Jews, all for a Jew,* i.e. nothing for the Jews as a group, but all for the Jews as individuals.[103]

---

[102] Sprawozdania stenograficzne Sejmu Ustawodawczego [Stenographic reports from the Legislative Sejm], pos. 185, November 16, 1920, ł. 59.

[103] K. Burnetko, *Getto: od azylu do zagłady,* w: „Historia Żydów – Trzy tysiące lat samotności" [*The Ghetto: from asylum to extermination,* in: 'A History of Jews – three thousand years of solitude], 'Polityka', special edition, Warszawa 1/2008. The French Revolution's attitude towards Jews is described in the following way: "Finally comes the French Revolution with its idea of emancipation and freedom of an individual regardless of their origin. As for the position of Jews, the originator of changes was Henri Baptiste Gregoire, a priest, deputy of

In the period between the two World Wars, the Poles did not prove to be as consequent as the French had been over one hundred years before. In the independent Poland of 1918-1939 every individual Jew received full civil rights. Furthermore, as an ethnic and a religious group, the Jews acquired conditions necessary for the cultivation and development of the religious, cultural, educational and political communities, including the right of representation in the Parliament. The Poles did not agree only to the creation of Jewish autonomies in Poland. Another matter is the question why the Jews demanded autonomy only from the Poles. Why did they not dare to make such a request to the rulers and the parliaments of France, England, Germany or United States?

There is no doubt that the attitude displayed by Polish Jews with regard to the captive and reconstructed Polish State, to the utmost degree, dictated Polish-Jewish relations during both the twenty-year period between the wars from 1918 to 1939, as well as during the years of the Second World War.

As far as the shape that Polish-Jewish relations took during WWII, the differences in attitude of both nations concerning Communism were not without significance. This emanated rather profoundly in the term that was coined on the cusp of the XIX and XX centuries, "żydokomuna" (Jew-Communist). The general meaning of this term expresses not only the stereotypical view that Poles at the time had as far as the attitude of Polish Jews towards Communism, but it also articulated the difference in both Jewish and Polish perceptions with regard to the concept of freedom. In a word, aside from the afore mentioned issue pertaining to the attitude of Polish Jews when it came to Poland's independence, understanding Polish-Jewish relations as they existed during the first half of the twentieth century requires coming up against yet another, albeit equally confounding

---

Constituent Assembly and Convention, a social activist, a lawyer, a powerful individual, a member of, for example, the Society of the Friends of the Blacks; he is also a fighter for Jews' freedom. It is he who coined the slogan: 'Nothing for Jews, everything for a Jew'. In December 1789, Clermony-Tonnerre, the same party deputy, drafts a bill concerning this matter. He kept saying: 'One has to deny everything to Jews as a nation but has to grant everything to Jews as individuals'. The dispute over the equality of Jews had lasted for the next two years. In November 1791 the bill is authorised by the king. Only then were Jews granted equal civil rights.

conundrum, which itself was overgrown with stereotypes from both sides, the matter of Polish Jews' participation in the Communist movement.

Although the XIX century in Poland was marked by, above all, Poles' fight for independence, there was another fight running along a parallel course, that for a new social presence in the country. On the cusp of the XIX and XX centuries, the awakening political movements garnering an ever more expansive forum were growing stronger among them the Socialist movement was gaining the lead on Polish lands with slogans of social and national equality, curtailing Capitalist exploitation, and providing a dignified life for all. The Polish Socialist Party, which was founded in 1892, was welcoming both Poles and Jews into its ranks. Socialist slogans of battling with Capitalism and of rebuilding social structures to the benefit of oppressed social groups, laborers and peasants, had very different meanings to both Jews and Poles, just as a different meaning was assigned by each of these national groups when it came to the concept of freedom. As much as these social changes made sense to Poles only within the framework of reconstructing an independent Polish State, freedom meant, above all, freedom for Poland. For Polish Jews enveloped into the ranks of the The Polish Socialist Party, the concept of a Polish State as such had very little significance. The only thing that mattered to them were social classes and the ideals that stretched beyond nationality, whose fruition was to bring with it freedom for the Jewish nation which was understood to be freedom from the influences of the Jewish caste, from national states (including Poland), and from anti-Semitism and Capitalist exploitation.[104]

---

[104] Poles and Polish Jews who belonged to the Polish Socialist Party were sent by the tsarist authorities into exile to Siberia. Side by side went the representatives of both nations. However, while Poles considered the exile as a punishment for their fight for Poland's freedom, Jews regarded it as a punishment for their fight for a bright socialist future of nations – including the Jewish nation – and in their plans there was no place for the independence of the Polish homeland. An excellent example of such a distinction is a conversation recorded in 1901 in the family of Maksymilian Horwitz, who had been sent to Siberia. 'Why had uncle Maks been exiled to Siberia?' – asked the children. 'Because he fought for a free Poland!' – said Janina, my future grandmother. 'No!' – Kamilka corrected her. – 'Because he fought for socialism.' Poles did not have any doubts why somebody had been exiled to Siberia. For the last hundred years one could have been sent there purely and simply because of his fight for

It seems that, upon weighing the centuries-old cultural and linguistic isolation of both these nations, during the first years of their common struggles within the ranks of the Polish Socialist Party, neither Poles nor Jews had any awareness of the differences in perception on either side with regard to the standard canons of their party. They would refer to concepts of freedom, but everyone understood what they wanted to understand in that regard, based on whatever influences were brought in from the traditions and needs of their respective nations. This dual nature of perception with regard to freedom that was prevalent among those socialists enveloped into the ranks of the Polish Socialist Party, very aptly depicts the life paths of two renowned and significant historical figures, whose vital impact is not limited to the Polish history alone: Józef Piłsudski, pseudonym "Wiktor", and Maksymilian Horwitz –Walicki, pseudonym "Wit".

In 1904, comrade "Wit", that is Maks [Horwitz], asked that comrade "Wiktor", that is Józef Piłsudski, be a witness at his wedding. That seems implausible today – the future co-creator of the Polish Communist Party and the future Commander of the reconstructed Polish State socializing in so intimate a fashion? [Although, already:] ... in March of 1905, at the VII conference of the party [the Polish Socialist Party], "the young ones", with Horwitz as their leader, forced through the resolution to set the proposition regarding Poland's independence aside to a later date. "The slogan for today" was supposed to be in support of the revolution in Russia and a demand for greater political and citizen autonomy from the tsarist government. The resolution had been passed by a majority vote, despite protests by Piłsudski and his followers. In June of 1905, at the Polish Socialist Party Council, Horwitz was elected to head the new, leftist Central Labor Committee, while the old party leadership [led by Piłsudski – note E.K.] *had been cast aside.*[105]

Poland's independence. Quotation after: J. Olczak-Ronikier, *W ogrodzie pamięci* [In the garden of memory], Kraków 2002, p. 89.

[105] J. Olczak-Ronikier, *W ogrodzie pamięci* [In the garden of memory], Kraków 2002, p. 117. Besides, Encyklopedia Gazety Wyborczej [Gazeta Wyborcza Encyclopaedia], Warszawa 2005, Vol. XIV, p. 505 says: 'In the time of escalation and the outbreak of the 1905 Revolution, in PPS there were three competing parties: the so-called Old Fraction (J. Piłsudski, W. Jodko-Narkiewicz, L. Wasilewski, B. Jędrzejowski, Perl), who suggested that social reconstruction should be subordinated to the fight for independence, and the so-called Young Fraction

It is not uncommon to hear that Marshal Józef Piłsudski got off the train called *socialism* at the stop called *independence*. Maksymilian Horwitz, on the other hand, remained on that train. Why is it that in the beginning, they were on the same train together for a while? Most likely because, in using the word FREEDOM, neither was aware what meaning the other was injecting into it. For Piłsudski, freedom meant, above all, the reconstruction and independence of the Polish State. For Maksymilian Horwitz, freedom meant equalizing the rights of the Jewish nation with the rights of other nations, breaking free of the restrictive boundaries of the Jewish caste system, and the fall of capitalism. That sort of freedom for Jews and other nations could only have been ushered in through socialism. In a pamphlet entitled *The Jewish Question*, written in 1905, Horwitz wrote this, among other things:

The un-assimilated Jew, the Jew not yet elevated to the same level of dignity as a Pole, was some sort of sub-human. [...] The Jew, in order to attain human status, was supposed to cease to be a Jew, was supposed to become a Pole... [...] So it is in fact possible to make that step from Jewry to humanity. It was the Jew-socialists who carried the torch of social class awareness to the Jewish mass. With Talmudic verse on their lips: Who shall help you, if not you alone? What kind of strength can you possess if you live in isolation? And when, if not today? They went to the Jewish laborer and taught him about solidarity and the fight, they taught him to feel, think and live. Their once lowered heads were now raised, their drooping necks straightened up, their sad extinguished gaze shone with new spark... The idea of the fight shattered the traditional image of the Jew who clung to life at the surface only thanks to the flexibility of his neck, and through the fusion of seeming humility with undying cunning. Through action, the centuries-old images and prejudices regarding the "Jewish spirit" were contradicted... Through this very action, what was enhanced in all its grandeur and beauty, was the new Jew-human.[106]

(Horwitz, Kelles-Krauz, F. Sachs), who advocated equality of social and national aims as well as the need of Polish and Russian revolutionists' cooperation in order to overthrow tsarism. This conflict divided PPS into the Polish Socialist Party – Left (Young Fraction) and the Polish Socialist Party – Revolution Fraction (Old Fraction). The division was officially announced in November 1906 during the party' congress.

[106] J. Olczak-Ronikier, op. cit., p. 121-123.

As a result of the elections which took place at the threshold of the XX century, Marshal Józef Piłsudski took over power in Poland on November 11, 1918, and he went down in the annals of the history of the Polish nation as the one who gave Poland back her independence. In the annals of European history, however, he is noted as the one who saved the continent from the deluge of Communism.

As a result of the elections which took place: ... *in December of 1918, Maksymilian Horwitz-Walecki became a member of the team of the Central Committee's newly formed Communist Labor Party of Poland (Komunistyczna Partia Robotnicza Polski – KPRP).* **Its intention was to break the ruling apparatus of the bourgeois [Polish] state through fierce revolution, bring down democracy, dismantle the parliament and replace it with the creation of a proletarian dictatorial regime which is looking to enter into alliance with Soviet Russia.** In his political journalistic publications, Maksymilian Horwitz-Walecki did not spare his former party colleagues, the Poles, who had just regained their independence, any insults, nor did he wish them well: *[these]... clowns, servants, imposters, sellouts, parasites, kowtowing to festering and hideous bourgeois politics.* He also called for the Poles and the reconstructed Polish State to be: *Destroyed! Defied! Ruined! Overthrown! Annihilated! Reduced to ash! Blown up!*[107]

If we were to accept Józef Piłsudski and Maksymilian Horwitz as personifying the stances of Poles and Jews with regard to Poland in the early XX century, then it must be stated unequivocally that, in 1918, playtime was over. Poles were able to forgive Jews their many transgressions, but they were never able to forgive two things: their lack of solidarity during the 123-year-long lonely battle for the freedom of Poland, and the betrayal of Jewish socialists (communists) in their attempts to subjugate the agonizingly reconstructed Polish State to Soviet Russia.[108] As a result,

---

[107] Ibidem, p. 156.

[108] Maksymilian Horwitz and his communist party did not abandon the idea of destroying the reborn Polish state. The Red Army was a considerable help. On 2 July, 1920, Tukhatchevsky commanded as follows: '*Soldiers of the Red Army! The time has come to settle accounts! The Army of the red banner and the army of the predatory Polish White Eagle have faced each other before the fight for life and death. The way to global conflagration leads through the corpse of White Poland. On our bayonets shall we bring happiness and peace to the working masses. Go west! The hour*

on December 11, 1920, the Ministry of Military Affairs in Warsaw issued a warrant for the arrest of Maksymilian Horwitz.

Maksymilian Horwitz, the once former Jewish friend of Marshal Jozef Pilsudski, managed to find his way to the Soviet Union several years later, where he had found his long sought after freedom, a beloved homeland, and death at the hands of Stalin.

Today, it is difficult to say how the figure of Maksymilian Horwitz contributed to the creation of the Polish stereotype of the Jew-Communist (żydokomuna). In this case it seems that the year 1905 was much more significant, for it was in 1905 that the wave of strikes and demonstrations that passed over Polish lands revealed the national and social scope of appeal that socialist ideas carried. This is how that year was recorded in Jewish memory:

In October of 1905, upon hearing the news of the strikes in Moscow and Petersburg, a widespread strike broke out throughout the entire kingdom. [...] The Tsar's manifesto also declared amnesty for political prisoners. On November 1, crowds gathered in front of the Warsaw prisons, the town hall, the Pawiak, and the citadel, and demanded that all of those being held under arrest be released. Among those released that day was Max [Maksymilian Horwitz]. Mania Beylin [a member of the Horwitz family] described this day: "It was exceptionally warm and beautiful for that time of year. In the afternoon, growing louder and louder, the buzz and singing of a large crowd of people started to fill the room through the open windows. The startled residents ran out onto the balcony. They saw the parade of marching demonstrators approach. A gray and black multitude. Men in work helmets, women with scarves on their heads, university and secondary school students in their uniforms, everyone was carrying red flags and singing the Warszawianka".[109] *[...]*

This day was described by my grandmother, in a short story entitled "Stacho", as happy and sunny, full of hope despite its tragic end: "Everybody dropped what

---

of the attack has come. To Vilnius and Minsk, and to Warsaw! Forward!'. Poles, together with their leader Józef Piłsudski, won the battle for life and death. They defeated Soviet Russia and prevented Europe from being flooded by communism. [Tukhatchevsky's order quoted after: J. Olczak-Ronikier, op. cit. p. 166].

[109] Warszawianka – a song written by a prisoner while serving a sentence in the Tenth Pavilion of the Warsaw Citadel for socialist activity.

they were doing and ran out into the streets in droves... These were not the same people who only a day earlier passed alongside each other as strangers, indifferent, often downtrodden and hostile. Today, there were no strangers, no masters or servants, no differences. For all people – equal rights – after all, our obligations are equal. And people were talking to each other like brothers, like comrades. They understood and agreed with each other immediately. For this was the first time that they were able to take a deep breath." The protagonist of this story, "Stacho", who is really the ten-year-old Gucio Bychowski, as he drifts off to sleep, imagines that: *"Things will always be like this, that people will now live as brothers and comrades, that no one will ever harm another ever again..."*. And in his sleep he muttered: *"Long live freedom."*[110]

10. A May-Day march of Jewish Socialists in Warsaw. Poland, 1936.

An eyewitness to the same demonstration in 1905 in Warsaw, Michał Sokolnicki, the Polish socialist, remembered the events of that day a bit differently:

... with unparalleled astonishment, I had to state that this crowd was not Polish. All around me I could see, above all, gathered into unbelievable masses of people from [Jewish streets] Nalewka, Gęsia, Nowolipki, who upon hearing

---

[110] J. Olczak-Ronikier, op. cit., p. 113.

the given slogan, after agreeing to the same promises in solidarity, started to move towards the center of Warsaw. In many places I saw many Russians, and I heard Jewish jargon or Russian, but very little Polish (...). On November 1, Warsaw witnessed socialism. For a great many socialists, including myself, that day has remained as a dark nightmare.[111]

That same year, 1905, looked very similar in the town of Dubienka in Lublin territory, although not nearly on the same scale as it had only about five thousand inhabitants (including more than four thousand Jews). In the memoirs of the descendants of the Rottenberg family, who had a fantastic way of describing the atmosphere within the lives of typical Jewish religious families in Poland, we read the following:

In the house of grandpa Szmul, there were probably close to 40 people living there at the time. Taking charge of everyone was done by grandpa personally. He governed autocratically, which ultimately had to lead to conflict with the youngest generation. The first to raise the flag of rebellion was the granddaughter, Hanna. She was born in 1886, so she can't have been older than 18 when the wave of revolutionary outbursts finally reached Dubienka in the turbulent year of 1905. It was with astonishment, at the very least, that the Dubienka Jews claimed, that participating in the labor manifestations, under the red banners, was none other than the granddaughter of the Skryhiczyn heir. It is obvious that something like this could not remain a secret for very long. The exact conversation between the grandfather and granddaughter had never been relayed to me. I know only that Hanna did not knuckle under to her grandfather, as she ran away from home.[112]

It seems that the revolution of 1905, in a very exacting manner, did have an impact on the creation of the Polish stereotypical term "Jew-Communist", and that the Jewish character of the 1905 revolution most likely is the key to understanding the reluctance of Poles as far as the socialist movement, and all other similar leftist movements that followed during the XX century, are concerned. Michał Sokolnicki, who was very closely associated with Józef Piłsudski, professed that: *For a great many*

---

[111] M. Sokolnicki, Wspomnienia [The memoirs], quoted after: J. Olczak-Ronikier, op. cit., p. 125.

[112] I. Kowalska, I. Merzan, op. cit., p. 106.

socialists, including myself, that day has remained as a dark nightmare. No doubt this day was perceived to be a dark nightmare by all the other Poles who bore witness to these socialist demonstrations. From here it's a mere hop, skip and a jump to the creation of the stereotype.

11. A May-Day march of Jewish Socialists in Chelm. Poland, 1932.

The term "Jew-Communist", which was assigned to Polish Jews on the threshold of the XX century, was offensive in that, no matter how you looked at it, it applied to a mere few percent of the Polish Diaspora. The greater majority among Polish Jews were religious Orthodox Jews, the majority of whom were Chasidim. For them, communism posed just as great a threat as it did to Poles. With regard to the ideas of Marx, Lenin and

Stalin, Jewish religious leaders, no doubt, expressed the same sentiments they had with regard to Napoleon: *Let them all perish for they are leading us into temptation and sin!*[113] The participation of Polish Jews in the socialist and communist movements was not a matter of quantity, that is to say that the problem regarding the creation of the Polish stereotypical term "Jew-Communist" was not associated with the number of Polish Jews who expressed their leftist views. The problem lay in the fact that it was this very leftist movement (socialist) that unveiled, in the most dramatic fashion, the chasm that divided Poles and Polish Jews at the threshold of the XX century.

---

[113] While speaking of the origins of the stereotype of the 'zydokomuna' (Jew-Communist) among Poles, one has to remember that at the turn of the XIX and XX century the atmosphere in cities and villages differed. What was typical in wealthy Jewish families in big cities, in small villages it was still an uncommon scandal. Admittedly, when the authors of the quoted memoirs of the Rottenbergs had grown up, in the thirties they followed their cousin Hanka's footsteps. Nevertheless, they still were merely exceptions in the Rottenbergs enormous family clan. Therefore, in the evaluation of the Polish stereotype of the Jew-Communist one has to distinguish between the situation of big centers of Jewish workers (e.g. in Lodz, Warsaw, or Bialystok) and the rest of the Jewish society, living mostly in small towns. The latter group was aware of political novelties and did not hesitate to take red banners out to the streets; nevertheless, the process of adoption of leftist novelties took an old, usual course. The big city streets crowded with Jewish workers carrying red banners were a well known image. It was also an image which for Poles was more noticeable than the Dubno Jews' indignation at red banners, and which was the origin of the Polish stereotype of 'zydokomuna'. It is obvious, however, that the basis of the evaluation of the scope of communism among Polish Jews should be religious circles' attitude towards communist ideas and not the streets of Warsaw or Lodz, or not even a few hundreds of Jewish communist members of the Communist Polish Party.

In view of the above facts, even though the subject of 'zydokomuna' is undoubtedly attractive, I do not consider it appropriate to attach undue attention to it. Jewish communists played an important role in the history of Poland only in the years of 1944-1968, but their ideas and commitment to communist ideas during World War II, which is the period of the main topic of the present discussion, was of almost no consequence for Poland and the Poles. Still, once a stereotype is coined, it lives its own life and has survived already as long as one hundred years. Despite the fact that Jews have not been living in Poland for already half a century, this stereotype shows its dark side over and over again. Stranger is always first to blame. That is why Feliks Dzierżyński – a Pole and an architect of communist terror – was called merely 'a red hangman' and left alone (his family lived in Poland undisturbed), while to this day we are not able to forgive Jewish communists their leftist beliefs and we always interpret them as treason and assault on Polish Republic's freedom.

The collision of Polish experiences and traditions of perceiving and understanding the concept of FREEDOM in which Poland's independence played the most important role, with the flow of Jewish experiences and traditions associated with the concept of freedom of Polish Jews for whom the freedom of their mutual homeland, Poland, was an unfathomable burden, in addition to the 123 years of lack of solidarity in the fight for freedom, were the reasons why Poles rejected the Jewish nation as fellow-citizens within the free Polish State. At the time, Poles, including both those who had rightist and leftist convictions, understood that, in the matter of freedom (as a concept and a goal of general national actions), Polish paths and Jewish paths shall never coincide. Starting with Kościuszko and Mickiewicz, and ending with the Galician intellectuals and early Piłsudski, they still believed that freedom was the one thing that, for both Poles and Jews, would constitute a cornerstone of unification and brotherhood, the early years of the XX century and the free Poland of 1918-1939 dispelled all those illusions. They were already able to recognize that Jewish freedom was something completely different from Polish freedom. They were able to see that there was no common ground between them. Therefore, the idea that was gaining popularity among Poles was that of designating Jews as burdensome tenants, foreigners in the Polish State who, through emigration to Palestine, for instance, must be eliminated, removed from public life and deprived of their strong economic standing. This Polish defiance against the eternal Polish Jews foreigners had always been perceived by Polish Jews to be anti-Semitism, which we, apparently, suckle with our mother's milk.

Perhaps Polish Jews were right. There is no point in trying to conceal the fact that Poles living between the years of 1918 and 1939 had enough with the burdensome Jewish tenants. Their desire was that Jews leave Poland alone, and find some other *Polin* in which to lead their lives in prosperity and success. In that sense, they certainly were anti-Semites.

Just as with all other matters pertaining to the appraisal of Polish Jews, there is no simple unequivocal answer to the question of whether Polish Jews, at the time the Second World War broke out, were in fact foreigners in Poland, or citizens. Therefore, the answer which comes closest to the truth is that of them being fellow-citizens and foreigners simultaneously.

This means that a small portion of those among them, through their words, actions and feelings, were citizens of Poland. The greater majority of Polish Jews that remained were foreigners with Polish citizenship stamped into their passports.

Władysław Bartoszewski writes that, in Poland, on the eve of the outbreak of WWII: *130 publications in the Jewish language or in Hebrew appeared, among them were 11 academic periodicals and 94 information or literary journals. During 1937, throughout all of Poland, 443 non-periodical publications appeared (book and pamphlets) in the Yiddish or Hebrew languages, with a total of 675,700 copies in print. There were 15 Jewish theatres and smaller playhouses in operation. It can therefore be stated that the cultural and intellectual lives of Polish Jewry was in full bloom during the period immediately preceding the outbreak of WWII, and rightfully so considering the significant proportion that Jews in Poland constituted as far as the worldwide Jewish Diaspora. At the same time, Polish intelligentsia of Jewish heritage played an active role in Polish community life. A great many scholars and scientists, artists (writers, painters and sculptors, musicians, theatre people), journalists, doctors, lawyers, etc. all contributed to reawakening of the intellectual movement in the reborn Polish State, and to the development of academia and art. Jews also actively participated in Polish political life as members, very often even as leading activists, of the democratic and socialist parties, including the Polish Communist Party, which although it functioned, it was outlawed at the time. There was no shortage of Jewish intelligentsia or bourgeois within the various political groups inside the camps of the Piłsudski followers, such as the Non-party Bloc for Cooperation with the Government (BBWR). Jewish political parties, including the Socialist Bund, as well as rightist and leftist Zionist and conservative-religious groups, were represented in the Polish Parliament, and they had fairly extensive representation within the territorial self-government (for example, at the outbreak of WWII, there were 20 councilors representing the Jewish population in Warsaw, 17 in Łódź, etc....*[114]

Polish Jews, during the period of 1918 to 1939, were exceptionally active in all fields and practically exhausted all the significant criteria that, in most

---

[114] W. Bartoszewski, Z. Lewinowna, op. cit., p. 8.

democratic nations, constitute citizenship. They led an active social and cultural life, and actively participated in the economic and political arenas of the Polish State. But, in order to regard Polish Jews as fellow-citizens of the democratic Polish State, there is still one very salient element missing, that of appropriate relations within the configuration of citizen-nation. The relationship between a citizen of a democratic country and the state assumes that, in general, there exists a mutuality of rights and obligations. The situation was not much different in pre-war Poland. Every citizen of the Polish State, including Polish Jews, was granted certain rights by the state, and in accepting these rights, was obliged to take on certain responsibilities that were specified by law with regard to that state. That situation had existed in the Polish State from the beginning of time. This framework of democratic governmental structures had been established in Poland even as early as the XV century. Meanwhile, Polish Jews were demanding the maximum in terms of citizen rights, but did not feel obliged to fulfill their citizen obligations with regard to the Polish State. They did not feel that loyalty with regard to the Polish State, or the fight for Poland's independence, were the duties of a Jewish citizen. Therefore, it's fair to say, that, as far as the Polish State is concerned, they behaved like foreigners.

Whatever explanation we choose to accept for the absence of a citizens' stance on the part of Polish Jews as far as their obligations with regard to the Polish State, it can be said that during the years 1795-1939, they were both fellow-citizens and foreigners at the same time, one of us and yet strangers on Polish lands. In showing their concern over the cultural, political, economic and social development of the Jewish nation, in fighting for deserved citizen rights for all Polish Jews, they were fellow-citizens. In remaining indifferent with regard to matters of Polish State's independence, and in recognizing freedom but not considering the need for the existence of a Polish state, within the Polish State, Polish Jews had earned their label of being foreigners.

CHAPTER III

SURROUNDING STEREOTYPES: JUDAS AND HAMAN STOOD UNDER ONE ROOF

The religious, cultural, political and linguistic separateness of Polish Jewry – including that of assimilated spheres of Jews – brought about an understanding that Jews had of Poles and that Poles had of Jews that was based solely on superficial views of each others' mutual behavior. Judgments formulated upon these superficial observations lie at the foundation of reciprocal stereotypes which, up until the outbreak of WWII, were assumed by a greater majority of both the Polish and Jewish communities. Despite extensive studies performed by both Polish and Jewish researchers on the matter, knowledge of the genesis and function of stereotypical impressions of Poles and Jews in both communities continues to evade a decisive definition; continues to be incomplete and does not allow for an ultimate understanding of the phenomenon that have resulted from it.

The main characteristic of the Jewish stereotype that circled within the Polish community was that of duality. In accordance with that, for the Poles, Jews were both damned and sacred at the same time. Their religion was laughed at, but their religiosity was held in great esteem; Jewish cleverness was thought of as being something undesirable, but their wisdom and intelligence was revered. Because it was believed that Jews possess supernatural powers, their presence at various ceremonies and rituals was seen as a good omen, but based on the same reasoning, it was suspected that Jews have the power to interfere with the regular course of history (this stereotype, among others, is the basis for the conspiracy theory of the ages, which circulates to this day, and of which Jews are believed to be the perpetrators). Within the Polish stereotype of Jews, the only unequivocally negative judgment stems from commerce and avoiding military service.

In literature dealing with the mutual Polish-Jewish stereotypes, it is evident that there is clearly a disproportion between the knowledge regarding the Polish view of the Jews and the Jewish view of the Poles, much to the disadvantage of the latter.[115] In other words, possessing a rather extensive knowledge regarding the Polish stereotype of Jews, we know very little or we possess a very fragmentary knowledge regarding how the Christian inhabitants of Poland were seen by Jews. Meanwhile, the issue of mutual stereotypes is especially crucial in light of what was brought on by WWII, for it is these very stereotypes that played a primary role in shaping the foundations of both nations with regard to the tragedy that played itself out before their eyes or affected them directly. Therefore, it is worth taking a second look at – comparatively in the sense of what effect the quality, genesis as well as scale and type – Jewish and Polish impressions are contained within Polish Christmas carol (representations) and Purim representations, the most festive of Jewish holidays.

The birth of Christ is an especially significant event in Christian tradition. In Polish tradition, Christmas is a momentous holiday which over the course of a thousand years of Christianity, has taken on a series of cultivated rites/ rituals steeped in great piety which continue to this day. A significant element of Polish Christmas celebration is the folk tradition of caroling understood to be skits performed by groups of young people who go from home to home during the holiday season in costumes and put on/act out revues related to the Birth of Our Lord interwoven with those that had been updated

---

[115] M. C. Steinlauff, *Mr Geldhab and Sambo in Peyes: images of the Jew on the Polish-Jewish Stage, 1863-1905*, in: „Polin – A Journal of Polish-Jewish Studies", Volumen IV, Year 1989, p. 110-118.

by following generations and taken from daily life of any given region of Poland. Generally, the custom of caroling was kept very much alive in the period between the world wars. One of the timeless characters portrayed by Polish carolers in their skits was that of a Jew. This tradition is perceived to this day within Jewish circles as a manifestation of anti-Semitism. In order to understand the reason and origin of a Jewish character in Polish caroling skits, and take a closer look at the characteristics assigned to this character, it is necessary to explain where the Polish tradition of caroling comes from to start with and the place of the Jewish character within the framework of the Christmas holidays that existed between the wars.

For the Poles, the concept of caroling [*kolędowanie*] has three meanings: singing Christmas carols, the visit paid by a priest in the house of the parishioner, and a Nativity Play performed in the houses of the congregants. The latter custom is the subject of the present discussion.

The genesis of Polish caroling is deeply rooted in medieval mysteries, that of encompassing the western Christian world of putting on performances in churches or church cemeteries, and monastic churchyards. Their pageantry was meant to reflect scenes from the New and Old Testaments, apostolic teachings and the lives of the saints. The mysteries were performances whose theme was almost historical, or at least that is the way they were seen in the eyes of the creators and spectators. As a variety they appeared in Europe in the XII century.

In the history of Christmas mystery development, similar to the history of European Christianity as a whole, the XIII century played a significant role. At the time, the Catholic Church propagated a new type of pastoral in which a dominant role was played by turning the attention of the faithful toward the human qualities of Christ the Lord as well as bringing up the faithful through personable examples drawn from Evangelical scriptures in an effort to reach the widest spheres of the community. It paid close attention to the human, realistic representation of the elements accompanying His birth.[116] It is difficult to overrate the role of St. Francis

---

[116] E. Kurek, *Średniowieczny kult Dzieciątka Jezus jako inspiracja procesu dowartościowania dziecka* [The Medieval Cult of Baby Jesus as an inspiration of the process of raising the importance of a child], in: „Summarium", Lublin 1979, p. 248; see also: E. Kurek,

in running the quasi propaganda campaign for the benefit of popularizing and increasing the attractiveness factor of Christmas. He created new forms of Christian prayer, thought and love. In 1223, in a small church in Greccio, he gathered the local peasants and shepherds, and together they, for the first time in the history of the world, celebrated Christmas with a manger next to which he placed dubious ox and donkey.[117] The Franciscan manger, most likely as early as the century in which it first made its appearance, did reach Polish lands with the monks. The first Franciscan monasteries in Kraków and Wrocław were founded in 1236 and 1237.

In Poland, the earliest traces of Christmas liturgical dramas being performed in cemeteries, churches and monasteries can be found in two sources dated from the XIII century: the brief of Innocent III to (Archbishop) Henryk Kietlicz which talks about indecent games played by the children of priests of cathedral churches on Christmas Day, whereas the performances and processions of Krakow students at the Benedictines in Tyniec on Christmas Day are mentioned in the brief by Gregory IX. Furthermore, in the synodal statutes of Andrzej the Bishop of Poznań dated 1412-1426 we find: *also on Christmas Day, performances and superstitions, which, unfortunately, are deeply rooted in this country, should be forbidden.* The bishop's ban is evidence that this was not in reference to a single random incident, but rather to a tradition that was being generated growing quite spontaneously.[118]

The Franciscan spirit and Franciscan view of the world are responsible for the flourishing of Polish liturgical dramas in which the Christmas Day mysteries became the most attractive element and the one best able to withstand the test of time. The completely autonomous quality of the

---

Średniowieczny kult Dzieciątka Jezus jako inspiracja procesu dowartościowania dziecka, MA, Lublin 1979, Główna Biblioteka Katolickiego Uniwersytetu w Lublinie.

[117] E. Delaruelle, *Wpływ świętego Franciszka na religijność ludową* [The influence of St. Francis of Assisi on folk religion], in: „W drodze", No 10, Poznań 1976, p. 34-37; N.G.M. Doornik, *Franciszek z Asyżu – prorok naszych czasów* [St. Francis of Assisi – the prophet of our times], Warszawa 1981, p. 91. On the images of the Nativity see also: J. St. Partyka, *Apokryfy w sztukach plastycznych* [The Apocrypha in Fine Arts], in: „Znak", No 275, Kraków 1977, p. 531.

[118] *Kodeks Wielkopolski* [The Wielkopolska Code], Vol. I, p. 58; The Diplomatic Code of Tyniec, Wyd. Smolka i Kętrzyński, No 12, p. 34.

mysteries had already been achieved by the XIV century. The richest Polish mysteries were composed in the XV and the beginning of the XVI centuries. The expansion in size of the performances as well as incorporating scenes that were of realistic-variety in character, comical-satirical, grotesque-farcical resulted in the mysteries turning away from its source, the church, losing their devotional function with regard to religious celebrations, and their patronage was taken over by guild organizations.

In the XVI century, the Polish school of pious dramatic spectacles ceased at a certain level of development – the time of the Renaissance was also the end of the mysteries as a creative phenomenon. The dialogues of the mysteries during the XVII and XVIII centuries, when new literary modes were in vogue, fell into the hands of peasants and small-town communities. Plays of passion disappeared from the repertoire along with worship of the saints, and the only remaining theme was that of Christmas Day. From the original texts, the more complicated intellectual scenes were eliminated and in their place came newer characters drawn from a reality of immediate surroundings which affected religious dialogue to sound more like folk literature. The transformed mystery spectacles connected with Christmas Day survived the critical time of censorship (which proved to be detrimental to other types of mysteries) during the aesthetic-mannerist time of the Enlightenment, only to be reduced to the level of folklore in the XIX century and survive in the form of carol performances which had absolutely nothing in common with religiosity or art, to the present day.

No one is capable of recreating the regional mutations of medieval-renaissance mystery texts that were created over the course of centuries in the carolers' dialogue. The authorship of endlessly re-composed stanzas which over time became overgrown with qualities specific to almost only one region's alterations or additions that can only be ascribed to anonymous provincial rhymesters. They built the carol drama based on the canvas of earlier mystery dialogues, yet completed them with realistic scenes drawn from their own view of reality and experience, and transformed old texts according to their given Polish region's and generation's aesthetic sensibilities and tastes. All of their forms over the course of XII to XX centuries, from liturgical dramas to rural peasant caroling, the Christmas mysteries were an egalitarian phenomenon affecting vast spheres of the population.

Now, only a superficial analysis of Christmas mystery dialogues and performances allows us to grasp the long lasting core of archetypes and in that the prototype of the Jewish character. In the XII century Spanish mystery about the Three Kings, *Anto de los Reyes Magos*[119], Herod turns to the Rabbis:

Herod: Well, read out to me and tell me if the one sought by the Magis has been born yet?

The First Rabbi: I beseech you, My Lord, that there is no mention of this in the scriptures.

The Second Rabbi: Hamihalá, what a cheater you are! Who deemed you a learned one? Do you not know the prophecy? Do you not understand what Jeremiah proclaimed? According to the law, we have gone astray. Why had we not reminded ourselves of this? Why did we not reveal the truth?

The First Rabbi: I do not know the truth, if I must be frank.[120]

The rabbis summoned by King Herod can also be found in the oldest Polish mystery dialogues from XVI century. In the *Dialogus Brevis pro Festo Nativitatis Domini Nostri Jesu Christi* [*Short Dialogue for the Holiday of the Birth of Jesus Christ Our Lord*] we read:

---

[119] A more in-depth study will probably lead to the discovery of other western European prototypes of Polish mystery plays, which will assuredly be similar to the Spanish ones. The mystery play of Benediktbeuern may be one of such prototypes. Professor Olga Mulkiewicz-Goldberg from University in Jerusalem wrote about it as follows: 'Already in the thirteenth century mystery play from Benediktbeuern Herod is summoning the elder of the synagogue, that is a contemporary character. Besides, apart from quoting Biblical texts, the anonymous author of the play introduces new comical elements that enrich the Jewish plot. The main scenes, which are based on the Bible, are preceded by the speeches of the prophets announcing the birth of Christ. In that moment a rabbi and his followers appear. His cane tapping loudly on the floor and his body moving vehemently, the rabbi tries to shout down the prophets and prevent them from prophesying the birth of God. After the exchange of arguments with St. Augustine and listening to his carol, the rabbi steps down. [See: O. Mulkiewicz-Goldberg, ... „Zeszyty Naukowe Uniwersytetu Jagiellońskiego - Prace etnograficzne" (The Volumens of Jagiellonian University), Vol. 34, Year 1996, p. 113.]

[120] J. Lewański, *Misterium* [Mystery Play], in: „Średniowieczne gatunki dramatyczno-teatralne" [Medieval theatre genres], Wrocław-Warszawa-Kraków 1969, p. 222.

When asked by the Three Kings about the place Christ was born, Herod answers:

I haven't yet heard from you such news,
I haven't anything until this hour,
That a king of sorts should be born here.
It would be difficult for him ever to be in agreement with me.
I am the king of Jewry; aside from me alone
I do not sense a greater monarch within my kingdom,
But to be sure, so as not to go astray,
I shall not pass judgment based on my understanding.
[to his servants]
Run and bring to me the rabbis, schooled in scriptures
And in all prophecies well versed.
If anyone, these, to be sure, know for certain,
Who sit day and night over their books.
But they almost (didn't) arrived on time:
Welcome among us guests, the rabbis were expected!
This is the reason why you were summoned:
I wish your advice in matters of great opinion.
These good men are going to see the Lord,
The Jewish King as he is referred to.
With gifts of riches they diligently seek him out,
Enquiring with me as to his birthplace.
I tell them that no other king than myself
Shall they come upon. Tell me based on your scripture,
What you understand about the birth of this new one?
Say everything honestly, if something you know.

The Head Rabbi:

Among all such prophecies we have this one matter,
That a Messiah in this world is expected by us;
A King of great fame whom our tribe
In glory shall lead to the Promised Land.
From the virgin he shall be born in the city of David.
That we know from the prophecies about the king.

But whether this time has come upon us,
Is a difficult conversation and no small discourse.
The Second Rabbi:
In Bethlehem, it so happens, this king was born.
Because Isaac agreed with your tale.
That star according to the scripture brightly lights the way,
And to this new king we go.
Follow her to Bethlehem without a place to stay,
There you have the matter of essence of prophetic statement.[121]

This is neither the place nor the time for a probing linguistic analysis of medieval European Christmas mystery texts. If one considers that the oldest mystery texts were written in Latin which, during the Middle Ages, served as the language of Europe extending beyond nations recognized above all within ecclesiastical spheres, if one considers the enormous capacity for mobility, in its day, of this ecclesiastic and its international character, it is not difficult to imagine that these mystery texts being the creation of Italian, Spanish or French monks, within a matter of a few years of their inception, managed to find their way into the possession of the Polish clergy. Appearing in their Latin version, and later, due to the dwindling knowledge of Latin among the devout, being altered to accommodate the conditions of the native language, western mystery texts would find their way to Polish monastic stages and from there would enter the populace who further flavored them with some local color and energy. The figure character of the mystery Jew also entered the populace, and over the course of the following centuries accompanied the Polish mysteries through all its phases of existence, including the pre-war folkloristic (tradition of) caroling. The difference between Poland and Western European countries when it comes to Christmas mysteries is that inasmuch as the custom of putting on mystery performances has disappeared from most European countries and never really passed into the phase of the ritual of public caroling, and even if it had, it did not survive to the XX century. The medieval mysteries survived in Poland to this day even if only in fragmentary form in some regions of the country.

---

121 J. Lewański, *Dramat staropolski* [Old Polish Drama], Vol. II, Warszawa 1959, p. 383-385.

The results of research conducted on the matter leaves very little doubt as to the fact that the custom of Christmas mystery presentations which contained the figure character of a Jew reached Poland from Western European countries. In light of this, it's time to put to rest with the bedtime stories the widely circulating allegations within many Jewish circles that at the core of the figure of the Jew appearing in Polish caroling exhibitions lies Polish anti-Semitism. Only from the juxtaposition of the two fragments of mysteries cited above can one deduce that, the idea of introducing the figure of a Jew into Polish Christmas mysteries was not concocted by Polish brains, but rather it was brought to Poland in the Middle Ages along with the western performances of this type that had been in vogue at the time.

And here is the scenery of preparation and the content of dialogues expressed in the thirties of the XX century by the caroling Jews to the caroling Jews in the pre-war small-town community of Wołyń-Powursk:

The boys already in the fall were assigning roles, preparing costumes, rehearsing, collecting money for wardrobe and masks. Fiedika always played King Herod, Felek the devil, Janek Bogulak the Jew, and Death was played by Heniek Klimczak with his squeaky voice. There was always someone who volunteered for the parts of the halberdiers, the marshal, the Turk, the angel and Herod's wife. Rehearsals, making of props and sewing costumes all took place in the evenings either at Kucharuk's or the Babińskis'. The most ornate and most important was the costume of King Herod: a long, deep purple overcoat, a scepter, a gold crown, tall high-shined shoes, red stripes on his pants, a glistening silver-and-gold studded armor plate. As for the rest of the actors, each one was responsible for their own wardrobe: armor, sword and shield. Death, the Jew and the devil all wore masks which needed to be purchased before Christmas at Cyn's (a local Jew – E.K.). He had them brought in before the holidays from Kowel.

The carolers took their performances only to the homes of Poles as the Jews would not accept them anyway and the Greek Orthodox had their own holiday two weeks later. Clanking their swords, spurs and chains, surrounded by swarms of children, they passed from home to home. First, the angel knocked softly on the door. The invited rang the little bell like an authentic messenger sent from heaven. He folded his hands piously and humbly asked: – Will you accept King Herod? – Welcome! Welcome! we answered in chorus. The angel stepped forward, and a moment later, without knocking this time, the door opened with a great ruckus, and in an energetic gait of clanking spurs, the marshal made an entrance. – A chair for King Herod! came the command, not a request by now. The awaiting chair was swiftly placed in the middle of the kitchen next to the wall. He saluted, clicked his heals, clanked his spurs and returned to the vestibule. Within moments, a rumpus opened the door completely and heralded by his armored halberdiers, the king paraded in. With a confident, swift stride, he approached the awaiting, not chair, but throne. His halberdiers placed his purple overcoat on the backrest as altar boys would a ministerial cloak during vespers. And thump – the halberds hit against the floor. And stomp-stomp – the sound of heavy shoes.

12. A contemporary Christmas Carol performance in Poland.

Fiedika – no, he's not Fiedika anymore, but the real King Herod sprawled in his throne. His knees wide apart, and on them his hands were resting. In one hand his royal orb, in the other his scepter. – Here I am, the king of the world – he began the performance with his lofty introduction. – A thousand rivers, a thousand fields! The halberdiers are keeping rhythm hitting their halberds against the floor. Upon completing his royal oration, his subjects chanted: – This day is yours, Herod the King! This day is yours, Oh! Grand one! This day is for rejoicing, not shedding tears!

The marshal appears ready to accept every command: I stand, I stand before you, oh great one! Whatever you command me to do, it shall be your will!

The three kings in long, flowing wraps. The king with black paste smeared all over his face is unrecognizable. The kings inquire about the place of birth. Herod does not know, but shall ascertain momentarily: – Summon to me the Jew Rabbi! – he calls out in the direction of the vestibule. There is already thud, shouts and commotion coming from that direction. – Oy vey. Oy vey! In a moment he shall be arriving. The elder holy-man shall make his way! He shall perform the Sabbath and stand before you! Oy vey, Oy vey!

He is pushed along by the soldiers, trips on the threshold and falls on his face. – Oy vey, Oy vey! Such hiiigh plaaanks you have - he emphasizes playfully and melodiously – someone can easily break all four feets!

The Jew is wearing a long black smock. On his head a tiny yarmulke, on his face a mask purchased at Cyn. The mask has a huge, crooked nose, red cheeks and long peyos. He walks stooped over with a hump made of hay stuffed under his smock which is girdled with a piece of rope. He is all over the place dodging around, dancing and rubbing up against the stove so that more dust fills the air during the pounding. He's talking nonsense: -- Peas and plum butter, pickerel with soap! – He's saying anything and everything in order to avoid revealing the location of the Messiah's birth. Whenever possible, he tries to sideswipe anyone he can with his hump. There are loads of laughs and cheers in response to this frolicking Jew. At the beckoning of King Herod, he is called to order by a fierce soldier who is not speaking but singing: – Jew, Jew, shortly I shall teach you a lesson! When I thrash you about over the head with this club! – he pounds the Jew on his hump. Clouds of dust fill the air. The Jew wails and runs away. Oy Vey! Oy gevalt! (Oh woe is me) What a row this is! Have they gone mad, these soldiers? Fear God! Ley, ley, ley! Fear God!

The Jew who had just been called to order finally proclaims that Bethlehem is the place where the Messiah is to be born. Upon ascertaining this, the three kings depart.

The second appearance of the Jew is connected with the final accent of traditional caroling – the offering and payment for services. The author of these memoirs describes it in this way:

The performance has come to an end. Everyone is rejoicing with the angels at the arrival of this most joyful holiday of the year. Even the little Jew wheedling his way into favor is collecting their reward in his yarmulke: – Perhaps some change to spare so as to purchase some galoshes, a new pair? Perhaps some vodka, a tiny sip, just enough to wet my lip?[122]

The caroling Jew from a place called Łapa near Łomża:

… was dressed in a black overcoat with a hump on his back. He had an old worn hat full of holes. Such a wise, old Jew.

Herod: Summon to me the little Jew, Little David, Lejba, the smart one. Let him explain to me the dream I had that goes like this: am I to rule, am I to reign, am I to step down?

Marshal: Hey there, Jew, the king summons you!

Jew: Just a moment, sir.

Marshal: Hey there, Jew, the king summons you!

Jew: It's the Sabbath, sir. Just a moment, sir. The king was a doofus, and is a doofus!

The Jew – appears before the king and says to everyone: So, the old lump is on his way, he'll sprawl himself, come milk him. A clean brew will advise, or it won't advise. A good evening shall not descend.

The Jew – pulls out Moses' Bible: Dear King, in the city of Bethlehem, the virgin Mary delivered a son who shall rule over the Jews, the lords and all living beings. And his lordship shall lay like a dog beneath my feet. Your scepter and crown will be dragged by black crows – dangling off their tails.

Herod: Be gone Jew, get out of my sight! Here I have a sharp sword that I will break upon your bones!

Jew: Oh, yeah! A big shot you are! To hell with you!

After the king's (Herod's) death, the Jew turns to the military: Perhaps I, you idiots, will be your king? I shall take to court, bring the kettle, guzzle vodka, deceive you, you'll have a drink and I'll be living off of you. And your king I shall be.

---

122 J. Zięba, op. cit., p. 40-45.

The Soldiers: Go ahead and be, Jew!

The Jew seats himself in a chair: How happy I shall feel that the king in my claws I've reeled![123]

In asking around about the pre-war caroling traditions in the areas surrounding Lublin, I was lucky enough to be able to recreate a fragment of a pre-war performance:

The choir: Oh, Jew! Oh, Jew! The Messiah is coming! The Messiah is coming! He shall soon, He shall soon set the people free!

The Jew: And where He is, and where He is?

For I would love to set eyes on Him, for I would love to set eyes on Him!

I shall be greeting, I shall keep a look-out – if something worthwhile, if something worthwhile...[124]

The few afore cited poems bring to mind stanzas from the theatrical production of "Polish Bethlehem" by Lucjan Rydlo, whose opening premier took place on December 28, 1904 in Lwow. The image of the Jew appears twice in Rydlo's production. In the first scene, after the curtain falls, the Jew Lejba steps out onto the proscenium arch/apron before a singing Jędrek-Mędrek/Andy-Smarty-Pants playing the fiddle:

Jędrek-Mędrek/Andy-Smarty-Pants – noticing his presence, turns towards him: Jew, Jew, the Messiah is being born, Tis' up to you, tis' up to you to greet him graciously.

Jew: And where Him be? And where Him be? Would like to see that one! We's be greetin', we's be bowin', if it's something worthwhile. Lay, lay, lay! If it's something worthwhile!

Jędrek-Mędrek/Andy-Smarty-Pants: Jew, Jew, in the town of Bethlehem, He lay there, He lay there, in the manger on some hay.

Jew: Don't talk nonsense, silly fool, have you drunk too much? To hell with you, yokel! A Master so great, a Master so great, what would He be doing in a manger?/ Lay, lay, lay! What would He be doing in a manger?

Jędrek-Mędrek/Andy-Smarty-Pants: Jew, Jew, Kings are greeting Him, myrrh, gold and frankincense they are offering Him.

---

[123] A. Cala, *Wizerunek Żyda w polskiej kulturze ludowej* [*The image of a Jew in Polish popular history*], Warsaw 1992, p. 122-123.

[124] Accounts of the inhabitants of Zemborzyce near Lublin, personal collection.

Jew: All this I know, all this I know: they came to my stall, A bit of myrrh and frankincense they bought from me./ Lay, lay, lay! They bought from me.

Jędrek-Mędrek/Andy-Smarty-Pants: Jew, Jew, you therefore see clearly, why's you, why's you so shy of the Messiah?/

Jew: The elder God I know the way I should, But this tiny one I do not yet understand. Lay, lay, lay! I do not yet understand.

Jędrek-Mędrek/Andy-Smarty-Pants: Jew, Jew, in no time I shall teach you, when from the back, when from the front with this fiddlestick I thrash you out.

Jew – protecting himself with his hands: Oy Vey gevalt! Oy Vey gevalt! Is this here a brawl? What are you doing, stupid yokel fool! Fear God! Lay, lay, lay! Fear God!

In the second scene, already after the death of King Herod, the Jew also appears in front of the curtain.

A Jew shyly opens the curtain and enters wearing a fox-tail spodik/shtreimel, a long overcoat and white tights, carrying tallow candles and singing: Now the Jew shall dance, Jew shall dance, Because the devil kissed the king, Because the devil kissed the king; He shall perform the Hebrew dance/ the Jewish Krakowiak. Ajdum, tajdum, taranda, He shall dance till dawn.

Jew – dancing and singing:

A poor little Jew was I, poor little Jew was I, and some way overpriced inventory had I, some way overpriced inventory had I, just as sure as I was able to hoard some goods away, a thief stole it all away. Ajdum, tajdum, taranda, A thief stole it all away. Everything from the clips off a Polish nobleman's coat, - nobleman's coat, to gilded stick pins, gilded stick pins. Just as sure as I was able to hoard some goods away, a thief stole it all away. Ajdum, tajdum, taranda, A thief stole it all away.

Pan Twardowski enters with a cape thrown over his shoulders and a glass of wine in his hand; dressed in Polish style, with a sword at his side, limping heavily on one leg: Hey, out of my way you wretches, can't you see that nobleman, Pan Twardowski is approaching?

Jew: So? Why shouldn't I clear the way? I am bowing at your feet.[125]

---

[125] L. Rydel, *Betlejem polskie [Polish Bethlehem]*, Kraków 1983, p. 36-41 and 87-88.

The above cited fragments were derived from various social circles and different parts of Poland. The Wołyn and Lomza texts were created in the small-town and rural/provincial environment of Wołyń and Podlasie and its people, to whom they were addressed. "Polish Bethlehem", although based on folklore motif, is the creation of a poet and from the moment of its premier performance, it reached, above all, metropolitan circles of the intelligentsia, although they were probably performed by provincial amateur school and popular/folk theatres. In this form or another, carol texts consequently reached nearly every generation of Poles which had to face surviving WWII. Therefore, the presence of the stereotypical Jew contained within (these texts), which was well suited to the viewing Polish population's reality, appears as being especially significant and meaningful. He is the way that he is (appears and is presented the way he is) because in reality he was subject to many local and epochal transformations, whose roots are very firmly grounded in the oldest western Christian traditions.

Originally, the medieval mystery plays were written in Latin and only then were they translated into national languages. Bearing in mind that in the sphere of western Christianity medieval Latin was a language both sacred and official, and that various texts circulated rather freely at the European princely courts and in monasteries, it is not impossible that both Polish and Spanish mystery texts had the same ancestor. Nevertheless, tracking down the travel of the Jewish character in the medieval mystery texts requires more thorough research in the domains of history, literature and linguistics.

In the XII century Spanish mystery, which though not directly, but most likely serves as one of the major western-European prototypes of later Polish mysteries, the Jew participates above all because Christ was a Jew born on Jewish lands and the most important, even in the way of understanding at the time, the only witnesses to His birth were Jews.[126]

---

[126] For two thousand years Christianity emphasized the Jewishness of Jesus in a variety of ways. Although the Catholic Church did not necessarily stress this fact, it never denied it. There are plenty of examples of liturgical texts where Jesus is regarded as a Jew. In the New Testament the people call Him 'Rabbi'; the Magi address Him as 'The Jewish King', and Jesus so calls Himself before Pilate; the inscription on the Cross read 'INRI'. It appears that the

Their role as witnesses of the Birth of Christ in Polish Christmas carol performances is expressed in a very straightforward and poignant manner eight centuries later by a resident of Trześniow near Krosno who said: ...*He had to be a Jew because the Birth of Christ happened in a Jewish country.*[127]

Professor Olga Goldberg-Mulkiewicz from the University of Jerusalem, says: *A Jew [in a medieval mystery play] is not solely another ludic character. [...] He is essential for the performance because he expresses its deeper contents. Above all, he brings the Evangelical narrative closer to the public and helps to assimilate the myth of the Birth of Christ; he is the personage most essential for the understanding of the Biblical story. [...] Doubtlessly, it was the Bible that was the primary inspiration for introducing a Jew into a medieval mystery play. The gospel according to Matthew says that during the visit of the Magi at Herod's court, the latter, having heard about the birth of a Jewish king.... is horrified, as is the whole of Jerusalem. Therefore, Herod gatheres all high priests and scholars, and inquires of them about the place of the Messiah's birth... [Matt. 2: 3-4, the Bible... 1980]. Those scholars could only be the inhabitants of Jerusalem, that is Jews.*[128]

The images of rabbis from XVI century Polish mysteries are a far cry from those presented in the Spanish prototype. At first the king expresses the great esteem in which he holds their wisdom (*learned in the written word, they no doubt know best of all, for all their days and night are spent perusing books*), and afterwards he accepts them with deserved deference (*We welcome you, our guests, dear Rabbis!*), and it was the rabbis who without mystery or concealment, tell the king the absolute most sincere truth. The dialogues of the XVI century mysteries in this aspect appear to be not so much a reflection of the western-European prototypes, so much as they are warped onto the canvas of the prototype into a description of actual relations taking place at the Cracovian royal court. That is why

Jewishness of Christ was more obvious in the Middle Ages than in the 20th century, which is proved by the mystery plays quoted above.
[127] A. Cala, *Wizerunek Żyda w polskiej kulturze ludowej* [*The image of a Jew in Polish popular history*], Warszawa 1992, p. 122.
[128] O. Goldberg-Mulkiewicz, *Postać Żyda w teatrze obrzędowym okresu Bożego Narodzenia* [The character of a Jew in the ceremonial theater of the Christmas period], in: „Zeszyty Naukowe Uniwersytetu Jagiellońskiego – Prace etnograficzne", Vol. 34, Kraków 1996

King Herod is more reminiscent of Polish kings Kazimierz the Great or Zygmunt August than of the cruel biblical figure, and the rabbis are more like the loyalist bankers and doctors faithful to the Polish throne rather than the witnesses to the birth of Christ. Four centuries later, in small-town and provincial carol performances, the figures of the Jews are still actually portrayed in the role of witnesses to the birth of Christ as well as royal advisors and prophets. However, the remainder of their attributes has undergone a significant metamorphosis. The above quoted resident of Wrzesniow adds: *A Jew He had to have been – just for the sake of diversity. He was a salesman/dealer of merchandise for show, he was funny. The devil was always aggressive, but the Jew and the beggar man always funny.*

The main reason why Jews had found their way into the XII century Christmas mysteries and had endured in Polish carol performances up until the XX century that remained invariable was: Jesus was born *in a Jewish country.* The only figure that was subject to evolution of form was the image of the mystery Jews. In Poland, from the distinguished guests that up until the XVI century had been addressed with deference by the king *Dear Rabbis,* were transformed into familiar folksy kindred folk: *the Rabbi Jew, the little Jews – David and Lejba, the wise one/wise head.* Maintaining the quality of wisdom, at the same time stripped of the sense of distinction and seriousness, the figure of the caroling Jew was ascribed by Polish folklore as that of being the clown and jester whose first and main purpose was to cheer up the crowd and bring an element of fun to the entire event.[129] This type of metamorphosis finds its justification both

---

[129] Professor Olga Goldberg-Mulkiewicz, *Postać Żyda w teatrze obrzędowym okresu Bożego Narodzenia Narodzenia* [The character of a Jew in the ceremonial theater of the Christmas period], in: „Zeszyty Naukowe Uniwersytetu Jagiellońskiego – Prace etnograficzne", Z. 34, Kraków 1996, p. 113, notices that comical features of the Jew in Polish carols originate from the medieval mystery plays. She says: 'The anonymous author of the thirteenth century mystery play from Benediktbeuern introduced new comical elements that enrich the Jewish plot. [...] The updating of the Jew's dialogue [that had been underway throughout the centuries] occurred on many levels and was connected with different historical periods. [...] The mixture of epochs, places and times is accompanied by the disruption of the previous balance of the performance. Most importantly, the language of the performance is changed. The Jew almost always expresses himself ungrammatically: his Polish is full of grammatical faults and incorrectly used, and borrowings from Yiddish and Hebrew. The text is often interrupted by

in the annals of Polish Jews, who in their sheer mass – in the sense of both number and status in the community – in the XIX and XX centuries in a fundamental manner deviate from the community of their forefathers from the times when the archetypal Polish mysteries had been born for the Polish carolers, as well as in the afore mentioned annals of the mysteries alone, which had already existed for a few centuries solely in the folklore of rural and small-town culture.

In Poland, the confrontation of images contained within the mystery dialogues and that of the surrounding reality, the clash of images of XVI century Jews, royal advisors, wise and distinguished rabbis *who live inside books and know everything* with the observant everyday Jewish neighbors who, though in fact did live inside books and perhaps did possess a lot of knowledge, but above all they observed the Sabbath, dressed somewhat funny and spoke funny Polish, all of which contributed to an actualization of a vision of the caroling Jew. In the evaluation of this actualization it is necessary to remember the specificity of Polish folklore culture in which wisdom and humor to this day, for appearances sake only, remain at odds.

The figures speaking funny Polish and draped in odd apparel which, due to their fondness for books, did not in fact lose their attribute of wisdom. To the country bumpkin or wise man alike, the caroling Jew was given more allowances than other "actors". He was allowed to harass members of the audience as well as reproach the king. In Polish tradition, only a clown was able to behave in such a manner. The role of the clown was played by the caroling Jew who combined in his role concealed under his overcoat of silliness and snappy cutting retort towards Herod and his soldiers with a repartee possessed only by a clever rabbi of Jewish wisdom in peculiar clownish garb and peyos as well as a hysterical manner of twisting the Polish language.[130] In the age old role of a jester, his first and foremost

---

emotional exclamations such as *Och, Ach, Aj waj, Aj waj mir*, which support the actor's vivid gesticulation. **The aim of all these elements is to amuse the public**'.

[130] The role of a Jew-Jester in Polish Nativity plays has been noticed also by e.g. Chone Szmeruk, *Majufes*, in: „The Jews in Poland – Jagiellonian University Research Center on Jewish History and Culture in Poland, TVol. I, Kraków 1983, p. 463-467; Olga Goldberg-Mulkiewicz, *Postać Żyda w teatrze obrzędowym okresu Bożego Narodzenia* [The character of a

purpose was to make the people laugh. The only role of the caroling Jew – aside from bearing witness to the birth of Jesus – was to make the people laugh and bring an element of happiness and joy to the occasion of the Christmas holidays: sometimes with wisdom, sometimes with silliness, occasionally through scoffing, and always with a fantastic costume and outrageous language.

Contrary to popular belief regarding the existence of Polish stereotypes concerning that of Jewish wealth, from the caroling image of the Jew comes forth the very sharp prevalent vision of Jewish poverty. The Wolyn Jew has neither gold nor treasures, but still wanting to appear dignified before the king, the poor jester also has his own unshakable principles worthy of praise and awe. Summoned into the realm of the king he responds that yes indeed, but first: *he will celebrate the Sabbath*! He is therefore religious and with his uncompromising observance of religious principles he inspires a recognition which is not very orthodox in the daily life of the Polish community.

The performances of the carolers in Poland during the period between the wars were an enduring widely prevalent element of popular folkloric Christianity. In the face of a widespread lack of mass media sources which we possess today – the press, radio, and television – as well as extraordinarily meager prospects with regard to entertainment available to the masses, it is with absolute certainty that until the end of the nineteen-thirties of the XX century, these performances were a very important artistic event in the lives of the population (mainly rural and small-town). Not only that, but they also served as an effective and lasting source of propaganda resource. Therefore, the stereotype of the Polish Jew contained within – that of the poor, devout and wise jester – appears as exceptionally significant and evocative.

It is difficult to state today how aware Polish Jews were as to the importance of the role the Jew played in the Polish caroling tradition, including the storekeeper, Cyn, who imported masks for the carolers to

---

Jew in the celemonial theater of the Christmas period], in: „Zeszyty Naukowe Uniwersytetu Jagiellońskiego – Prace etnograficzne", Vol. 34, Kraków 1996, p. 117.

the Wolyn town of Powursko. It seems, however, that they were not at all sentient in their perceptions of the real picture; no doubt they were able to infer that this was a humiliating image exaggerating some Jewish traits, but entirely devoid of anti-Semitic aggression.[131] Consequently, in rural and small-town Jewish environments, there must have existed a sort of consent and tolerance for Polish carolers – indeed, the Jews also amused themselves in a similar fashion once a year during Purim.

Of all the Jewish holidays, not only in rank and religiosity so much as in atmosphere and ceremony, Polish Christmas is most similar to Purim. The comparison of Christmas to the festival of Purim is equally criticized as is supported. Perhaps some will say that Christmas is terminologically closer to the Feast of Channukah (the festival of light, the myth of the miracle that saved the nation). What is important for my analysis, however, is the form of the celebration of the feast rather than its religious contents. For the Jews Purim means carnival and fun (*a parade, masks, men dressed as women, which means the break of a very strong taboo etc.*). Also for Christians Christmas is a beginning of the carnival and entertainment, which have been forbidden during Advent. For Christians it is the time of joy, of New Year's Eve, masked carnival balls, country-side carolling etc. The atmosphere of happiness and merriment connects the celebrations of Christmas and Purim festivals, whose customs intertwine in many surprising ways. As in my research I limit myself to suggesting possible directions of future study, I leave final conclusions to these questions to Jewish and Polish historians and ethnographers.

During the Jewish holiday of Purim, in synagogues and Jewish homes alike, fragments of the Bible from the book of Esther are read, a special holiday meal is eaten (the"ears" of Haman among other things) and a festive dinner is prepared after which the consumption of alcohol is permitted, merriment and Purim related presentations and skits are performed in homes by Purim jesters. During Christmas, in Polish churches and Catholic homes, fragments from the Bible pertaining to the Birth of Jesus are read,

---

131 The accusations of an anti-Semitic and missionary character of Polish Nativity plays and carollers frequently appear in the debates with Jewish historians. For the author of the present book they have become the main inspiration for the closer research of this subject.

during the holiday meal of Wigilia a special course of food is eaten (Wigilia Ears – small "ear-shaped" dumplings – among other things)[132], after which alcohol consumption is permitted, merriment as well as Christmas plays or caroling, that is presentations of Christmas performances by carolers. A joyful atmosphere and the rich setting of the Polish Christmas as well as the ceremony surrounding the Jewish holiday of Purim, both create an immensely important foundation for the comparison of stereotypes of Jews and Poles.

Because the genesis falling on the cusp of February and March of the Jewish holiday of Purim (the holiday of "Lots", Lottery), commemorating the history of the Biblical Esther, it is not widely known outside the Jewish community, I will cite an abridged version of its nineteenth century description:

During the Babylonian enslavement, the deported Jews from Jerusalem (597 B.C.), crossed paths in Elam and Susa with previous exiles from the tenth generation nation of Israel (from 720 B.C.) whose offspring had retained in their hearts a certain attachment to the religion of Moses. They had not yet become mixed in with the local population, and were more drawn to their earlier arrived brothers from Palestine. Both these groups were outgrowths from the same tribe: Israelites and Jews, enemies within their homeland, but sympathetic to one another on foreign land. They were scattered about over the entire Persian-Median lands, the separateness of their religion and their customs distinguished them from the natives, their tribal hatred towards each other was aroused. For ages, under the reign of the Persians, an historical fact occurred. [...] King Ahasuerus (Xerxes), in his capital city of Susa, prepared a feast for the princes and dignitaries. During the feast he summoned his wife, Vashti, in order to show pride in her beauty before his revelers. When she did not obey the king's command by not making an appearance, the king took his revenge for the disregard being shown him by deposing his wife from his royal eminence and ordered that all the fairest virgins in the land be brought before him to the capital in order that he can select another wife to replace Vashti.

---

132 It is difficult to establish whether a traditional Polish dish *uszka* (dumplings resembling 'ears') comes from the Jewish Purim custom of eating 'Haman's ears'. Many facts suggest that the study of Polish and Jewish traditions could bring many unexpected results...

At that time, Mordecai, one of the Jewish exiles, was living in Susa. He had with him his uncle's daughter, Esther, who was fair of form and had a beautiful face, whom he had adopted as his own daughter. So along with the virgins, Esther was taken to the royal palace where she was very much to the king's liking. She received the crown and was named the queen in place of Vashti. She accomplished this without betraying her heritage or her nationality, as Mordecai had suggested she do.

It so happened that two royal servants were plotting against their king in order to dispose of him, a plot about which Mordecai had come to learn from spending all his time at the royal gate. He warned Esther of this conspiracy, but she did not rush to inform the king in Mordecai's name. An investigation was conducted, the guilty parties were hanged and the entire matter was recorded in the royal annals.

The highest position in the official hierarchy was held by Haman, before whom all royal servants bowed their heads to the floor and to whom they surrendered everything they had. Mordecai alone did not show Haman the slightest degree of respect, nor did he even bow in his presence. When this behavior came to Haman's attention, in addition to learning of Mordecai's nationality, he conceived the criminal notion of putting to death all of his fellow coreligionists who resided in the land.

Upon offering 10,000 talents to the royal coffers, Haman was able to win the king's approval for his spiteful plan, and soon enough, a command was issued to all the authorities in the land that the 13th day of Adar is the day – which was selected in a lottery system by a lot (pur) – on which all the Jews shall be put to death: young and old, children and women. A great fear had spread among the Jews, a fasting was instituted, prayers were organized, tears and lamentation were all around. Everyone donned a sack and rolled themselves in ash.

Upon learning of all this straight from Mordecai's lips, Esther decided to avert the catastrophe. With this purpose in mind, she appeared before the king while he was seated on his throne. When he noticed her, the king extended his scepter toward her, which she touched as she approached. Upon completing this royal ceremonial etiquette, the king inquired as to Esther's desire, adding that even if she asked for half his kingdom, he would fulfill her request. Esther replied with a humble request that the king along with Haman accept her

---

invitation for a feast the following day. Haman, flattered by this honor, boasted before Zeresh, his wife, not concealing in this the sadness he feels over the sight of Mordecai's constant presence at the royal gate. Zeresh replied by suggesting that he prepare the gallows and obtain permission from the king to hang Mordecai, and with no qualms, immediately thereafter, proceed to Esther's feast.

The night before the feast, the king, unable to sleep, instructed that the royal annals be brought to him for a reading. It was there that he came upon the record of his life being saved by Mordecai after two palace conspirators had planned to have him killed. The following day, when Haman appeared before the king to extract the highest order for the hanging of Mordecai, the king cut him off by posing a question: what should be expected for a person that the king would like to honor? Haman, with the notion that this question can only be in reference to him, answers with this: "A person whom the king wishes to honor ought to don the royal array, exhibit the crown on his head, mount a royal horse, be led through the streets by one of the nation's most esteemed dignitaries, and he should be preceded by an announcement: this is what happens to a person whom the king wishes to honor".

Ahasuerus (Xerxes), agreeing with Haman's conclusion, suggested that he, without delay, perform everything he had just stated without omitting one single word, on Mordecai who can be found sitting at the royal gate. The king's wish had been fulfilled, Mordecai was honored in royal fashion, and Haman returned home grief-stricken with his head hanging low. As if complaining to his wife and friends about what had transpired wasn't bad enough, he had to listen to their sad prediction: "If Mordecai, before whom you've now started to fall, is a descendant of the tribe of the Jews, then you shall never be victorious over him; instead, you shall fall even deeper".

Haman had not yet recovered from the impressions of the day when the royal service began to pester him about attending Esther's planned feast. Here, with regard to Haman, the king turned to Esther with a question: "Whatever is your heart's content, Queen Esther! Whatever you desire, even if it is half my kingdom, your wish shall be granted. To this Esther replied: "If I have found grace in your eyes, my dear king! If the king be so gracious, please grant my life be spared at my request, and my nation – such is my desire; as I and my nation/people were sold so that we could be put to death, be murdered and destroyed; if we had been sold as slaves, I would remain silent; but our enemy cannot repay the king any suitable amount for this loss".

She barely finished speaking when Ahasuerus/Xerxes asked his queen: "Who and where on earth is this one whose heart has been rendered so insolent as to behave in this manner?" Here, Esther pointed to Haman and stated: "'Tis' this spiteful one here who is the tyrant and enemy". Upon hearing this utterance, Haman lost his balance. The king, on the other hand, rose from the table impetuously and went for a walk in the royal garden. In the meantime, Haman took advantage of the opportunity to beg the queen for his life, knowing how he had offended the king. After returning from the garden to the chamber where the feast was taking place, the king noticed Haman sprawled on the rug where Esther was sitting. In his anger he yelled out: "And now you want to perform a rape on the queen in my home?" As soon as these words spilled from the king's lips, Haman's face was immediately covered (in accordance with the custom in the East). Suddenly, Charbona, one of the royal servants, spoke: "The gallows is prepared as it had been by Haman for Mordecai, who had the kingdom's best interest at heart". And the king said:"Hang him on it". And so Haman was hanged on the gallows that had been readied for Mordecai. And in this way the king's anger was assuaged.

That day, the king offered Esther the home of Haman, enemy of the Jews. Mordecai was granted permission to visit the king from then on because Esther finally revealed what her relation to him was. The king gave Mordecai a ring which had been confiscated from Haman, and Esther placed Mordecai in charge of running the former home of Haman.

After that, Esther threw herself at the king's feet and through wistful tears begged him to revoke the malicious plan that had been instituted by Haman against the Jews. The king, issuing a free hand, authorized Esther and Mordecai to compose a rescript regarding this matter in his name with the royal seal stating that that which is written in his name and carries the royal seal may not be annulled. The royal scribes were gathered, a proclamation was composed and dispatched to the Jews and to all the authorities in the land, stating that the king has allowed the Jews to assemble and defend themselves against murder or destroy any army of any people or nation which represents a threat against them, not sparing children or women, and to then plunder their booty.

This entire drama was due to take place on one day in the entire nation, the day of 13 Adar – the timeframe in which the enemy was preparing an attack. Meanwhile, they were taken by surprise by the Jews. On that day, 75,000 enemies of the Jews were lost; the booty, however, was not plundered. In the capital of Susa alone, 500 people had been killed and 10 sons of Haman had been hanged. The following day, the 14th in the province, but the 15th of Adar in Susa, a merry celebration ensued after this joyous incident by preparing a copious feast, sending rounds of gifts among friends, and distributing alms among the poor. All of these details were carefully recorded by Mordecai and later an order was given that this celebration is to take place every year. It was called "Purim", from the word "pur", which means lot, which is the day of 13 Adar, the day chosen by Haman through a lottery.[133]

13. The performance of the Purimszpilen in Poland, XVII century.

This is how the genesis of the celebration by the Jews, dated from the II century B.C., called Purim – also called the holiday of "lots", fasting or Jewish carnival – is presented in the Biblical book of Esther. Despite the fact that king Ahasuerus is often identified with Xerxes, there is no

---

[133] H. Nussbaum, *Przewodnik Judaistyczny obejmujący kurs literatury i religii* [*A Judaic guide including the course of literature and religion*], Warszawa 1893, p. 124-130.

information about a Persian king who had taken a Jewess as a wife. Over one hundred years ago, one Jewish author described the tradition of the Purim holiday that had been cultivated in Poland in this way: *To this day they celebrate Purim as a joyful day during which they read out the drama of Esther in synagogues everywhere, they hand out alms to the poor, and make their day more pleasant by exchanging gifts with friends. In the evening, as tradition dictates, they feast lavishly, and after the festivities, there is music, a masquerade or theatrical skits from the episode of the drama of Esther, in which a caricature of Haman plays the leading role.*[134]

Based on the Christian mysteries, mainly perhaps influenced by the Christmas mysteries in which the figure of the Jew appears, students of the Yeshiva in Poland started to present their own version of Jewish mysteries from the XVI-XVII century – *Purim spiel [Yiddish: Purimszpilen]*, commemorating the recorded story of Esther from the Old Testament.[135] The creation of Purim spiel in Yiddish in a way constitutes a direct response to the needs of the Jewish community, in which women and lesser educated men, since they did not understand the sacred language of Hebrew which was used in synagogues, they were deprived of the opportunity to listen to the stories of the book of Esther. Andrzej Żbikowski writes: *In the street and in homes people joked, argued and held discussions using the everyday language of most Polish Jews – Yiddish. Upon crossing the threshold of the synagogue, Jews passed through a curtain of sorts behind which the sacred language of Hebrew resounded (Yiddish: łoszn kojdesz – holy language). Their likes and needs had to be taken into account. Therefore, there were ever newer adaptations of "the book of Esther" developing constantly.*[136] Purim Spiel, at first was performed by random individuals wearing costumes, occasionally beggars, with time they expanded their repertoire to include other stories from the Bible and evolved into the domain of professional musicians, and in the 1870's entered the first professional Jewish theatre of Abraham Goldfaden in Poland.

---

[134] Ibidem, p. 264.
[135] I. Schipper, *Geshikhte fun der yidisher teater-kunst un drama fun di eltste tsaytn bis 1750*, Warsaw 1923, p. 168-169.
[136] A. Żbikowski, op. cit., p. 159.

From distant times, the main villain of Purim had been Haman. At the outbreak of WWII, Jews had been celebrating Purim for 2,200 years. In Jewish communities throughout Europe, a custom that had been passed down from Babylonian Jews was that of hanging and burning Haman in effigy. There also exists an old Jewish custom of making noise with rattles and graggers during the reading of the Book of Esther when Haman's name is mentioned. There is also holiday food associated with the figure of Haman the villain: sweet Purim dumplings are called "the ears of Haman" (Yiddish: hamentashen). Haman was also the main character of the *Purimszpilen*. Polish Jews dressed the Purim Haman in a cassock. By doing so, the biblical villain and enemy of the Jews came to resemble a Catholic priest in Poland.[137] In order to understand why Haman took on the characteristics of a priest in the *Purimszpilen* skits presented by Polish Jews, one must be able to answer at least two questions: what experiences

---

[137] A. Żbikowski, op. cit., p. 159, says: 'Even in the XIX century Jews were accused of taunting Christians because the theatrical Haman was consistently dressed as a priest. At that time, street brawls were not an uncommon view'. Dressing Haman in a cassock is another unexplained aspect of Polish-Jewish relations that requires a detailed interdisciplinary research. At present, it is a little known and delicate subject that is rarely brought up in historical and ethnographical studies. In her private letter to me, which was a kind of a preliminary review of my theses, professor Olga Mulkiewicz-Goldberg takes up the problem of Haman dressed as a priest and says: 'Perhaps dressing Haman in a cassock really happened somewhere, but [Żbikowski] does not bother to mention the source of this information. But – UNFORTUNATELY – in 99 per cent of the performances, Haman is dressed as an armored soldier. On the decorated Megilas there are dozens (if not hundreds) of Haman's images, where he is regularly represented as a soldier. Besides, the manuscripts are often dated according to the type of armor he is wearing.[...] He is beaten as a personification of EVIL, and not because he is a priest. [...] He had not 'taken the shape of a priest'; perhaps - once in a blue moon - he could have been dressed in something that only resembled a cassock. [...] It is a well known fact that already in 5th century Rome (accusations of burning a Christian boy), and, if I am not mistaken, in 14th century London, the rabbinate forbade the burning of Haman for fear that it would be understood as burning a GENTILE (because they would not burn anyone from among themselves). But it did not catch on.' [The letter comes from the private collection of the author]. Since historians and ethnographers disagree on the evaluation of the phenomenon of dressing Haman in a cassock, I accept Żbikowski's information – despite professor Olga Mulkiewicz-Goldberg's reservations – as trustworthy because it is confirmed by the sources quoted below. The ultimate resolution of the dispute requires in-depth research and analyses of Polish and, above all, Jewish sources.

had Polish Jews had with the Catholic clergy at the time the Jewish custom of *Purimszpilen* was born, as well as whether the negative attitude towards the Catholic clergy was limited solely to Polish Jews, or was this more widespread among European Jews, which in Poland – due more to the localized custom of *Purimszpilen* – took on this additional element.

Kraków on the cusp of the Middle Ages and the Renaissance in the XVI century was the capital of the Polish State, the center of culture and education – a city in which the most important matters of the state and church took place, from which royal commands were dispatched to the rest of Poland, along with diverse religious and cultural currents, fashion and modes of behavior regarding all matters of greater and lesser importance concerning good of the Polish people. Kraków also played a similar role for the community of Polish Jews that had settled there. The Jews of Kraków represented the largest community in its time, where the highest Jewish authorities and centers of Jewish culture and education resided. If we were to compare the afore cited sources pertaining to the custom of Poles performing Christmas mysteries originating in Kraków, so to speak, it is entirely plausible that Kraków was the birthplace of the custom of the *Purimszpilen* performances based on Christian mysteries, and from there the idea of dressing up the straw figure of Haman in a cassock to associate the ancient enemy of the Jews with the modern day Catholic clergy.[138]

The second half of the XV century was for the Jews of Krakow a string of calamities whose apogee in the form of being exiled to Kazimierz took place in 1495. It is not difficult to comprehend that two consecutive banishments from their occupied area in Krakow occurring almost one after another separated by roughly one generation (1469 and 1495) did have a lasting effect on the collective memory of the Jewish community, and that during the century that followed – the time when the custom of *Purimszpilen* performances was born – it did remain an open and

---

[138] The note dated 1377 includes the expenditures for the organization of mystery plays. The costs were covered by the city of Kazimierz near Karakow, which later developed into the Jewish town. The note is an evidence of the fact that mystery plays had been known to the citizens already in the XIV century. See: S. Windakiewicz, *Dramat liturgiczny w Polsce średniowiecznej* [Liturgical drama in medieval Poland], Kraków 1903, p. 7.

unhealed wound of injustice. A natural course of events was that the Jewish community needed someone to blame for their misfortunes. Based on the assessment of Polish Jews as well as Jewish historians, in the matter of Jews being exiled from Kraków, the king was involved, the Krakovian middle class, but above all the Catholic clergy.[139]

In accordance with the archetype contained within the Purim holiday as well as the Biblical directives for Jews: *Even among your friends, do not curse the king, and do not wish any ill will on the potentate even in your own bedroom.*[140] The Polish king – despite being the one who ultimately in 1495 made the decision to exile the Jews from Krakow – was outside the realm of suspicion. Even if he had armed the Jews, he was not their enemy, but rather the instrument of power which truly desired the doom of the Jewish nation. The middle class was in reality the direct and natural enemy living off of Jewish trade and commerce which was evident from the constant battle with the Krakovian middle class within the framework of the law (lawsuits and court cases) and outside the law (constantly repeated violent outbursts). But the middle class was not cut out for a symbolic enemy of Krakovian Jews for two reasons: they constituted too insignificant a political power to exert any influence on the king's decisions in any way; moreover, since the middle class of Krakow was fighting for exactly the same things the Jews were fighting for – being self-sufficient and able to support their families – the position of the middle class, though exacting, was socially and economically justifiable and clear to the Jews. The only socio-political force in XV century Kraków which possessed enough power to influence the king's decisions and had a strong enough ideological motive to exile the Jews were – according to the Jews – the Catholic priests.

For the Catholic priests of the day, Jews were the descendants of the devil and, as such, ought to be destined to live in degradation and contempt. For the Jews, the priests were the embodiment of all possible evil that flows for Judaism and Christianity. Because XV century Poland was

---

139 M. Bałaban, *Dzieje Żydów w Krakowie i na Kazimierzu 1304-186 [A History of Jews in Krakow and in the Kazimierz District 1304-1868]*, Kraków 1912, p. 31-36, 43-45, 50-51 and 56.

140 H. Nussbaum, *Przewodnik Judaistyczny obejmujący kurs literatury i religii [A Judaic guide including the course of literature and religion]*, Warszawa 1893, p.314.

abundant with significant political and intellectual personalities, Bishop Zbigniew Oleśnicki, Canon Jan Długosz and the royal brother of Cardinal Fryderyk were all encumbered with the responsibility for the banishment by the exiled Jews. The first two were guilty because, through cultivating royal sons and anti-Jewish propaganda, they lay the foundation for such activities; the third because he directly convinced the king to the exile of Jews from Krakow to Kazimierz.

Even if we were to accept the claim of Jewish historians that the Polish clergy alone were responsible for the exile of Jews from Kraków as accurate, it is not possible to defend the theory that this experience alone lay at the foundation of the Jewish custom to dress Haman up in a cassock expressing a negative attitude of Jews towards the Catholic clergy. One must keep in mind that the XVI century in Kraków was already the sixteenth centennial of experiences with European Christianity for the Jewish people, and at least the sixth century of experience, in a territorial and political sense, with current Polish clergy. The experiences of Krakovian Jews in their contacts with Catholic clergy were, therefore, a secondary phenomenon in relation to the experiences which the collective memory of European Jews that had been recorded in bygone centuries.

Without understanding the language of Polish Jews (Yiddish), it is very difficult to clarify the problem of the function and genesis of the Jewish stereotype of the priest-Haman, which appeared in Poland within the context of the above described custom of dressing up the figure of Haman in a cassock in a *Purimszpilen*. I am, therefore, leaving the matter of the final conclusion regarding this question to Jewish historians. A certain, significant amount of light had unexpectedly been shed on this subject during an attempt to answer the question of why Polish Jews did not know how to speak the Polish language. For this reason, setting aside the reflections upon the matter of Jewish *Purimszpilen*, I will dedicate a little bit of attention to this question.

Majer Bałaban, at the beginning of the XX century, evaluated the level of culture and knowledge of the Polish language among Galician Jews in this way: *...the stature of their enlightenment was very low. In truth, there was not a Jew in any city or town who did not read and write in Hebrew, or in*

Yiddish. But even in the Talmud, a greater knowledge, a creative knowledge, was not being applied in XVIII century Poland. The matter of acquiring the culture of the country, or of having an adequate command of the Polish language among the Jewish middle class was out of the question. Merchants and brokers spoke a very broken Polish out of necessity, but those Jews who could write in Polish were virtually nonexistent; the Jewish council had to pay Christian secretaries and legal advisors to draw up reports for government authorities. It is with great likelihood that we can claim that Pinkas Szyjowicz, legal advisor to the Jewish consistory of Krakow during the years of 1770-1790, was the first in his profession who had a relative command of the written and spoken Polish language. The reason for this cultural distinctness, was the separateness of life, as well as the Jewish consistories and schools. Jews did not attend public, parochial or parish schools at all. Synod Budeński as early as 1279 clearly forbade such a thing. From its inception, the Academy of Krakòw did not accept Jews. It should come as no surprise, therefore, that at the time, after being rejected and turned away from nearly every institution of higher education, Jews had to create their own schools and academies, in which only the Talmud was taught. [...]

With the Austrian Constitution of 1867 and the law passed on May 25 1868, both of which pertained to the regulation of attitudes of the church with regard to state, the matters of Jews fighting for equal rights were settled, and it was the beginning of a normal life within regular conditions. The Jewish youth threw themselves into schools with full impetus, and the numbers are the best evidence of how the local culture had been accepted among the Jewish population in Galicia: in 1830, there were 408 Jewish children in elementary schools throughout Galicia; in 1900, there were 110,269; in the year of the Constitution (1867), there were 556 students in Galician secondary schools, in the school year of 1910/11, there were 6,600 (from 20 to 51%), in non-classical schools the number soared from 125 to 735 (21%). In 1867, all the Austrian universities had a total of 769 Jews, and in 1904, the two state universities alone had 904 Jews, not including the students of technical schools. But one who would infer that Chasidism was on the decline based on these numbers would be mistaken; these numbers are only a one-sided measure of a country's culture, as there existed enormous beaten-down masses of Orthodoxy outside of these numbers, very far removed from public schooling and any new way form of forward-thinking.[141]

Despite legislation in all three partitions of Poland from the second half of the XIX century enabling Polish Jews to partake in an education in all non-Jewish learning institutions, the twenty-year period between the wars (1918-1939) is characterized in Poland by a spontaneous flourishing in education and there is no evidence of limitations with regard to access to Polish schools by anyone[142], the state of affairs from the beginning of the XX century as described by a Jewish historian, especially *the beaten-down masses of Orthodoxy, very far removed from public schooling and any new form of forward thinking*, remained virtually unchanged up until the outbreak of WWII. Marian Milsztajn, who was born in 1919 in Lublin, captured the character of the linguistic relations which prevailed in Jewish neighborhoods of Polish cities in the twenty-year period between the wars:

The place where we lived [...] I never heard a single word uttered in **Polish. I didn't know that such a language existed.** *As for its existence, I knew that it was the language of the goys.* **Poland? No idea.** *I first encountered the Polish language when I was seven years old. When I entered the first floor of the Talmud-Tora, the first grade [of the Jewish school]. There they had the Jewish (Yiddish) language. Writing in Yiddish, a little bit of history in Yiddish, arithmetic and Polish. And in the first week of classes, the teacher spoke in Polish, and we did not understand a single word. And we started screaming: "Talk the way we do, talk the way we do." We caused such an uproar that the shammes had to intervene. The shammes turned to us and said: "Children, you must learn the Polish language because we are in Poland." [...] We suffered. We had to learn a, b and c. [...]*

I was drawn to the language of the goys. When I started working, I became a member of the unionist library and there they had both Jewish books and Polish books. The worst part was that the accent was just horrible. What was one to do with all this? I couldn't grasp the accent or proper pronounciation.

---

[141] M. Bałaban, *Dzieje Żydów w Galicji [The History of Jews from Galicia]*, Lwow 1914, p. 7-10 and 210-211.

[142] M. C. Steinlauf, *Pamięć nieprzyswojona [Unassimilated memory]*, Warszawa 2001, p. 30-31.

I can see the distance between me and my wife, who despite being Jewish, was raised in the Polish culture in Kraków. She does not speak Yiddish, and I for so many years never spoke the language of my homeland. There were millions like that. **In small towns, Jewish youth did not know the Polish language at all, only Yiddish or Hebrew.** *Young people did not speak Polish, and if they did, they spoke it they way I did – very poorly.*[143]

This report is confirmed by the residents from the Bug river region who lived in a large city, and who would travel to visit their families in the 1930's:

During our vacation, we attempted to teach our cousins and all the backward Jewish children the Polish language. We brought Polish literature to their lives, and at the same time a sense of belonging to history in time, place and cultural realm.[144]

In an extraordinarily realistic manner, the above cited relations present the linguistic situation of Polish Jews in the pre-war Polish State. The opportunity to learn Polish was available either to those Jews who had been Polonized, or to those who, as the author expressed, were drawn to the language of the goys. The opportunity to know the Jewish language, on the other hand, was available only to those select individual Poles who lived inside the Jewish neighborhoods and performed some sort of specific professional tasks or functions. I have not come across information in any source regarding Poles who had learned the language of Polish Jews in any other form or for any purpose other than that described above. It is, therefore, only appropriate in this case, to agree with the Jewish historian Aleksander Hertz, who writes: *...in Poland, where everyone 'was dealing with' the Jewish matter, it is possible to count on one hand the number of people who actually knew the language [of the Polish Jews] which was being used by three million citizens of the Polish State.*[145]

---

[143] *Ścieżki pamięci [The path of recollection]*, ed. by Jerzy Bojarski, Lublin 2002, 69-70.

[144] I. Kowalska, I. Merżan, *Rottenbergowie znad Buga [The Rottenbergs from the Bug River region]*, Warsaw 1989, p. 68.

[145] A. Hertz, *Żydzi w kulturze polskiej [The Jews in Polish Culture]*, Warsaw 1988, p. 45. One could have an endless discussion whether the Poles should learn the language of the Jews, or the Jews should learn Polish. One thing is certain: it would be better in every respect if the Jews and the Poles were able to communicate. Besides, looking from the perspective of World

On the eve of the outbreak of WWII, barely 15% of the Jewish population had knowledge of the Polish language. Why was this? Why was the personal equation of a commonly shared millennium in Poland so tragic with regard to language? Why didn't Polish Jews know the Polish language? Why is it that a people who had been using language in the written form for so many millennia and a people being predisposed to having excellent linguistic abilities were not capable of grasping the Polish spoken language and some twenty or so characters of the Latin alphabet?

In posing this question I was very well aware that it is not enough to place all the blame on Polish anti-Semitism, the Polish educational system, or the pre-war "bench ghetto" system (which officially segregated Jewish students from Polish students in learning centers – translator's note) and the such. All of this took place and existed, but it does not explain- as Majer Bałaban relates- why it took the Jews a good 700 years before a person was born among them who learned the Polish language in spoken and written forms well enough to replace the Christian that needed to be hired by the Jewish consistory.

In the foreword to the first schoolbook to learning the Polish language, which was written by father Gintyłło in Vilnius in 1817, we read:

Just as it is very important for all the citizens and residents to know to read and to speak the language of the land, so it is for the believers in the Old Law [the Jews]. And, since knowledge of one language helps in learning another one, the native born who know written Hebrew, can learn to read and write Polish quite easily, especially since they are familiar with that language from everyday use.

This learning, as needed as it is easy, was, in time past, completely neglected by our believers in the Old Law. They lived in the native country like recently arrived foreigners, not knowing how to read papers which sometimes were of greatest importance to them. It is easy to understand how it caused them great discomforts and, frequently, damage. Only very infrequently someone could be found among them who by chance learned to read and write Polish and, consequently, was considered a very learned man, skilled in matters of this world, although he didn't differ much from the common folk. To other believers

---

War II, the knowledge of the Jewish language among the Poles until 1942 would have rescued many of them from roundups and saved many lives, while the knowledge of Polish among the Jews after 1942 would have saved many Jewish people.

in the Old Law it seemed to be an exceedingly difficult and almost inaccessible art. The government of the country and the educational authority (from its conception) provided neither caring protection nor aid. It was sometimes mistakenly presumed that the believers in the Old Law either do not need to learn the country's written language or are obstinately unwilling to acquire it, or consider it contradictory to their religion.[146]

Father Gintyłło was very much mistaken in his accusations with regard to those who suspected that the Polish language of Polish Jews was interpreted as a slight and an attack on their religion, because in the heat of the matter, those suspected did not lose their way as they were closest to understanding that the first and foremost reason for the unwillingness of Polish Jews to learn the Polish language is deeply rooted somewhere beyond the Polish educational system being unfavorable to the Jews; that the Jewish reason existed long before the Polish educational system was even barely in its infancy, which at that time was centuries away.

It is widely accepted that the year of 966, the year when Prince Mieszko accepted Christianity, is the same year that the Polish nation was created. Accepting Christianity signified that Poland was now included in the realm of Western Christianity, which today is called the western European realm. From its inception, the official language of the Christian cultural sphere that had been built on the ruins of ancient Rome was Latin, and the written word had for centuries signified the domain of people of the Church, the sole administrator of the ancient legacy of intellectual culture. Poles – similarly to Celtic and Germanic peoples, as well as other Slavic nations – actually possessed their own culture at the time of accepting Christianity, but they got along without writing. With time, following the example of other nations of Roman Christianity, they adapted the Latin alphabet to suit their needs, which in turn was responsible for the birth of written Polish literature.

Poland accepted Christianity relatively late. This fact together with its vital native culture and common law, as well as lacking a strong governmental shoulder and church organization, explains the slow pace at which cultural currents based on written language rose on Polish land. It

---

[146] Ch. Schmeruk, *The Esterke Story in Yiddish and Polish Literature*, Jerusalem 1985, p. 48.

is not until the middle of the XII century that the written words in Poland begins to seep out beyond the strict realms of the church and begins to enter the circles of the more brilliant persons of magnate status, which in turn bloomed into the creation of the oldest written song in the Polish language, the *Bogurodzica*, on the cusp of the XII and XIII centuries. It was at once a Polish paean of the church, as well as knightly hymn, which to this day captivates the attention and emotions of Poles. As for the father of the Polish written language, it was not until Mikołaj Rej (1505-1569), who stated *that Poles are not geese, and they possess their own tongue,* first composed and realized a program of generalizing the Polish language thus making it more prevalent. For Latin, this marked the beginning of its final and irreversible return to behind the confines of the doors of Roman-Catholic churches.

At the onset of the XII century at the latest, ancient Jewish peoples began to settle on Polish lands: merchants, bankers and craftsmen. The newcomers practiced their own religion, different from both the Christianity that had been transplanted to Polish lands and the pagan gods of our forefathers. They had a well developed social structure, spoke their native language and everyone used their uniform written form of the language. At this time in the XII century, Poland had barely a two-hundred-year existence behind her – narrow in content and with a limited social scope – the elite cathedral and monastic schools of Latin operated under the protectorate of the Piasts and the Catholic Church. The Jews arriving in Poland had been using the written language for several millennia; for dozens of centuries there had not been an illiterate among them. The ability to write among Poles, outside of the spheres of the church, was an uncommon phenomenon even within the elite circles of Piast dynasty princes and noblemen. At the same time, according to contemporary concepts, acquiring the skills of reading and writing was a rite of ennoblement: "an adept in this art – *homo litteratus* – stood out in the crowd of *idiotae*, as the illiterates were referred to". Consequently, using the medieval terminology of the day, Polish lands had been inhabited by the illiterate population *idiotae*, as Poles were called, while the lands were beginning to be settled by the Jewish peoples composed exclusively of *homo litteratus*.

Among the oldest historical sources claiming Jews present on Polish lands are located on brakteaten (one-sided denars; coin shaped decorative disks – translator's note), which had been coined by Jewish minters commissioned by the son of Bolesław Krzywousty, the Duke of Greater Poland and the Duchy of Kraków, Mieszko III the Old (circa 1126-1202). The information that the denars had been coined by Jewish minters is presented directly from the coin itself which, next to the image of the Duke, reveal words in Hebrew. It is not difficult to find the reason for this seemingly uncommon occurrence. It is highly probable that the Jewish minter was a member of the *homo litteratus*, if not within the entire environment surrounding the court of Mieszko the Old, which may have consisted of the *idiotae*, then certainly among those using the mintmark of the Duke. In other words, the Jewish minter, being the only person who, because he new how to write, was capable of executing the writing on the coins of the Duke. And because the Jewish minter knew only the Hebrew alphabet, he would write the Polish words in Hebrew.

In order to correctly read the information contained on the denars of the Polish Duke Mieszko the Old, we cannot apply the contemporary coin manufacturing standards well known to us today. Rather, we need to consider what, aside from a form of currency, did a monetary coin signify to people who lived 800 years ago. Professor Brygida Kurbis has written the following about Poland of the XII century: *If it is appropriate to say such a thing, a more popularized propaganda [more so than the liturgy or documents] of the written form was represented by the monarchal coin with the image of one's lord [during the Middle Ages]. The writing on said coin, the legend that is, also played a role in signifying ownership. Because minters were craftsmen from the secular world, the coin is our oldest trace of an active connection to the writings of people from secular circles.*[147]

If we are to weigh, that in the first centuries of Poland's existence, and no doubt during the XII century as well – applying our contemporary way of thinking – that coins were a more effective method of communicating

---

[147] A. Kurbis, *Pisarze i czytelnicy, [Writers and readers]*, in: „Polska dzielnicowa i zjednoczona", [Poland sectional and united], Warszawa 1972, p. 162.

information advertising the written word than the competing church and chancelleries could provide. The Jewish minters possessed more power in advertising their Hebraic alphabet than the clergy did for the Latin alphabet and the chancelleries preparing documents. The only denars to have survived to our times are those of the Duke Mieszko the Old. Therefore, no one will ever be able to answer the question of the scale and far-reaching capabilities of this phenomenon: was the coining of denars with Hebraic wording in the royal mint of the Piasts commonplace, or is it perhaps that the denars known to us today were an isolated incidence which had never been copied in other mints? If the coining with Hebraic wording was so commonplace an occurrence in minting, then why is it that in the final outcome, the Latin alphabet prevails? Whatever the reason, the XII century in Poland was most likely a time during which the fate of the Polish written language hung in the balance. It was also the time in which it had been determined which alphabet – the Hebraic or Latin – would be used to record the Polish spoken tongue.

Deeper research into the functioning and endurance of the stereotypical reluctance towards the Polish language among the Jews, as well as into the role played by the spread of Hassidism in this matter, and to a lack of access to Jewish sources on the topic, it is best left to Jewish historians to sort out. But even superficial attempts to research the problem allow us to conclude that the widespread lack of knowledge of the Polish language among Polish Jews on the eve of the outbreak of WWII was not solely the result of Polish anti-Semitism, nor of a flawed educational system, nor of all the other Polish faults that have been commonly attributed in historiography in an attempt to discuss the matter. Rather, it was also very present within the far-reaching, deeply rooted Medieval Jewish stereotypes and prejudices toward the Christian world. Carried over into the vast Polish geography and into the cultural-political reality, these stereotypes and prejudices toward the Latin alphabet had been planted and endured up until the annihilation of the Polish Jews who lacked the ability to understand the Polish language.

The mystery of why the Polish Jews were so reluctant to learn the Polish language was explained by Jewish historian Professor Chone Shmeruk, who died a few years ago, and who wrote the following about this phenomenon: *While Yiddish-speaking Jews knew the language of their non-Jewish neighbors, they either did not know or did not wish to learn the Latin alphabet. Regardless of the language in which it was used, this alphabet was associated with Christianity, as is clear from the term 'galkhes' (from galekh, Christian priest) the Ashkenazi [Jews] designation for the Latin alphabet.*[148]

Professor Chone Shmeruk was too great an erudite, and rather too great an expert of the history and culture of Poland, as well as that of Polish Jews to mislead his readers. In the light that his words have shed, the politics of the educational powers that be, from the inception of the very first school in Poland up until the critical year of 1939, were neither the sole nor most important reason why knowledge of both the spoken and written Polish language remained a rarity among religious Jews. The reluctance of Polish Jews with regard to learning the Polish language in no way reflected their attitude towards the Polish language, culture or nation. In this way, the conventional belief of the stereotypical view that persists to this day among historians that Polish Jews did not know the Polish language because Poles had not allowed them to access their educational institutions. The truth of the matter is that Polish Jews did not know the Polish language because it was written in a Latin – "clerical alphabet". In addition, as it has been proven by the above cited relations, this language served absolutely no purpose to them within the closed Jewish communities.

The pejorative term "galkhes" used to identify Latin as "the language of the Christian priest" was formed in the Jewish language in Yiddish, about which we read: "... the language of the Ashkenazi Jews, which was born of colloquial speech, and later also served as a literary language. [...] The lexical structure of Yiddish was 75% influenced by German, 15% by Hebrew, and approximately 10% by Slavic languages. The written form of this language is recorded using the Hebraic alphabet. [...] It was created among Jews who had been residing in Nadrenia, under the influence of an Old High German dialect. The first recognition of Yiddish as a separate, distinct language is usually dated to the IX century".

---

[148] Ch. Schmeruk, *The Esterke Story in Yiddish and Polish Literature*, Jerusalem 1985, p. 48.

The key to understanding the history of further Polish-Jewish relations, especially as it pertains to the history of Polish Jews and their knowledge of the Polish language, seems to be the XIII century. For the purposes of recording their language, at the beginning of the XIII century, Poles ultimately selected the Latin alphabet, which was referred to in the Jewish language as the *galkhes* alphabet, the "clerical alphabet", since a member of the Christian clergy is known as *galekh*. The only thing is that the Latin alphabet that had been chosen by the Poles was not a Polish invention; it had been known to Jews and had been named by them long before they arrived in Poland.

Jews came to know this "clerical" alphabet during Roman times as well as from its worst side in Western Europe: in Germany, France and Spain. They did not want to learn this alphabet because they associated it with the persecutions they had to endure in these countries by Christian authorities and clergy. With Christianity and persecutions, Jews always associated the German, French and Spanish languages first, and then the Polish language. In this way, the reluctance among Polish Jews in learning the Polish language was not specifically attributed to the Polish factor, but rather a recurring phenomenon of aversion which they had brought to Poland with them with regard to the reigning Christian Latin alphabet throughout Europe; it was more of an element of dislike with regard to Christianity, as it were, than to Poles and their language.

Consequently, the Polish educational system is one element which lies at the root of why Polish Jews lacked knowledge of the Polish language, but above all, it was the cultural-religious pre-conditioning of the Jews. The written form of the Polish language was only accessible to those Jews who were willing to break the centuries-old tradition of reluctance to learn the "clerical alphabet". An alphabet which, no doubt similarly to other matters associated with Christianity, carried with it the stigma of something contaminated and unclean in its form, and therefore not worthy of the attention of a devout Jew. The first Polish Jew in Poland to break through the reluctance towards the *galkhes* alphabet was, if we believe Majer Bałaban, the one who, in the years of 1770-1790, served as the legal advisor to the Jewish consistory of Kraków, Pinkas Szyjowicz.

Due to the times in which he lived, he can be considered a precursor to the Jewish Haskahla, the Jewish Enlightetenment. Among the Jews of Western Europe, and sometimes among Polish Jews as well, this produced the result of assimilating with the cultures and the languages of the countries in which they resided.

The fact that Pinkas Szyjowicz, and the promoters of Haskahla after him, did not find many followers among Polish Jews was decided by the fact that in Poland, at the end of the XVIII century, Hassidism was born and enjoyed a dynamic growth spurt. Within the next few decades, communities of Polish Jews, with a great majority of followers of Hassidism, created *a giant, beaten-down mass of orthodoxy, far removed from public schools and any form of forward thinking.* It was this very Hassidic *beaten-down mass of orthodoxy*, which never would have survived under less than favorable conditions, but which managed to store away all the Medieval prejudices toward the "clerical" alphabet, and in turn was responsible for the fact that, on the eve of the outbreak of WWII, barely 15% of Polish Jews were able to function in the Polish language.

It is here, it seems, that we have reached the essence of the problem. By shedding some new light on the issue of the utter lack of knowledge of the Polish language among Polish Jews, and allowing for a better understanding of the figure of Haman dressed up in a cassock in the Purim spiel sketches, brings together the two matters inside the Jewish stereotype of the Catholic priest as Haman. The roots of the stereotype do not necessarily come from good or bad Polish-Jewish relations in XV-century Krakow, so much as they result from the negative attitude of Jews toward Christianity. It would be unfair to lay the entirety of the blame on the priest for their participation in expelling Jews from Krakow, or even the greatest release of negative emotions, which brought about the dressing up of the life-size caricature of Haman in a cassock. "The fault" of the Polish Catholic priests compared to the earlier experiences of this nation in countries of Western Europe (Spain, England, Germany) seems negligible. The memory of the clergy in the role of perpetrator during the entire drama of expelling Krakovian Jews on top of their earlier prejudices towards Catholic priests, which is apparent in the term "galkhes", and the customary reluctance of

Jews to the Latin alphabet, was passed on to the following generations. In XVI-century Krakow, when the tradition of *Purimszpilen* was born, the biblical Haman was dressed up by Polish Jews in the cassock. In this way, the ethos of EVIL from the Book of Esther was drawn on and had been personified, up until that point in time, by Haman.

During the XVI century in Poland, it became actualized and, over the course of the next four hundred years, in the consciousness of Polish Jews, it became the figure of Haman and of the Catholic priest – with no regard for the actual attitude of the latter – melded together into one tangible EVIL present in the everyday life of all generations to come, an EVIL which just lies in wait for the doom of the Jewish people. This personification of haman-esque evil had endured in Poland for centuries. What also stood the test of time was the custom of putting on the *Purimszpilen* sketches, which similarly to the Christmas mysteries, was the spring-board for the Jewish theatre as well. Immediately before the outbreak of the war, during Purim, there existed the tradition, among Polish Jews, of going from one Jewish home to the next dressed in costumes, similar to those of carolers. From the homes of Jewish families living in Skryhiczyn on the Bug:

In the evening, during dinner, they would burst in dressed in costumes – the Purim spiel performers. They sang cabaret songs about the good old days, and they composed new ones. Everyone celebrated and had fun, and no one could foresee that there was an enemy approaching who was more dangerous than Haman.[149]

The Jewish author of the memoir does not mention whether the figure of Haman dressed in a cassock was present among the *Purimszpilen* performers visiting her family. Both Jewish historians and Jewish authors of memoirs, for reasons that need not be explained, are reluctant to write about the widespread negative stereotypes, among Jews, of the Poles or Christians at all. Polish historians, on the other hand, due to the language barrier, are not capable of accessing the information contained in the sources written in Yiddish. It seems to be quite evident, however, that

[149] I. Kowalska, I. Merżan, *Rottenbergowie znad Buga [The Rottenbergs from the Bug River region]*, Warsaw 1989, p. 205.

without the figure of Haman, the *Purimszpilen* performances would be pointless. Somebody had to personify that Haman. It is well known, that up until the XIX century, the *Purimszpilen* Haman was definitely dressed in the cassock. It is probable, though, that because the cassock-clad Haman was the reason for street brawls that had been started by Christians, that Jews during the twenty-year period between [the wars, ceased to display so blatant an anti-Catholic character during Purim, and instead of a priest, they threw any old Christian into the embodiment of Haman. Polish sources mention utilizing this sort of solution. This is the way in which Purim was recalled by Poles residing in provinces and small towns during the period immediately preceding WWII:

[Jews] dressed up in different ways, in some sort of rags, and they paraded about as though they were going caroling. From one Jew to the next, and once there, they would do something. On the Haman holiday, they rented out some person and chased him out of town. On the Jewish holy day, they paid some farm hand so that they could poke him and beat him with reeds, just like (they did) Jesus. The Jews then paid some Christian so they could beat him with birch rods, they spit on him. They called that rented-out Christian "Haman". They paraded and pushed him around while beating him with reeds – just like (they did) Jesus. They made triangle-shaped dumplings (pierogis) filled with kasha and onion and called them Ham-an-ears.[150]

From the Jewish *Purimszpilen*, as well as from the whole of Purim, a very sharp and important stereotype pertaining to Polish-Jewish relations emerges: the personification of their greatest enemy, equal to the biblical Haman, for dozens of generations of Polish Jews, was the Catholic clergy as well as Catholics in general. The stereotype of the Haman-priest and the Haman-Catholic had been presented to Polish Jews from their earliest years, and – it is necessary to convey this clearly and openly – unfortunately, was not spared any hatred. Hatred had been written into the Holy Scriptures and celebration of the Purim holiday, renewed and re-saturated with the arrival of every spring, ingraining and fixing into

---

[150] A. Cala, *Wizerunek Żyda w polskiej kulturze ludowej* [*The image of a Jew in Polish popular history*], Warszawa 1992, p. 62-63 and 85-89.

the memories of generations of Polish Jews the image of their impending EVIL.[151] And their conditioning towards Catholic priests and Christians in general took place in exactly the same manner. In truth, this is a very powerful and shocking stereotype. One thing is certain, it was well known to them and all the pre-war Polish Jews had been raised with it.

The stereotypical perception of Polish Jews with regard to the Catholic clergy, and the personification of Haman clad in a cassock, were also accompanied by an equally negative image of Jews, whose personification among the Poles was that of Judas. Father Jędrzej Kitowicz (1728-1804), in his guide to the Polish habits and customs of the times of king August III, included the following passage:

On Holy Wednesday [...] boys [...] upon making an idol from some old rags stuffed with hay to resemble Judas, dispatched it, along with one or two from among themselves, to the church tower, while the others, with sticks at the ready, stood in front of the church. Since Judas had been thrown down from the tower, immediately, one (of them), grabbing the tether tied around Judas' neck, dragged him through the streets, running here, there and everywhere with him; the others, giving chase after him, beat him with the sticks, incessantly screaming at the top of their lungs: "Judas!", until said idol was ripped to shreds. If by chance some unsuspecting Jew, unaware of this ceremony, happened along, the fake Judas was abandoned and the real Jude was beaten so sincerely and so long as he did not find some house into which to save himself. But this prank the boys had grown accustomed to – during which they had harmed houses of worship, servants of the church and poor little Jews – after the intervention of school professors and public advisors, lingered for a short while longer, but eventually ceased.[152]

Father Jędrzej Kitowicz was mistaken. It had been around from at least the XVIII century, and in the custom introduced by the *boys' prank* associated with Judas, with the passing of time, not only had it not ceased, but over the next 150 years, it evolved considerably. And this *prank*, during

151 Encyclopedia Judaica, Jerusalem 1972, Vol. XIII, p. 1395; The New Standard Jewish Encyclopedia, New York 1977, p. 833.
152 J. Kitowicz, *Opis obyczajów i zwyczajów za panowania Augusta III* [The description of customs and habits in the times of August III], Kraków 1925, p. 360.

the twenty-year period between the wars, grew to include, in all seriousness, some of the most important representatives of small towns who had allowed themselves to be dragged into it. In a place called Kańczuga, near Przemyśl, this custom was practiced before WWII in the following way:

On Holy Thursday, the Poles constructed a Judas-dummy. They dressed it in things they had stolen from the Jews. They hung him from a pole in the middle of the town square. On Good Friday, the Catholics, after their Mass, along with the priest, an apothecary and a doctor, all went to the square and they cut Judas down. They dragged (him) on a rope and then threw him in the water. [or] On the evening of Holy Thursday, hooligans hung a Jew-dummy in the square. Jews were forced to give the clothing and materials for the dummy. The Jews were furious (about this). He hung in the square overnight. On Friday, after Mass, the whole pole was cut down. They dragged him to the river, set him on fire and threw him in the water. The tradition lasted up until the occupation. The dummy's outfit: a fur-trimmed hat – a shtraymel, a fox or nutria fur coat. And of course peyos, a beard, a long, black frock, white socks and black shoes.

In a place called Studzian: *On Good Friday, Judas was hung across the street from a Jew's house. The Jew had to pay to have the dummy removed. It was said: "So greedy are you, Judas, for money – like a Jew". And that is why he was hung.*

In a place called Urzejów: *On Holy Thursday, nasty old boys, sometimes went and hung Judas from a tree in front of a Jewish house. His pants were stuffed with hay, he had an old hat, a stick inside and a sign that was written on...*[153]

The origin of the Polish custom of hanging, burning and drowning Judas needs to be tied to, above all, to the history of Judas' betrayal recorded in the Evangelical scriptures. But it is also very likely to be linked with the celebration of Purim in some Jewish communities. In the traditional celebration of this holiday, the custom practiced by some Jewish communities (e.g. Kaukaz and Tchorny) as far back as Babylonian times,

---

153 A. Cala, *Wizerunek Żyda w polskiej kulturze ludowej* [*The image of a Jew in Polish popular history*], Warszawa 1992, p. 130-131.

of a public hanging of a dummy of Haman from the gallows, and then setting it on fire.[154] There exists a great probability that, at some point, this custom had reached Polish lands and later became the prototype for the Easter ritual of hanging Judas. The answer to these questions remain open: by which route did this custom penetrate into the community of Polish Jews, and when was it, in fact, adopted by the Poles? The fact that this type of penetration – despite a rather impervious language barrier – on Polish lands had been taking place over the course of all the centuries, at least explains the origin of the creation of *Purimszpilen*.

A practically identical ritual (hanging and setting on fire) in the case of Haman and Judas can, of course, be the result of pure convergence of the fates of each of these figures – (the hanging) and an effective method of annihilation of evil, in the populaces' understanding, (fire). The Jewish tradition, had been well known and practiced with regard to Haman dozens of centuries before the formation and Christianization of Poland, probably possesses a somewhat primeval character as far as the Polish ritual connected to Judas is concerned. The ritual of hanging Judas could also have been, in some sense, in response to the profanity of the cassock in the Jewish custom, a symbol of Catholic spirituality, in which the Polish Jews dressed Haman. At the present time, there is a lack of foundation to further unravel the riddle regarding the origin and all the possible mutual influences of the Jewish custom of hanging Haman and the Polish custom of hanging Judas. It is, therefore, with utmost certainty that only one thing can be claimed, that without the cooperation of both Polish and Jewish historians, we will continue to wander crashing upon historical research pertaining to the unexplainable phenomena and the difficult to understand behaviors of both Polish Jews and Poles in an era when Poland was the shared homeland to both peoples.

Without getting too caught up in the intricacies of justifying an ultimate equity in analyzing the origins of both customs, the following

---

154 Encyclopedia Judaica – Das Judentum in Geschichte und Gegenwart, Berlin 1927, Vol. VII, p. 885-886. See also: M. Bendowska, *Swieta i posty judaizmu, [The Holidays and Fasts of Jews],* in: „Kalendarz Zydowski 1984/85" [The Jewish Calendar 1984/85], Warsaw 1984, p. 54.

claim can be made – that even if it was drawn from the Jewish custom, it is still deeply rooted in the foundations of the Christian religion – the custom of hanging Judas, in an exceedingly theatrical and memorable manner, propagated the stereotypical image of the Jew-Judas into the minds of the Polish community. Similarly, even if drawn from Catholic rituals, it is very deeply rooted in the Jewish religion – the custom of dressing Haman up in the cassock for *Purimszpilen*, propagated the stereotypical image of the Catholic-priest-Haman in an exceedingly theatrical and memorable manner in the minds of the Jewish community.

In contrast to the stereotypical impressions of Polish Catholic priests and Christian Poles that had been personified by the biblical cruel Haman, there existed the stereotype of the fair-minded Polish king that had most likely been the creation of Polish Jews somewhere on the cusp of the XV and XVI centuries. In this case, not unlike with the stereotypical impression of the Catholic priest, biblical images were mixed with historical figures. Majer Bałaban, in his book, claims that when it comes to Jews in Poland it was the *kings who took the most care of them*, and the reign of Polish kings with regard to them was *fair*. These words were written by the Jewish historian in 1912, which means 30 years prior to the Holocaust. We must interpret these words, above all, as an important thesis in the way of historical research, but because historical monographs tend to carry with them the stigma of the epoch during which they were born, we must consider them as bearers of popular judgments and stereotypes that existed among the author's generation at the time, in this case the stereotypical impressions that Polish Jews had with regard to Polish kings.

As far as it can be presumed, the archetype of the stereotypical image of the priest-cruel Haman was, for Polish Jews, the aversion to Christian clergy expressed by a disinclination to Latin as the "alphabet of the clergy" (galkhes) which had been brought over from Western Europe. This was further compounded by the inspiration for the expulsion of Krakovian Jews which is attributed to the fifteenth-century ministry of Kraków. One thing is for certain, that the archetype of the stereotype of the fair king was the reigning king of the XIV century, Kazimierz the Great (1333-1370).

14. Polish King Kazimierz the Great (1333-1370) gives privileges to Jews.
Artur Szyk

As a result of the privileges that had been granted to the Jews, Kazimierz the Great was regarded as the benefactor and protector of Jews by generations of Polish Jews (that followed). Because such a stance was unheard of at the time in Europe, as other European rulers of the day burned, sold and expelled the Jews living on their lands. The Jewish people rewarded Polish king Kazimierz the Great by giving him a legend in which he was assigned a Jewish mistress, or rather a Jewish wife, as some liked to tell it, and in this legend the Polish king is equated with the biblical Persian king Ahasuerus from the capital city of Susa. The Polish equivalent of the biblical Esther, whose story is celebrated year after year during the spring holiday of Purim, was Esterka. She was a Polish Jewess famous for her beauty, who, according to legend, protected the Polish Jews and to whom the role of the key architect of the well known petition to grant Polish Jews privileges under Kazimierz the Great was ascribed by the Jewish population of the time. Because the myth of the Polish Esterka was so well-known to all Polish Jews during the period immediately preceding the outbreak of WWII, it is worth examining its history and role in Polish-Jewish relations of that time.

Documented sources of the history of Jewish settlements in Poland reach as far back as prince Mieszko III the Elder (c.1126-1202), whereas the oldest privileges granted to Jews are dated to the year 1264, when Kalish prince Bolesław Pobożny (Duke of Greater Poland, Bolesław the Pious) granted his Jewish subjects immunity, designating them as a free people, directly subordinate to him, possessing the rights of protection of their synagogues and cemeteries, as well as independent jurisdiction in civil matters in accordance with the Talmudic Law. In other matters, Jews were required to subjugate to the tribunal of the prince or officials of the royal tribunal. The Charter of Kalisz designated Jews by the term *servi camerae* (servants of the royal chamber) and regulated their professional activities in the trade-credit-monetary spheres, as well as protected against the willfulness of their Christian neighbors. King Kazimierz the Great expanded the Charter of Kalisz to encompass the whole of Poland in 1334, and in 1364 and 1367 he ratified it again. Based on the legislation of Polish king Kazimierz the Great, Grand Duke Witold (Vytautas the Great) granted Lithuanian Jews similar privileges and liberties.

Based solely on the abridged calendar of events cited above, it is not difficult to arrive at the conclusion that the greatest role in Jewish settlement in Poland was played by the granting of privileges by Polish king Kazimierz the Great. If we were to weigh the fact that the Kazimierz privileges had been granted to the Jews during a time when their life throughout Western Europe was starting to become dramatically curtailed, when they had already lived through being expelled from England and France, and living conditions in their European countries did not bode a too optimistic future, the favor of the Polish king was, without reason, generating rumors and speculations not only among the Jews, but also among the Poles.

The king Kazimierz the Great (1333-1370) is described in this way in this anecdotal version of Polish history: *Above all, stories were told about Kazimierz as though about Don Juan, fawning over womanly charms and graces from his youth up until his very last days. In 1330, he arrived at the Hungarian court as still a prince. Charles Robert reigned [in Hungary] at the time, and the queen was Elizabeth Łokietek, the sister of Kazimierz. During his visit, the exceptionally beautiful Lady Clara, caught his eye. She was the daughter of one of the Hungarian knights. Kazimierz began to court her. Suddenly, one day, he left the Hungarian, and without bidding farewell to the lady of his heart, he left very rapidly, as though he were fleeing. He was headed for Krakow. The disappointed Lady Clara expressed her sorrow to her father, Felicjan the knight, who executed his revenge on the king and queen, [because he] suspected them, not without reason as far as Elizabeth was concerned, of collaborating in this crime. The king Charles Robert was not seriously injured, but the queen Elizabeth (the sister of Kazimierz) lost four fingers on her right hand for all eternity to the vengeful sword of the disgraced knight.*

Upon becoming Polish king, Kazimierz the Great paid homage to almost sultanic customs. He soon became bored with his second wife, Adelajda, and dispatched her under royal guard to a castle in Żarnów. In her place, he began to receive various concubines, both domestic and international. The spiteful even claimed that that was the reason why the king so often and so willingly traveled throughout the country, that he had a different mistress at every castle. This was indeed slander, or at least an exaggeration.

One time, while visiting with Charles IV in Prague, he had his eye on a certain beauty from Rokiczan, whom he brought back to Poland with him. The king was very much taken by this Czech beauty. However, the devil must have dispatched a nosy gentleman in waiting who sneaked a peek and saw that this royal concubine 'had a head very bald and not very clean'. Of course he quickly notified the king of his discovery because his tongue was itching to tell someone. Kazimierz did not want to believe this gossip at first, but the seed of suspicion had been planted. At the right moment, the king pulled his fair maiden by her hair. It must have been quite a shock when in his hand he was left holding… a beautiful wig. History did not preserve the dialogue which accompanied this scene. The fact of the matter is that Kazimierz the Great disposed of the beauty from Rokiczan, and in her place summoned the famous Esterka, about whom so many legends have survived.[155]

The legendary Jewish beauty, Esterka, who was born in Poland, the paramour of the Polish king, was not the first in the history of the Jewish people to bear the name, to whom the Jews owed their prosperity and favor. She had her archetype in the Bible. The Polish king Kazimierz the Great, who resided in his capital city of Kraków, also had a significant forefather in the Bible, *king Ahasuerus, who once upon a time resided in his capital city of Susa.* And just like his Persian counterpart, king Ahasuerus, was famed among his contemporaries and descendants for not only his favor with regard to the Jews, but also for his countless romantic dalliances. The privileges granted by king Kazimierz as well as the Persian attitude toward marriage and romances, about which word had spread like wild fire among the not yet so numerous Jewish community even if delivered by the residing royal banker, the Jew Lewka. Within the mass consciousness of Polish Jews, it must have been a very organic association between, above all, the favors granted to them by king Ahasuerus under the guidance of the biblical Esther, whose memory had been honored during the annual celebration of Purim that had, by now, been taking place for centuries. From here it is merely a skip and a hop jump to the creation of the legend about the Polish Jewess, chosen by the king himself, protector of her fellow-tribesmen and the main authoress of Polish king Kazimierz the Great's favor. There is no doubt that her archetype was the heroine of the biblical Book of Esther.

To further support the fact that the legend of Esterka was created among Polish Jews and not Poles is the fact that, above all, Catholics, to this day, have a very limited knowledge of the Bible, especially of the Old Testament. In contrast to followers of Judaism or other Christian denominations, Catholics, especially Poles, never really took to studying the Holy Scriptures. In contemporary Polish families, there exists the old tradition of reading the fragments pertaining to the birth of Christ from

---

[155] A. Tomkiewiczowa, W. Tomkiewicz, *Dawna Polska w anegdocie* [Ancient Poland in anecdote], Warszawa 1973, p. 47-48.

the Bible during Wigilia [Christmas Eve dinner], but that is the extent of thoughtful biblical meditation for the majority. In Catholic churches, readings from the Old and New Testament never pertained to the Book of Esther, therefore that biblical character is not known to Catholics as such.

In light of the above, it is without fear of making an erroneous statement that it can be stated, that the legend about the Polish Esterka was born within the Polish-Jewish community. This thesis is supported further by the gossip spread by the Krakow middle-class that the Jews gained the favors of king Kazimierz the Great thanks to the royal banker, Jew Lewko, who supposedly cast sorcery spells over the king, and that he possessed a magical ring with which he performed witchcraft. For a long time, the middle-class of Krakow was far from possessing knowledge about either the biblical Esther, or the Polish Esterka.

The oldest Jewish historical document regarding Esterka comes from a Hebrew chronicle published in Prague in 1595, which is roughly two hundred years after the death of Kazimierz the Great. It is difficult to claim with absolute certainty whether Esterka really did exist. And even if she had existed, it is rather doubtful that she had anything at all to do with the privileges granted to the Jews by king Kazimierz the Great. These doubts become more evident when one examines the dates when the privileges were granted (1334) and the alleged romance between Kazimierz and Esterka. According to the legend, Esterka was the successor of Christine of Rokiczan, a person who actually existed, whom the king most likely married in Prague in 1356, twenty two years after granting privileges to the Jews. It is not clear exactly, how long the relationship between the king and Christine of Rokiczan lasted. What is certain is that, it is possible to tie the character of Esterka to the confirmation of Jewish privileges (1364 and 1367), but not to the actual granting of said privileges. A Polish historian, an expert of the epoch of Kazimierz the Great, summed up the matter regarding the authenticity of the existence of the Jewess, the royal paramour in this way: *Długosz is the only source who confirms the above mentioned mistress of the king, Ester. Her existence cannot be denied, but it also cannot simply be accepted without reserve. If indeed king Kazimierz did have so many lovers as it is upheld from the time of Długosz, then it is entirely possible that one of them might have been a Jewess. But if this was in fact just gossip, and the tradition of word of mouth simply added a Jewess to the story in order to explain the good intentions of the king with regard to the Jews, and at the same time the creation of privileges for the Jews – these are the questions that will continue to be asked over and over.*[156]

Regardless of whether Esterka was in fact a historical figure or simply a creation of the human imagination, in the XV-XVI centuries, the myth of the beautiful Jewess was already widespread among both Poles and Polish Jews. As to whether the Poles were apt to blame their king for the favors bestowed upon the Jews as the result of an immoral relationship, they did give *Kazimierz the Great* the nickname *Small when it comes down to it* as a direct result of his connection to Esterka. The Poles did not make a big deal over the tales of his dalliance with Esterka so much as she became a permanent figure within the folkloric tradition among the Polish-Jewish community over the course of next few centuries. So strong was her presence, in fact, that during the Purim celebrations, Polish Jews often failed to contemplate the history of the biblical Esther, but celebrated the tales of king Kazimierz's dalliance with the Jewish "Polish Queen", Esterka. Over the years, this romance became the fabric of many a woven literary tale.[157]

The legend of Esterka was also very well known among Polish Jews during the period before the outbreak of WWII. This is the version as it was told to Karol Junosza in the early years of the XX century at the Jewish cemetery in Lublin:

– Over there you can even catch a glimpse of one stone on which there is much written, and not so much, and it is inscribed with one name! Do you know, Sir, which name? Ha! Ester! And do you know, Sir, who that name belongs to? She was a Jewess, of humble beginnings, in fact – the daughter of a tailor. But later on, she became the Jewish queen [in Poland].

---

[156] J. Wyrozumski, *Kazimierz Wielki* [Kazimierz the Great], Wrocław 1986, p. 212; see also: M. Bałaban, *Dzieje Żydów w Krakowie i na Kazimierzu 1304-1868* [A history of Jews of Kraków and Kazimierz], Kraków 1912, p. 11; Ch. Schmeruk, *The Esterke Story in Yiddish and Polish Literature*, Jerusalem 1985, p. 37 and 55-59.

[157] Ch. Schmeruk, *The Esterke Story in Yiddish and Polish Literature*, Jerusalem 1985, p. 56.

— Jewish queen [in Poland]? You are poorly informed, my dear Berek, as she was not the queen at all.

— Oh, yeah?! Perhaps, Sir, you will even venture to say that the Polish king Kazimierz was not a king either, and that that Jewess was not Jewish, that he did not sit next to her, and that she was nowhere near him. Everything with you people is backwards.

— But on the contrary, I absolutely admit that there was such a person and that she was, in fact seated next to the Polish king Kazimierz the Great.

— Well then, who has permission to be seated next to the king?! This is comical, by God! The seamstress is seated next to the tailor, and next to the king, the queen. Even a child comprehends that sort of arrangement.

— She is buried not far from Kraków, everybody knows that.

— Well then, let it be the way you say! I did not attend her funeral. For me it's enough that people say that there is such a stone and that on it is inscribed the name of Ester, and that this Ester was the Jewish queen. Why do I need to know more? It's enough for me. Whoever so wishes, let them believe, whoever doesn't want to, doesn't have to believe. There is no one forcing anybody to do anything here, no gun to anybody's head.[158]

There is no question that Kazimierz the Great, in the collective consciousness of Polish Jews, would have gone down in history as the monarch that was good to the Jews, even without the insertion of the legendary Jewish "queen". He was the example for later kings to follow, as well as for leaders of other nations. The myth of fairness and protection of Polish kings over Jews that had been created during the reign of Kazimierz the Great, the memory of promises of guaranteed protection of the Jewish people had survived within the consciousness throughout the partition of Poland (1795), which means over a period of time during which the monarchy itself was nonexistent, nor was a Polish state as such.

Over the course of my twenty years of study of Polish-Jewish relations during WWII, I was always struck and filled with wonder by the love and reverence that Polish Jews had for Marshal Józef Piłsudski, regardless of

---

[158] K. Junosza, *Cud na kirkucie – Z jednego strumienia* [A miracle at the Jewish cementary – From one stream], Warszawa 1960, p. 124-125.

their social status or degree of religiosity. The New York lawyer who died several years ago, Milton Kestenberg, University of Vilna alumnus, who left Poland in 1939, wrote the following:

I believe that the Marshal Josef Piłsudski (1918-1935) was one of the most important figures of Polish history. He was a heroic person, a person with a great political vision. Finally, he was a liberal – actually, he was a dictator having control over a nation, but his philosophy was always liberal. As far as anti-Semitism in Poland is concerned, he was a witness to its development, and I believe that he was the effect/result/outcome of a few basic causes/reasons/ factors. The most significant of which was the impoverishment of the countryside and the overall economic devastation of the country in the period following the partitions and a freshly ended war. This state of affairs required some hefty reforms, which Piłsudski understood very well. His reform program, however, was squashed due to the opposition of great land owners, as well as church circles, which wanted to turn attention away from the matters at hand and created a campaign against Jews.[159]

All other accounts contain, more or less, the same opinions as cited above:

During the period preceding the war, when the Polish Marshal Josef Piłsudski was still living, the posture and politics with regard to Jews was very proper. We were not yet so severely badgered or harassed. Once Piłsudski died, all the Jews throughout all of Poland cried as a result, as did we in Lublin as well. I remember this event very well. I was eleven years old at the time. At five o'clock, a Polish woman came with our milk delivery. She blessed herself and informed us that Piłsudski had died. We all cried. My entire family was crying. Me, too. We all knew that, for the Jews, he represented nothing less than a "savior". To this day, the memory of that event moves me very deeply.[160]

In contemporary publications dedicated to the history of Polish Jews we always find an unequivocal judgment of this figure: *Józef Piłsudski enjoyed the adoration and trust of the Jews. Upon his death, it was written: This nation's minorities, of which we, Jews, are members, have lost a person*

---

[159] E. Lesik [Kurek], *podajmy sobie ręce* [Let us shake hands], in: Nowy Dziennik – Nowy Jork, June 25, 1987.

[160] *Ścieżki pamieci [The path of recollection]*, ed. by Jerzy Bojarski, Lublin 2002, p. 84.

in whom we saw the image and embodiment of the most beautiful Polish traditions in the history of tolerance and the fight for freedom of all people.[161]

In the above cited fragments of documents and declarations, we find the same elements on which the popular stereotype of the kind and fair Polish king was formulated among Polish Jews. Just as the expulsion of Jews from Krakow and Lithuania was not at the hands of the Polish kings, because, in the opinion of a Jewish historian, it was done under pressure of the hateful clergy; just as the Marshal Pilsudski within the collective consciousness of Jews was free of responsibility with regard to the pogroms in Lwów, Pińsk, and in Krakow (1918/19); for the internment of Jewish commissioners during the Polish-Bolshevik war. As for who was at fault for failed reforms upon regaining independence and the ever-growing anti-Semitism, that fell onto the land owners, the middle class, and church circles which worked in direct opposition to the directives of Josef Pilsudski – the heir and champion of *the most beautiful Polish historical traditions.*

The quandary regarding the genesis of the posture Polish Jews held with regard to Marshal Jozef Pilsudski during the twenty-year period between the wars will require separate research in the future. Although it is possible even today, with a certain degree of certainty, to state that it was commonly accepted throughout the Jewish community, and that the belief that in Poland, it was *the kings who took the greatest care of the Jews* had endured for centuries. During the twenty-year period between the wars, upon regaining independence, and in the absence of restitution by the monarchy, this feeling was transferred to the charismatic Marshal who, in the minds of Polish Jews, has gone into history as the *savior*, the savior from anti-Jewish policies of the occupiers, who reinstated the once favorable Polish reign toward the Jews. Because at the hands of the occupiers, especially under the Austrian and Russian rule, the manner in which Jews had grown accustomed to being treated under the reign of Polish kings had shifted in a very dramatic fashion. The source of attributing the stellar qualities of a reigning Polish monarch to Jozef Pilsudski most likely stem from yearning for the guaranteed freedoms they had enjoyed as a Jewish community by

---

161 A. Żbikowski, op. cit., p. 196.

the decree of kings under the Polish State, up until its fall of 1795. It was also a longing for the genuine royal personal protection and care afforded by the Polish kings. Since the free Poland was not reborn as a monarchy in 1918, Polish Jews transferred these royal attributes onto the persona of the Marshal, the undisputed creator of a nation reborn and leader of the Polish nation. Bringing to mind the most just of all fair kings, Kazimierz the Great, Polish Jews "assigned" the Marshal Jozef Pilsudski a Jewish wife, as tradition dictated. Both the Polish and Jewish pre-war Poland rattled to the rafters with the gossip that one of the Marshal's wives is Jewish, which was supposed to explain his alleged favors, and decent attitude, with regard to the Jewish minority.

It is difficult to assert with absolute certainty that this unfounded hearsay did originate inside the community of Polish Jews. Very telling is the fact that the Polish-Jewish community did assign Józef Piłsudski the name of monarchial attributes *savior*, which lends support to the notion that it did originate inside the Jewish community. For emphasis, in summoning up the memory of king Kazimierz's paramour, Esterka, the Marshal was assigned a Jewish wife as well.

15. Polish Jews greet Marshal Jozef Pilsudski in Deblin with traditional bread and salt.

Marshal Jozef Pilsudski died in 1935. Polish Jews were entering the time of the Holocaust without a "monarchial" protector or "savior". There was not a single leader in the Nation of Poland who would be able to replace him; not a single one who, in the hearts of Polish Jews was worthy of such respect and devotion. Among Polish Jews, with regard to the widely spread stereotype of the fair leadership of Polish kings, compounded by the death of the Marshal – the last of the "Polish kings" – there was a fracture in the longstanding Polish-Jewish relations that had endured unbroken since the beginning of our mutual history. Interrupted by the period of partitions, the epoch of monarchy had ended. History has not afforded the Poles or the Jews the opportunity to write the next chapter. Ten years after the death of the monarchial Marshal Jozef Pilsudski, the nation of Polish Jews was no longer among the living.

Poles entered WWII with the widespread stereotypical notion that Polish Jews had betrayed the Polish matter – Judases. Polish Jews entered WWII with feelings of abandonment after the death of the monarchial Marshal who symbolized the protector of the Polish State, as well as with the stereotypical perception that Poles, especially the Catholic clergy, as being Haman – the enemy of the Jewish people. The widespread stereotypes among the Jews, and their lack of knowledge of the Polish language, created a reality in which Polish Jews lived inside the same country, but at the same time they lived in a world separate from the world of the other residents of Poland. This was a world completely isolated from that of the Polish "goyim" which for hundreds of years had been so airtight, that at the turn of the XX century, not everyone was even aware that they are living in Poland. The result of these very traditions was no penetration into the consciousness of understanding even between communities which, by their very nature, are not supposed to recognize any national or linguistic barriers.

From the perspective of half a century gone by; from the perspective of knowledge regarding how a mutual existence of Poles and Jews on Polish land did come to an end, it must be said that, living alongside one another without a mutual understanding of each other; and with absurd stereotypical impressions of the Jew-Judas and the Pole-Haman on top of that; with the medieval prejudices of Polish Jews with regard to the

Polish language and the waiting for the arrival of a medieval "monarchial protectorate" of the Polish State, made absolutely no sense at all. It was a carelessness and thoughtlessness worthy of criminal prosecution on the part of both the Poles and Polish Jews which, during the time of the war, no doubt, enabled the German realization of their felonious acts all that much easier to accomplish.

CHAPTER IV

1939-1942:
THE UNDERGROUND POLISH STATE,
THE OPENNESS
OF UKRAINIAN AND BIELORUSSIAN
NATIONAL STRUCTURES AND
JEWISH AUTONOMOUS PROVINCES[162]

World War II started on September 1, 1939 with the invasion of Poland by Germany. England and France, despite earlier guarantees, limited themselves to declaring a so-called "paper war" on Hitler. Some two weeks later, the Polish State had to face yet another deadly enemy: on September 17, 1939 Poland was invaded from the east by the Soviets. On September 23, 1939, the occupiers issued a mutual

---

[162] The term **'Jewish autonomous provinces'** has been drawn from the proposal of the article 113 of the Polish Constitution which had been put forward by Izaak Grünbaum, the Jewish member of the lower chamber of the Parliament of the Polish State, in the Constitutional Committee in November 1920. The full version of the proposal in: "Druki sejmowe: Sejm Ustawodawczy – Komisja Konstytucyjna 1920", [The Polish Parlaiment Prints: The Legislative Parliament – The Polish Constitutional Committee 1920], print No 1883. The whole excerpt is quoted in Chapter 2.

communiqué regarding the establishment of delimitation lines between the German and Soviet armies. The treatise signed in Moscow on September 28, 1939 "pertaining to the borders and friendship" recognized the lines of delimitations as the ultimate "border of mutual interests of the States" of Germany and the Soviet Union.

The Soviets, who occupied the part of Poland to the east of the delimitation line, incorporated the eastern territories of Poland to the Soviet Union. The Germans, who occupied the part of Poland west of the delimitation line, divided their occupied territories into two parts: the northern and western territories were called the "New Reich" – as opposed to the "Old Reich" from before 1937 – and it was directly incorporated into the Third Reich. From the remaining central territories of Poland, however, they created the so-called General Gouvernement [Generalna Gubernia] an area of 96,000 square km which was divided into districts: the Warsaw District, Radom District, Kraków District, and the Lublin District.[163]

Once again in its history, Polish State had disappeared from the map of Europe.

The multi-national nature of Poland was the reason why, when the Polish State found itself in a state of war with the Germans and the Soviets in September of 1939, this did not pertain to all of the people residing on its land. For the Poles who identified with the Polish State, the loss of a defensive war meant a loss of freedom. However, for those who identified with the minority population within the Polish State, the outbreak of WWII signified not only a wartime drama and hardship, but above all the creation of new types of political and military possibilities which provided the impetus to undertake attempts of realizing hitherto impossible ideas and intentions connected with the creation of their own independent forms of national status.

Because deliberations pertaining to the subject of Polish-Jewish relations during WWII geographically encompass the area of the Polish

---

163 After the outbreak of Soviet-German War in June of 1941, when Hitler's army expanded its conquered territories far to the east, the area of the General Gouvernement [Generalna Gubernia] increased to 145,000 square km. The former provinces of Lwów, Stanisławowo and Tarnopol were renamed by the Germans to the Galicja District, and as the fifth administrative body of its kind, it was added to the General Gouvernement [Generalna Gubernia].

State 1918-1939, in which Poles and Jews lived among the other national minorities, it is only possible to understand them against the backdrop of the posture of the two remaining ethnic groups living in Poland: the Ukrainians and the Bielorussians. Therefore, in comparing the socio-political campaigns run by these nations in the first three years of the war, from 1939 to 1942, we are provided with the backdrop without which an understanding of Polish-Jewish relations during the years of the Holocaust from 1942 to 1945 would be impossible.

At the outbreak of WWII, the Polish State was almost 1000 years old. The crossing over the borders by the Germans and by the Soviets in 1939 ignited something in the Polish people mechanisms of citizen behavior that had been cultivated over generations. The most important one of all – defending "your country" and battling the occupiers – dictated and subordinated all the other social and national mechanisms.

In September of 1939, in the face of imminent danger, the well-practiced mechanism of citizenship went into full force. This meant that Poles needed to be prepared to sacrifice bloodshed or personal fortune for the purpose of regaining their freedom. Undertaking a defensive war against the Germans on September 1, 1939 and against the Soviets on September 17, 1939 ended in calamity. The battles of the defensive war had not yet died down by the time the Poles had already prepared a concept of war against the invaders.

Because the entirety of Poland's territory was occupied by foreign armies, in an effort to maintain the structure of national leadership in tact, those highest in authority within the Polish State decided to emigrate. The Polish President, Ignacy Mościcki, who together with his cabinet members and central institutional staff crossed the border into Roumania after the Soviet invasion on September 17, 1939, was interned there. In accordance with the rules of law, he named Władysław Raczkiewicz, who was in France, as his successor. The new president dismissed the existing government and the highest ranking military personnel, and assigned the task of creating a new government to General Władysław Sikorski. The premier, Władysław Sikorski, was also given the title of commander-in-chief by the president. The Poles who remained within their country, citizens of the Polish State, went underground and formed a conspiracy movement to create an underground structure to their Underground State.

Poles dedicated the first three years of the occupation to building the Underground State. WWII historians in Poland have accepted this caesura: 1939-1942 as the period of construction for the Polish Underground State, and 1942-1944 as the period of its full development. Because the most penetrating and thorough look at the quandary of the Polish Underground State was put forth by Professor Tomasz Strzembosz, I am taking the liberty of citing it in its entirety:

Researchers of WWII are all in agreement when it comes to the Polish Underground State being an exceptional phenomenon within the scope of German occupied Europe, that is in the area from Moscow to the Canal de la Mancha. It was in a country that had to surrender under the pressure of occupying forces that were far more severe than in any of the occupied countries of Western or Central Europe, but equally as treacherous as in the territories of the Soviet Union; in a country under the threat of biological warfare, where millions of its citizens had been murdered; it was here that, in a matter of three years, a perfectly capable and functioning Underground State system was created. An Underground Polish State, which thanks to its own authority, had an actual impact and influence on the day-to-day goings-on and postures of a greater portion of citizens of the pre-war Poland. A state which stood in the face of occupying forces as a real entity and force to be contended with, which in conspiracy prepared vital legislative and organizational elements necessary to ensure the functioning of a future Polish democratic system in post-war Poland, and realizing human rights based on Christian ethics for people living in freedom. (...)

The task of a modern state, at least in the form in which they are developing in Europe, are always based on defending oneself against an outside enemy, guaranteeing internal peace and order, directing those areas of public life (included in this is the economy), which a given society has put in the hands of national leaders, stabilizing a legislative order. In democratic situations, the carrying out of these tasks is divided among legislative, executive and judicial institutions. Have these tasks been performed by some unusual state living in an occupied country?

The role of the armed forces was performed by the Home Army [the Armia Krajowa; AK], within the designated or possible capacity, having in its reserve a greater number of citizens than the Polish Army did during peacetime. The role of highest authority was performed by Government Delegate to the Country [Delegatura Rządu na Kraj], in greater part taking the place of the premier, and towards the end it was in the rank of Vice Premier. It gave orders to a series of district and county delegates – a substitute administration. It had at its disposal a state police in the form of State Security Corps. There were also other functioning branches of executive power. Judicial Power in the name of the Polish State was executed by Special Civil and Military Courts, passing out sentences which were no less harsh than at any other time. The Political Committee of Knowing, which had already been set up in February of 1940, represented the main functioning political parties in the Underground, and later on, the Home Political Representation and the Council of National Unity were formed. They had an authority, perhaps even greater than any diet.

The underground state apparatus had a clear connection to the conspiratorial political and social subgroups, and had a direct impact and influence on their operations. It also supported them on numerous planes, in the form of a protector, no less significantly than any government authority. It gained the recognition of the majority of social organizations, as well as, most importantly, of the simple people scattered throughout the country. (...) Not only did the Polish Underground State organize opposition to both occupiers; not only did it protect and care for its citizens, it protected historical structures of Polish culture and saw to it that they increased in number; it supported a subversive education, and such; it also prepared the necessary legal dossiers for the post-war period of a liberated Poland. Therefore, the Polish Underground State, to a greater extent, performed all of the functions that a nation should.

Only a fraction of pre-war citizens of the Polish State identified with it in trying times, or identified with the Polish Underground State. It is only that portion that can be considered as "citizens of the Underground State", that is of a certain reality within, above all, moral parameters. As professor Jan Szczepański once put it: this was a citizenship with a "humanistic element" as well as being a state to which one belonged not due to ones place of residence – as a result of some international arrangement, under political pressure or outright physical pressure – but rather a State whose citizenship one obtained on the path of an internal decision and for which one agreed to a sacrifice and great effort. Being a member was something very private, personal and without force.[164]

The Ukrainians, citizens of the Polish State 1918-1939, did not include themselves in the building of the Polish Underground State, for they had been fighting for their own independent nation for the last three hundred years, and their true attitude toward the Polish State had been expressed quite clearly during the almost entire twenty-year period between the wars. This posture was characteristic not only of the Ukrainian population, but also of almost every Ukrainian political party. The posture the Ukrainians would take with regard to the outbreak of war between Poland and the Germans, as well as between Poland and the Soviets, was easy to predict. Because they felt no connection to the Polish State, and because they did not identify with its borders or governmental structures, the Ukrainians could not take the stance of citizens, nor could they consider the invasion and occupation by Germany and the Soviet Union as a cause worth fighting for.

Outside of the political environment surrounding the Ukrainian National Democratic Unification, the Ukrainians residing in pre-war Poland took the stance of foreigners with regard to the war in 1939. For the longest time they did not conceal the fact that a free Poland was not their goal, but rather an independent Ukraine. The geo-political conditions of Central-Eastern Europe created a situation in which the two main directions of Ukrainian independence movements were, for a long time prior to the outbreak of the war, geared towards Poland's enemies: the Germans and the Soviets.

During the years of 1939-1941, when all the Ukrainian territories constituted an integral part of the Soviet Union, the Ukrainians were concentrated within the OUN [Organization of Ukrainian Nationalists – translators note], and in 1940 they split into OUN-R ("revolutionary fraction") under the direction of Stepan Bandera, and OUN-M under the

---

164 Prof. T. Strzembosz, *Rzeczpospolita podziemna [Polish Underground State]*, Warsaw 2000, p. 8-9 and 39. Strzembosz was a historian, an expert on WW II and wrote much on this subject.

leadership of Andriej Melnyk. They were in no position whatsoever to realize the goals they had set for themselves. These possibilities did not present themselves until June of 1941 with the outbreak of the Soviet-German war. Following the footsteps of the Germans, a group of Ukrainian political activists from OUN-R arrived in the Ukraine, with an understanding they had reached with the Metropolitan, Szeptycki, proclaiming Ukrainian independence on the day of June 30, 1941; and Jarosław Stecko was assigned the mission of creating a government. The Germans, who had no intention of supporting the Ukrainian goals of building an independent state, reacted quite swiftly. Already in the first half of July of 1941, the newly formed government and a slew of OUN activists were arrested and transported to Berlin. Erich Koch, who took over the function of deputy of the Reich in matters pertaining to the Ukraine, proclaimed that leadership over the Ukrainians will be accomplished with *the help of inferior tobacco, vodka and a knout.*

The announcement of severe German rule did very little to dissuade the Ukrainian nationalistic environment from willingly collaborating with the occupier. From 1941, the Ukrainians participated in German extermination campaigns (as in the murder of Polish professors of the University of Lwów) as well as provided the special German groups (Einsatzgruppen), with proscriptive lists, and occasionally even replaced the Germans in murdering of those considered to be of most value, especially the members of the Polish intelligentsia. The Ukrainians also willingly participated in the extermination of the Jewish population. Many Polish Ukrainians were also found in the ranks of the Ukrainian assistant police that were called upon by the Germans. There were two Ukrainian battalions, "Rolland" and "Nachtigall", supporting the German forces on the front, and as of April 1943, the SS rifleman division, "Galizien," famous for its cruelty, under the leadership of General I. Freytag, which consisted of four regiments and subsidiary divisions.

In 1942, the Ukrainian nationalists shouted the slogan: *Death to the Jews, death to the Poles, only then it will be good for us [Smert Żydam, smert Lacham, tu de bude dobre nam!],* and they began an ethnic cleansing campaign in what had, from 1939, been the Western Ukrainian lands. A wave of slaughter came over tens of thousands of human beings: Poles and Jews, as well as representatives of the various nationalities that had been residing on these territories.

The posture taken by the Ukrainians with regard to the outbreak of WWII and the occupation of Polish lands by the Germans and the Soviets is critical as far as Polish-Jewish relations are concerned with regard to at least two aspects: as an example of the attitude of foreigners taken by minorities with regard to the Polish State, as well as the threat of death flowing from the Ukrainians towards Poles and Jews alike. In other words, the Polish State, and during the years of the war its continuation in the form of the Polish Underground State, not only because it could not count on loyalty from the Ukrainians citizens living within its borders, but also because of the active movements towards an independent Ukraine after the outbreak of the war, was perceived by the Ukrainians as a deathly enemy with whom, just as with its non-Ukrainian citizens (the Poles and the Jews), an unforgiving war is being waged. Due to the reasons cited above, the Poles and Jews residing on the lands that the Ukrainians were claiming as their own, found themselves in a situation facing a double threat: one from the German invaders and the other from their neighboring Ukrainians.

Similar to the Ukrainians, although far more lenient in form, the Bielorussians also took the stance of foreigners with regard to the Polish State at the outbreak of WWII. The Bielorussians, as Zachar Szybieka, a Bielorussian historian, writes, in a defensive war that had been lost by the Poles in September of 1939 "found reasons to rejoice" in the fact that their lands were being reunited under the colors (of the flag) of the Soviet Union. However, at the outbreak of the Soviet-German war in June of 1941, they undertook the far-reaching collaboration efforts with the Germans: *They wanted to take advantage of the German occupation in order to usher in a local Bielorussian administration, develop their sense of national consciousness, and create their own army. (...) The truth of the matter is that many of them entered into this collaboration not due to ideological callings, but rather because they stood to gain materially.*

The plans the Bielorussians had made became possible when, as a representative of the Third Reich, *The exceptional Gauleiter, Kube, appeared on the scene in Bielorussia. He believed that in order to successfully crush the Bolsheviks, it was necessary to cooperate with the Bielorussians.* According to one Bielorussian historian, *the exceptional* Gauleiter Kube, over the next few years, transformed the Bielorussian Popular Self-help Organization, which had been established in 1941 and had been under the direction of Iwan Jermaczenek, into a substitute of Bielorussian government and administration. *The organization had district and regional field offices, as well as a House of Commons. Gauleiter allowed the Self-help Organization to occupy itself with not only performing good deeds, but also to engage in cultural-educational activities. In July of 1942, a twelve-member panel of the Main Protection Council of the Bielorussian Popular Self-help Organization (BPSO) was formed with Iwan Jermaczenek at its head. A few departments were created along with it: political, military, school, culture, propaganda, public health. The councils of BPSO with their respective departments started to function in every sphere. (…) In March of 1943, the congress of the Bielorussian Popular Self-help Organization voted on the memorandum regarding the Autonomy of Bielorussia, the creation of a Bielorussian government and Bielorussian army, and going to war with the Soviet Union.*[165]

Aside form the administrative apparatus collaborating with the Germans, from the beginning of 1942, there had existed Bielorussian political units which were subordinate to the Germans[166], and in June of 1942, at the initiative of Gauleiter Kube, the Bielorussian Defense Force was created, Bielorussian military units which were overseen by German officers. A substantial influx of Bielorussian volunteers allowed for the creation of approximately twenty battalions. In the Bielorussian Defense Force, the Bielorussian commanders saw *the seed of the future Bielorussian army.*[167] The broad spectrum of the Bielorussian collaboration with the Germans was supplemented by a twelve-thousand-five-hundred-members-

---

[165] Z. Szybieka, *Historia Białorusi 1795-2000 [The History of Bielorussia]*, Lublin 2002, p. 331-335.

[166] The functionaries of the German-subordinated Bielorussian police were mainly recruited from among the prisoners of war and were unofficially called the 'Russian People's Army' or *narodnicy*. In March 1943 these formations were joined with the Russian Liberation Army commanded by General A. Vlasov.

[167] Z. Szybieka, *Historia Białorusi 1795-2000 [The History of Bielorussia]*, Lublin 2002, p. 345.

strong Bielorussian Youth Association, which propagated fascist and anti-Semitic ideologies. The Bielorussian military units participated alongside the Germans in extermination campaigns of the Jewish population as well as numerous pacifications.

One trait that the Poles residing within the Polish State 1918-1939 shared with the Ukrainians and Bielorussians was having to reside within specifically delineated contain territories, to which these nations were assigned based on rights of occupation (of said territories) and historical tradition, and as a result, they felt a sense of resentment towards one another, sometimes justified, sometimes not. The only minority residing throughout the entirety of the pre-war Poland and not having any assigned historical connection to any specific region of Poland were the Polish Jews. Merely lacking territorial reasons did not signify lacking a model of Jewish lifestyle which, mainly due to religious reasons, had always been isolated from the Christian world. Because the Jewish population, from their earliest settlements in Poland, had always been mainly city dwellers, over the course of residing here for several centuries, they had created Jewish enclaves in nearly every city. In other words, they had established neighborhoods which in a very organic manner delineated the territorial reach of the Jewish world. As a result of a growing national-political consciousness among Polish Jews along with favorable political conditions within the Polish State that had been rebuilt in 1918, Polish Jewry, as an ethnic minority, for the first time in history, made territorial demands with regard to Poland in 1920. Articulated in the Constitutional Committee by the Jewish member of The Lower Chamber of the Polish State, Izaak Grunbaum, the proposition pertained to the transformation of Jewish residential neighborhoods into *autonomous provinces* whose relation to the Polish State were to be determined by separate laws.[168]

---

168 The question of the Jewish autonomy in Poland has been exhaustively presented by Jolanta Żyndul in her book *Państwo w Państwie? - Autonomia narodowo-kulturalna w Europie Środkowowschodniej w XX wieku* [A state within a state? – The National and Cultural Autonomy in Central and Eastern Europe in the twentieth century], Warszawa 2000, p. 83-156, in the chapter entitled 'Próba wprowadzenia autonomii narodowo-kulturalnej dla mniejszości żydowskiej w II Rzeczypospolitej' [The attempt to introduce the cultural and national autonomy for the Jewish minority in the Second Republic of Poland]. The project

In the political-national and religious sense, on the eve of the outbreak of WWII, Polish Jews were split into a few basic political-religious units. The largest amongst them was represented by the Orthodox religious Jews (approximately 85%) having had practiced isolating themselves from the Christian world for centuries, for whom autonomous provinces, regardless of party affiliation, were an optimal solution. Among the remaining 15% Jewish minority in Poland, the most important were the nationalists promoting the idea of building a national state in Palestine (the Zionists) and Autonomy in Poland (the Folkists), as well as socialists concentrated around the Jewish Laborers Union (Bund), all of whom claimed that Autonomy would be the optimal model for the Jewish lifestyle within the Polish State. Jewish communists, Christians of Jewish descent, and assimilated Jews (i.e. not baptized, but living solely within Polish circles from 1939), lived as marginalized groups within Jewish communities, amongst whom the last two groups were not even associated with Jews before the war. For a variety of reason, they had very little influence over the political decisions that were being made by Polish Jews between the years of 1939 and 1942.[169]

Therefore, aside from the nationalist group (the Zionists) who collectively constituted a rather large, albeit marginal, Jewish community, for the majority of Polish Jews, the optimal model for a Jewish lifestyle within Poland was being postulated in 1920 by the Jewish member of

---

of the article 113 of the Polish Constitution had been designed to include all the minorities of the Second Republic but, as it originated in the circles of the Polish Jewry, it concerned mainly the needs of the Jews.

[169] The assimilated Jews and Christians of the Jewish nationality had been excluded from the Jewish life already before the outbreak of the war. Thus, in 1939 they were not entitled to make any political decisions as regards the relations between the Jewish community and the occupying authorities. They had bound their future with Polish nationality and with the Polish State, and sometimes also with Christianity. Therefore, they were Poles. In 1940, the Nuremberg Laws, which applied to the Polish Jews upon the occupation of the country, forced them into the Jewish circles that were unfamiliar to them. Jewish communists, although visible in the Jewish community, not only denied Poland the right to independence but also denied the Jews the right of choosing their own political way. Their sole aim was to build communism. Due to the above reasons their attitudes cannot be equated with those of the Jewish nation and as such they are excluded from the present considerations.

The Lower Chamber of the Polish State, Izaak Grünbaum, in favor of *autonomous provinces*. Polish Jews had spent the entire twenty-year period between the wars waging parliamentary and propaganda battles over the realization of Jewish Autonomies. From the start, this was a lost battle. Neither the Poles nor the Polish State was willing or able to meet the demands of the Jews. Polish Jews were allowed to practice their religion in Poland without limits, to form political parties, to run schools, publish books and newspapers, etc... In other words, they were able to live an independent, limitless religious-cultural-political life, but they were not able to count on Poles issuing them autonomous provinces from Polish lands, for the scope of demands was a threat to the interests of the Polish State. The Jewish Autonomy factor in Poland was the proverbial bone of contention between Poles and Jews during the years of 1918-1939, and to a large degree, dictated the state of relations between the two nations.

Into this cauldron of extremely complicated social-political-national and religious Polish-Jewish circumstances within the pre-war Poland, September of 1939 brought with it the war. The Poles, Ukrainians and Bielorussians undertook to create a new political-military reality for their people under the severely strained conditions of a two-pronged occupation of Poland. They undertook to build underground state structures, or as in the case of the Poles, be it clear, forms of statehood within the shape and borders that had been created as a result of collaboration with the occupants (the Bielorussians and the Ukrainians). In the fall of 1939, under German occupation, Polish Jews had also already set out to create a new quality of political-national life.

There is no doubt, that before the Germans instituted the "Final Solution" with regard to the Jewish question, i.e. the Holocaust, and before it became clear for the Jews and the Poles what the occupiers had really in store with regard to the Jewish people, three years of the war had gone by. During those first three years of the war, Polish Jews, as a minority residing within the territories of the Polish State, had first to come to terms with the fact that the war had in fact started, and later had to face the reality of losing the defensive war in 1939 and of the occupation from 1939 to 1942. In the first three years of the war, the political-religious elite of Polish Jewry continued to occupy certain positions with regard to certain problems, continued to make political, military and administrative decisions, and continued to give shape to the social and cultural aspects of the lives of their people. In a word, they were making certain choices which directly impacted both the shape of Jewish life and relations with the forces occupying Polish lands, the Germans and the Soviets. They also had an effect on the shape of the deliberations which are the topic of my book, Polish-Jewish relations. **It is important to emphasize that the postures taken by Polish Jews in the years 1939-1942, as well as the decisions that were being made and campaigns being pursued were not in any way based on the perspective of the Holocaust. For only a handful of Germans sitting in the highest command within the structure of the German nation had any knowledge of this.**

In order to understand the complexity of the information contained within Jewish sources, in order to understand the atmosphere and conditions under which Polish Jews were making their decision during the years of 1939-1942, it is crucial to address a few fundamental questions. These are the same question we pose with regard to the other peoples of pre-war Poland, that being the Poles, the Ukrainians and Bielorussians. Just as it is not possible to comprehend the existence of the Polish Underground State during the years of 1943-1945 without the first three years of its formation; just as it is not possible to understand the Ukrianian-Polish and Bielorussian-Polish wars reminiscent of the years 1943-1945 without understanding everything that had happened in the first three years of the war. In order to grasp the Holocaust of Polish Jews and Polish-Jewish relations during the years of the Holocaust, one must reach as far back as to the years of 1939-1942, to the period when, no one apart from the Germans had any idea regarding the fate that the occupying Hitler had readied for Polish Jews on Polish lands. The first of these questions pertains to the stance taken by Polish Jews with regard to the defeated Polish State in September of 1939.

Attempting to find not only an answer to the question of the stance taken by Polish Jews with regard to the outbreak of WWII and the catastrophe that Poland had had to endure, but also, what sort of a political-military and administrative-social vision were they trying to realize through the campaigns they were waging and the decisions they were making for themselves in the first three years of the war. These are matters of great significance and consequence, without which searching for answers concerning the years that followed, i.e. the Holocaust and Polish-Jewish relations during this time, is pointless and warps reality.

Excluding the communists, Christians of Jewish descent and assimilated Jews, the first group on the list were the ones to replace being Jewish for the idea of Communism; the second group, in reality, were Poles, a trait which they shared with Polish Jews regardless of their political beliefs or form of practicing their religion, was that at the time WWII broke out, on the one hand they were a united front with regard to the above cited model of Jewish lifestyle within Poland, meaning striving for the autonomous provinces proposed in 1920; on the other hand, their attitude to the world around them in which they had for centuries expressed a specific classification of incidents, both political and military in nature, with regard to "Jewish matters" and "Polish matters". It was this classification that dictated the direction of the campaigns Polish Jews were undertaking: identifying the problem as "the Polish matter", dictated passiveness; however, identifying the problem as "the Jewish matter", dictated taking action and resulted in undertaking campaigns that stood to benefit the betterment of the Jewish nation.

Communicating using one language, practicing one religion, and being shaped by one culture, the Jewish nation, of which the Polish Jews constituted a significant portion, stretched from Vladivostok to Paris, according to some; according to others, from Odessa to Warsaw.[170] Its specificity was characterized by a lack of allegiance to any specific land or statehood.

Without land or a country, the Jewish nation did not exactly have a legitimate packet of so-called "Jewish matters" that could be recognized by Polish historians to this day. These "Jewish matters" served as a sort of national bonding agent for the Polish Jews. Very rarely, if ever, were

---

170 Mark Edelman, in: Grupińska A., *"Ciągle po kole"* ["Still Round the Circle: Talks with the Soldiers of the Warsaw Ghetto"], Warszawa 2005, p. 36; Vidal-Naquet P., *Zbieram obelgi z różnych stron* [*I receive insults from different sides*], in: 'Gazeta Wyborcza', 12-13 October, 2002.

"Jewish matters" identified as "Polish matters". This means that the Polish Jews perceived the social-political-military campaigns of the country in which they were residing as rolling masses of volcanic lava, and they only, if ever, participated in these campaigns if they were, in some way, capable of being associated with "Jewish matters". As for the remaining matters that had not been identified by them as "Jewish matters", Polish Jews positioned themselves as outsiders. A perfect example of this Jewish posture is Marek Edelman, one of the last surviving participants of the Warsaw Ghetto Uprising, who lived in Poland. As he himself says, throughout most of his life, he has moved in circles of "Jewish matters". It was not until thirty years after the war had ended that he included himself in "Polish matters":

*On the cusp of 1975/76, independent opposition circles in Warsaw organized protests against an attempt to write amendments into the Polish Constitution regarding the directorial role of the Communist Party as well as our friendship with the Soviet Union. Wiktor Woroszylski dispatched Teresa Bogucka, a journalist, to Łodz in order that she get Marek Edelman's signature (this protest will be recorded by history as "List 101"). Bogucka remembers him asking: „Why exactly do you come to me? And what, if anything, do I have to do with this matter? **After all, this is not a Jewish matter**". Bogucka responded: „This is true, this is neither a Jewish matter, nor is it a Polish matter. This is a just matter". He signed it. „In this way – Edelman later said – in the form a frozen through-and-through Tereska Bogucka, because it happened to be a very, very cold day, Poland came to me".[171]*

Poland did not come to Marek Edelman before the war.

Poland did not come in September of 1939.

Poland did not come to the Warsaw Ghetto in the days of the Holocaust.

Poland came to Marek Edelman thirty years later.

It seems that the above mentioned classification by Marek Edelman, which confirms the very sharp delineation of matters into "Polish" and "Jewish" by the Polish Jews, is the key to understanding the posture taken

---

[171] J. Szczęsna, *Ostatni Mohikanie i nowy naród [The Last of the Mahicans and the New Nation]*, in: „Gazeta Wyborcza", Warsaw, June 28/29, 2003.

by Polish Jews with regard to the outbreak of WWII in September of 1939. Because if he, a Polish Jew born and raised in Poland, who had consciously connected his entire life with this country, more than thirty years after the war still continued to strictly segregate the world that surrounded him into "Polish matters" or "Jewish matters", then this sort of segregation process must have been commonplace at the outbreak of WWII. This type of understanding of things is confirmed by other Jewish sources. As to whether the outbreak of WWII was solely a Polish matter, or was it in fact a Jewish matter as well, Emanuel Ringelblum writes the following:

*Recently, there has been a surge in historical awareness. In dozens of instances, there is a connection to the Middle Ages. I have spoken with a learned Jew. Jews have created a separate world for themselves in which they have forgotten about the tragedies all around, and they will not let anyone inside this world. [...] I heard an **interesting theory** [..]. The Jews are the ones waging the war and therefore must suffer casualties.*[172]

At the time Emanuel Ringelblum, somewhat shocked, recorded this "interesting theory" he had come upon, that the war currently being waged is also a Jewish war, in turn a "Jewish matter", the German-Soviet occupation of Polish lands was barely in its second year. The theory that WWII is also a Jewish matter must have developed very slowly in a Polish-Jewish environment and most likely never made it beyond the narrow circles of Ghetto historians or chroniclers. This theory is confirmed by yet another fragment in Ringelblum's *Diary* dated on the cusp of 1942/1943, during the period when the fate of the Polish Jews was no longer a secret to anyone. In this fragment, the author reveals the person behind the "interesting" theory:

*The question which millions of Polish Jews ask themselves daily, will I be lucky enough to survive the war, will Hitler's murderers stop the slaughter, or will they bring their plan of exterminating all the Jews to its fruition, comrade [Szachno Efroim] Sagan had an **original** response: 'We, the Jews, are the side with which Hitler is waging this war. We are on the front lines'.*[173]

[172] Ringelblum E., *"Kronika getta warszawskiego wrzesień 1939 – styczeń 1943"*, Warszawa 1983, p. 189-190 and 269. [See also: "Notes from the Warsaw Ghetto" by Emmanuel Ringelblum, paperback, Ibooks Inc., 2006].
[173] Ibidem, p. 539.

Szachno Efroim Sagan was of the few Polish Jews who believed that WWII was in fact a "Jewish matter" as well. He was so isolated in his manner of thinking that his views survived only within the realm of chronicle entries as "original" and "interesting" theories.

In the defensive war in September of 1939, *roughly 120,000 Jews, Polish citizens, actively participated in the ranks of the Polish Army in the battle against the Germans. 32,216 soldiers and officers perished, while 61,000 were imprisoned by the Germans.*[174]

Among the Polish-Jewish soldiers, there was a small group of people who, in the first few days of the war, took the citizen-stance and determined that the outbreak of war is the war of Polish Jews as well, in other words, they continued to practice the "original" and "interesting" theory that Szachno Efroim Sagan had put forth. It was these Jewish people, mainly soldiers of the Polish Military, who extablished the Jewish conspiratorial organization called „Dawn" ["Świt"] in the autumn of 1939. With time, this organization morphed into the Jewish Military Union [Żydowski Związek Wojskowy - ŻZW], a conspiratorial military organization equal in its goals and activities to the Polish conspiratorial army, the Home Army [Armia Krajowa – AK]. Lieutenant Dawid Apfelbaum stood at the head of the Jewish Military Union. The soldiers of the Jewish Military Union maintained contact with the Polish Home Army and with other Polish conspiratorial organizations, and with an estimated 150-400-strong well armed soldiers, they fought in the Warsaw Ghetto Uprising in 1943.[175]

Szachno Efroim Sagan and a handful of Jewish soldiers concentrated within the Jewish Military Union, took the citizen-stance with regard to WWII and determined that the ongoing war is very much a "Jewish matter". It is not entirely out of the realm of possibility that there did exist other small groups of Polish Jews, whose memory did not survive to this day, who also supported the citizen-stance with regard to WWII. Their number, however, barely surpassed a fraction of a percentage point when

---

[174] W. Bartoszewski, Z. Lewinowna, op. cit., p. 9.

[175] The Judaic Lexicon *[Słownik Judaistyczny]*, Warszawa 2003, Volume II, p. 865. See also: J. P. Eisner, *Nadać sens śmierci [To Give a Sens for the Death]*, in: „Wprost", Warsaw, June 8, 2003.

compared to the number of Polish Jews who, with tremendous dedication and dignity, while serving under the command of Berek Joselewicz, supported the Poles in their fight for independence one hundred fifty years earlier. The remaining Jews, the greater majority, classified the outbreak of WWII as they did all the other wars that had been fought on Polish lands in its almost 1000-year-old existence, strictly as a "Polish matter".[176] The posture of the greater majority of Polish Jews with regard to WWII can, without qualms of being mistaken, be described in the following way:

- since the side with which Hitler is waging war is the Polish State and the Poles, this war is strictly a "Polish matter", and it is the Poles who must suffer casualties;
- since Polish Jews are not the side with which Hitler is waging war, the declaration of war on the Polish State is not a "Jewish matter", and Jews are not obligated to suffer casualties.

Interpreting WWII as an issue not falling into the category of "Jewish matters" proves that almost all Polish Jews, just as the Ukrainians and Bielorussians, did not identify with the Polish State. Claiming that the masses of Polish Jews did not identify with the Polish State, just as they had in many other instances, reflects only a partial truth. This is what the difficulty in understanding Jewish problems is based on: there is no known template that would fit their way of being. For if I claim that the Ukrainians did not identify with the Polish State and that during WWII they undertook to create their own nationhood, I am stating an undisputed fact. If, however, I express the same sentiment with regard to the Polish Jews, that Polish Jews did not identify with the Polish State, intuitively I know that that is not the entire truth of the matter. Where can the words of Adam Czerniakow be inserted? How can the words of the Polish senator

---

[176] Historians take for granted the fact that since the consequences of World War II were most tragic for the Jewish nation, this war must have been a Jewish one. One can agree with this reasoning with one restriction: through the death and the Jewish blood shed during the war, it has also become a Jewish case – the war of the Polish Jews. However this is not to say that it was so understood by the Polish Jews at the moment of its outbreak in September 1939.

and wartime-mayor of the Warsaw Ghetto be classified and understood, along with the words of several like him, all of whom said the following about their fellowman: *He indeed loved Poland, just like all Polish Jews did, with every fiber of their souls, with a love that was not circumstantial. He did not shame himself, however, by escaping from the people from whom he grew. [...] Anyone who imagines that digesting the quandary of bi-nationalism within oneself, that assimilating the two elements and creating a valuable alloy upon melting it together is an easy matter, is mistaken...*[177]

Therefore, the statement about Polish Jews which comes closest to the truth seems to be that Jews loved Poland as the place they had designated and chosen to live in (*Polin*), and that they identified with the Polish State only so far as it was a form of a guarantee which allowed them to lead a Jewish lifestyle, but not as an idea for which it was worth bearing the burden of casualties. Consequently, in judging Polish Jews in the categories of citizens-foreigners, it must be written that, because Polish Jews were foreigners who loved Poland, they interpreted the threat of WWII to Poland as a general misfortune which must be endured under the best of conditions, but not as a "Jewish matter" that is worth dying for.

Anyone who imagines that digesting the quandary of bi-nationalism within oneself [...] is an easy matter, is mistaken. These words were uttered by Adam Czerniakow one year prior to the outbreak of the war. Surely, he had no inkling whatsoever that it would fall upon him to be tested on his "Polishness" and "Jewishness" simultaneously, and that this would prove to be the most challenging exam of his life. Anyone who believes that understanding *the quandary of Jewish bi-nationalism* is an easy matter, is also mistaken. Except that, regardless of the degree of difficulty involved, an attempt to grasp said *quandary of bi-nationalism* should be undertaken, especially since it does hold the key to understanding the Holocaust and Polish-Jewish relations during WWII.

The foreigners of the Polish State gave an account of the politics of their motherlands (the Germans, the Latvians), or attempted to build their

---

[177] A. Czerniakow, *Udział Żydów w odbudowie zniszczeń wojennych w Polsce* [The Jews' participation in rebuilding of the war damages in Poland], in: „Głos Gminy Żydowskiej", Nr 10-11, Warsaw 1938, p. 267-278.

Ewa Kurek

own nationhood (the Ukrainians and Bielorussians). Polish Jews, at least the residents of Warsaw and Łódź, since the war that was being engaged in by the Poles with its German occupier was not a "Jewish matter", set foot on their own national-political path in the autumn of 1939 which differed from the Polish path. A key figure which affords an understanding of the chronology, logic and weight-factor of the Jewish choice resulting in concrete postures taken during the years of 1939-1942 is the pre-war senator of the Rzeczpospolita, Adam Czerniakow. He was the president of the Jewish Faith Council, later the Chairman of the Warsaw Judenrat and Mayor of Jewish Autonomy of Warsaw Jews, colloquially known as the Warsaw Ghetto, who accepted the title of *Verwaltung des Jüdischen Wohnbesitzes,* administrator of the Jewish residential neighborhood. First and foremost, because Warsaw was the Capital and the city with the largest concentration of Jews, the decisions made by Adam Czeniakow, as well as the actions taken, served as an example of postures and behaviors for all other concentrations of Jewish people. Secondly, because Adam Czernikow, from the outbreak of WWII until his death, kept a daily journal which survived almost in its entirety to this day, and which serves as an irreplaceable historical source allowing for the grasping of chronological and problematic Jewish-German and Jewish-Polish interactions of 1939-1942, which in turn constitutes the key to understanding the Holocaust as well as Polish-Jewish relations between 1942 and 1945.[178]

During the twenty-year period between the wars, Adam Czerniakow

---

[178] Before analyzing Adam Czerniakow's notes it must be underlined that it is not true that his diary (*'Dziennik'*) contained ciphered messages because he 'could not write about everything straight and used irony or coded facts in case the notes fell into the Germans' hands.' [P. P. Reszka, J. Cywiński, *Kurek: getta założyli Żydzi [Kurek: The ghettos were built by Jews],* in: „Gazeta Wyborcza" August 19/20, 2006.] The statement of the 'Gazeta Wyborcza' journalists that Czerniakow 'coded facts' suggests that he conspired because he did not trust the Germans. The thesis that Czerniakow used any conspiracy techniques (coding) does not withstand the confrontation with the source itself, i.e. with Czerniakow's *Dziennik* ['The Diary']. The Czerniakow's diary is full of names of Jews, Germans and Poles, and of political news that – if the author used the basic rules of conspiracy or did not trust the Germans – should not have appeared there at all. The thesis that Czerniakow coded the messages in his diary also does not withstand the confrontation with the accounts of reliable witnesses such as Marek Edelman, according to whom Adam Czerniakow: *...did not like that Underground,*

190

was honored with the dignitary status of Senator in The Upper House of the Parliament of Polish State [in Poland evolved from royal council in XV century]. In every democratic country, the mandate of a senator is conditioned upon the possession of social prestige applied to obtaining the required number of votes. On the one hand, the elected deputy's or senator's dignitary conduct obliges them to represent the interests of the voters with regard to the state; on the other hand, exhibit loyalty to the state whose legislative authority they represent. The obligations of Polish Parliamentary senators or deputys were equal for all: not only for those representing the Poles, but also for those representing minorities. Included in this, of course, was the Jewish minority. This is the way it was in the Polish State, and this is the way it continues to be in other multi-national countries, as in the Unites States, for example: a senator of Polish descent that has been elected by the American people has the same obligations with regard to the nation of the United States as does a senator elected by the American people regardless of whether he is of Jewish, Chinese or Thai descent. In addition to that, in Poland there exists a tradition that once a deputy or senator has been elected, they maintain their Parliamentary status for the rest of their life, if only in the titular and moral sense. In order to understand the posture and dilemmas of Senator Adam Czerniakow, who was one of the very few to have experienced the difficulty of reconciling the tendency among Polish Jews of the *quandary of bi-nationalism,* let us compare them to the posture and activities of a Polish Warsaw Deputy with regard to the outbreak of WWII. In a most significant manner, they both left the stigma of the wartime Polish-Jewish history of the Capital, and their postures in the clearest of manners constituted a model of behavior for Polish and Jewish communities throughout all of Poland.

Stefan Starzyński (1893-1944), was a deputy to The Lower Chamber of the Parliament of the Polish State during the years of 1930-1933. In September of 1939, he was the president of the city and the Civil Commissioner to the Warsaw Defense Command. He has passed into

---

those newspapers that they brought him. He was afraid of all that.[Grupińska A., *"Ciągle po kole"* ["Still Round the Circle: Talks with the Soldiers of the Warsaw Ghetto"], Warszawa 2005.

history as the one who exhibited exceptional dignity and bravery in the face of adversaries during the most trying days that the city had seen. In September of 1939, the deputy, Stefan Starzyński, mobilized the community to fight and he became the head of the fighting capital. Subsequently, he was arrested by the Germans on October 26, 1939 and murdered in 1944. Up until the moment of his arrest, he was a veritable presence at the Town Hall and he took the responsibility for the entire Capital upon himself with regard to the Polish authorities, as well as for the more than 300,000 Jewish residents. The last known directive from President Stefan Starzyński to the residnts of the Capital was dated October 19, 1939, and was announced in the "Dziennik Urzedowy m.st. Warszawy" [The Bulletin of the Capital City of Warsaw] on October 21, 1939. Before Stefan Starzyński was arrested, he had managed to play the exceptional role of co-creator of the administrative foundation and structures of the Polish Underground State.[179] Functioning in the role of President of the Capital, up until the moment of his arrest, the deputy represented the highest

---

179 W. Bartoszewski, *1859 dni Warszawy* [Warsaw's 1859 days], Kraków 1974, p. 77, says: 'On October 26 [1939] in the town hall, Gestapo arrested president Stefan Starzyński, who after a few days (October 30) was put in prison at Daniłowiczowska Street and then in the Pawiak prison. Stanisław Lorentz recalls that moment as follows: "At 2 p.m. on the 26th of October, when I was in the president Starzyński's office, two Gestapo officers – one of a high military rank - suddenly entered the room and asked which one of us was the president of Warsaw, Sefan Starzyński. They told him to get dressed and go with them. One could not doubt that the President had just been arrested and that he would not return from the interrogation. President Starzynski went to the washroom where he kept his personal belongings, and not closing the door, put on his winter coat and took his hat in his hand. [...] The President shook my hand without a word and left the room first; the two officers went after him."' Encyklopedia Gazety Wyborczej, Warszawa 2005, Vol. XVII, p. 457, says: 'Stefan Starzyński, born on August 19, 1893 in Warsaw, died in 1944. [...] 1930-1933 The Lower Chamber of the Parliament of the Polish State' deputy; in September 1939 a Civilian Commissar at the Defense of Warsaw Headquarters; he mobilized the society against the enemy and became the leader of the fighting city; co-author of the guidelines and the structure of the administration of the Polish Underground State; arrested by Germans on the 27th of October 1939, imprisoned in the Pawiak prison, then moved probably to Berlin and to the potassium mine in Baelberge where he was murdered; his symbolical grave is at the Powązki Cementary in Warsaw'.

authorities of the Polish State: the Government in Exile and the authorities in command of the Polish Underground State.

Pedagogue, social and political activist, member of the Commission of the Jewish Community Administration of Warsaw and the Chairman of Central Union of Jewish Laborers, Senator Adam Czerniakow, in The Upper House of the Parliament of Polish State, represented the Jewish minority. Elected by the votes of the Jewish organizations to serve as an Advisor to the City of Warsaw as well, Senator Czerniakow was the epitome of "being Jewish", and for Polish Jews, the embodiment of Jewish government and authority. On September 23, 1939, Adam Czerniakow was selected by the President of the Capital to take the position of the President of the Jewish Community Administration of Warsaw. He wrote the following in his journal: *I have been nominated by President Starzyński to the office of Chairman of the Community of Jewish Faith of Warsaw. This is an historic role in this city under siege. I will do my best to live up to the task.*[180]

Through this, Senator Adam Czerniakow became the representative of over 300,000 Jews residing in the Capital. As mentioned earlier, his behavior under extreme conditions served as a model for the remaining community of Polish Jews to follow. Just as the behavior of Polish deputies and senators constituted a model for the Polish community to follow. After the outbreak of the war, Adam Czerniakow did not actively include himself in the defense of Warsaw. As he recorded in the journal he was keeping, on September 10, he did sign up for the Citizens' Patrol[181], although it is

---

[180] All quotations from the Adam Czerniakow's diary have been taken from: *Adama Czerniakowa dziennik getta warszawskiego 6.IX.1939 – 23. VII 1942 [Adam Czerniakow's diary from the Warsaw Ghetto 6.IX.1939 – 23. VII 1942; edited and supplied with notes by Marian Fuks]*, Warszawa, 1983 [See also: Hilberg *"Warsaw Diary of Adam Czerniakow – Prelude to Doom"*, Ivan R. Dee Publisher,1998]. Since the quoted excerpts have day dates, I do not give the pages of the quotations.

[181] W. Bartoszewski, *1859 dni Warszawy* [Warsaw's 1859 days], Wydawnictwo Znak, Kraków 1974, p. 28, says that on the 6th of September 1939, the Civilian Commissar of the Warsaw's Defense President Stefan Starzyński 'takes up action against first symptoms of confusion and chaos in the city, caused by the departure of the Government Commissar for the city of Warsaw Jaroszewicz and a part of the police forces and administration authorities; [the president] orders the establishment of the Civilian Guard as a public security force. Reserve major Janusz Regulski is appointed the commander of the Guard; Dr Jan Gebethner

difficult to imagine that he actively participated in the campaigns that were undertaken, especially since on October 14, 1939 he noted: *In the corridor of the SS, I encountered an unknown Commissioner of the Citizens' Patrol, Regulski was his name. He and his companions confiscated my Citizens' Patrol armband and I.D. I shall refer this matter to Starzyński.*

The unknown *Commissioner Regulski* mentioned in the author's notes, was no more or no less than the mere Commander-in-Chief of the Citizens' Patrol of Warsaw, the very same in which Adam Czerniakow, Chairman of the Community of Jewish Faith of Warsaw, had been a member of since the last week of September; and with whom, if only by virtue of belonging to the Patrol, he should, by that time, have been in cooperation. The posture of the Chairman of the Administration with regard to an embattled Warsaw was summed up by Emanuel Ringelblum in the following way: *They (within the Jewish Administration of Warsaw) were in possession of a certain amount of monies (the Germans found 90,000), and nothing was done with these funds during the time of the siege.*[182]

Senator Adam Czerniakow did, in truth, accept the nomination to the position of Chairman of the Community of Jewish Faith of Warsaw from the President of the Capital at the end of September 1939. He did not, however, establish any permanent contact with Stefan Starzyński despite the fact that, until the moment of his arrest, he did represent both the State Government of conquered Poland, as well as the structures being created for the Polish Underground State within its limited form during the time of the occupation. From the notes taken in his journal it is clear that in September 1939 he met with President Starzyński only on the day of accepting his nomination.

The following meeting was initiated by Starzyński, but not until after the Germans had entered Warsaw on October 2, 1939, and the meeting

and Bronisław Barylski are his deputies. Starzyński announces an appeal to the people about the organization of the Civilian Guard and its tasks. At the same time appears the announcement of the First Chief Command of the Civilian Guard regarding the volunteers for this formation.'

182 Ringelblum E., *"Kronika getta warszawskiego wrzesień 1939 – styczeń 1943"*, Warszawa 1983, p. 57-58. [See also: "Notes from the Warsaw Ghetto" by Emmanuel Ringelblum, paperback, Ibooks Inc., 2006].

pertained to an announcement to the Jewish people with *the goal of trying to convince them to maintain order at the time of daily fare distribution* as well as at the time of *rationing out of food.* The very last time that Senator Czerniakow met with Stefan Starzyński was October 12. The details of the conversations between the two statesmen remain unknown.

What is apparent from the entries contained in the journal of Adam Czerniakow is that all forms of contact with Polish government officials had already ceased in the middle of the second month of the war. At the same time, almost every day from the moment the Germans had invaded Warsaw, the former senator, Adam Czeniakow, spent his days in the headquarters of the SS negotiating the conditions of collaboration with the German authorities, at which time, with the greatest of precision, he immediately proceeded to implement them into daily life. In light of the Jewish Senator's later entries, as well as commonly known historical facts from the years 1939-1942, it becomes evident that, under the concept of conducting negotiations with the Germans regarding "the conditions of collaboration", it is understood that these negotiations pertained to administrative-legislative forms and to the territorial construction of a Jewish Territorial Autonomy in Warsaw.

In the case of Polish Jews, especially of Warsaw Jews, conditions were particularly conducive with regard to this matter as: *The Jewish community in Poland was in an exceptional situation as they had at their disposal a well developed network of their own institutions – denominational communes which, with an expansion of competence, could have served as the fundamental element of a national autonomous structure. The Jewish community in Poland never really functioned strictly as a religious organization; it was involved in a series of matters pertaining to the conduct of loosely connected religious worship. This fact was taken advantage of by the advocates of the Jewish Autonomies.*

The battle of Jewish secular communities over turning the Jewish commune into a national institution had already started towards the end of nineties in the XIX century. The Warsaw municipality was an experimental ground. From the seventies, its administration had laid in the hands of an assimilatory-Hassid coalition. The communication between these two obviously different, in fact opposing, groups were based on a division of power. The assimilators handled representation

195

of the commune with regard to the outside world – the Polish community and government, as well as philanthropy; whilst giving the Orthodox-Hasidim a free hand in the sphere of religious matters as well as religious education.[183]

The notion of building Jewish Autonomies within Poland in 1939 was hardly a new idea, as the model of Jewish autonomous structure, whose fundamental elements were supposed to have been the devotional communes that had already been worked out towards the end of the XIX century, and were later articulated in the proposal of the article 113 of the Polish Constitution which had been put forward by Izaak Grünbaum, the Jewish member of The Lower Chamber of the Parliament of the Polish State, in the Polish Constitutional Committee in November 1920.

Let us return to the diary of the Jewish Senator. From only four fragments of entries by Adam Czerniakow dated October 1939, we can surmise that both he and those under his subjection had still been living in Poland, and that alongside "Jewish matters", in Warsaw some sort of "Polish matters" seem to have existed.

The path to isolation from "Polish matters", Polish authorities and the Poles had already been chosen by Senator Adam Czerniakow in the first days of German occupation. Following the example of the Jewish Senator from Warsaw, this posture was taken on by the entire community of Polish Jews. I know of no city or town in Poland occupied by Hitler in which, in 1939, the Jewish community refused to cooperate with Germans in the broadest sense, and at the same time failed to recognize them as the new governing power.

In 1939 Polish Jews did not greet the Germans by erecting triumphal gates in their honor as their ancestors once had to honor the Austrians in Brody near Lwów. A characteristic trait of their posture was that they failed to treat the German occupiers as the enemy, but rather as an admittedly stern, but legitimate authority with which one carries on discussions and negotiates the conditions of coexistence. Emanuel Ringelblum, who sedulously recorded the prevailing atmosphere amongst the Jewish population, wrote the following in the years of 1939/40:

---

[183] J. Zyndul, *Państwo w Państwie? - Autonomia narodowo-kulturalna w Europie Środkowowschodniej w XX wieku* [A state within a state? – The National and Cultural Autonomy in Central and Eastern Europe in the twentieth century], Warszawa 2000, p. 106.

A lady passes in front of a German of distinction (who asks her) why she isn't wearing an armband. She explains, in the end (he) kisses her hand. [...] [The Germans] do not scoff at the Jewish language; on the contrary, they aptly use Jews as translators. [...] A few weeks back, I was told the story of a certain German commander who gave a Jewish child some money – to a pedestrian huckster, and told him to go home. (...) Recently, that is in the middle of March (1940), there has been an influx of groups of Jewish prisoners-of-war from Germany; a group arrived from Olsztyn (Eastern Prussia). Some say that those (over there) treated them very well. [...] The attitude of the Germans towards the Jews is good, friendly. They addressed doctors as "buddy"; but Poles have not forgotten. They wanted to pounce on Rusinek because he wanted to recite the poem of a Jew, Tuwim. [...] I have heard about more than 2,300 Jewish prisoners-of-war, about how well they have been accepted throughout several German cities they had been transported through. Some German had said: 'If we had as many Jews as you, then Germany would be the wealthiest nation". Another German said: "You arrived here as the cursed Jews, and you leave here as the dear children of the nation of Israel". Knowledge of the German language was a very important component in getting closer to the Germans. [...] Mr. Icchak [Giterman] believes that in Stargard, 95% of the Germans are decent people. [...] **The symbiosis of German and Jewish craftsmen**: *they lend money to each other with interest. [...] [The attitude] of the representatives of German authority isn't bad.*[184]

A Jewish street, as Jewish sources tell us, far outdid itself with praise of culture, elegance and German kindness – and even with love in regard to the Jews. Because since Jews are not waging war with the Germans, because they feel closer, if only due to the language, to German than to Polish culture... The term *symbiosis* which Ringelblum used to describe the Jewish-German relations of the first few months of WWII seems to relate to the atmosphere between Polish Jews and the German forces occupying Poland in full.

Let us return, however, to the chronology of incidents of 1939. The Germans occupied Warsaw on October 1. From that moment, Adam

---

[184] Ringelblum E., *"Kronika getta warszawskiego wrzesień 1939 – styczeń 1943"*, Warszawa 1983, p. 36, 40, 53, 65, 92, 110-111, 134. [See also: "Notes from the Warsaw Ghetto" by Emmanuel Ringelblum, paperback, Ibooks Inc., 2006].

Czerniakow did not feel obligated to consult with representatives of the
Polish State with regard to his activities. In his journal entry dated October
4, 1939 he dryly records:

*Upon entering the Jewish Commune I was stoppel by Germans, and for
the time-being, there isn't a lot I can do. I was driven out to Aleja Szucha, and
there I was instructed to select twenty four people to consult on the board of
the [new] Jewish commune, and that I am to stand at its head. I have worked
out a statistical questionnaire.*

The effect of this initial German-Jewish conversation was the immediate
undertaking by Senator Adam Czerniakow to create a twenty-four-member
Judenrat [The Jewish Commune]. The following day, on October 5, 1939,
when Hitler was reviewing the German victory troops in Warsaw, the
Senator wrote: *All morning it was impossible to get across the Aleje (Avenue)
Jerozolimskie until 1pm. I was sitting in the garden. [...] I have convened the
session regarding the twenty-four for tomorrow morning at 9.*

In the result of the actions of the first ten days of October 1939, from
the hands of the second-in-command of Group IV Operational Security
German Police and the Police Service (IV Einsatzgruppe der Sipo und SD),
Josef Meisinger, the representative of the new "leaders" of Poland, Adam
Czerniakow accepted the position of President of the Warsaw Judenrat.
Following the example set in Warsaw, all other centers of Jewish life
abided. *In Łódź, the so-called Jewish representation had already been called
upon in October of 1939. Writings dated from the 13th and 14th of the
current month, the [German] president of the city, Leister, appointed M. Ch.
Rumkowski as the Head of Jewish Elders (Ältester der Juden) and authorized
him to dismantle the old Administration of Jewish Municipality.*[185]

The difference between Jewish leaders of the Municipality of Religion,
which had for centuries conducted itself as a spiritual governing body over
Jewish communes in Poland, and the Judenrats which dictated a way of life
after having been called upon in the autumn of 1939 under the terms of
the German-Jewish understanding, is that the pre-war Jewish authorities

---

[185] L. Dobroszycki, wstęp do: *"Kronika getta łódzkiego" ["The Lodz Ghetto Diary - preface"]*,
Łódź 1965, p. XVIII.

had been chosen by the Jewish community and occupied themselves with matters pertaining to religious worship and ritual (public welfare, elementary education, religious judicature, etc.), whereas the Judenrats were instituted by the German occupiers from among individuals displaying a willingness to engage in a multifaceted cooperation with them, and the scope of their authority, as granted by the Germans, digressed substantially from the traditional capacity of Jewish municipalities, and had, with the passing of time, expanded.

In Łódź, for example: *Rumkowski, along with his nomination to the position of Head of Jewish Elders, was also granted a wide range of authorizations within the internal administration of the municipality. All of its agendas were subordinated to him. Every Jew was obliged to absolute obedience with regard to the leader. It was also simultaneously proclaimed that any opposition against or insubordination to him will be punished by the German authorities. The German authorities also gave Rumkowski permission to move about the city at any and all times, and granted him authorized access to German institutions. He was exclusively charged with selecting his own co-workers who would constitute the Counsel of Elders, as well as creating new Jewish administrative cells.*[186]

In this way, aside from matters falling under the scope of activity of the old Municipalities of Religion, the Judenrats, whose network in the first few months of the war covered all Polish lands under German occupation, above all handled areas such as: employing and directing Jews to forced labor for the benefit of the Germans, food supply, the department of health, police force, and prisons. The manner of behavior engaged in by the leaders of the Judenrats was also something new. As practice soon would reveal, the Judenrats fulfilled an exceptionally important dual role in the lives of Polish Jews: for the Germans, it was an executive power of sorts, an extension of German authority in Ghettos and a "Jewish gendarme" supervising over the fulfillment of German orders; for the Jews, it was the sole authority in whose hands all aspects of Jewish life were concentrated.

To summarize, in the autumn of 1939, Polish Jews, just as the Ukrainians and Bielorussians, with regard to a Poland defeated in a

---

[186] Ibidem, p. XVIII.

defensive war, took on the stance of foreigners. This manifested itself, on the one hand, through terminating all contact with the last representatives of the official government of the Polish State and with not establishing contact with the newly forming Polish Underground State; on the other hand, through the immediate establishment of lively permanent contacts with the German occupying forces as well as undertaking the construction of Jewish Territorial Autonomies on Polish lands under the tutelage of the Germans, colloquially known as Ghettos.

The answer to the question regarding the form and shape the Jewish Autonomies were to take after Warsaw Jews had negotiated them with the Germans, as well as the chronology of its construction can be found in a careful and penetrating reading of Senator Adam Czerniakow's diary:

December 16 and 17, 1939 – I open the Department of Hospitals.

January 5, 1940 – Attempts at setting up a Jewish bureaucracy.

May 6, 1940 – The municipality is recognized as having a right to existence.

May 17, 1940 – (German) Laschtoviczek in the morning, the Judenrat, self-government with executive power. The Magistrate is supposed to have officials to do this. He recommended composing an executive charter.

June 25, 1940 – 9 o'clock in the morning to (German) Leist. I was seen by Braun – he declared that within 3 to 4 weeks the "Selbstverwaltung" (self-government) of the Jews will be worked out.

*September 5, 1940 – I was paid a visit by Rumkowski in the company of an SS-man and the director of the Łódź Ernährungsamtu([Office of Food). He claimed that that he **has the ministries** and that his budget is worth 1,500,000 Mk.*

*September 20, 1940 – At the conference, L[eist] introduced me to some higher-up official from the district. [...] We are to be awarded "**Selbständige Autonomie**" (independent autonomy)*

*May 5, 1941 – **Only the Judenrat is to be a self-governing authority, with the Obmann (Chairman) as its mayor.***

*May 7, 1941 – Gencwajch reports that **there exist questions within the community as to whether or not the current Chairman of the Council will be named Mayor, or not.***

May 8, 1941 – At 4 P.M., at Mohns. He said that ghetto is to receive a budget of 24,000,000 zł.

*May 11, 1941 – I went to see Aurswald. He demanded the organizational plan regarding the officials of the Council which will be subordinate to me. **I am to be granted the rights of the Mayor.***

May 14, 1941 – The Municipality in the morning. (German) Mohns informed me that the Governor had nominated me for Mayor of the Jewish Quarter (in Warsaw)].

*May 19, 1941 – A day full of experiences. (....) Dr. Auerswald declared that **I had been nominated for Mayor.***

May 23, 1941 – Auerswald (. . .) declares that all departments of the (jewish) municipality should be condensed into 6 departments.

May 24, 1941 – Auerswald suggests that the directors of 6 or 7 departments (of the Jewish municipality) receive salaries.

May 31, 1941 – Auerswald was mulling over my title. He arrived at the conclusion that I should put "Verwaltung des Jüdischen Wohnbesitzes (Headquarters of Jewish Property) on the letterhead.

August 19, 1941 – apparently, a budget with certain changes has been approved.

A penetrating analysis of Adam Czerniakow's entries leaves very little doubt that the network of Jewish Ghettos that had been built on Polish lands were not solely the result of the Germans' Holocaust plans being realized, but at least in equal degree, the result of Polish Jews' plans with regard to constructing Jewish territorial autonomies in Poland being realized.

Written openly, the term *"**Selbständige Autonomie**"* (Independent Autonomy) appears for the first time in Senator Adam Czerniakow's entries dated September 20, 1940. Surely, it was not a coincidence that two weeks prior, there was a visit in the Warsaw Judenrat by the community director of Łódź Jews, Chaim Rumkowski. As Emanuel Ringelblum wrote:

*Today, September 6 [1940], Rumkowski arrived from Łódź, they call him "King Chaim" over there. [...] He told the highest of tales in the Ghetto. There is a **Jewish State** over there with 400 policemen and 3 prisons. He has a ministry of foreign affairs and all the other ministries as well. [...] Rumkowski,* *during his visit to Warsaw couldn't boast enough: "Have a look, in a year or two, I will have the best Ghetto in Poland."*[187]

From the sources presented above, it is clear that aside from the agreed upon terms from the first weeks of the war, it was in the autumn of 1940 that the most intensive German-Jewish discussions were taking place regarding the final shape and form of the Jewish Territorial Autonomy in Warsaw, and that it was not only the future mayor of the Warsaw Jewish Territorial Autonomy, Adam Czerniakow, who participated in these discussions, but also the leaders of other Jewish Autonomies from different cities. In May of 1941 it was decided that: *only the Judenrat is supposed to be a self-governing authority, and Obmann its mayor.* This meant that, the Judenrats had reverted in function to their traditional self-governing style similar to that of pre-war Jewish municipality administration, where Jewish mayors became state officials representing the authorities of the German State with regard to residents of specific Jewish Autonomies.

On May 19, 1941, Adam Czerniakow accepted the nomination to the position of Mayor of the Jewish Autonomy of Warsaw from the hands of the Germans, and thus began to use the title of *"Verwaltung des Jüdischen Wohnbesitzes"* [the Mayor]. In the formal-legal sense, from that moment, the Warsaw Jewish Autonomy and all other Jewish autonomies in Poland, became part of the composition of the III Reich and the former Senator of the Polish State, Adam Czerniakow, along with other mayors of Jewish autonomies, became the state officials representing the German authorities with regard to residents of the Jewish autonomie in Poland.

Based on the suggestion of the Germans, the administration of the Jewish Mayor in Warsaw *was reduced to 6 departments*. However, the term "department" was not mandatory, for the same administrative rung, which in the Jewish Autonomy in Warsaw was designated a department, in the Jewish Autonomy in Łódź was called a ministry. The application of terms played absolutely no role in this. What was important to the

---

[187] Ringelblum E., *"Kronika getta warszawskiego wrzesień 1939 – styczeń 1943"*, Warszawa 1983, p. 154. [See also: "Notes from the Warsaw Ghetto" by Emmanuel Ringelblum, paperback, Ibooks Inc., 2006].

Jewish Autonomies was that the newly named *"Verwaltung des Jüdischen Wohnbesitzes"* (Mayor) in government and all its departments not have the character of a self-governing authority, but rather that as the highest leadership of the Jewish Territorial Autonomies, it also be a state government of the III Reich.

The budget for Warsaw Jews had been approved by the German government on August 19, 1941, which ultimately put an end to the several-month-long process of building the Jewish Territorial Autonomy within the capital of Poland. The structure of other Jewish Autonomies on Polish lands, colloquially called Ghettos, under the auspices of the Germans, was similar to each other. At the end of 1941, the authorities of the Autonomy of Warsaw Jews were an enormous bureaucratic apparatus, which consisted of more than two thousand employees, which included subordinate institutions. The situation was similar in Łodz, Krakow, in Silesia and other centers of Jewish life. It is not known whether the Judenrat Chairmen of other Jewish Autonomies (Ghettos) had accepted the title of Mayors. If so, they did not boast of this, but rather remained with the title of chairmen or supervisors, as in the case of Adam Czerniakow. Chaim Rumkowski in Łodz went by the title of Supervisor of Jewish Elders. He, therefore, called the Jewish part of Łodz subordinate to him a "Jewish State" rather than an Autonomy; the Jewish population referred to him as king or prince. A similar nickname was given to Meryn in Silesia. Regardless of the titles that had been accepted or used, the Mayors, Superintendents or Chairmen of all Jewish Territorial Autonomies (Ghettos) on Polish lands possessed unlimited authority over the Jewish population.

Returning to the structure of authority within the Warsaw Jewish Autonomy, it must be said that, as of May, 1941, it consisted of two institutions: the Mayor, i.e. *"Verwaltung des Jüdischen Wohnbesitzes"* and his subordinate departments, as well as the Judenrat. In Warsaw, Łódź and all other large Autonomies, the function of Mayor and the Judenrat Chairman was fulfilled by the same person. Before Adam Czerniakow became the Mayor of the Jewish Territorial Autonomy of Warsaw, in the first twenty months of Hitler's occupation of Poland, he was the

Chairman of the Judenrat. The twenty-four-member Jewish Counsel of the Elders (Ältestenrat), which was called the Judenrat, was the ruling body of the Jewish Autonomy during the time of its construction, in other words, giving the Autonomy its final shape. At the moment that the Jewish Autonomy of Warsaw took on its final shape, on August 19, 1941, the Judenrat became the sole self-governing authority. In the legal and administrative sense, its role became limited. In the practical sense, aside from its official name, everything else remained the same. Adam Czerniakow was the *"Verwaltung des Jüdischen Wohnbesitzes"* [the Mayor] and Chairman of the Judenrat simultaneously. The entirety of Jewish authority over the residents of the Jewish Autonomy rested in his hands.

The Jewish Territorial Autonomies that had been built in the years of 1939-1942, based on the Autonomies of Warsaw and Lodz, had a mixed character: that of a self-governing-nation, as their self-government structure was covered, to a large extent, by typical structures of a national administration. Henryk Makower assessed it in this way:

[The Jewish Warsaw] Municipality, out of necessity, transformed a rather small religious, educational and self-help institution into an expansive self-governing apparatus which stood at the head of a new administrative element which was named "Der Jüdische Wohnbezirk in Warschau", and at whose head the "Obmann des Judenrates-Warschau" stood with mayoral authority: Adam Czerniakow, engineer. The Germans boasted of how the Jews had never had it this good, as during the time of their ruling.[188]

At the head of the Jewish Autonomies stood individuals who possessed unlimited authority with regard to the Jewish population: Jewish leaders who functioned both as Chairmen of Jewish self-government and as national clerks of the III Reich. This is what the Ghetto in Lodz looked like:

The internal goings-on of the Ghetto are reminiscent of the feudal system of the Middle Ages, let's say at the estate of a wealthy Russian boyard. Everything

---

[188] H. Makower, *Pamiętnik z getta warszawskiego [The Memoirs from Warsaw Ghetto]*, Wroclaw 1987, p. 13.

around the court is surrounded by deep gloom and mire. The plebs are the personal property of the Duke (Rumkowski) and are solely a labor machine. They came into this world and live for only one purpose: so that the Duke can extract benefits and satisfaction. The Duke, therefore, in this case our own Duke [Rumkowski], likes to appear before his subjects in his full glory. Our Duke is untroubled. He hops from one resort to the next, from one office to the next. Everywhere he goes, among office workers, supervisors, laborers, security and errand-boys, he spreads fear and dread. What should come as no surprise, as it occurs rather infrequently, is that during such an "inspection", without rhyme or reason, just like that, someone should suffer. So an office clerk gets slapped across the face or deprived of his employment for a long period of time, if not till the end of the Rumkowski Dynasty, unless the barbed wire surrounding the Ghetto were to disappear sooner. And these are the types of sadistic and mad interplay Rumkowski engages in with great pleasure in the presence of this or that "minister". They should shake a little in their own boots over their own fate.[189]

There was not a single Jewish Territorial Autonomy in Poland during the years of 1939 and 1941 that would not see its own native Duke. In Silesia, this was Mojżesz Meryn, in Lublin, Szama Grajer, *who is remembered by all those who had survived the Ghetto.* Jewish sources also indicate that the Jewish authorities in the Ghettos, in an unequivocal manner, modeled themselves after the style of German authority. *They are impressed by the might and posture of the others,* one Warsaw chronicler had written with regard to the attitude exhibited by his own brethren executing authority toward the Germans[190]. "The system of ruling over the Łódź Ghetto was shaped based on imitating Hitler's Germany", was the assessment posed by one Jewish historian twenty years later.[191]

Rumors of creating a Ghetto in Warsaw, of delineating the borders

---

[189] Leon Hurwitz, *Pamiętnik z getta [The Memoirs from the Ghetto]*, in: *Kronika getta lodzkiego [The Diary of the Lodz Ghetto]*, Lodz 1965, p. XIII.

[190] Ringelblum E., *"Kronika getta warszawskiego wrzesień 1939 – styczeń 1943"*, Warszawa 1983, p. 203. [See also: "Notes from the Warsaw Ghetto" by Emmanuel Ringelblum, paperback, Ibooks Inc., 2006].

[191] L. Dobroszycki, wstęp do: *"Kronika getta łódzkiego" ["The Lodz Ghetto Diary - preface"]*, Łódź 1965, p. XXI.

of a Jewish Territorial Autonomy, had already surfaced in the autumn of 1939.[192] Originally planned for November of 1939, the Warsaw Jewish Territorial Autonomy (the Ghetto) was not created until October 2, 1940. Jewish sources seem to indicate that, as much as the construction of open Jewish Territorial Autonomies went against the ambitions and plans of both the Germans and Polish Jews, the limiting of Autonomy expansiveness realized, above all, the goals of the Germans. This does not mean, however, that putting up walls to surround the Jewish Territorial Autonomies gave rise to widespread opposition by the Polish Jews. Using this angle to read into the most reliable of Jewish sources, we shall attempt to trace the history of the construction of the largest Jewish Territorial Autonomy in German occupied Poland, the Warsaw Ghetto. According to the words of Emanuel Ringelblum from 1940, the preparations for the closing off of the Autonomy proceeded as follows:

Today [March 29, 1940] rumors were circulating that brick walls will be replacing the existing perimeter of the Ghetto territory. (…) March 30, the information that the Jewish Municipality [in Warsaw] has received an order to put up brick walls in place of the existing barbed wire that had, until now, separated Seuchengebiet from other areas has been confirmed. (…) Today, March 2 [actually April 2, 1940 – E.K.] the work of putting up a brick wall around Seuchengebiet has begun. This has made a strong impression. They are starting to see the emergence of a de facto Ghetto in this. There is absolute peace on the streets. (…) April 26, 27, 1940 – the **construction of thick brick walls at the corners of Próżna Street and Złota Street etc is costing the Jewish Municipality [in Warsaw] a quarter of a million Zlotys**".[193]

192 L. Landau, *Kronika lat wojny i okupacji [The Diary of the war and occupation]*, Volume I, p. 57.
193 Ringelblum E., *"Kronika getta warszawskiego wrzesień 1939 – styczeń 1943"*, Warszawa 1983, p. 106, 14, 116, 128, 137, 139, 141, 143, 147, 154, 158 and 161. [See also: "Notes from the Warsaw Ghetto" by Emmanuel Ringelblum, paperback, Ibooks Inc., 2006].

16. Jews putting up a brick wall around the Warsaw ghetto, 1940.

The information of the Warsaw chronicler is confirmed by Adam Czerniakow:

April 1, 1940 – Morning at the [German] Laschtoviczka's. He has advised that I go see Leist regarding the matter of the brick walls. (…) Leist – the problems: 1) the walls, 2) the post (…) Krochmalna Street up to Nr. 38 is closed off, a portion of Rynkowa Street and Walicow Street. Ciepła Street at the intersection with Krochmalna ought to be closed. 1-38 make 3 locations (not a brick wall but board it up with wooden planks and stakes). (…) the brick walls ought to be put up in various places throughout the city. Tomorrow Laschtoviczka will inform me of who will cover the costs.

April 4, 1940 – Morning at Braun's (Leist's assistant). **"The walls are there for the purpose of protecting the Jews from excesses being committed [by Poles]".** *The bricks can be brought by the Jews themselves, each one between the ages of 10 and 60 can carry a few.* **The idea of the Ghetto.**

April 9, 1940 – Have been summoned to the SS for 8:30. (…) I brought up the matter of the walls. I submitted the materials.

April 10, 1940 – At a dozen or so locations, the Municipality started erecting the walls.

April 13, 1940 – We shall pay for the walls.

May 10, 1940 – Today I received "the Sketch of the closed area of Warsaw".

August 20, 1940 – The plan of the (expanded) Jewish quarter has been signed.

*September 30, 1940 – **The working out of the fortification of the Ghetto area** (Złota, a wedge of the Hale Mirowskie, the Old Town, etc.)*

November 8, 1940 – Kunze has requested a letter regarding the financing of the walls by the community.

November 22, 1940 – We are to build a wooden bridge on Chłodna Street.

November 13, 1941 – Part of the Ghetto has walls, part has barbed wire.

Just as in the case of several other matters, utilizing a series of well-established stereotypical imaginings, historians of the Holocaust accept as an obvious certainty, that the Ghettos were solely the result of German extermination policies with regard to the Jewish population; that their construction took place without the participation of the Jews and against their will. Meanwhile, as the above cited Jewish sources indicate with regard to both the process of delineating borders of the Jewish Autonomies, that is the Ghettos, as well as during the process of enclosing them within brick walls or barbed wire, the authorities of the Jewish Autonomies were willing participants. Shocking is the fact that the separation of the Jewish Autonomies from the outside world (the erection of brick walls and the construction of a barbed wire abates) was financed out of the budget of the Jewish Autonomy as well as community monies. This means that the isolation of the Jewish Territorial Autonomy in Warsaw, colloquially referred to as the Ghetto, from the Poles living outside its walls fit perfectly into the parameters of the Jewish idea. Henryk Makower summed up the end result of the process of territorial delineation of borders of the Jewish Autonomy in Warsaw in this way: *We, therefore, did have a reason to rejoice, because* [the Germans – note by E.K.] *gave us such a large and beautiful Ghetto in the downtown of Warsaw.*[194]

---

[194] H. Makower, *Pamiętnik z getta warszawskiego [The Memoirs from Warsaw Ghetto]*, Wroclaw 1987, p. 13.

17. A street in the Warsaw ghetto, 1941.

The closing off of the Jewish Autonomy borders was assessed in a similar manner by representatives of other community groups. Antoni Marianowicz, who came from a Polonized Christian Jewish family, wrote the following about the first months within the brick walls:

Everyone had set themselves up pretty well. There was an atmosphere of relaxation... The optimists were triumphant. Even when, on November 15, the de facto closing off of the Ghetto had taken place, we were not overly concerned about that. The perspective of cutting ourselves off from the world, on the other hand, created the illusion of being isolated from the threat of the Germans. There was no shortage of circulating opinions that here, intra muros, we will be able to survive the war in peace.[195]

Adam Czerniakow, in his journal, recorded that *the walls are there for the purpose of protecting the Jews from excesses being committed,* that the plans for *the working out of the fortification of the Ghetto area* are in progress. If we keep in mind that these words had been written in 1940,

---

[195] A. Marianowicz, *Życie surowo wzbronione [The Life Strictly Forbidden]*, Warsaw 1995, p. 48-49.

that is during the time that the German-Jewish *symbiosis* was in full bloom, a time when Polish Jews had not even an inkling as to what would await them at the hands of the German Holocaust, it seems obvious to state that both erecting brick walls as well as planning to fortify the area of the Jewish Autonomy (the Ghetto), were designed to protect the Warsaw Jews not from the Germans, but from the Poles.

Jewish Territorial Autonomies in Poland between 1939 and 1942 possessed an independent structure of authority, administration and budgeting. The leaders of the Autonomies (the Ghettos), the Mayors and Judenrats had, among other things, the right to impose taxes on Autonomy residents. "The Jewish Newspaper", in September of 1940, wrote this regarding the system of taxation established by the Warsaw Judenrat:

The Municipality can attribute today's revenue to a variety of random circumstances which are felt most painfully among the broad pauperized layers of the community. This system is unfair. The Warsaw Municipality was, for example, the first to have the idea of imposing taxes directly [...] on bread ration cards. In the history of the Jews, various taxes had been implemented, but a tax on bread is the first of its kind in our history.[196]

Functioning on the premise of dependence solely on the German State, Jewish Territorial Autonomies in select cities had at their disposal nationwide Jewish organizations among which the largest activity was displayed by JUS – Jüdische Unterstützungsstelle – the Central Jewish Aid which operated in Kraków. Adam Czerniakow writes this, among other things:

June 23, 1940 – Nominations to the 7 members of the JSS [Jüdische Soziale Selbsthilfe – the Jewish Social Self-help] presiding officers in Kraków;

June 26, 1940 – our own Jewish Ambulance Convoy under German direction.

The Jewish Territorial Autonomies that had been constructed in Poland during the years 1939-1941 were geared toward the greatest possible self-sufficiency which would underscore their Jewishness and independence. Alongside its own Social Services and Department of Health, which

---

[196] "Gazeta Zydowska" [The Jewish Newspaper in Warsaw Ghetto], Nr 15, Warsaw, September 10, 1940.

happened to be in accordance with Jewish tradition, the Jewish community and authorities took great care and put a great deal of effort into building other attributes of an independent Jewish Nationhood. From the journals of Adam Czerniakow, the following picture of the above process emerges:

January – June, 1940:

Conversation with Leist's assistant. [...] The matter of the post will be reviewed at the session tomorrow; Laschtoviczka [...] recommends going to Schubert in the district regarding the matter of the post. Braun agreed to see us. [...] The matter of schooling was brought up. Braun agreed to see us. [...] The matter of the rabbinate was touched upon.

July – December 1940:

In Lodz, supposedly Rumkowski produced his own money, "Chaimki"; *Steyer declared: 1) the post office Zamenhof 41. As of January 15, 1941, it will be the Jewish Post Office; the Trade School of Dance in the "Melody Palace". The only one outside of the nursing school in the hospital; I agreed to see the delegation of school organizations; At 11 o'clock at Schulrat on Daniłowiczowska Street. He declared that schools may not be private, but rather subjugated to the Municipality. The language of instruction, for the time being, shall be reverted to the Municipality, 7-department. It is necessary to put together a School Committee; After lunch, I called a conference regarding the matter of mobilizing schooling. I came forth with the proposition: trade schooling – the Municipality; primary schooling – school organizations and private initiatives; At the conference, L[eist] introduced me to some higher-up official from the district. [...] The official suggested I organize 3000 peace-keepers. L[eist] claimed that the entire Polish Police consists of 3,000 members, therefore, we should make do with 1,000. (...) The regulations manual of the peace-keeping service will be signed by him; I was advised to create a Jewish Militia consisting of 1,000 members; Yesterday, I committed lieutenant colonel Szeryński to director of peace-keeping security.*

January – June 1941:

We are submitting our request for movie theatres. [...] We are submitting our request for concerts with the goal of employing musicians; The idea of creating a Rabbinate and of appointing a Head Rabbi has emerged; Rabbi Kanał had made an appearance and requested that, if there should be a Head

Rabbi, he would like it to be him; The Jewish detention center has been made operational. Lewkowicz is its director.

July – December 1941:

*Schools will be allowed on Mondays, the day after tomorrow; I have allotted a series of stipends in the amount of 50 zł per month for the duration of 6 months as well as relief awards of 50 zł.; Finally, today the authorization for opening primary schools arrived; **[The German] Auesrswald (...) expressed the opinion that creating [in Warsaw Ghetto] a roulette in such trying times will weigh on our consciences;** Nossig put together a meeting regarding the repertoire of Jewish theatres in the Ghetto; I toured the Jewish detention center on Gęsia Street. It's much better kept than Pawiak (a Warsaw prison famous under all occupations – translator's note); The Jewish Municipality in the morning. At 8:30 Kamlach arrived. (...) we took a look at the police command post, the police station and Jewish detention center. There is nothing but order and cleanliness all around.*

From Adam Czerniakow's entries it is apparent that in the first half of 1940, the attention of the authorities of the Jewish Autonomy that was being built was focused mainly on the problem of making Jewish schools, the post and the Rabbinate operational. In the Jewish Autonomy in Lodz, Chaim Mordechaj Rumkowski put a public German Mark into circulation throughout the city which was called a "Mark-Quittungen", colloquially referred to as "chaimki" from the name of its creator and realizer. In Warsaw at the same time: *Jewish trams appeared, painted yellow, with the Star of David on every side as well as the sign "Only for Jews".*[197]

Warsaw Jews spent the second half of 1940 over discussions and, together with the Germans, the creation of a concept of a Jewish school system as well as the formation of a Jewish police force division which was brought to life on the day before the Ghetto was closed off; the Jewish Order Service (Jüdischer Ordnungsdienst) took its posts in the Warsaw Ghetto on November 28, 1940. Part of its duties was to: stand guard at points of entry, direct street traffic, implement forced labor and

---

[197] Ringelblum E., *"Kronika getta warszawskiego wrzesień 1939 – styczeń 1943"*, Warszawa 1983, p. 216, 243 and 252. [See also: "Notes from the Warsaw Ghetto" by Emmanuel Ringelblum, paperback, Ibooks Inc., 2006].

deportation, and act as the anti-epidemic service. Jewish police forces arose in all localized Ghettos on Polish lands; the Jewish policemen were charged with assisting Jewish Judenrat clerks in exacting their own orders from the Jewish population, as well orders given by the Germans.

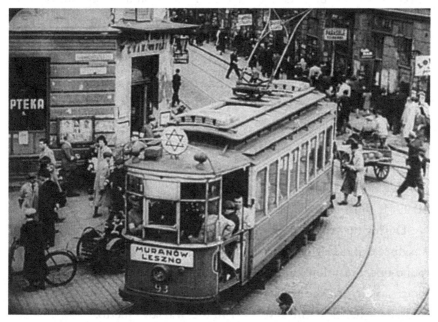

18. Jewish tram inside the Warsaw ghetto, 1941.

The following year of the war, aside from the establishment of Jewish State authorities (the Office of the Mayor), the year within the Jewish Autonomy in Warsaw passed with further development of Jewish institutions. The Jewish detention center on Gęsia Street was created which generally housed only Jews in the beginning, but with time, Christians of Jewish descent and Gypsies also found themselves there. Jewish schools and cultural institutions started to operate: cinemas, concert halls, theatres; there was even the idea of creating a Jewish casino.

In Kraków, as of July 23, 1940, the "Gazeta Żydowska" (Jewish Newspaper) started to appear. Published under German supervision, printed in the Polish language, it was an organ of the authorities of Jewish Autonomies throughout the Generalna Gubernia (the General

Governorship). With time, despite the fact that the editorial staff and publishing headquarters were located in Kraków, the "Gazeta Żydowska", to a greater extent, was dedicated to the matters concerning the Warsaw Autonomy; the Warsaw office of the newspaper was located on Elektoralna Street. "Gazeta Żydowska" appeared on Tuesdays and Fridays, and during a certain period of time, even three times a week; it was anywhere from 6 to 16 pages thick. Aside from official German orders, "Gazeta Żydowska" printed several items pertaining to daily life in the Ghettos that had been formed throughout the Generalna Gubernia (the General Governorship). "Gazeta Żydowska" continued to appear up until the time of the Holocaust, that is up until July of 1942.[198]

The Lodz Ghetto also had its own newspaper, the "Getocajtung". This was the official Jewish-language weekly newspaper of the Chairman of Jewish Elders in Łódź which was printed non-periodically until September 21, 1941; 18 issues had been printed.

During the years of 1939-1942, the Warsaw of the Goyim, i.e. of Poles, was dismal and sad. The population living there was harassed by German round-ups, executions and deportations to concentration camps. During those same years, the Jewish Territorial Autonomy, the Warsaw Ghetto, enjoyed itself. The carnival of 1941 in the Warsaw Ghetto:

"Melody Palace" held its carnival ball with the contest to see who had the most beautiful legs. The Ghetto is dancing. [...] The "lifeless Hassids" on Nowolipie Street have put up a huge banner: "Jews, do not lose hope!" The Jews over there are dancing the way they did before the war. Despite the fact that the carnival has long since ended, in the Ghetto: *There are more and more entertainment clubs opening up. (...) On the other side [of walls] Poles are saying: "He/she is enjoying her/himself like Polish Jews do in the Ghetto". The Ghetto is dancing. The number of nightclubs is multiplying endlessly. On Żelazna Street – "Palermo" with private rooms, at Nowolipie 18 – "Casanowa". (...) Jewish policemen fill the most elegant clubs [in the company of] beautiful women. They dictate the tone of all the parties. Women*

---

198 The complete set of "Gazeta Żydowska" [The Jewish Newspaper in Warsaw Ghetto] is present in The Jewish Historical Institute in Warsaw.

are impressed by their elegant, shimmering, tall officer's boots, as is quite evident.[199]

A crowning of sorts, of Jewish life inside the Jewish Territorial Autonomy in Warsaw, was the implementation, in place of Sunday, of the free Saturday as the Jewish holiday. Adam Czerniakow noted this in his journal:

May 1, 1941 – Photography studios, as well as barbers and hairdressers, are requesting permission to have their businesses open on Saturdays;

May 3, 1941 – Today is the first Saturday of general rest;

May 4, 1941 – The Rabbis appeared with Michelson at their head and thanked (us) for Saturday. I tried to convince them to create a Rabbinate and advised them to select a head rabbi, and to take to restoring the synagogues.

From the entries made by Mayor Adam Czerniakow it is clear, and has been confirmed by all other Jewish sources, that in the middle of 1941, the Jewish Autonomy of Warsaw had taken on the shape that had long been desired by Jewish leaders. Despite being burdensome, the Jewish population accepted the Jewish Autonomy that had been built thanks to their cooperation with the Germans. In virtually every Jewish source we are able to find praise for being isolated from the Christians, i.e. the Poles. Chroniclers and diarists had noted that, in the Ghetto:

In general, people feel more secure. If not for the fear of food and coal shortages, it would be possible to live so-so. [...] Images from the tram. A Jew wearing a cap with a visor and a red scarf around his neck is answering a Jewish woman who has addressed him in Polish: "One speaks Jewish aboard the Jewish tram". Another butts in: "What about in Hebrew?" "In Hebrew as well". [...] To the Jewish tram, The Star of David and other signs of the Jewish population, the Saturday day of rest in Jewish establishments is added. It seems that Saturday will be the designated day of rest in Jewish businesses, just like in Tel Aviv. [...] The Orthodox are satisfied with the Ghetto. They

---

[199] Ringelblum E., *"Kronika getta warszawskiego wrzesień 1939 – styczeń 1943"*, Warszawa 1983, p. 233, 240 and 254. [See also: "Notes from the Warsaw Ghetto" by Emmanuel Ringelblum, paperback, Ibooks Inc., 2006].E. Ringelblum, op. cit., p. 233, 240 and 254.

believe (Rabbi, descendant of Szmull Zbytkower) that this is the way it's meant to be. Jews are among their own.[200]

Life in the Ghetto "among your own" had a positive connotation not only for the Hasidim and Orthodox Jews, but also for the secular. Antoni Marianowicz says, that he felt rejuvenated in the Ghetto:

...Jewish fanaticism and nationalism. (...) I remember an incident that took place while I was in the process of looking (for an apartment) when I came upon Nowolipki 14, the apartment occupied by a certain Izaak Lejpuner. This Lejpuner, a doctor by profession, was an activist, which I did not know, of the marginal faction of Jewish nationalists. When I asked about a room for rent, he looked at me with hatred and yelled: "Here, we do not speak Polish! This is now our own place and we speak our own language!"[201]

Deserving of its own attention is the economy of Jewish Autonomies. Henryk Makower wrote this shortly after the war:

A problem of vital significance (within the Ghetto) was establishing an exchange of goods with the "Aryan" neighborhood. The direction towards the Ghetto was essential in order for there to be anything to eat; the direction away from the Ghetto was also necessary so that the food could continue to flow in, so that the Ghetto didn't expend its entire cash-flow on food. In a word, in order to achieve what was close to a balanced state, it was necessary to organize, not only import for the Ghetto, but also export from the Ghetto.[202]

The equivalent of the ministry or department of economy and trade in the Warsaw Jewish Autonomy was an institution called **Transferstelle**, i.e. the relay station post which served to facilitate the exchange of goods between the Jewish neighborhood and the outside world. *Transferstelle* became operational immediately following the closure of the Jewish Autonomy borders, despite the fact that the German order regarding permission to operate did not come down until April 14, 1941. As for the purpose and function of *Transferstelle*, Adam Czerniakow wrote:

---

[200] Ibidem, p. 216, 243 and 252.

[201] A. Marianowicz, *Życie surowo wzbronione (Life Strictly Forbidden)*, Warsaw 1995, p. 46-47.

[202] H. Makower, *Pamiętnik z getta warszawskiego [The Memoirs from Warsaw Ghetto]*, Wroclaw 1987, p. 20.

October 13, 1940:

I called a session of the Counsel at 9 A.M. this morning. A committee was formed to work out economy matters etc. of the possible Ghetto.

November 20, 1940:

At 10 o'clock in the morning at the Umsiedlungsamcie. (The Germans) Schoen, Mohns, Fabish (from Daniłowiczowska), Steyer declared: [...] 3) A Transferstelle will be created near the Ghetto. We are to furnish 20 rooms. We will cover the monthly 10,000 zlotych. The deadline is December 1, 1940. We have until November 28, 1940 to present a compendium of necessary articles and food. Foreign currency (dollars) are to be an equivalent along with prefabricated inventory. The Transferstelle is to issue orders to craftsmen and laborers. The Transferstelle is to take care of German and Polish creditors [...]. The Transferstelle is to take over the arbeitereinsatz with the representatives of Arbeitsamt.

November 24, 1940:

Schoen's orders: 1) at 7:30 on November 27, 40-50 craftsmen who will refurbish the Transferstelle office (23 Królewska Street), 2) furnish 20 rooms with new office furniture, hanging and standing lamps, curtains, 2 rooms of luxury items. A table for 30. Writing materials, etc., 6 new Continental machines, a telephone exchange, 3) Deposit 26,000 zł into the bank, in that 6,000 zł for Opel-Olympia (for a car for Czerniakow).

May 5, 1941:

We were paid a visit by Gater and Meder (the higher-up German officials of the Hauptabteilung Wirtschaft economy department in the General Government) regarding work productivity in the Ghetto etc. They support the idea of buyers in the Ghetto communicating directly with sellers on the other side, in order that a Jewish cooperative be created inside the Ghetto.

May 8, 1941:

At 4 in the afternoon, at Mohns'. It is necessary to create a cooperative savings bank (not a bank of emission). The bank of emission will have a branch. (...) German Mohns has declared that we are to have 10% revenue from the houses etc. The German Governor(of Poland) is supposedly relinquishing his revenue from the Jewish houses for the benefit of the Jewish Council.

The developing exchange of goods between the Warsaw Jewish

Autonomy and the Poles, and with the rest of the world, demanded a proper means of transportation. It is, therefore, why the authorities of the Warsaw Jewish Autonomy had made the decision to connect a secondary railway line within the vicinity and set up a transfer station called the *Umslagplatz,* which during the years of the Holocaust, gained the dismal notoriety for being the place from which transports of people departed heading for the gas chambers in Treblinka. Adam Czerniakow enters these incidents with these words:

November 20, 1940:

At 10 in the morning in the Umsiedlungsam. [The Germans] Schoen, Mohns, Fabish (from Daniłowiczowska Street), Steyer declared: It is necessary to organize the transfer station [Stückgut Warenlade – Verladungstelle] for food supplies near the train station as well.

November 24, 1940:

Preparing the personnel roster for the transfer station.

November 25, 1940:

It is necessary to set up a transfer station (Markstelle) near the Gdańsk train station. Conduct the conversation with the railway people regarding hooking up a (secondary) railway line.

July 4, 1941:

I toured the Umschlagplatz. A huge area, a solid plant, large personnel. A reserve of inventory for productivity is abundantly stocked.

In the middle of 1941, the construction of the Jewish Autonomy in Warsaw was nearing its end. The economy, although with difficulty, was in fact developing, which became evident once the production line of a series of articles designated mainly for outfitting the German army was set into motion. At the time, no one was aware that the secondary railway line and Umschlagplatz that had been built by the Jews would be utilized by the Germans in a year for a completely different purpose.

The Judenrats within the Jewish Autonomies fulfilled a dual role: they were a self-governing authority ruling the Jewish Autonomy and an executive power fulfilling the orders of the Germans. From the moment Poland was occupied and the Judenrats were created, the Germans bestowed the Jewish councils with the further assignments, which the Judenrats performed with exceptional conscientiousness and often at their own cost. In the autumn of 1939, a census of the Jewish population was taken, and at the beginning of 1940, the registration of Jews capable of performing labor took place. Emanuel Ringelblum noted the following:

February 19, 1940:

The information regarding the re-registration for forced labor. In every location there will be a Jewish doctor who will be responsible for diagnosing illnesses. The Jewish Municipality is responsible for affirming the people registering themselves. Every craftsman and industrial worker ought to report their tools. ***They (the Germans) will print up this declaration in German at the Jewish Municipality's expense.***

February 23, 1940:

The order for the second registration of Jews ages 14 to 60 was announced in two parts: the first – March 1 pertains to people between the ages of 16 and 25; and the second – to the rest. One is required to report their tools of the trade. The Chairmen of Jewish Elders are responsible for (authenticity) of the information provided.[203]

A natural human reaction is the desire to maintain one's personal fortune and the fortune of the community to which they belong. How can one explain the fact that the Jews themselves provided the Germans with information of their own fortunes? The chairman of the Warsaw Judenrat Adam Czerniakow noted:

December 12, 1939:

The Jewish Municipality provided [the Germans] with the addresses of wealthy Jews with the goal of requisitioning of furniture, lamps, bedding etc.

February 2, 1940:

A new inquiry has been published with regard to the matter of Jewish fortunes (clothing).

---

[203] Ringelblum E., *"Kronika getta warszawskiego wrzesień 1939 – styczeń 1943"*, Warszawa 1983, p. 85,94 and 96. [See also: "Notes from the Warsaw Ghetto" by Emanuel Ringelblum, paperback, Ibooks Inc., 2006]. To contrast Polish and Jewish attitudes one has to underline that the information about Poles who were fit to work had to be obtained by Germans themselves. Poles did not catch Poles and did not hand them over to work for the Germans. No Pole, no senator of the Second Republic, unless engaged in an active fight against the occupant, ever supplied information about Polish society or caught Poles to work for the Germans!

Emanuel Ringelblum confirmed this information and filled some of the blanks further:

Today, a command regarding Jewish property appeared in Warsaw. Those who are in possession of more than 2,000 złotys are obliged to report the surplus of funds. The problem with registering one's property: report it – no good, don't report it – also no good. Poles, in the face of such a problem, would opt for the latter.

The Jewish Municipality also outdid themselves when it came to serving the Germans and delivering various accessible goods:

The Jewish Municipality was advised to provide enough furniture for 100 apartments, 15 grand pianos. (...) The (representatives) of the (Jewish) Council arrived from Lublin in an effort to assist them (that is, the Germans); they went out of their way to obtain a train car for the goods. As it turns out, based on the information (received) from the provinces, in every city there are those Jews who supply the German authorities with everything they need. Some provide food stuffs, others provide clothing, and the such. (...) Recently, an interesting type of people has surfaced. Young Jewish activists, under thirty, thirty-five, completely unknown before the war; (...) They are capable of establishing a relationship with them (that is, the German)]. They do make a pretty penny doing this.[204]

From Jewish sources, it is possible to endlessly multiply the supply of descriptions of what Jewish life was like in the Jewish Territorial Autonomies (the Ghettos) located on the Polish lands that had been occupied by the Germans during the years of 1939-1942. The Autonomy in Łódź – the Jewish State, as it was referred to by its "king", Chaim Rumkowski – isolated itself completely from the surrounding Christian world. Other Autonomies officially, some not so officially, took care to ensure a balance of imports and exports (they tended to look the other way when it came to the smuggling of food, the selling off of one's personal valuables and the selling of Jewish manufactured goods). In the first three years of the war, none of the Jewish Territorial Autonomies had made any attempts

---

[204] Ringelblum E., *"Kronika getta warszawskiego wrzesień 1939 – styczeń 1943"*, Warszawa 1983, p. 46, 78, 79 and 103. [See also: "Notes from the Warsaw Ghetto" by Emanuel Ringelblum, paperback, Ibooks Inc., 2006].

whatsoever to establish communication or remain in contact with the Polish Underground State or the Polish Government-in-Exile in London – the rightful authorities of Poland. In Marek Edelman's opinion, Adam Czerniakow: *did not care for this underground, or their little newspapers that they kept delivering to him. He feared all of this.*[205]

The Poles did not fear the underground or the little underground newspapers. The years of 1939-1942 were devoted to the construction of a "virtual" Polish Underground State which, to be honest, was not very visible on the surface, but it did exist and it did, despite being concealed, quite adeptly fulfill all state functions. The first and most fundamental form of defense against exposure of underground structures is the rule in which one avoids individuals of dubious character with regard to loyalty, especially those who are in contact with the enemy. In the face of the outright collaboration with the Germans by the Jews, Bielorussians and the Ukrainians during the years of WWII, Poles expanded this rule regarding individuals and applied it to all minority groups of pre-war Poland. In so doing, they transformed the Polish Underground State into a virtually homogeneous structure with regard to nationality. That is to say that, they excluded the Ukrainians entirely, and almost entirely excluded the representatives of the Bielorussian and Jewish populations from within the orbit of cooperation with the conspiratorial structures of the Polish Underground State.

For the sake of accuracy, it must be stated that, during the years of 1939-1942, with the exception of a handful of Polonized Jews, the Polish minorities did not interpret the stance taken by Poles as discrimination. For the Ukrainians, belonging to the Polish conspiracy was considered to be treason; for the Bielorussians, on the other hand, it was considered an act of stupidity as it would bring with it no tangible material or political gains; for the Jews, it made very little sense to expose Jewish Territorial Autonomies to any repressions at the hands of the Germans, and, in a sense, it was also much frowned upon by the Jewish authorities. The first

---

205 The interview with Marek Edelman, in: Grupińska A., *"Ciągle po kole"* ["Still Round the Circle: Talks with the Soldiers of the Warsaw Ghetto"], Warszawa 2005, p. 310.

three years of the war made one thing clear to the Poles, that in their fight for freedom they could not count on the support of the Bielorussians, the Ukrainians or the Jews who lived on Polish lands. As for their presence within the ranks of the conspiratorial structures of the Polish Underground State, it generated more risk than the benefits might be worth. Therefore, the Polish Underground State of 1942, in the ethnic sense, was a virtually homogeneous Polish structure.

Both the Ukrainians and the Bielorussians were similarly abandoned during the first three years of the war. They first recognized Poles and Jews as the deathly enemies; the latter recognized Poles to be a fallen government and an undesirable element. In mutual Ukrainian-Bielorussian relations, neither ever found sufficient enough support to realize their goals of building their own independent states.

The abandonment of the Jews on the threshold of 1942 had a specific character. For as far as the Poles, Ukrainians and Bielorussians, all of whom wandered along independent political-military paths, they all had support within specific, ethnically identifiable contained territories. Within the framework of a conspiracy or outright state structures, they possessed channels of communication that were not controlled by the Germans. The Jewish Territorial Autonomies (the Ghettos), on the other hand, were isolated from the outside world. They were self-contained islands of Jewish self-government which, not only did not possess channels of communication independent of the Germans or the outright conspiratorial structures of the Poles, Ukrainians and Bielorussians, Polish Jews did not possess secure channels of communication independent of the Germans between their own Jewish Territorial Autonomies (the Ghettos). In addition, because, in the first months of WWII, Polish Jews had accepted the tactics of absolute cooperation and subjugation to the conditions within the Autonomies that had been set by the Germans, they lacked not only weapons (in the summer of 1942, in the Warsaw Ghetto which consisted of close to a half million Jewish people, there was one gun), but also any concept of defense against an occupying force. Indeed, the only concept of defense with regard to the Jewish Territorial Autonomy that Polish Jews possessed pertained to defending the surrounding brick walls against the Poles...

The winds of war always carry death and destruction with them. They also verify the political declarations that had been composed during times of peace, and they brutally unveil the values of moral and religious postures. In the multi-national Poland, which lies between the East and the West, wars have always been very dramatic, but so have the most telling gauges of the postures taken by its residents: postures of citizenship, understood as loyalty and trust with regard to the side engaged in a war for the freedom of their state; as well as the posture of foreigners which carried itself over into indifference with regard to the fate of Poles; and ethnic egotism, which means steadfastly maintaining such postures in the face of war, and which, with regard to the outbreak of war, take advantage of the newly created conditions and strive to realize their own ideas of a political-national nature.

A perfect example of this type of situation was during WWI. Interpreted from the perspective of the century as a fratricidal war of the Europeans, it erased certain nations (e.g. Austro-Hungary) from the map of Europe, while opening the way towards rebuilding their own countries for others (Poland, among others). The Poles, who as a result of the partitions of 1914, resided in Russian, German or Austrian areas, took the posture of foreigners with regard to the occupying forces and took advantage of the conducive political-military situation that had been created by the war. They rebuilt the Polish State which had not existed for 123 years.

For the same reasons that in 1918 signified an end to the multi-national Austro-Hungary, the outbreak of WWII, right from the outset, and aside from reasons that are military in nature, turned out to be deathly for the nationhood of the multi-national Poland. For those minorities that had been residing in Poland, a political situation had emerged in which they could attempt to realize the hitherto impossible idea of building the most suitable forms of their own statehoods for themselves.

In other words, the Poles devoted the years of 1939-1942 to preparing for the ultimate political-military contest with the Germans. The Ukrainians and Bielorussians, on the other hand, under the aegis of the Germans, undertook to attempt to build their own states. Despite a long developed collusion with the occupiers, they did not remain defenseless, and as the years that followed would reveal, they managed to utilize the weapons they had received from the Germans against the protectors (the Ukrainians). It was only the indiscriminate Polish Jews who, to the very end, entrusted themselves to the Germans and recognized that the fourth partition of Poland, that of September 1939, combined with the distribution of its territories among the Germans and the Soviets was the best moment for realizing the construction of Jewish autonomous provinces on Polish lands. After three years of the war had passed, they had their desired autonomous Jewish structures, granted they were scattered throughout all of Poland, but they had Jewish trams, Jewish children were learning the Jewish language in Jewish schools, they paid for things with Jewish currency, criminals were caught by Jewish police and imprisoned in Jewish jails, a Jewish mailman delivered their letters, Jews were enjoying themselves in Jewish theatres and cafes, and they had their designated day of rest – the "free-Saturday". But in the political-military and mentality senses, they were defenseless and had been abandoned. They were doomed to rely solely on themselves and each other, and on the good graces of the Germans.

A prudent reading of the most somber of Jewish sources dated between the years of 1939-1942, especially the *Warsaw Ghetto Journal of Adam Czerniakow* which is written almost entirely in Polish, *The Chronicle of the Warsaw Ghetto* by Emanuel Ringelblum, which has been translated from Yiddish to Polish, as well as the *Chronicle of the Łódź Ghetto*, leaves very little doubt as to the circumstances surrounding the creation of the Jewish autonomous provinces in the first two years of the war. Referred to as Ghettos in both colloquial and academic jargon to this day, they were the result of, not only German plans of repression with regard to the Jewish population being realized, as has been the belief until now; but rather, above all, the result of the idea of *Jewish Autonomous Provinces*[206] that had been brought to fruition by Polish Jews under German tutelage, as a form of Jewish Statehood. This most certainly was the case as far as

---

[206] The idea of *Jewish Autonomous Provinces* was born and presented to the Poles by Izaak Grünbaum, the Jewish member of the lower chamber of the Parliament of the Polish State, as the proposal of the article 113 of the Polish Constitution in the Constitutional Committee in November 1920.

the Warsaw and Lodz Ghettos are concerned. Jewish historian, Michael C. Steinlauf, writes about the Jewish Ghettos in Poland 1939-1942: ...*created at the behest of German directives and functioned under German supervision, invoked the age-old tradition of Jewish autonomy.*"[207]

---

[207] Steinlauf M. C., *Pamięć nieprzyswojona* [*Unassimilated memory*], Warszawa 2001, p. 42.

CHAPTER V

BEYOND THE LIMITS
OF SOLIDARITY OF THE JEWS

In documentation relating to the Holocaust, the matter of collaboration between Polish Jews and the Germans is rarely touched upon, or rather, the cooperation of European Jews with German authorities in Hitler's Germany when it comes to the extermination of the Jewish nation. Meanwhile, everything points to the fact that this very issue holds the key to understanding the Holocaust in general, and in turn to understanding the extermination of Polish Jews specifically. In other words, one must try to answer the question of whether the Germans would have managed to murder so many millions of Jews had it not been for the fact that, from amongst the Jews themselves, they found eager collaborators and perpetrators of criminal acts. Certain standards of behavior of the Jewish community with regard to Hitler's Germany can be dated to well before the start of WWII. For example, Dr. Joseph Löwenherz, as early as 1938, ...*managed to transform the entire Viennese Jewish community into an institution servicing the Nazi authorities exclusively. He was also one of the few activists of this sort who, for his services, was rewarded by being allowed to remain in Vienna until the end of the war, at which time he emigrated to England, and from there to the United States.*[208]

Jewish historiography, as well as Polish, European and world historiography, in its perception of the Holocaust, operates within commonly accepted linear narrative deriving from legal nomenclature in which the two main roles played are by the concepts of executioner and victim. These concepts, in no uncertain terms, designate the side using violence and the side succumbing to said violence. According to the dictionary, an executioner is defined as one who performs executions, as well as exacts corporal punishment, torture, and such; colloquially, it describes someone who treats others inhumanely. Respectively, this very same dictionary defines the victim as a person or thing yielding to another's force, becoming their prey.

From the moment WWII ended, in the vernacular of Holocaust historiography, it has been unanimously and unequivocaly accepted that the extermination of 6 million European Jews was carried out by one nation, Germany, who played the role of executioner, while the exterminated Jewish population was the victim of the afore mentioned executioner. Following such a linear narrative, this would not be the first time, or the only time, that historians have applied commonly accepted norms when assessing these events. As it turns out, this would not be the first time, or the only time, that such simplistic presuppositions would lead an historical fallacy. For if one were to read more deeply into Jewish sources, read more carefully into chronicled writings that were kept up to date in the ghettos formed on Polish territories; as well as Jewish memoirs and journals – especially those written during the war or immediately following the end of the war; as well take into account the ever bolder most recent findings, one can see the picture of the German executioner and that of the Jewish victim fall apart. That is to say, the role of the German executioner remains unchanged. However, what is revealed ever more definitively is the role of Jews not only as victims, but also as executioners of their own people.

As the American historian Brian Mark Rigg has found, *Not everyone*

---

[208] H. Arendt, *Eichmann w Jerozolimie*, Kraków1987, p. 394; [see also: *Eichmann In Jerusalem: A Report on the Banality of Evil*, The Viking Press, New York 1964].

of Jewish descent fell victim to the death camps. Not every German officer was a pure Aryan. There could have been at least 150,000 Mischlings (persons of Jewish ancestry; German cross-breeds – note by E.K.) serving in the Wehrmacht. There is also evidence that not one, but many, became high-ranking officers, and some even achieved the ranks of generals and/or admirals.[209] The matter that remains for future historical research to assess is how significant the impact 150,000 Jewish soldiers serving in the Third Reich really had on shaping its military successes, as well as establishing if, and in what capacity, did Jews in German uniforms participate in the murder of the Jewish nation.

Therefore, in order to understand how it was possible for such an atrocity to be perpetrated in the heart of Europe, how it was possible for the murder of three million Polish Jews and three million other European Jews to take place before the eyes of the world, we must try to answer the question of what role Jews themselves played in the genocide of their own people. Above all, one must determine if all the Jews murdered on Polish lands, Polish Jews and European Jews alike, were in fact victims. The most straightforward answer that comes to mind is that since they were murdered, no doubt they most certainly were victims. Except that prior to becoming victims, they could very well have been executioners as well.

Jewish sources demonstrate that it was in fact the case. A certain percentage of European Jews who perished during the last war, including Polish Jews, before dying an agonizing death, had themselves been the executioners of their own people. **It was before the eyes of these Jews, the victims, that their brethren murdered other Jews or led a helpless Jewish people to their death. It was these Jews who first assigned the title of executioner to the Jewish murderers.** Emanuel Ringelblum noted:

When the relocation was put in into effect in Warsaw in July of 1942, and the Jewish Ordnungsdienst (police) took over directing the campaign, (Szachno Efroim) Sagan was not overcome with indignation. He felt that the Jewish community, despite German threats, should have refused to participate in the

---

[209] B.M. Rigg, *Żydowscy żołnierze Hitlera: nieznana historia nazistowskich ustaw rasowych i mężczyzn pochodzenia żydowskiego w armii niemieckiej*, Warszawa 2005, s. 71. [see also: *Hitler's Jewish Soldiers: The Untold Story of Nazi Racial Laws and Men of Jewish Descent in the German Military,* University Press of Kansas 2002].

campaign. It would have been better if the Germans did it themselves. Sagan went to the Judenrat to file his complaint against the disgraceful manner in which they were behaving in taking on the role of executioner and assistants to the murderous SS, the infamous Juden-Sieger.[210]

Calling the Jews who actively participated in the Holocaust executioners is not a term that was coined in contemporary vernacular. It was not created by historians, nor was it put into use by representatives of other nations. The title of executioner that was given to Hitler's Jewish partners came from the Jews who saw the Jewish drama unfold before their very eyes, and who generally experienced violence from Jews firsthand. The afore mentioned Szachno Efroim Sagan (1892-1942), the head activist of the Jewish party, Poale Syjon-Lewica, publicist, organizer of civilian resistance and conspiracy, named the Jewish torturers executioners of their own people. Emanuel Ringelblum in the summer of 1942 wrote about him:

... he couldn't stand by and watch as the Jewish Ordnungsmänner (policemen) captured Jewish children and shoved them into the back of the trucks bound for Umschlagplatz. He couldn't bear the sight of women being dragged by their hair by their Jewish captors from the Ordnungsdiens. On one such occasion, after witnessing such a brutal act take place, he intervened. The Jewish "boys", enraged by his actions, wanted to load him up onto one of the trucks and ship him off to Umschlagplatz. There was one among them, however, who recognized him and released him.

Szachno Efroim Sagan, both as witness and victim of crimes committed by Jewish executioners, had a certain right, a right which he claims to this very day – the right to call things by their proper name. Because soon enough, Emanuel Ringelblum writes:

The day of August 5, 1942 had arrived. This was during the first weeks of the relocation campaign. This so-called "campaign" rested in the hands of the Ordnungsdiens (the Jewish Order-keeping Service). That past Friday, Szachno Sagan had been visiting friends. By the time he returned home, his family was already assembled in formation, waiting dispatch to Umschlagplatz. He

---

[210] Ringelblum E., *"Kronika getta warszawskiego wrzesień 1939 – styczeń 1943"*, Warszawa 1983, p. 71. [See also: "Notes from the Warsaw Ghetto" by Emanuel Ringelblum, paperback, Ibooks Inc., 2006].

wanted to share in the fate that awaited his family, the fate of his wife and two children. He placed himself in the queue, in formation, headed for certain death.[211]

In analyzing the problem of Jewish participation in the annihilation of Polish Jews, one must, above all, find the answers to three basic questions:

- Firstly, one must try, at least, to arrive at a rough estimate of the percentage from among Polish Jews who made up the ranks of Jew-executioners of Jewish people. Especially because the majority of them, despite their loyalty to the Germans, were, after all, murdered, and therefore are treated by history as the victims of the Holocaust as perpetrated by the Germans.
- Secondly, one must establish what Jewish spheres these Jew-executioners who cooperated with the Germans in annihilating their own people came from.
- Thirdly, it is high time to finally consider how significant an impact Jewish technical support proved to be in facilitating the Germans during each phase of realizing their plan to murder Polish Jews.

The best measure of the number of Jew-executioners, or rather the percentage from within the general Jewish population in Poland, is in the statistical data for the city of Łódź. At the outbreak of WWII, there were approximately 250,000 Jews residing in Łódź. In the excruciating year of 1942, the year of the "Final Solution", when transports of those sentenced to death were departing from the ghettos practically daily, *the population of the ghetto consisted of 162,681 persons (66,978 men and 92,703 women).*[212] **Lucjan Dobroszycki, a prominent WWII Jewish expert, writes** this regarding the Lodz ghetto: *Rumkowski, in a period just short of five years, as **the Chairman of Jewish Elderls, taking advantage of the privilege assigned to him by the occupiers of the autonomy**, created a massive network of administrative cells which, in its heyday, employed more*

---

[211] ibidem, p. 539-540.

[212] *Kronika getta lodzkiego, [The Lodz Ghetto Diary]*, preface and notes by D.Dąbrowska and L. Dobroszycki, Lodz 1965, p 360.

than 10,000 office clerks and laborers. Aside from public service institutions such as the board of health, education, and public welfare, food supply and public kitchens, he developed an extensive militant apparatus in the form of a multilayered police force (including a secret service division assigned to combat those in opposition), a prison and court system.[213]

The end of 1941, the start of 1942 was the peak of the Lodz ghetto's success. Among the give-or-take 163,000 residents, more than 10,000, or roughly 6%, of its inhabitants represented the workforce of the Jewish administration. From among that 6%, every single member, as a result of performing a variety of anti-Jewish German commands, was a de facto executioner of his or her own people. If one takes into consideration the fact that the majority of those answering to Rumkowski and the Germans were men, this is an indicator that the number of executioners from among Jewish men was roughly 15%. Because of the high turnover within the administration itself, which was directly linked to the deplorable living conditions in the ghetto, as well as a result of the throngs of Jews collaborating with the Germans outside the realm of the official administration, the nearest, most likely estimation of the number of Jew-executioners appears to swing between 6% and 10% of the Jewish population at large.[214]

Who were the Jews that did not hesitate to play the role of executioners of their own people? As I mentioned earlier, Polish Jews were a nation, a caste, or a social group very distinctly stratified, not only according to material wealth, but also in the degree to which they were assimilated, the manner in which they practiced their religion, and the language they spoke. The vast majority, according to the widely referred to census report of 1931, roughly 85%, were Orthodox Jews, Hasidim, living mainly in their own world. The absence of established norms of interacting with the outside world, the Hassid attitude toward an introspective life, the lack of

---

[213] L. Dobroszycki, *Wstęp*, w: *Kronika getta lodzkiego*, [*Foreward, Chronicle of the Lodz Ghetto*], Lodz 1965, p. .XX.

[214] Obviously, the above estimates need to be precisely defined. I quote them not because they are irrefutable but because I would like them to become the subject of Polish and Jewish research. The aim of their presentation is thus not to eventually settle the problem but rather to attract the researchers' attention, as this issue is an extremely important one for the question of the Holocaust.

the Polish language, being poorly oriented in the outside world of politics, socialization and economics, were all responsible for bringing a state of condemnation of this group under the conditions that existed within the Jewish autonomy where the representation of the entire Polish Jewish nation, with regard to the German authorities, was taken on by educated members of the community who came from the more assimilated group of Jewish intelligentsia.[215] In his chronicle, Emanual Ringelblum often writes about the social group from which the Jews who played the role of executioners had emerged:

Warsaw [the getto] is divided into three parts: the aristocrats – Leszno, Elektoralna and Chłodna streets; the mensches – Sienna Street; the scabs – the rest [of streets]. [...] The Jewish community in Warsaw is characterized by, other than a wide range of "attributes", its being a den of revolting assimilation. 95% of the office clerks [of the Judenrat] speak Polish to the applicants even though they don't understand what is being said to them.

Today, March 23, (1941), the McDonald Relief Committee came to visit. The Jewish clerks [in the Judenrat] were not even able to say how many letters the Jewish alphabet consists of. And even those who attempted to throw some numbers out there were mistaken (21). Those who accompanied the McDonald party could not get over the fact that the employees of a Jewish institution didn't understand their own language. (...) The leaders in the department of labor of the Jewish community [the Judenrat] are former assimilates and such.

(In 1942) Jewish community employees [the Judenrat and others] played the role of "catchers". Doctors and others wearing "Umsiedlungsaktion" armbands (relocation campaign).[216] (...) The Jewish policemen pointed out hideouts, basements, and attics to the Germans. Outside of the Jewish police, Jews were

---

215 Since the 1890s, the tasks of administering and representing Jewish communities were traditionally divided between the assimilators and the orthodox-Hassidic circles of the Warsaw community. The former represented the community before the outside world and the latter dealt with education and religious issues. This pattern had been adopted by other Jewish communities. [See: J. Zyndul, op. cit., p. 106.].

216 The Judenrat's officials and other clercks who were ordered to take part in the deportation of Jewish people wore armbands with the inscription 'Umsiedlungsaktion' ('the resettlement action') and the Judenrat's stamp.

caught by the employees of the Jewish emergency services, Jewish funeral homes, and Jewish community clerks.[217]

According to his words, the majority of the Jewish police were from the intelligentsia, and were lawyers before the war. An entry from the chronicle of the Łodź ghetto dated December 2, 1941 says:

Open enrollment into the Order-keeping Forces (the Jewish Police). In the last 8 days, about 100 new members were accepted into the Order-keeping Forces. They were selected from men recently relocated to the ghetto. They are exclusively former German, Austrian and Czech army officers. For the time being, they have all been enlisted as lowly privates. From among those selected there are 2 former squadron leaders.[218]

19. Jewish police lining up for instructions in Lodz ghetto, 1942.

This picture depicted above is filled in further by Władysław Szpilman:

217 Ringelblum E., *"Kronika getta warszawskiego wrzesień 1939 – styczeń 1943"*, Warszawa 1983, p. 39, 217, 251 and 426. [See also: "Notes from the Warsaw Ghetto" by Emanuel Ringelblum, paperback, Ibooks Inc., 2006].
218 *Kronika getta Lodzkiego [Chronicle of the Lodz Ghetto]*, Lodz 1965, p. 286.

It was May [1942], and even in the gardens scattered few and far between throughout the ghetto, lilacs were in bloom. [...] The Germans have once again been reminded that we exist, however with one small difference this time: they alone were not going to be managing us. The responsibility of executing the round-ups has been transferred to the hands of the Jewish police and the Jewish Board of Employment. Henryk was right in refusing to join the ranks of the police calling them a band of criminals. **It was composed of mostly well-to-do young people.** *We used to move in the same social circles with many of them and, therefore, we are filled with even greater revulsion when we realize that these decent people of not so long ago whose hands we used to shake and whom we treated as friends have turned into rascals.*

They have become infected with the winds of the Gestapo. It seems the only way to describe it. The moment they donned their uniforms and took the clubs in their hands, they turned into animals. Their most important goal was to get into cahoots with the Gestapo, wait on them hand-and-foot, parade up and down the streets alongside them, impress them with their knowledge of the German language, and show off the brutality they are capable of towards the Jewish population in front of their higher-ups. [...] When it came time to execute the round-up in May, they surrounded the street with the sharp precision of seasoned, pure SS-men. They were running around in their stylish little uniforms, barking loudly and fiercely as expertly as the Germans, and they beat people with their rubber clubs.[219]

The above recorded sources, which have been verified by countless archives, journals and memoirs, have allowed us to put forth a thesis that the role of executioner of the Jewish population in Poland was played almost exclusively by representatives of the Jewish intelligentsia. It will, therefore, most likely not be erroneous to state that since, during WWII, the Jewish intelligentsia composed no more that 15% of the Jewish population from among Polish Jews, whereas 6-10% of the entire Jewish population fulfilled the role of executioner – at least 1/3 or, what is more likely, 2/3 of Jewish intelligentsia (lawyers, doctors, clerks, etc.) fulfilled

---

[219] W. Szpilman, *Pianista [The Pianist]*, Krakow 2003, p. 85.

the role of executioner of its own people. The question still remains of how significant an impact, in terms of technical support, did the Jews make in facilitating the Germans during each phase of realizing their plan to murder Polish Jews.

20. The Jewish police inside the Warsaw ghetto, 1942.

From the point of view of technical solutions, the process of genocide with regard to Polish Jews consisted of at least seven steps:

1. Intermediate extermination: gathering up the dispersed Jews from throughout small towns and village settlements within autonomous territories and concentrating them in larger urban areas;
2. Keeping the Jews convinced the deportation is directly linked to finding work in the East in areas specifically designated by the Germans;
3. Capturing the Jews designated for death (which to this day, for no apparent reason, is referred to by historians as "deportation") and bringing them to the appropriate location for re-loading – such as

to the place from which trains departed for the death camps, as well as loading up those designated for death into the train cars;

4. Transporting the Warsaw Jews to the death camps in Treblinka, and the Jews from other cities to other death camps;

5. Preparing the condemned for death (cutting off their hair, confiscating their valuables, baggage, etc...) and raking up any belongings left behind by the murdered;

6. The killing of the Jews;

7. The destruction of bodies of the dead.

In order to further understand the role of the Jewish executioners in Poland during the Holocaust, it is necessary to examine each of the above mentioned steps of genocide of the Jewish people one by one:

Ad 1: Intermediate extermination: gathering up the dispersed Jews from throughout small towns and village settlements within autonomous territories and concentrated them in larger urban areas. The first and most important step of the German Holocaust plan was implementing a sort of census of the Jewish population and gathering up of the dispersed Jews and placing them into Jewish territorial autonomies localized in larger urban areas. What implementing this meant for the Germans was that, first of all, they had the foundation for exploiting the Jewish workforce (work camps), and that further down the road, for preparing a suitable region on the outskirts of town that would technically facilitate the Holocaust plan (localization of the death camps, transportation to and from, etc...) As it is irrefutably proven from the most esteemed of Jewish historical sources, Jewish authorities actively and eagerly participated in the execution of all German commands as they related to this particular step. Emanuel Ringelblum writes:

The deportation of 150,000 Jews from Sosnowiec, Będzin, Katowice, Cieszyn (1200 people), Zawiercie. The plan was brought forth because "Joint" (the Jewish organization), which was assisting Jews from neighboring towns, suggested that they take on the execution of the deportation. (...) Should it not work out, then (Mojżesz Maryn, Chairman of Elderly Jewry in Sosnowiec – E.K.) will organize the deportation. (At the time of registering the Jews, those gathered in Judenrats)…did everything that was asked of them by the Galej (the Germans). During general registration, for example, they did everything they were told to do, even if it was not always in the best interest of the Jews. They're saying that the assassination in Otwock was the result of Judenrat intervention which could not manage all the Jews designated for the work camps; they didn't want to go there. They brought in the SS-men in order to curb the revolt against the Judenrat. That's what they're saying about Otwock.[220]

The execution of German commands in the Lodz ghetto was similar. In the Łódź ghetto chronicle dated December 3, 1941 we read: *Census of the residents of the collective. Today, the census of all residents of the collective was executed. (…) The census was carried out (by) the Prażans* [inhabitants of Prague; Jews from Prague deported to Lodz – E.K.] *who have recently been employed by the Registration Bureau. They came around all the commonly occupied homes in pairs, starting at 9 P.M.. In accordance with the orders in place, the night of Tuesday into Wednesday, all residents of the collective had to be at home. Those who worked at night left their I.D.'s. On average, each collective houses 1000 people. The census was completed after 3 A.M.*

The same chronicle, under the date of December 6, 1941, among other things, describes a round-up of Jews being executed by Jews: *Rounding up for labor. (…) The "rounding up" began at exactly 5 P.M.. This campaign was carried out by service functionaries of the Jewish Order-Keeping Forces and the Jewish Central Prison. The captured were held in the district courtyards. It wasn't going to take place without several beatings or a series of unpleasant incidents brought on by the commotion involved, excessive bloodshed of the Jewish functionaries as well as the overall darkness that was rampant throughout the entire ghetto, even thicker than usual this evening because of the fog. In general, around 2000 men were detained.*[221]

Ad 2. Keeping the Jews convinced the deportation is directly linked to finding work in the East in areas specifically designated by the Germans. This often overlooked step in the genocide process, which is

---

[220] Ringelblum E., *"Kronika getta warszawskiego wrzesień 1939 – styczeń 1943"*, Warszawa 1983, p. 81-82, 108, 142 and 150. [See also: "Notes from the Warsaw Ghetto" by Emanuel Ringelblum, paperback, Ibooks Inc., 2006].

[221] *Kronika getta Łodzkiego [Chronicle of the Łódź Ghetto]*, Lodz 1965, p. 291 and 297.

based on keeping the Polish Jews in a state if misinformation by other Jews for the purpose of massive deportations, perhaps played the most important role in maintaining a posture of passivity, essential in efficiently bringing the Holocaust to its fruition. In this step of bringing about the realization of the Holocaust, when it comes to the role of Jewish authorities in Jewish autonomies (ghettos) in Poland, as well as that of the Jews themselves in both overt and under-cover collaborations with the Germans, we find these references in almost all of the most reliable historical sources.

In the chronicle notes that were made in the Lodz ghetto we find that in January of 1942, the head of the Lodz Judenrat, chairman Rumkowski, who was very well aware that he was sending them to their death, told his fellow brethren:

At present, we are deporting 10,000 persons from the ghetto. (...) The fate of those expelled will not be as tragic as is commonly believed throughout the ghetto. They will not end up behind barbed wire, and in participating they will have some farm work thrown their way. On the sidelines of the deportation campaign, gossip has been running rampant. I can't condemn this disruption to public peace strongly enough.[222]

In Warsaw, on July 24, 1942, while the two-day-long campaign of deporting Jews to the Treblinka gas chambers was taking place, the Jewish community (Judenrat), very well aware of where these trains filled to capacity with Jews were heading, in an effort to quiet growing fears of the neighborhood residents and avert a potential revolt, released an official decree which stated:

The deportation of the population that is otherwise useless or less than productive in the Jewish neighborhood within Warsaw to eastern territories is indeed taking place.[223]

Emanuel Ringelblum, in judging the posture of Jewish office clerks, has noted:

The shameful document of the community [Judenrat]. Regarding the rumors concerning the deportation out East. The Jewish Employment Board

---

[222] *Ibidem*, p. 398-399.

[223] Ringelblum E., *"Kronika getta warszawskiego wrzesień 1939 – styczeń 1943"*, Warszawa 1983, p. 409. [See also: "Notes from the Warsaw Ghetto" by Emanuel Ringelblum, paperback, Ibooks Inc., 2006].

knows it's a death sentence. (…) Lies regarding the East. The alleged letters from Pińsk, Brześć and other towns. They knowingly spread such rumors immediately after the campaigns began in order to create confusion. Nobody ever saw these letters. Who was spreading these rumors? Jewish Gestapo agents. The same rumors were being spread throughout towns in the provinces.[224]

Ad 3: Capturing the Jews designated for death (which to this day, for no apparent reason, is referred to by historians as "deportation") and bringing them to the appropriate location for re-loading – such as to the place from which trains departed for the death camps, as well as loading up those designated for death into the train cars. The deportation of Jews to the death camps took place in a nearly identical manner throughout all the Jewish autonomies (ghettos) in occupied Poland. Władysław Szpilman recalls:

The worst started in July – the deportation of an entire neighborhood of half a million, an absurdity it seemed, that no one was able to fathom. In the first days the campaign was carried out in a lottery system. Homes were surrounded at random, sometimes here, sometimes in another part of the ghetto. With one whistle, the residents evacuated out into the courtyard and every single person, without exception, was loaded onto the trucks regardless of sex or age, everyone from infants to elders, up into the trucks and transported off to Umschlagplatz. There, the lambs for the slaughter were stuffed into train cars and dispatched into the unknown. In those first days, the campaign was being carried out exclusively by the Jewish police with three chiefs: colonel Szeryński, and captains Lejkin and Ehrlich. They were no less dangerous or merciless than the Germans, perhaps even meaner and more base than them. When they found people who had hid rather than come down to the courtyard, they were easily bribed. But they accepted only money. Neither tears, nor begging, nor the heartbreaking screams of children were enough to move them.[225]

In a passage dated May 7, 1942, in the "Biuletyn", which occasionally appeared inside the Lodz ghetto, the chroniclers of the Lodz ghetto described, pretty accurately, how Jews were dispatching their brothers to death:

---

[224] Ibidem, p. 409 and 418.
[225] W. Szpilman, *Pianista [The Pianist]*, Krakow 2003, p. 86.

The 4th day of deportations. Today, exiled Jews from Hamburg and Düsseldorf were dispatched from the ghetto. All belongings, including even the smallest of packages, are still being confiscated. The only thing that is allowed to be kept is bread, and sometimes other types of food. The delivery of human cargo takes place in the following way: during the afternoon hours, the deportees are brought to the Central Prison, or to buildings surrounded with barbed wire on Szklana St., here they remain overnight. The following day at noon, they are lined up in groups and convoyed to a camp in Marysin which is located in a school complex on Jonschera St. and in five buildings on Okopowa St. at the assembly place, they receive provisions which consist of a ration of bread, coffee and soup. Each person receives a loaf of bread for the trip free of charge. At 4 A.M., an expert team of the Jewish Police specializing in carrying out such responsibilities, transports the deportees in trams to the train station on the Radogoska line. A half hour before the train departs, which is at exactly 7 A.M., functionaries of the German secret police arrive by car to assist the regular police. Up until that moment, the deportees are handled by the Jewish Police Forces, divided into groups of 10, and placed to stand in front of the small train compartment doors at a distance of two meters from the train cars. Under the watchful eye of the German police, they proceed to occupying their places on the train. It is at this point that they are instructed to dispose of any carry-on belongings. Larger packages and pieces of baggage have already been confiscated by the Jewish Forces at the gathering point. Those items, along with the ones taken at the train station, will ultimately make their way to the offices on Rybna St. The ill and advanced in age are carried into the train cars by porters. There are personal hygiene stations located at the gathering point, and there is a hygiene official on duty at the train as well. It's worth straightening out the information circulating throughout the ghetto regarding the beatings of the deportees. These accidents, with some minor exceptions, do not occur. As in the all previous deportations, the train is made up of third class cars. Every one of the deportees gets a seat. The train makes its way back the very same day at 8 P.M.[226]

There is a scene in Roman Polanski's film, *The Pianist*, in which Wladysław Szpilman is paired up in a queue with other men who are

---

[226] *Kronika getta Łodzkiego [Chronicle of the Łodź Ghetto]*, Lodz 1965, p. 515-516.

dressed in uniforms, and along with his family, is approaching the train. This is the final road the Warsaw Jews will walk down. The train cars will go to Treblinka. To the uninformed spectator who generally operates within the linear narrative with regard to the Holocaust, as do historians, has the concept of the German executioner and the Jew victim. They generally fail to notice that the uniforms worn by those awaiting the arrival of trains are not German uniforms. They are Jewish uniforms. Władysław Szpilman, whose journals became the canvas for the screenplay of Polanski's film, describes that scene in these words:

On August 16, 1942 it was finally our turn. A selection took place at the gathering point, and only Henryk and Halina (the brother and sister of the author – E.K) were declared fit to work. My father, Regina and I were advised to return to the barracks. When we arrived there, the building was surrounded and a whistle was sounded. (…) We were getting dressed when we heard screams coming from the courtyard along with gunshots meant to get people to hurry up. Mother bundled and wrapped some things that were handy and we proceeded down the stairs. The square (Umschlagplatz) for reloading was located in a remote area of the ghetto. There were a few side streets that led to the square and conveniently connected it with the rest of the city. The thru streets had been blocked off and the entire area could now accommodate up to 8,000 people.

When we got to the square it was still relatively empty. (…)Having found a perfectly decent place to settle, we waited for the train. (…) Every once in a while, trucks would pull up to the entrance gates of the square and unload crowds of people designated for deportation. (…) Along with the influx of people within the square, it was getting more and more crowded and it was becoming increasingly more difficult to avoid groups of those standing as well as those lying on the ground. Everybody was talking about the same thing: where are we being taken, and is it really for work as the Jewish police was trying to convince everyone was the case.

It was already noon when yet another group of deportees was forced into the square. With horror, we noticed Henryk and Halina were among them. (…) Word of our deportation had reached them and they simply volunteered to be taken to Umschlagplatz as they wanted to be together with us. This was an idiotic rush of emotion on their part. I decided to get them out of here at all costs because their names were not on the list of deportees and they could very well be left behind in Warsaw. They were brought over by a Jewish policeman who knew me. I was counting on being able to reach his conscience, especially since, obviously, there was no sensible reason or necessity for these two to be deported to start with. Unfortunately, I overestimated the situation. He wanted to hear none of it. Like all the other Jewish policemen, he worked under the threat of being deported himself were he to disobey the order which stated that he was obligated to bring five people to Umschlagplatz daily. Halina and Henryk were his fourth and fifth of the day. Because he was tired, he had no intention of letting them off. Otherwise he would have to go back out on another round-up. Such a round-up was no easy task as nobody really wants to assist in making the job of the Jewish police easier. They hid. (...)

21. A Jewish policeman who caught a Jewish woman, hands her over to a German. Warsaw ghetto, 1942.

At about 6 o'clock, a very uneasy feeling settled upon the square. A couple of cars of German military police pulled up and they started pulling the young and strong out of the crowd that was designated for deportation. (…) The Germans got the workforce they were looking for and left. Soon afterwards, somewhere in the distance, we could hear the train whistle and the rattling of the train cars steadily approaching. A few more minutes passed and we were able to spot the train. Probably a dozen or so cargo cars were approaching, the kind used for cattle. Blowing from the same direction was an evening breeze which carried with it a wave of nauseating stench, the stench of chlorine.

At the same time, the chain of Jewish police and SS-men surrounding the square started to tighten, to push inward, and once again we heard warning shots being fired. From the densely packed crowd, loud, pleading screams of women and children started to rise. We moved forward. What were we supposed to be waiting for? The sooner we are inside the train cars, the better. A few feet in front of the train cars, a double row of Jewish police was formed, which created a wide passage way for the crowd. There was only one outlet at the end of this passageway which led directly up to the doors of the chlorinated train cars.

Half the train cars were already behind us when suddenly I heard someone shouting: "Look! Look! Szpilman!" A hand grabbed me by the collar and I was thrown outside of the police cordon. Who on earth had the audacity to treat me in such a manner? I didn't want to be separated from my own. I wanted to be with them!

The only thing I could see now was a wall of Jewish policemen's backs. I threw myself at them but they wouldn't give. Over their heads I saw my mother and Regina being held up by Halina and Henryk as they entered the train. Meanwhile, my father was looking around trying to find me.

"Father!" I shouted.

Once again I lunged at the wall of policemen with all my might.

"Father! Henryk! Halina!"

I was screaming at the top of my lungs like a madman, overcome with fear, that at this most critical moment, I won't be able to reach them and that we will forever be separated.

One of the Jewish policemen turned around and looked at me angrily:

"What the hell are you doing? Why don't you save yourself?"

"Save myself? Save myself from what?"

In an instant I realized what awaited all those people being stuffed into the train cars. I took a look around. The square was vacant of people. Just beyond the train tracks and ramps, there were outlets out onto the streets. I started running away in that direction, driven by an uncontrollable, almost animal fear. I managed to blend in with a group of community laborers, who where just at that precise moment leaving the square, and with them I passed through the gate.[227]

The image conveyed by the pianist, Wladysław Szpilman, fills in some of the blanks of the Warsaw ghetto chronicle notes of Emanuel Ringelblum. Ringelblum, who describes the role of Jews in the liquidation of the largest group of European Jews, the massive deportation of Warsaw Jews to the Treblinka death camps which commenced on July 22, 1942, writes:

Umschlagplatz (reloading square). Szmerling (a Jew, commander of Umschlagplatz – E.K.), tormentor with a whip. The criminal giant, Szmerling, with a horsewhip in his hand. He has entered into the good graces of the Germans. The loyal executor of their commands. [...] The Jewish police had a bad reputation even before the deportations began. Unlike the Polish police which did not participate in the work camp round-ups, the Jewish police engaged in this repugnant act. They were the epitome of corruption and demoralization. They couldn't possibly have sunk to new lows than they did while the deportations were taking place. Not one word of protest was uttered against their despicable function which entailed leading their own brothers to slaughter. The police were spiritually dedicated to this filthy job and, therefore, performed it willingly and eagerly. At present, you really have to rack your brain to try to solve the riddle of how this was able to happen. How did it happen that Jews, usually the intelligentsia, former lawyers (most of the officers (in the Jewish police force) were former lawyers), willingly had their hands in the extermination of their own people; that Jews dragged women and children, the elderly and the sick into trucks knowing that all of them were headed for the slaughter? (...)

---

[227] W. Szpilman, *Pianista [The Pianist]*, Krakow 2003, p. 92-101.

It was the Jewish police who most willingly and eagerly executed the German commands with regard to the deportations. The fact remains that, during the deportations, the Jewish police daily exceeded their quotas. This was referred to as stocking up your supply for the next day. The faces of these policemen did not reveal any sadness or pain at having to perform this repugnant job. Quite the contrary, they appeared proud, satisfied, cheerful, well-fed, loaded with the loot they had pillaged in concord with the Ukrainians.

The cruelty of the Jewish police was often far greater than that of the Germans, the Ukrainians, or the Latvians. There were more than just a few hiding places that were "sniffed out" by the Jewish police. They always wanted to appear plus catholique que le pape in order to suck up themselves to their occupiers. The victims who managed to go unnoticed by a German were caught by a Jewish policeman. (…) A common occurrence was one where these bandits would take women by their hands and feet and toss them onto "Kohn and Heller" trucks, or just onto ordinary trucks. They treated anyone who showed even the slightest resistance without mercy. Breaking the resistance (of their victims) was not satisfying enough for them. No, they punished the "innocent", who did not want to go to their deaths voluntarily, very, very severely. (…) There were groups and organizations outside the police which voluntarily showed their support for and participated in the deportation campaign. At the top of this list was the Gancwajch Ambulance Service, a faux institution in amaranth hat, which not once, not ever, provided any medical attention to a single Jew. (…) This criminal gang of troublemakers volunteered to do the ungodly job of sending Jews to the other world. It was this gang that was the epitome of brutality and inhumane acts. Their red hats became covered with the blood spatter of the unfortunate Jewish masses. Aside from the Gancwaj Ambulance Service, the deportation campaign was helped along by (various) Jewish Community office/administrative assistants/clerks, as well as by the KOS Ambulance service.

As far as they were concerned, it all came down to a "headcount". On days when they were given a quota, they traded "heads". They kept track in little notebooks by writing, "I delivered this many "heads"". He would show up at 3 Dzika St. and ask for bread because he had delivered more "heads" than his quota required. Some lawyer was bragging to me about how he had loaded 1,000 Jews onto the trucks. Now, at the end of October 1942, the Jewish police were trying to figure out how to catch some Jew and bring him down to Umschlagplatz. (…) From among the Germans, the SS-men were the ones taking part in the campaign. Their "fame" is justified. (…) How were 50 SS-men (some say even fewer than that) with the help of some 200 Ukrainians and an equal number of Latvians able to pull this off so smoothly?[228]

22. Jews leading their children to the lorry, destined for death. Lodz ghetto, 1942.

One of the most moving of Jewish sources regarding the Holocaust are the poems of Icchak Kacenelson. In a most transparent manner, he offers the nightmare of crimes perpetrated by Jews on Jews with the sensitivity possessed only by poets. In his poem, *Oh Pain of Mine*, we find such stanzas:

---

[228] Ringelblum E., *"Kronika getta warszawskiego wrzesień 1939 – styczeń 1943"*, Warszawa 1983, p. 404, 407, 410 and 426-428. [See also: "Notes from the Warsaw Ghetto" by Emanuel Ringelblum, paperback, Ibooks Inc., 2006].

I'm the one who saw, who observed from up close
As children, wives and husbands, and my grey-haired elders
Like rocks and scraps were tossed/crowded onto trucks by the oppressor
Who beat them without a hint of compassion, insulted them with inhumane words.

> *I watched this from behind a window, I saw gangs of murderers –*
> *Oh, my God, I saw those beating and the beaten who were going to their deaths...*
> *And I folded my hands in shame... shame and humiliation –*
> *The hands of Jews assigned death to the Jews – the helpless Jews!*

Traitors who ran up the empty streets in their shiny shoes.
As though with the Swastika emblazoned on their hats – they charged angrily wearing the Star of David
Wild, with arrogance on their mouths that uttered broken words they did not understand,
They threw us down the stairs and dragged us from our homes.

> *Ripping doors off their hinges and forcing their way inside, goons,*
> *With their clubs raised ready to strike – into the homes overcome by fright.*
> *They beat us, chased our elders, hurried our youngest*
> *Somewhere onto the streets of dismay. And they spit God straight in the face.*

They found us inside closets and dragged us out from under the beds,
And cursed, "Move it! God damn it! To the umschlag! That is your place!"
All of us were dragged from our homes where they later lingered and went through our things,
To take what last bits of clothing, bread and grits remained.

> *And on the street – madness! Take a look and freeze in your tracks,*
> *Because this is a dead street, with one shout it turned into horror –*
> *Empty from end to end, and completely full like never before –*
> *Trucks! This is a heavy load of despair and screams for these trucks...*

There are Jews inside! Tearing their hair from their heads and folding their hands.
Some are quiet – their silence even greater than the screams.
They look... Their eyes... Is this a dream? Perhaps just a nightmare and nothing more.
And next to them the Jewish police – cruel and wild thugs!

And looking on from the side – a German with a slight smile on his face,
A German has paused and looks on from a distance – he is not getting
involved,
He is assigning death to My Jews by Jewish hands![229]

23. German watching the departure of Jews for death camps.
Lodz ghetto, 1942.

For Icchak Kacenelson, an eyewitness to the crimes, whose poetry constitutes an undisputed historical source, *the oppressors* who *beat without a hint of compassion, insulted with inhumane words,* were his fellow Jews. Jews were also the ones who *assigned death to Jews – helpless Jews!* There are, of course, those historians for whom a poem is hardly a trustworthy, reliable enough source suitable for judging the events of history. It is, above

---

229 I. Kacenelson, *Piesn o zamordowanym narodzie żydowskim [The Song of the Murdered Jewish Nation]*, Warszawa 1982, p. 23. Itzhak Katzenelson (1886-1944) – an outstanding poet, a playwright and a Hebrew translator. He conducted a secret educational activity in the Warsaw Ghetto. Deported to a concentration camp in April 1943, he was killed in 1944 in Auschwitz; an author of a terrifying *The Song of the Murdered Jewish Nation*. **Katzenelson claimed that his nation had been murdered.** Out of respect for the victims, the murdered Katzenelson's terminology is closer to me than that of the Jewish post-war opinion-forming circles.

all else, an emanation of the poets emotions and talent, and occasionally even the product of his fantasy – hardly proof of the past. Except that, there are quite a few Jewish sources which confirm the poetic truth presented by Kacenelson regarding the extermination of the Jewish people. Quite a few Jewish historical sources are in agreement with the fact that the most brutal as well as most important part of the German plan to exterminate the Jews – daily quotas for capturing a certain number of people destined for death, delivering them to the location from which the trains departed, loading them onto the train – was all performed by Jews. The Germans, in the Lodz ghetto for example, showed up a half hour prior to the departure of the trainloads of Jews that had been prepared by Jews.

Ad 4. Transporting the Warsaw Jews to the death camps in Treblinka, and the Jews from other cities to other death camps. The trains which transported the Warsaw Jews to Treblinka, just like other trains carrying Jews to other death camps, were usually operated by Polish engineers and conductors in so much as it was Polish trains, Polish tracks and Polish railway side-tracks that were used to transport the cargo of Jews destined for death, as the actual extermination of Jews that was performed by Germans was conducted on Polish territory. The logistics behind running the transportion of Jews to the death camps was in the hands of German administration. The train cars were escorted by Germans along with Ukrainians serving in military formations and collaborating with the Germans. Jews did not participate in this phase of the extermination of their own nation.

Ad 5: Preparing the condemned for death (cutting off their hair, confiscating their valuables, baggage, etc…) and raking up any belongings left behind by the murdered. As far as the role played by Jews on the final path of the Jews, we can find a series of memoirs and documentation on the matter. Similarly as in other camps, at the death camp in Sobibór, Jews performed a whole array of functions. Thomas Toivi Blatt recalls:

My heart was paralyzed with panic and fear. Sobibór! I was in the death factory. From the loft, through a wide gap, in the place where the slanted roof met the wall, looking down I saw the camp grounds. A labyrinth of squares surrounded by barbed wire and lookout towers. (…) Shortly thereafter, the empty square opposite the barrack was full of prisoners. I was looking for someone I could talk to. (…) I felt someone pulling at my sleeve. I turned and saw an old friend. "Józek!" I shouted. We embraced. (…) "Tell me something, Józek. What am I supposed to be doing here? What kind of place is this?" (…) "This is the death camp. There is no selection here. Your transport found its way to the camp, not the gas, because a few days ago, the Germans killed seventy two Dutch Jews who attempted to escape. You're taking their place." (…)

Józek gave me some advice on who to look out for, what to do and what not to do, but I didn't listen to him. He asked if I wanted to meet his girl. The womens' barracks weren't too far away. We went inside and climbed up into the loft. There were a couple of girls sitting up there, among them was Józek's girl. She was absolutely beautiful and couldn't be more than seventeen years old. Józek introduced us to each other, we talked a bit and then went outside together. The sound of music reached our ears. We followed the sound to the back room of a tailor's workshop. In the middle of this dreadful place there was a small orchestra playing and a couple was dancing the tango! (…) "Józek, what is going on here? How can they be laughing, dancing, chatting and thinking about women? Look around… There's barbed wire here, there, everywhere you look. We will never get out of here." "Toivi" he answered, "why are you surprised? Barely a few hours ago you were free. Given enough time, you too will get used to this. We all know what's awaiting us. Do you see that fire over there? As we speak, your entire family is being turned to ashes. Just as my mother was six months earlier. I didn't cry. You're not crying either. You want to say that you no longer have what it takes to cry, that you have no tears left? That's not the reason. You're not crying because we've all become automated. The animal instinct to survive has kicked in and taken over. If we were to think, feel and act like normal people, we would go mad. (…)

The Supplier of Raw Material. In the middle of the night, I was rudely awakened by the noise of a screeching whistle. My companion from up on the upper level informed me that a new convoy of Jews has arrived – Jews from Holland. The convoy from Holland sometimes arrived at three in the morning.

While Jews from Eastern Europe came to Sobibór by truck or overloaded cargo train, the Dutch Jews arrived on passenger trains. The Jewish administration in Westerbork, in Holland, where the convoys of Jews originated, was concerned about transportation conditions. There were doctors and nurses aboard the trains to care for the sick, as well as childcare and care for the disadvantaged. Inside the attached cargo wagons, there were ample supplies of food or medicine.

Bunio, the kapo stormed into the barrack and, as he turned on the light, barked, "Baggage handlers and hairdressers – get ready!" A group of prisoners immediately jumped down from the loft. They quickly got dressed and stepped outside into the courtyard. Clearly they were expecting a larger than usual convoy as the kapo pulled some extra prisoners down from the upper level. I was included in this. A few of us were designated as "baggage handlers", a few as "hairdressers". The whole camp was brightly lit. As we were being led to our work stations, I noticed a commotion taking place on the unloading platform. The arriving Jews were exiting the train, a dump truck pulled up. As I later found out, all the oversized and heavy baggage was thrown onto the dump truck along with the sick, old, and crippled people, and those unable to get around on their own. The rest followed an SS-man to a long barrack.

Our group of eight was brought to this barrack and we were told to wait for the Jews. This was a large barrack with no windows. It had a wide, open entryway and exit. Two prisoners were set up at the entrance, four in the middle of the barrack, and two more at the exit. We were supposed to inform the Jews entering the barrack that they were to deposit all carry-on baggage and ladies handbags here.

The first group of the condemned was approaching. The women were walking in front. They were elegantly dressed. I felt numb and paused for a moment. It was very early in the morning and many of the women were carrying sleeping children in their arms. They had not the slightest clue that they were heading for death.

Suddenly, the smack of a horsewhip reminded me that I am not a passive observer in all of this. The more seasoned, more experienced prisoners mechanically repeated their sentence in Dutch, informing the people passing by to deposit their personal belongings here. I started to imitate the words they were saying. An SS-man was posted at the exit. When he noticed someone exiting the building with some sort of package or bag, in an infuriated voice, he reminded us of our responsibilities. (...)

A parade of approximately five hundred people passed through the barrack. New wagon cars were entering the side tracks. It was necessary to evacuate the premises. The barrack in which I was standing was connected by a side wall to three pairs of doors leading to smaller barracks. A few prisoners entered through those doors. Together we loaded stacks of baggage onto blankets and carried them into the adjoining rooms. There were tables set up in the middle, and there were women standing around each of these tables sorting through the raked up plunder. We were emptying the blankets one by one. Soon enough, the large temporary barrack was empty and the sand floor was cleaned and smoothed with a rake.

Now the SS-men walked us to the gate of the locked courtyard and told us to wait. We could hear a single German voice coming from inside the courtyard. We heard the end of an announcement. After some time, the gate was opened and we stepped inside. The courtyard was now quiet and empty. The only things left were small piles of neatly folded clothing and pairs of shoes tied together by their laces. We threw everything onto the blankets and pulled them out through the same gate. Following the others, I found myself inside a large passageway that was constructed from two barracks that were connected to each other. We threw the clothing down onto some large low tables. I figured out that all of these things were left behind by the Jews who were told to undress their clothes.

Because there was another group of Jews approaching from the train platforms, we were ordered to return to our previous stations inside the large barrack where personal baggage was confiscated. The entire procedure was repeated. Afterwards, we once again walked up to the gate to the courtyard and waited for the SS-men to let us inside. (...)

I heard the growl of an exhaust engine, and immediately following was one horrifying, albeit muffled, sound of people screaming. At first, the sound of the voices was greater than the roar of the engines, however after a few minutes it gradually dissipated. I froze. I was convinced that the people currently getting undressed in the courtyard heard the noises and screams. However, I don't think they realized what they signified. The wailing, although drowned out by the sounds of the growling engine, and the thick walls of the gas chamber, could have been mistaken for the sounds of a thunderstorm approaching. (...)

These naked people, just like those that came before them, entered onto the path the Nazis spitefully dubbed "the Path to Heaven" [Himmelfahrtstrasse]. The path which had already been stomped down by hundreds of soles was bordered on both sides by barbed wire. It led to the barrack where women had their hair cut off. From there, the lambs for the slaughter went directly to the gas chambers.

Our work had reached its conclusion. SS-Oberscharfuhrer, Karl Frenzel, selected four prisoners, among them, me. He walked us over to the barrack which stood about ten meters away from the gas chambers. Inside, there were some wooden benches and chairs. The dark-haired, not so tall SS-man, Josef Wolf, was standing in the middle of the barrack. I was handed a large pair of scissors and I just waited. Naked women started to pour into the barrack. I didn't know how to act. "What am I supposed to do," I asked a friend? "Just cut their hair in clumps. It doesn't have to be cut too close to the scalp. If one of them has braids or something, just cut the braids off."

I was very shy. I had never even seen a naked woman before. Of course, like any other fifteen-year-old, I was very interested in the opposite sex, but seeing these naked, humiliated women, I felt embarrassed and abashed. I tried to avoid making any eye-contact. The women looked very dejected. They kept their eyes lowered and tried to cover themselves up as best they could with their hands. (…) They were due to die in a matter of minutes and there was nothing we could do. The women left the barrack, we put all their hair into empty potato sacks, and later carried them out to a storage room.

After about three hours of work and the death of more than two thousand people, the SS-men instructed us to return to our barracks. (…) In the morning, another group finished up the sorting and raking of the plunder.[230]

The plot of the movie directed by Claude Lanzmann in the eighties, the documentary, *Shoah*, contains a thread in the story of a Jew who, during the last war, similar to the author quoted above, in a death camp cut the hair of Jewish women prior to their entering the gas chamber. In this manner, he prepared almost all the female members of his own family for death. The hair-cutter of the camp survived the war. He moved to Israel

---

230 T. Blatt, *Z popiołów Sobiboru, [From the Ashes of Sobibor]*, Chelm 2002, p. 89-95.

and opened his own hair salon. At the time Lanzmann was making his film, he was still cutting hair of Jews in his hair salon on a daily basis.

Ad 6. The Killing of the Jews. Jews in the death camps did not operate the gas chambers.

Ad 7. The destruction of bodies of the dead. As it is described by a prisoner from Sobibor, as well as according to the memoirs of people similar to him, Jews most certainly took part in the process of clearing out the gas chambers of their murdered brethren, and in disposing of their dead bodies:

As we approached our barracks, we heard the rhythmic, deafening pounding. It sounded as though someone were throwing stones into a metal bin. The sounds were coming from around the vicinity of the gas chambers. I later learned what that sound was. The prisoners who worked at the crematorium were throwing remains into a narrow-tracked dump truck which then drove the corpses to a place to be burned.[231]

Jews, with the exception of transporting the condemned to death in the death camps and having a hand directly in assigning them death in the gas chambers, actively participated in five of the seven steps of the extermination of the Jews. It is necessary to emphasize their unequivocal participation in certain steps. Inasmuch as the participation of Jews in the two final steps - the "preparation" of those going to their deaths and the disposal of their bodies – were conducted on the premises of the death camps, under coercion, they do not carry with them the character of actions as an executioner. One can try to consider the mindset of people who survived, whose lives were spared by "preparing" those closest to them for death, but the mere reality of their imprisonment and the ever-present threat of death does remove the stigma of executioner from them. Even more so, however, it is important to separate the first three steps with absolute clarity (containing the Jewish population in large Jewish autonomies located within greater Polish cities; disseminating German lies as to the true nature of the "deportations"; rounding up people and loading them onto various modes of transportation), all of which were performed by Jews willingly, and that does qualify them as executioners of their own nation.

---

[231] Ibidem, p. 95.

The principles of executing the first phase (in historiography it is called intermediate extermination), the gathering up of dispersed Jews from throughout small towns and village settlements within autonomous territories and concentrating them in larger urban areas, were established during a time when Poland was still fighting a defensive war. September 21, 1939, at the council of Berlin, the Germans decided on how to proceed with regard to population recognized in Nazi nomenclature as Jews. In the famous telephone message from the head of the main office, R. Heydrich, which outlined the main goals of German policies with regard to Jews, as well as specified the role Jews themselves would play in bringing to fruition the German plans:

Regarding the session of today's council meeting, I am once again pointing out that the planned dual movement (that is the final solution) must be held in absolute secrecy. It is imperative to distinguish between: 1. the final solution (which requires more time), 2. from the steps leading to the final solution (which will be brought about in shorter periods). (...) The first step in achieving the final solution is the concentration of Jews from provincial areas into larger cities. (...) A Jewish Council of Elders (Judenrat) must be established within every Jewish community. Every Council [Judenrat] must carry the burden of full responsibility, in every sense of the word, of timely and efficient fulfillment of all instructions given.[232]

· A salient point is that in the entire area of Poland that was occupied by the Germans, there was not one single Jewish community that did not conform to the first and key command, dispersing from within an administrative structure which is prepared to govern the Jewish population and cooperate with the occupying forces. In the months that followed, in every locality where Jewish communities existed, Councils of Elders started to appear. They were called Judenrats and they took over all the hitherto eternal functions that once belonged to the community authorities (imposing taxes, giving orders), as well as carrying on negotiations with the Germans regarding the conditions of building, functioning and

---

[232] *Eksterminacja Żydów na ziemiach polskich w okresie okupacji hitlerowskiej - zbiór dokumentów, [Extermination of Jews under the German occupation of Poland – document collection]*, Jewish Historical Institute, Warszawa 1957, p. 26.

management, and the subordination of Jewish autonomies to the Germans, and diligently carrying out German orders.

The most ludicrous form authority in the Jewish autonomy, but at the same time the most helpful to the Germans in realizing their plans for the Holocaust, was assumed by the Judenrat in charge of the Lodz autonomy. Already in the middle of October of 1939, Chaim Rumkowski[233] accepted the position of Superior of the Jewish Elders [the Judenrat] from the hands of the Germans. He dissolved the existing governing body of the Jewish Community and proceeded to construct a "Jewish Nation" in Lodz which he ran based on the example set by Nazi leaders.[234]

The situation was similar in other autonomies and ghettos. The obedience of Jews with regard to the Judenrats was absolute in many respects, including the death penalty. In other words, there was a group of Jews in every Jewish autonomy on Polish land that was prepared to cooperate unconditionally with the Germans and to fulfill every German command. In every German community during WWII, one was able to find a group of Jews for whom following German commands was more important than the greater good of their own nation. Emanual Ringelblum writes:

W(ajn)traub from Luków, a slovenly creature, a Jew with a beard and corkscrew curls, with his usual vest on top, a regular with regard to connections – everything that takes place does so with his mediation. How did he win the favors of the mayor – it's a mystery to everyone. He's the one who decides who gets work and where. (...)

In the Katowice region the certificate of leadership of the Jews has been seen. He can receive 20,000 zlotys, he can say which Jews get arrested, he can move around freely anytime, day or night. (...)

---

233 Until the outbreak of the war, M. Ch. Rumkowski was little-known and an inconspicuous person. Born in 1877 in Russia, during World War I he settled in Łódź, where he was a merchant. He had no other education than 4 or 5 classes of a Tsarist school. In the 1920s and the 1930s he was the president of the Jewish Orphanage in Helenówek near Lodz and the member of the Lodz Jewish Community on behalf of the Zionists. In August 1944, together with the 70 thousand of the remaining inhabitants of the Lodz ghetto, he was deported to Auschwitz and gassed.

234 Dobroszycki L., *Preface* to: *"Kronika getta łódzkiego"* ["The Lodz Ghetto Diary"], Łódź 1965, p. XIX-XXI.

The story about chairman of Warsaw Jews Czerniakowy and the horsewhip went something like this: when the horsewhip broke during the beating of Jews who arrived late for work, he ordered that it be sent to the saddler for repair and then returned to his office at nine o'clock.[235]

The first two years of the war, 1939-1941, were a time during which, on the one hand, Jewish authorities (Judenrat chairmen, mayors, and such) developed the structure of authority (the police, emergency medical services, a communication system, the postal service, the prison system, public welfare and such) and transformed Jewish communities into autonomies which were colloquially referred to as ghettos, which answered to them directly and to the Germans indirectly. On the other hand, they became experts at enforcing authority and exacting from the Jewish population both German commands and their own German-style commands. Concurrently, this was a period when, thanks to the productive help that resulted from the cooperation of the Jewish authorities, they executed the plan of intermediate extermination (they concentrated the Jewish population in large urban areas), and in accordance with the guidelines cited above, were able to adhere to "the final solution" regarding the matter of the Jews, the annihilation of the Jews.

On June 22, 1941, Hitler undertook aggression against the Soviet Union. Six to eight weeks later, Eichmann (a high-ranking official of the Third Reich – E.K.) was called to Heydrich's office in Berlin. On July 31, Heydrich received a letter from Hermann Göring, a Reich marshal, plenipotentiary of matters relating to the four-year plan, and last but not least, Hitler's second-in-command in the national apparatus (as opposed to the party apparatus). This letter commanded Heydrich to prepare 'the global solution (Gesamtlösung) of the Jewish matter in the European spheres of German influences', and also to present 'the general solution (Endlösung) of the Jewish matter'. The moment Heydrich received these instructions, 'he had prepared some time earlier – as he explained in his letter to the army's higher command dated November 6, 1941 – the final solution to the Jewish problem, a project that had been

---

[235] Ringelblum E., *"Kronika getta warszawskiego wrzesień 1939 – styczeń 1943"*, Warszawa 1983, p. 41, 54 and 120. [See also: "Notes from the Warsaw Ghetto" by Emanuel Ringelblum, paperback, Ibooks Inc., 2006].

delegated to him years before', and from the beginning of the war with Russia, has been directing massive murder (campaigns) in the East carried out by Einsatzgruppen. Heydrich started his conversation with Eichmann with 'a short speech on the topic of emigration,' (...) he then declared, 'The Führer has ordered the physical liquidation of the Jews.' (...) The official codename for the extermination will be 'the Final Solution' – this was determined during the ongoing Eichmann trial in Jeruzalem.[236]

In 1942, the Germans undertook the complete annihilation of Polish Jews. When they commanded Jewish policemen and officials to deliver (round up and deliver) a certain number of residents of the Warsaw autonomy to the trains heading for the death camps, senator Adam Czerniakow, chairman of the Warsaw Judenrat, Mayor of the Independent Jewish Autonomy in Warsaw [**"Selbständige Autonomie"**], upon realizing the bankruptcy of the Jewish policies of collaborating with the Germans, did not want to have his hands in the annihilation of his own brethren. He committed suicide.

Adam Czerniakow saved his honor.

Adam Czerniakow was an exceptional figure.

The authorization to send Warsaw Jews to their death was signed by other members of the Judenrat.

A fine example of a chairmen for all the other ghettos in German occupied Poland was chairman Rumkowski in Lodz who did not hesitate to carry out even this command from his occupiers. When the Germans continually demanded tens of thousands of victims, he personally participated in preparing the list of the condemned. He did not hesitate even when Germans commanded him to release Jewish children for the slaughter. In the name of deranged theories of subservience with regard to the Germans, and the equally deranged theories of sparing the lives of a portion of the Jewish population at the price of the lives of other Jews, he surrendered that which every nation deems its most precious asset: its own children. Marek Edelman says:

---

[236] H. Arendt, *Eichmann w Jerozolimie*, Kraków1987, p. 107-108; [see also: *Eichmann In Jerusalem: A Report on the Banality of Evil,* The Viking Press, New York 1964].

Today, Mostowicz (Arnold) says that Rumkowski acted justly because he saved the lives of a certain number of Jews who did not perish in the Death March. It's unheard of that one can be prepared to take the responsibility for killing people because maybe ten out of a hundred will survive... If that is morality, then too bad.[237]

Did he not realize that he was, in fact, only the person who carried out Nazi commands, a blind instrument in their hands? – this was a question posed by the Jewish historian, professor Lucjan Dobroszycki regarding Rumkowski's stance twenty some years after the war.[238]

When the Germans undertook the "Final Solution", the mass extermination of the Jewish population, when the time of the Holocaust had arrived, all the administrative structures of the independent Jewish autonomy in Poland (Judenrats, officials of the Jewish police, emergency services workers and officials of other departments) actively participated in: lying to the Jewish population as to the purpose and direction of the deportations, depriving them of any chance to escape or pose any sort of opposition; selecting members of the Jewish population based on estimating the order of certain social groups, and occasionally even people for the transport of death; executing the round-ups and delivering the captured residents of the ghettos to the location from where the Germans dispatched them to the death camps.[239]

The tragedy of the position the Jewish authorities within the autonomies and ghettos had found themselves in lies in the fact that, the Germans, even without them, would have deported, and did deport, Jews. Such was the opinion of Jewish historian Professor Lucjan Dobroszycki.[240] The

---

[237] Marek Edelman, in: Grupińska A., *"Ciągle po kole"* ["Still Round the Circle: Talks with the Soldiers of the Warsaw Ghetto"], Warszawa 2005, p. 309.

[238] Dobroszycki L., *Preface* to: *"Kronika getta łódzkiego"* ["The Lodz Ghetto Diary"], Łódź 1965, p. XIX-XXI.

[239] H. Arendt, *Eichmann w Jerozolimie*, Kraków 1987, p. 117; [see also: *Eichmann In Jerusalem: A Report on the Banality of Evil*, The Viking Press, New York 1964]. H. Arendt writes: „Sonderkommandos (special forces), which consisted of Jews, took part in the extermination everywhere".

[240] Dobroszycki L., *Preface* to: *"Kronika getta łódzkiego"* ["The Lodz Ghetto Diary"], Łódź 1965, p. XIX-XXI.

first portion of this thesis is not really subject to dispute. With or without the help of the Jews, the Germans would most certainly have taken on the realization of the "Final Solution", or would at least have begun the deportations of Jews. It is not so certain that the Germans would have been able to realize their plan to annihilate the Jewish nation without the help of the Jews, or that they would have successfully managed the deportation of this population because:

- How many tens of thousands of German soldiers would have had to be utilized by the Germans between the years 1939-1941 in order to deport the number approaching millions of Polish Jews to large cities, and to maintain order and see to it that their orders/ commands were carried out within the autonomies (ghettos) had it not been the Jews themselves who carried out that part of the plan for the Germans? Had the Jewish leaders not executed the deportations themselves, would the Germans even have been able to lock the Jewish population up in the ghettos to start with?

- How many millions of (Deutsch) Marks would the Germans have had to spend and how many laborers would they have had to employ in order to surround the autonomies and ghettos with walls to hide them from the Christian world if the Jews had not agreed to finance and build these walls? Had the Polish Jews refused to finance and build the walls around the Jewish ghettos and autonomies, would the Germans have succeeded in isolating the Polish Jews from the Christians?[241]

- How many tens of thousands of German soldiers would the Germans have had to remove from the German fronts in 1942 in order to capture three million Polish Jews who were hiding out in forests or in their own homes (in wardrobes, bunkers, etc...), and then deliver them to the train stations and load them up onto the

---

[241] E. Ringelblum says: 'Today, on the 30th of March [1940] the news has been confirmed that the Jewish Community had been ordered to build walls in the place of barbed wires [...]. A number of streets have been closed. [...] To build thick walls at the corners of the Próżna and Złota Streets will cost the Jewish Community 250 thousand zlotys.'

train wagons had the Jews themselves not done the dirtiest of the dirty work for the Germans? Or would the fact that the Germans had been fighting a war on two fronts by June 1941, and the tactics of war involved, even allowed the Germans to pull off such an operation at all?

Questions such as these can be multiplied endlessly. Military, financial and bricklayer experts are capable of answering these questions precisely and professionally. One needs not be an expert, however, in order to conclude that without the help of Polish Jews, it would have been extremely difficult for the Germans to realize their plan of annihilating Polish Jews. Within the Jewish autonomy in Lodz, there were barely a handful of Germans that participated in the annihilation of the Jews, *who arrived a half hour prior to the departure of the trains.* Their role was more supervisory with regard to the departure of the trains loaded up with Lodz Jews being taken to the gas chambers at the Chelmno death camp on the Ner river. Preparing the lists of those sentenced to death, capturing the doomed, confiscating their baggage and delivering them to the trains was carried out by Jews alone. The situation was similar in the Warsaw autonomy where, according to Emanuel Ringelblum: *50 SS-men (some say that even fewer than that) with the help of about 200 Ukrainians and an equal number of Latvians,* was sufficient in supervising the round-ups being conducted by Warsaw Jews, and in bringing about the death of three hundred thousand people…

A great number of Jew-executioners had, by the end of the Second World War, become victims. Once the Jewish collaborators had performed their assigned tasks, the Germans did kill them. In August, 1944, Chaim Rumkowski, the head of Jewish Elders in Lodz, along with his entourage and their families, the executioners of Lodz Jews, including some 70,000 people, were transported by the Germans to Auschwitz, and nearly every single one of them perished. In this way, a greater portion of these Jew-executioners from Lodz, found themselves in the same queue as their victims.

From among the Jew-executioners, those who managed to escaped the Holocaust with their lives, in the sixty years since the end of WWII, have done and continue to do everything possible, to make

sure that the truth about their deeds in the role of executioners during the annihilation of Polish Jews never sees the light of day, never reaches the consciousness of future generations of Jews and the entire world.

There is absolutely no doubt regarding the fact that tens if not hundreds of thousands of Jew-exectioners (150,000 Jewish soldiers of Hitler; 10,000 in Lodz, etc.) are on an equal plane with the Germans when it comes to being guilty of the annihilation of 3 million Polish Jews and 3 million European Jews. From among the four categories of guilt as defined by Karl Jaspers, there is not a shred of doubt the Polish Jews are guilty of all four types for their deeds:

political guilt: the Jewish leaders who, through their decisions which were political in character, (constructing in Poland the Jewish autonomies under the auspices of the Germans and making them subservient to German rule), acquiesced the Germans in the annihilation of the Jews, therefore bear political guilt;

criminal guilt: all Jews whose crime consisted of actions objectively determined and being outside of unequivocal laws (participating in deceiving, capturing, uncovering hideouts, delivering other Jews to the trains, and such) bear criminal guilt;

moral guilt: all Jews, for the deeds which, on an individual basis, were committed against other Jews, bear a moral responsibility; Jews, as a rule, cannot hide behind the notion of "orders are orders"; a crime remains a crime even if committed as a direct order and is subject to moral punishment;

metaphysical guilt: in which, above all, God resides, for there exists a solidarity among men as human beings, that we are all universally responsible for every wrong and every injustice in the world.

x   x   x

Otto Adolf Eichmann, who, within the structures of Hitler's Germany, was responsible for transporting European Jews to the death camps, personally did not murder Jews. It could not even be proved that he had function similar to that of the Germans within the Jewish autonomies in Łódź, that of directly supervising the trains carrying Jewish people departing for the gas chambers. Despite that, when asked during the ongoing trial against him in Jerusalem in 1961, whether or not he had played a role in exterminating European Jews, he responded: *Of course, I played a role in the extermination of Jews, of course, if I hadn't transported them out, they would not have ended up in the hands of the oppressors. What is it exactly that I am supposed to be admitting to here?* – he asked.[242]

Emanuel Ringelblum, in describing the horror of Jewish crimes, summarized in this way: *Every Warsaw Jew, every woman and every child can cite to thousands of facts relating to the inhumane cruelty and the fury of the Jewish police. Those who survived shall never forget it, and it should be punished accordingly.*[243]

The will of the Jewish people, providing that the voice of the chronicler can be considered as expressing the will of murdered Jews, was to punish not only the German, but also the Jewish executioners. The German executioner, Otto Adolf Eichmann, who was responsible "only" for coordinating the logistics of transporting the Jews to the death camps, during the trial brought against him in Jerusalem testified that "if he had not transported them (the Jews)out, they would not have ended up in the hands of the oppressors". And concurred that the most suitable punishment for him would be the death penalty. That was the sentence that came down from the Israeli court on May 31, 1962 – death by hanging in Ramleh prison near Tel Aviv.

This is something somewhat absurd, as I have never, to this day, come across a situation similar to that of the Eichmann case where the Jewish executioner confessed. I have also never heard of such a case where they would request the death penalty for their cooperation in the Holocaust and the murder of (their) innocent brethren, or that such a punishment would be granted.

---

[242] H. Arendt, *Eichmann w Jerozolimie*, Kraków1987, p. 68; [see also: *Eichmann In Jerusalem: A Report on the Banality of Evil,* The Viking Press, New York 1964].

[243] H. Arendt, *Eichmann w Jerozolimie*, Kraków1987, p. 428; [see also: *Eichmann In Jerusalem: A Report on the Banality of Evil,* The Viking Press, New York 1964]. H. Arendt writes: „Sonderkommandos (special forces), which consisted of Jews, took part in the extermination everywhere".

Jewish executioners: donning German military formation uniforms, Jewish police uniforms or civilians sitting behind desks, whose actions are reminiscent of those performed by Eichmann.

In philosophical reflections pertaining to the Holocaust, two types of executions are identified: people who were directly involved in the various phases of the annihilation, as well as bureaucrats whose participation in the genocide was limited to making decisions from behind desks directly related to the realization thereof. This identification was, however, formulated with regard to the Germans, or Nazis, as such terminology is widely accepted by authors of various circumspections, but there is no doubt they also refer to Jewish executioners who colluded with the Germans in the annihilation of their own nation. For among them there were those who captured, chased down and loaded helpless Jews onto the trains (the Jewish police first and foremost), as well as those whose decisions from behind desks dispatched other Jews to their death (Judenrat clerks among whom Rumkowski from Lodz was a shining example).

The first person to bring attention to the murderers from behind desks was Hannah Arendt in her book, *Eichmann in Jerusalem*. In conducting an analysis of the model personal murderer from behind a desk, she put forth a series of extraordinary relevant propositions crucial to the understanding of the Holocaust, about which Alan Milchman and Alan Rosenberg wrote the following: ""First of all, she has disregarded the circulating wisdom which is rooted in the belief that those who were engaged in the Holocaust were solely sadists and pathological murderers. Second of all, she disregards the idea that in working in planning and implementing the "Final Solution", they had to have been fanatical Nazis or diehard anti-Semites".[244]

A penetrating analysis of Jewish sources with regard to the aspect of Jewish executioners in its entirety confirms the thesis put forth by Hannah Arendt:

- Not all the Jewish executioners who collaborated with the Germans were sadists and pathological murderers. Granted, the majority of

---

[244] A. Milchman, A. Rosenberg, *Eksperymenty w mysleniu o Holokauscie [The Experiments with Thinking about the Holocaust]*, Warszawa 2003, p. 179.

the Jewish police probably were, but not the representatives of the Judenrat who in giving orders, propagating German lies and preparing lists of the condemned were taking away the lives of other Jews. The embodiment of such an executioner was Rumkowski.

• It would be difficult to assign to the Jewish executioners fanatical Nazism or rampant anti-Semitism. Rumkowski and other leaders of the Judenrat emulated their own authority on the model exemplified by Hitler, but because they were Jews, it is hardly plausible that they were driven by anti-Semitism. The question is, if not anti-Semitism, then what is the proper name for the sentiment that was the driving force behind Jews sending other Jews to their deaths?

In the summer of 1942, three hundred thousand Jews were sent from Warsaw to the gas chambers in Treblinka. Ringelblum poses the question of how it was possible that fifty SS-men and the few hundred Latvians and Ukrainians who cooperated with them were able to execute such a despicable crime of such magnitude so smoothly. In the light of the Jewish sources presented above, confirmed by thousands of other reports and archival documentation, the answer to the question put forth by the chronicler is obvious: it was possible because the most hideous, the most disgraceful and brutal part of the genocide of the Jews was carried out by the Jews themselves.

It was the same in Warsaw as it was in all the other autonomies and ghettos in occupied Poland. Worth mentioning is the fact that, in making the decision to cross over to the side of the executioners, every single Jew who executed the commands (those that were given with regard to the realization of the first three steps of the Holocaust) did so as free people, and the freedom of their choice is the condition of their absolute responsibility for the deeds executed. Indeed, every Jewish policeman and bureaucrat, who through their actions enabled the annihilation of the Jewish people, had the option of not participating in them or abandoning them all together. In choosing not to do so, they were, and forever will be, known as executioners to their contemporaries and to their future generations. It is, therefore, useless to continue with the decades-old silence and diminishing of the role played by Jews in the annihilation of the Jewish nation.

As a result of the afore mentioned proof of participation of Jewish executioners with regard to the annihilation of the Jewish nation, the linear narrative regarding the annihilation of Jews in Poland as within the relation of German executioner and Jewish victim does not stand up in the face of scrutiny of historical reality. Insofar as the concept of executioner-victim has exhausted this quandary with regard to other nations in modern Europe, including those nations that were subject to the planned genocide by Hitler's Germany (i.e. Poles and Gypsies), the matter regarding the Jewish nation constitutes a source of misunderstandings and outright lies. A similar conclusion was reached by the American historian Bryan Mark Rigg, who wrote this about the 150,000 Jewish soldiers of Hitler, that these people: "were fighting for a system which not only deprived them of human rights, but also usually murdered their kin".[245]

If, consequently, Jews actively participated in the killing of their own nation, and a majority of whom were not only executioners, but also a military force supporting a German fascist totalitarianism, then all of the commonly accepted notions regarding the Jewish nation within the framework of the concept of executioner and victim are shattered. In that regard, if we wish to arrive at an understanding of the despicable days of the Holocaust, one must search for other explanations. Above all it must be stated that the role of executioner with regard to Polish Jews during the last war was played not only by Germans, but by all Jews who, for whatever reasons, participated in any of the steps of the annihilation of their own nation or who, through their service in the German military formations, supported the genocide by Hitler's Germany.

---

[245] B.M. Rigg, *Żydowscy żołnierze Hitlera: nieznana historia nazistowskich ustaw rasowych i mężczyzn pochodzenia żydowskiego w armii niemieckiej*, Warszawa 2005, p. 130 and 288. [*Hitler's Jewish Soldiers:The Untold Story of Nazi Racial Laws and Men of Jewish Descent in the German Military*, University Press of Kansas 2002]. See also: Jeremy Noaks, *The Development of Nazi Policy towards the German-Jewish „Misschlinge" 1933-1945*, in: „Leo Baeck Yearbook", Nr 34, Year 1989, p. 291-354.

Merely stating that some significant, albeit to this day unknown exact number, or part of the Jewish population played the role of executioner with regard to murdered Jews and that they were partners in the crime of genocide does not exhaust the quandary. Insofar as the Germans and their collaborating representatives from other nations are concerned with regard to the Holocaust, the dubious title of executioner has been attached to them permanently and for all of eternity, the majority of Jewish executioners will go down in the history of world events as victims. This is so because, in the end, the Germans did not spare the lives of the Jewish executioners. Upon jointly murdering millions of Jews, the Germans put their obedient partakers of genocidal commands to death. In this way, the Jewish executioners were automatically deemed victims, i.e., people who had fallen victim to German violence and force. To put it another way, by dying at the hands of German executioners, the Jewish executioners are added to the praise and glory of the pantheon of millions of Jewish martyrs, and as a direct result of their martyrdom, their previous atrocities as executioners fall by the wayside.

Although unheard of in historiography, in the sixty years that have passed since the end of WWII and the Holocaust, the only information that has passed into the consciousness of historians and the population at large is that of all the murdered Jews being victims. Despite the fact that the most serious, and from the point of view of the most indisputable and trustworthy of Jewish sources, scream that this is not the way it was, that Jews were also executioners of their own nation. And for dozens of years there has been a dead silence surrounding the matter of Jewish executioners. The only one who forty years ago had the courage to draw attention to this matter was Hannah Arendt.[246]

---

[246] Hannah Arendt was born in Hannover on the 14th of October1906. She spent her childhood and youth in Königsberg; she studied philosophy, theology and Greek in Heidelberg; at age 22 , she defended her PhD thesis under the direction of Karl Jaspers. After Hitler had come to power, she emigrated to Paris, where she studied, wrote and occupied herself with social work for Jewish orphans in Palestine. In 1940 she fled to the United States. As an editor in one of the New York publishing houses, she contributed to the publication of Franz Kafka's *Diaries* in America. In 1951 she published her three-volume work *The Origins of Totalitarianism*, which ensured her a prominent place among the philosophers of politics and political scientists. Her academic career in America includes the lectures at the

A Jewish woman, more philosopher than historian, in her book *Eichmann in Jerusalem – the Banality of Evil,* in the sixties of the previous century, was the first to draw attention to the afore mentioned matters.

Unveiling to the world a tiny selvage of a secret regarding the truth about the extermination of the Jewish nation, and drawing attention to the double role of a portion of the annihilated Jews (the executioners who, in the final analysis became victims) was already in disagreement with the stereotypes of the Jew-victims that had been promulgated throughout Jewish circles, and which was to become obligatory over the century that followed. That is why, Hanna Arendt writes: „„A vicious campaign was started which presented my book in a false light, a campaign which was organized within Jewish "directorial spheres" in Israel and the United States. There exist very few who are capable of withstanding such a campaign. (…) Public opinion, especially that which had been skillfully manipulated – as was the case here – possesses immense reactionary power. (…) The matter I dealt with was that of the cooperation between Jewish civil functionaries and those that executed the "Final Solution". This is a very inconvenient matter because it is unseemly to claim that they were traitors. (There were traitors to be found, however that is irrelevant.) In other words, everything that was perpetrated or not by Jewish civil functionaries up until 1939, even 1941, is understandable and justifiable. It's not until later that the situation becomes highly problematic. This matter presented itself during the trial, and, clearly it was my responsibility to document it. It constitutes an element of the so-called "past that is slipping away". (…) I am convinced that the only way we can reconcile with our past is by fulfilling this one condition: we begin to judge it and we will conquer it by telling the truth.""[247]

I have been dealing with the problematic nature of Polish-Jewish relations during WWII for the past twenty years. In the eighties, while I

---

renowned universities of Princeton, Columbia (the first female professor in the history of the university), Chicago, the University of California, Berkeley and the New School for Social Research. In 1958 appears her book *The Human Condition* and in 1963 *On Revolution* and *Eichmann in Jerusalem. The Life of the Mind* was published posthumously. She died in New York on December 4, 1975.

[247] H. Arendt, *Eichmann w Jerozolimie,* Kraków1987, p. 394-395; [see also: *Eichmann In Jerusalem: A Report on the Banality of Evil,* The Viking Press, New York 1964].

was researching the matter of Jewish children rescued by Polish convents, I came upon the problem of Jewish executioners of the Jewish nation. Because the entire matter seemed to me to be completely absurd and because it was in no way connected to the vein of my research, and my knowledge regarding Jews being somewhat lacking, I arrived at the conclusion that it is not my place to reach into fundamental Jewish matters so I left it where I had found it. Using the current historical problem as a gauge, that is in researching Polish-Jewish relations during WWII, at some point I arrived at the conclusion that if there is no attempt to resolve the problem which Hanna Arendt described as "a Jewish past that is slipping away", I shall never understand the Holocaust, nor Polish-Jewish relations. Therefore, despite the fact that I am completely aware that in writing this book, "the big guns" will be drawn and there will be various accusations brought forth against me, and since I am Polish – and that with my mother's milk I drank anti-Semitism – is why I am taking on the enormous task that had been attempted by Hanna Arendt, that of "reconciling to terms with our Jewish past." I am not reaching for this tumultuous Jewish past for some inexplicable reason or because I am haunted by ghosts of the past. I am reaching for it because I am an historian and I know that sorting it out will shed new light on Polish-Jewish relations between the years 1939-1945.

A probing read, Hanna Arendt's book, *Eichmann in Jerusalem*, has put me on yet another extraordinarily important trail. As a result of the trial described by the author, Eichmann, as a German criminal against the Jewish nation was lost. It is remarkable that the Jewish criminals against the Jewish nation did not bring about the same sentences.

In Israel in 1950, a law was passed requiring the prosecution of Nazi crimes against the Jewish nation, but parts X and XI of this law were written with Jewish executioners who collaborated with the Nazis in mind. They anticipated the possibility of vindication of all responsibility from crimes committed, on the grounds that it can be proved that they were committed "in an attempt to save themselves from the threat of imminent death" or in order to avoid "more severe consequences than actually existed".[248]

---

[248] ibidem, p. 394-395.

The original act from 1950, which is located in the Knesset Archives, reads:

10. שחרור מאחריות פלילית
אדם שנדרף שעשה אי שעמה או ואי שעמהו, והשעמה-אי ארבעה מהוווים יפל קוח הז, עמשה תושעמ ענמנ או עמשה השושת ,עמשה תא שה מא אי- (א)
רחשירי ביט השמפט מאחריות פלילית -
ואו ; עמשה , ובתי שמשפט שושכע שעש שמכטב ילכתו דכי ולעונ את ותואצרגמו לע ידי השעמה או אי-
; השמעה
(ב) או מא השע את השעמה או ענמנ עמשות ותמד כונוה לגמנו תוצאות ותמור רתי ותה מו ; אד הורואת אל הלא ולוחי ולבגי- , השמעה-אי וא השעמה, עמנו ונתא תוצאות השמעל ; אד העמש ידי לע וא אי- ארבעה מהוווים יפל ריבע 1 וא 2 (ו).

11. סביבות מקילות
בקביעת שנע ושל שיש אציש בייח לע וידל רביעה יפל קוח הז, היהי ביט השמפט רשאי להביא
: וובשחב ,סרוגמ המתקתה נוע,ש אתא הניסבות הבאה :
(א) מא דמ בער תא העריבה תובינסב ,אשר ,אלמלא עיפ 8, ויה ותורטוף ותא מאחריות פלילית
ואו ויה שממשות עילה ליחמת העריבה, והו אשע סמכט ולכתו דכי ולהקל תא חמות התואצות
;
(ב) העריבה לע ידי העריבה ; אד מא התיה וז העריבה לע יפ סעיפ ,1 אל טיל תיב השמפט לע העריירו
.נוע שא לק ממאסר של שבע שינים.

In Katarzyna Bednarska's translation from Polish to English the paragraphs of the Israeli act which has been mentioned by Hannah Arendt read as follows:

§ 10. Acquittal of criminal responsibility.

A person who committed a deed, or refrained from committing it, and those committing this deed or refraining from committing it constituted a crime according to the law, is taken to court. The court acquits that person of criminal responsibility:

   a.   If the person committed the deed or refrained from committing it in order to avoid the danger of death that threatened them, and the court is convinced that the person did everything to avoid the consequences of their deed or of refraining from committing it;

   b.   If the person committed the deed or refrained from committing it in order to avoid the consequences bigger than the consequences caused by their deed or refraining from committing it, and could remove the consequences of their deed; but these regulations do not apply to the deed or refraining from the deed that constitutes a crime according to § 1 or § 2

§ 11. <u>Extenuating circumstances</u>.
While determining the punishment for the person convicted according to this law, the court is entitled to take into consideration the following factors as contributing to the mitigation of the punishment:

1. If the person committed a crime under the circumstances that would - excluding § 8 – exempt them from criminal responsibility or served as a reason for their acquittal, and if they did everything to alleviate the consequences caused by their crime.

2. The crime was committed with the intention of removing the consequences bigger than those caused by the crime, and does remove them. However, if the crime applies to § 1, the court cannot impose a sentence less than 10 years of prison.

Luba Lis, who resides in Haifa today, recalls an anti-Jewish campaign in Przemyśl which she survived as a twelve-year-old girl: *The construction of the big shelter had begun. To enter, one had to pass through the water toilet`. Mommy and I hid in the bunker. A few days had gone by. At some point we heard a shot. Suddenly, after some time had passed, I saw the Gestapo entering. "Raus! Raus!", they were shouting. I remember it as though it happened yesterday. There were fifteen of them, maybe more. People started to exit. Mommy and I were standing toward the back of the bunker. Suddenly, mama pulled me into the chimney. We climbed up onto the brackets chimney-cleaners use. We stood there for three days. Once everything had settled down, we came out of the chimney. From our bunker where about five hundred people were hiding, only the two of us survived – mommy and me. Our bunker was given up by a Jew who probably thought that he would save his own life by giving us up. Interesting. Everybody knew what the Germans were doing. Despite that, they were counting on the fact that their own lives would be spared for a* *price – the price of the lives of others. The one who gave us up was shot on the spot by the Germans.*[249]

With his actions, the Jewish executioner who showed the Germans where the bunker in Przemysl was located deprived five hundred Przemysl Jews of their chance to survive. Because the Germans "rewarded" him by killing him for his cooperation, for all of eternity he will remain in the pantheon of Jewish victims along with those whom he had sold out. Had he survived, he would not have to suffer any consequences in Israel as, without much effort, he would have been able to prove that he had committed this act "in an attempt to save himself from the threat of imminent death". The explanation that by capturing innocent Jews and dragging them onto the train cars, killing them or giving up their hideouts he was avoiding imminent death, guaranteed his immunity from prosecution in Israel after the war where every Jewish executioner could seek refuge: catcher, murderer and snitch. In the eyes of Israeli law, their actions were excused.

In defining metaphysical guilt, Karl Jaspers wrote: „There exists a solidarity among men. (...) In the face of crimes committed against someone or when it comes down to the division of resources which are physically necessary to survival, there is a principle which applies to everyone everywhere, that they can only save themselves or perish together; it is a part of their very being".

This sort of compliance with the rules of humanity and being responsible for one another comes from being human; in Europe this was supported in Christian theology and philosophy. The European ethos of human solidarity in a life threatening situation, which Karl Jaspers used as a basis, was further elaborated throughout the two-thousand-year history of Christianity and was based on the most fundamental of Christian commandments, the commandment of love which Christ expressed using these words: "There is no greater love than that of one who gives his life

---

[249] The relation of Luba Lis, in: Kurek E., *Your Life is Worth Mine: How Polish Nuns Saved Hundreds of Jewish Children in German-Occupied Poland, 1939-1945*, by Ewa Kurek, Hippocrene Books, NY, 1997, p. 190/191; Kurek E., The documentary film: He *Who Saved one Life Saved all the Word*, The Polish Television canal 2, Warsaw 1998; Kurek E., *Dzieci zydowskie w klasztorach*, Lublin 2001, p. 171-175.

for that of a friend" (J. 15,13). The somewhat less dignified version is proclaimed by the French Musketeers: "One for all, and all for one."

Karl Jaspers was mistaken in stating in his definition that his principle applies "everywhere to all people". This principle is not for everyone, and in no way is it applicable to the principles elaborated in Jewish theology or tradition. Therefore, applying the European philosophical-religious conceptual apparatus to the annihilation of Polish Jews is misleading. Historical documentation which utilizes it not only does not achieve an understanding of the events of the Holocaust, but also obscures the picture presented to us by trustworthy Jewish historical sources.

There exists no other route. Only in reaching into Jewish theology, philosophy and tradition can one grasp the absolute lack of solidarity among Jews when faced with a situation in which their very existence as a people is threatened, as well as understand the stance taken by Jewish executioners. Only by reaching into Jewish theology, philosophy and tradition is it possible to understand the annihilation of Polish Jews and to grasp how it was conceivable, in the heart of Europe with minimal financial and military backing, for Germans to successfully accomplish the murder of three million Polish Jews and that of another three million Jews from all over occupied Europe. Out of reverence for my elder brothers in faith, I am far from usurping any right to pass judgment or to possess any opinion regarding matters so grave and fundamental as the determinations, theological-moral in nature, that flow from Jewish religion and tradition. My knowledge of this matter is more encyclopedic in nature, supported by Jewish sources and literature. As an historian, I am simply trying to find some answers to the following questions:

1. Why did Polish Jews, those who died as well as those who found themselves in the miniscule group that walked away with their lives intact, during those years of horror of annihilation of Polish Jews, find themselves outside the borders of Jewish solidarity?
2. Why did a greater portion of Jews, especially the Jewish intelligentsia during WWII, take on the roles of executioners of their own nation?

3. Why were Jews fighting and dying for Hitler despite the fact that he was murdering their nation?

4. In Israel, why were the Jewish executioners not punished accordingly to the crimes they had committed?

The answer to the questions posed above is not possible without reaching to the very foundations of Jewish religion and tradition which, like within all other nations and cultural spheres are dictated by the behavior of their people, in this case the Jews.

One of the theses that touch upon the matter within the context of the interdisciplinary problem of mass mentality and the role played by tradition claims that: "A nation is a synthesis that is not the creation of the now, but also of bygone centuries. (...) The true guides of people are their traditions. (...) Almost every action of man, being an element of the masses, depends on, above all, tradition, and even though his external expression may undergo frequent changes, the foundation remains virtually unchanged. (...) The most ardent followers of tradition are groups of people which we refer to as castes".[250]

No one is questioning the statement that the foundation of longevity and endurance of the Jewish nation has been, for thousands of years, a Jewish tradition. We must, however, be mindful when speaking of Jewish tradition, that we not assign to it the Polish or European understanding of the word.

For Europeans, for example, a shared tradition is the celebration of Christmas holidays. Catholics, Protestants and Anglicans alike, as well as all other Christian denominations, every year celebrate December 25 as

---

[250] G. Le Bon, *Psychologia tłumu* [The Crowd Psychology], Kęty 2004, p. 42-43. Gustave le Bon, a French doctor, anthropologist, sociologist, philosopher and a traveler. Considered a forerunner of social psychology and one of the main representatives of irrational psychologism in sociology. He explained social and political phenomena with the use of psychological analysis of the behavior of human assembly ('a crowd'). He proposed a prophetic thesis that political processes would be dominated by crowds driven by emotions and instincts. After Le Bon, the question of crowd behavior has been raised in countless studies. Nevertheless, German fascism and the extermination of the Polish Jews are the historical events that confirm Le Bon's theses, which a fact justifies quoting the works of this author.

the day Christ was born (the Greek Orthodox celebrate two weeks later). But aside from the customs of trimming a tree, exchanging gifts with loved ones and sending Christmas cards, there is no other common link in participating in the rituals surrounding this holiday. On Christmas Eve, Poles eat a meatless dinner after fasting, others bake a turkey, and the Irish go out to pubs for a beer.[251] The Christian version of the holidays is that of a religious experience. It is for that reason that every nation and every family develop their own traditions which are designed to suit them and are in accordance with their own spiritual needs and personal tastes. The situation is similar when it comes to all other traditions rooted in the Christian faith.

Within the realm of Christian traditions, the presence of an element of individuality in matters small and large has played a significant part for at least a couple dozen centuries, and has been of considerable importance. More than one war has been fought in defending it, and it is unfathomable that we would ever want to give it up. Consequently, Christianity, the religion that is, which shaped European traditions, and in turn, Polish traditions as well, never interfered with everyday human life. Giving up Christianity, choosing atheism or converting to another religion – unlike in the Jewish religion – did not result in, at least not in Poland, being excluding from the secular social structures that had been born from Christianity. Practically all areas of human life are subordinated to the

---

251 An account of Tom, in: *Polska w oczach Irlandczyków – Poland through Irish eyes*, B. Wagner (ed.), Lublin 2001, p. 117: *In spite of cold, I decided to stay here for Christmas. I had been invited to a Christmas Eve supper by one of the families and obviously I'd been looking forward to this event. You are probably wondering why I had been invited to a Christmas Eve and not to a Christmas Day dinner. Such is the Polish tradition. The Poles go to the Christmas Eve Mass and they have their Christmas supper on the same evening. It is more quiet than at home. All the families get together, sing carols, wish each other a Merry Christmas and have their supper, of course. There were so many courses that I couldn't remember them all. There was no meat. There were fish and pierogi (a kind of small dumplings filled with cabbage and mushrooms). Pierogi are delicious. Actually, I'm afraid I ate too many. Then, of course, desserts were served. There was alcohol served during the Christmas Eve supper. There is yet another difference between our [Irish] and their [Polish] Christmas celebrations. Where do the Irish go on the 24th of December? They go to pubs. And I went to church with Poles. At midnight. A very nice Mass. All that was completely new to me.*

same thing – (solely) man's free will, which in the context of human beings is colloquially referred to as individuality. At the source of the European genesis of individuality lies the idea of St. Augustine (354-430), whose philosophical theory regarding active freedom of will, upon which human actions are dependant, have shaped the Christian traditions of western cultural spheres.[252]

For Jewish religious-philosophical spheres, which created the foundations of Jewish traditions in Poland, St. Augustine's theory regarding man's active free will and all other Christian theories were foreign, unknown, and not suitable for being adopted. Therefore, in applying European world values and mentality to the traditions, mentality and the value system of the Jewish world, we will never understand what actually transpired during the annihilation of the Jews. We will never understand how the Holocaust took its shape or how it was even possible at all. In order to understand Jews during the time of the Holocaust, we must, above all, take a very in-depth look at Jewish traditions.

Religion, from the dawn of time, has always played a very significant role in the lives of Jews. It dictated their way of life in society from the cradle to the grave. The number of Jewish religious rules regarding even the smallest of things like how to dress and what to eat, not to mention

---

[252] St Augustine (354-430) was born in the city of Tagaste. His father was a pagan and his mother a Christian. Augustine was a rhetoric teacher first in his home town and then in Carthage, Rome and Milan. Cicero's works activated him into philosophical research. At the age of 41 he was nominated as Bishop of Hippo. St Augustine's views can be summarized in a number of key theses. Firstly, he postulated breaking with objectivism and advised to turn to the internal life of the subject, for one may doubt the existence of external things but one cannot doubt their own life. St Augustine: *You who want to know yourself, do you know that you exist? I do. How do you know that? I do not know. Do you consider yourself as a simple or a complex substance? I do not know. Do you know that you move? I do not know. Do you know you think? I do.* Secondly, he broke with intellectualism. For Augustine it was will – not reason – that was the essence of spiritual life. Behind this claim lay the statement that the nature of every thing is manifested if the thing is active, not passive. That is the first assumption. The second one is that reason, according to the unanimous opinion of the Antiquity, is passive. Hence the conclusion: human nature is constituted not by reason but by active will. Human nature is manifested not in what it knows but in what it desires. See: St. Augustine, *Wyznania [Confessions]*, Kraków 2003.

regarding more important matters religious, moral or emotional in nature, is astounding for someone from the European cultural spheres. The lives of Jewish women and men took place for thousands of years within a very narrow framework dictated by religion.

Any sort of departure from the convention which created this framework was virtually impossible – in Jewish life there was no place for individuality.

It seems that this very fact – the role of religion in the life of every religious Jew and the role of religion in the shaping of Jewish tradition – is the first premise which must be taken into consideration when attempting to understand the Jewish stance with regard to the Holocaust. The second premise is the tradition that was shaped by Jews living in the Diaspora over the course of millennia, that is the development of a certain type of behavior attributable only to a nation whose people function without belonging to any specific geographical region on Earth, lacking a sovereign nation, and whose existence would always be delineated by laws created by others – the laws of nations extending hospitality to the Jews residing on their borrowed land.

Religion and life in the Diaspora lay at the foundation to at least two Jewish traditions and laws which very clearly collide with the traditions and laws that are dictated within the cultural realms of western Christianity as explained by Karl Jaspers in his definition of guilt. Concurrently, a lack of understanding of these Jewish laws and traditions was detrimental to properly understanding the annihilation of the Polish Jews.

The first traditional law explains the option of sacrificing the lives of a few Jews with the purpose of saving the lives of the remaining Jewish community (sacrificing a portion of Jewish lives).

From the earliest of times, Jews have always lived according to the six hundred thirteen commandments of the Old Testament which must be abided by every devout Jew. Three of these commandments are very specific in stating that one must choose death rather than break one of them. They pertain to: 1. idolatry, 2. modesty, cleanliness, lust, 3. murder. Any Jew who chooses death over breaking one of these commandments achieves

Kiddush ha-Shem (sanctifying the name of God) i.e. the gates of paradise. Should he, however, not choose death, he is guilty of Hillul ha-Shem (disgracing the Name of God). From the II century, when the Council of Rabbis created the laws of martyrdom, dying to honor the Name of God was considered by Jews to have the same significance as a martyr's death. Martyrdom took on the name of kadosh and was given to one who is sacred. From that time, children, from their earliest years, being brought up in the Jewish tradition, were instilled with the notion that martyrdom is the ideal model of behavior. Kiddush ha-Shem, despite centuries of ongoing discussion, was a valid commandment which Polish Jews were expected to abide by during WWII.[253] There was another tradition in place, which was derived from Kiddush ha-Shem, the tradition of sacrificing the lives of a few Jews with the purpose of saving the remaining Jewish community.[254]

In light of the Jewish tradition presented above, the train of thought followed by Chaim Rumkowski and those like him was straightforward. In an extreme situation, as turned out to be the case within walls of the "Jewish country" he had constructed in Lodz (a Jewish provincial autonomy, a ghetto), the Germans wanted to keep alive only those Jews who were fit to work, and that not all Jews were fit to work. It was necessary to sacrifice the lives of those less productive and save the working part of the people.

The decision about who was supposed to play the role of the condemned and who the role the survivors in this horrible theatre of Jewish sacrifice and survival was made, in accordance with Jewish tradition, by the elite – the clerks within the Jewish community. And so, the Judenrat clerks, in this order, first dispatched the deportees from other ghettos to their death, then *the unproductive element – children to the age of 10 and the*

---

[253] Jewish historians point to Kiddush ha-Shem as the inspiration of the Polish Jews' attitude towards the Extermination. The most distinguished ones are: Lucy Dawidowicz, *La guerre contre les Juifs 1933-1945*, Paris 1977, p. 495, 501 and 547; R. Sharf, *Saints or madmen? – A meditation on Ephraim Osbry's – Response from the Holocaust*, in: "The Jewish Quarterly", London, January 1988.

[254] H. H. and B. S., *Kiddush ha-Shem and Hillul ha-Shem from the Holocaust*, in: "Encyclopedia Judaica", Jerusalem 1972, Volumen X, p. 978.

elderly over 60[255], followed by those who had lost their jobs, and finally their own wives, mothers-in-law, and mothers. They did all this with the undying hope that they would be spared, and that their salvaged life would somehow give the Jewish victims the Jewish significance of a martyr's death, Kiddush ha-Shem.

Only through the prism of this Jewish tradition do the decisions of all the Judenrat leaders in Poland become more transparent; the decisions of those who gave the authorization to deport groups of residents of the ghettos under their command to the death camps, including Rumkowski's decision to dispatch children to their death. For in accordance with Jewish religion and the foundation of Jewish norms that had been developed over millennia of living in the Diaspora, these decisions are in absolute accord with the Jewish tradition of sacrificing the lives of a few Jews for the purpose of saving the remaining Jewish community.

In other words, during WWII, some Jews were selected for condemnation by Jewish laws and tradition to be the victims, while others were condemned to be the survivors. Emanuel Ringelblum, who represented the upper echelons of Jewish intelligentsia, on the day before the Holocaust, wrote:

*In certain circles, discussions were taking place: what would one have to do, if it were possible at this moment, to send someone out into the great big, wide world? A conundrum was being discussed as to whether it would be necessary to send a list of the most accomplished individuals in order to obtain foreign passports for them so that they can be saved. Some said that the elite should stay behind with the pedestrian masses to perish along with them. Others still were calling upon examples from Jewish history and tradition which dictate the saving of at least one Jewish being. **The final decision rested on the notion was that every social group should attempt this for their (most) accomplished people and not for the whole, as it were.**[256]*

Speaking in more practical terms, in accordance with the Jewish

---

[255] Ringelblum E., *"Kronika getta warszawskiego wrzesień 1939 – styczeń 1943"*, Warszawa 1983, p. 392. [See also: "Notes from the Warsaw Ghetto" by Emanuel Ringelblum, paperback, Ibooks Inc., 2006].
[256] Ibidem, p. 391-392.

tradition, Jewish painters should select the most accomplished painter from their realm, musicians their greatest musical genius, historians their most renowned historian, doctors their greatest doctor, etc..., and then focus all their energy on securing their survival. But from among the Jewish elite, no one wanted to be considered second rate, so no one wanted to be the victim! Therefore, the notion *that every social group should make this attempt for the sake of their most accomplished people* led to nowhere.

The agreement to appropriate a certain portion of Jews for death was, during the last war, a very common occurrence inside the Jewish ghettos:

*A wealthy man in Warsaw was asked if he would agree to higher taxation for the greater good of the refugees. His response: "**This won't help a bit. No matter what, the lowlifes are going to die out**". (...) Public welfare will not resolve this problem, it only helps people for the time being. No matter what, they have to die. (...) A question comes to mind, would it not serve a greater purpose to use this money for the chosen, for the social activists, for the spiritual elite, etc... (...) A question arises, is it possible to utilize the tradesmen, laborers and valued/worthwhile people (...) in mass graves.*[257]

Forty years later, Marek Edelman explained this rule that functioned within the Jewish tradition (agreeing to sacrifice a portion of the whole) in these simple words:

With people it's like this, as with lions in a herd, when they throw their weaker ones out of the group. It's so the jackals that will come up will devour the weaker ones. It's the same with people. There's no difference. It's phylogenetic.[258]

Not all people on Earth follow the example of herding lions.

One thing is for certain, that during WWII, Polish Jews designated a portion of their nation for death. They did not undertake the task of attempting to save the Jewish people as a whole. An idea such as this, foreign to their historical-religious traditions though it might have been, never even entered their minds. Fighting the Germans during the last

---

[257] Ibidem, p. 268, 388-389.
[258] Marek Edelman, in: Grupińska A., *"Ciągle po kole"* ["Still Round the Circle: Talks with the Soldiers of the Warsaw Ghetto"], Warszawa 2005, p. 24.

phase of the annihilation of Polish Jews was taken on by a group of a couple of hundred youth fighters. The Jewish fighters did not fight to save the Jewish nation. It was too late for that. They were fighting for a death with dignity.

A caste society from the dawn of history, subordinate to the authorities within the Jewish community, almost without objection surrendered to the law of salvaging of a portion of the Jewish population at the cost of sacrificing the lives of others, with the understanding that someone from among the Jews must be the victim in order for the "most valuable individuals", from whom a nation of Jews will be born in the future. Operating within the guidelines of Jewish law and traditions, it was in this light that Rumkowski acted, by handing the children of Lodz ghetto over to the Germans destined for death. Based on this, all the autonomies and Jewish communities in occupied Poland behaved in this way, within the framework of Jewish law and traditions. It is necessary to know about this in order to be able to understand what really transpired in the years of annihilation of the Polish Jews.

If, therefore, we understand this vein of Jewish tradition conditioned by history and religion, the stance taken by Jews in life threatening situations in which there exists the option of sacrificing the lives of a portion of Jews for the purpose of saving the lives of the remaining Jewish community, then part XI of the Israeli law passed in 1950 regarding relieving the Jews who actively cooperated with the Germans during the Holocaust providing they prove that their actions were motivated by trying to avert "consequences far more serious than actually existed" becomes more transparent. Stating the idea of the Israeli law more precisely – because handing successive groups of people destined for certain death in the gas chambers over to the Germans was supposed avert consequences more sever than actually existed, that is the annihilation of the entire Jewish community – the decisions of the Judenrats to dispatch further groups of residents from the autonomies and ghettos under their rule was in accordance with the Jewish laws and traditions, and, therefore, justified. The unfortunate part rested solely upon the fact that, although it was meant to emulate the behavior of herding lions and follow the long-tested

Jewish norms of behavior developed over centuries, it proved to be quite disappointing during WWII. The Germans murdered almost all of those who usurped the right to save their own lives at the cost others, that is the Jewish executioners. From the 250,000 residents of the Lodz ghetto in 1939, 887 people remained by 1945.

The second Jewish law speaks about the unlimited right of Jews to save their own lives in the face of imminent death.

This Jewish law also derives from the above mentioned Kiddush ha-Shem (martyrdom for the sake of honoring the Name of God). It was, in fact, a new tradition created during WWII. In March of 1941, Emanuel Ringelblum wrote:

The Orthodox are pleased with the state of things in the ghetto. They believe (rabbi, descendant of Szmul Zbytkower) that this is the way it was meant to be. Jews are among their own kind. They are not, however, pleased with the events taking place in the ghetto. There are no accidental "kidusz ha-Shem", but there have been incidents of tearing out the Pentateuch by devout Jews and other incidents similar to that; [Jews] do not get involved by actively standing in opposition to (evildoers). "Kidusz haszem" currently appears in a sublimated form: aspiring to keep the Jewish population alive.[259]

The sublimated version of Kiddush ha-Shem, which was described by the chronicler of the Warsaw ghetto, in Hebrew was called Kiddush ha-chajim (sanctifying life), and was: ""An idea dropped in the Warsaw ghetto by Rabbi Izaak Nissenbaum (1866-1943?), which put the responsibility of self-defense and saving lives on the Jews. This thread was carried further by other Jewish spiritual leaders. Nissenbaum saw it as both a reversal and continuation of the Kiddush ha-Shem idea for the Jews who had encountered persecution in the past, whose executioners' goal was to destroy the faith which the martyrs had documented with their own deaths. In the matter of the Holocaust, the goal was to annihilate a nation. In this context, **saving one's own life** indirectly came to mean "sanctifying the

---

[259] Ringelblum E., *"Kronika getta warszawskiego wrzesień 1939 – styczeń 1943",* Warszawa 1983, p. 252-253. [See also: "Notes from the Warsaw Ghetto" by Emmanuel Ringelblum, paperback, Ibooks Inc., 2006].

Name (of God)".[260] The theological justification of the Jewish imperative to live is most likely rooted in, or at least is linked to, the words of the prophet, Ezykiel: "Then I passed by and saw you kicking about in your blood, and as you lay there in your blood I said to you, "Live! in your own blood, Live!" (Ezekiel 16:6).[261]

It is characteristic that that which derived from Jewish religion, experience and tradition, modified during WWII, the idea that Rabbi Nissenbaum dropped of saving Polish Jews from annihilation, did not call upon the solidarity of Jews in their misfortune and their common fight for survival – (instead) it called upon Polish Jews to *save their own lives*. As a result, in the face of the Holocaust during WWII, Polish Jews were saving their own lives in every conceivable way. Emanuel Ringelblum wrote:

The betrayal by the Judenrat, the Jewish Police, the Werkschutz, workshop management, at the cost of saving their own lives and those of their families. (…). They thought that various means lead to a goal, and the goal was to survive the war, even at the cost of the lives of other people. (…) The "Kohn-Heller" trucks with the captured. One of the most horrifying images. The cries and screams of the captured. The police beating people. The common people are scuffling with the police. (…) Warsaw – a city of heartless Jews.[262]

In the light of Jewish law and tradition, the shameful actions of Jewish executioners were excused. Part X of the Israeli law of 1950 freed them of all responsibility providing they were able to prove they actively participated in the annihilation of their own nation "in an attempt to save themselves from the threat of imminent death". Jewish law, tradition and religion, which are rooted in the premises discussed above, have also found excuses

---

260 The Judaic Lexicon *[Słownik Judaistyczny]*, Warszawa 2003, Volumen I, p. 775-776.

261 H. Arendt, *Eichmann w Jerozolimie*, Kraków1987, p. 26; (see also: *Eichmann In Jerusalem: A Report on the Banality of Evil*, The Viking Press, New York 1964), says: ""Mr Hausner (…) started his opening speech (which lasted for three sessions) from the Egyptian pharaoh and Haman's decree according to which 'Jews had to be destroyed, killed and wiped off the face of the earth.' Then he quoted the prophet Ezekiel (...) (Ez 16, 6) and explained these words as an 'imperative of the Jewish nation from the moment of its appearance in history'"".

262 Ringelblum E., *"Kronika getta warszawskiego wrzesień 1939 – styczeń 1943"*, Warszawa 1983, p. 411, 425, 426 and 477. [See also: "Notes from the Warsaw Ghetto" by Emanuel Ringelblum, paperback, Ibooks Inc., 2006].

for the 150,000 Jewish soldiers of Hitler. Bryan Mark Rigg writes: „„Being put before the fact that Jews served in the Wehrmacht, an orthodox Rabbi from New York, Chaskel Besser claimed: "At first glance, it may seem somewhat strange. However, I can understand that someone is capable of something like that in wanting to survive"".[263]

At this point we touch upon the essence of the contradiction between the standards of attitude developed through Jewish religion, experience and tradition and the standards of attitude developed through Christian religion, experience and tradition. I am going to allow myself, once again, to quote the words of Karl Jaspers, who, in expressing his thoughts based on the European Christian tradition, states: *there exists a solidarity among men as human beings. In the face of crime, only together can they save themselves or perish; it is a part of their very being.*

Consequently, from the sources presented above, it is clear that the Jewish religion along with the laws and traditions based on it, in extreme situations allow for the option of sacrificing the lives of a portion of the Jewish community in order to save the rest of the community; and also allow for the option of saving one's own life at the cost of the lives of other Jews. These allowances are, in their very nature, in direct contradiction to the European tradition of *solidarity among men as human beings* in its form as defined by the philosopher quoted above.

The picture which emerges regarding the time of the Holocaust as relayed by Jewish sources can be boiled down to one situation in which Jewish victims (Hasidim as well all the others from among the Jewish intelligentsia who refused to actively participate in the annihilation of their own nation), were up against two enemies: The Germans and their Jewish counterparts.

Hitler's Jewish collaborators – Jews in German military formation uniforms, Jewish executioners seated behind the desks of Jewish institutions and the Jewish police – are the key to understanding the events of the

---

[263] B.M. Rigg, *Żydowscy żołnierze Hitlera: nieznana historia nazistowskich ustaw rasowych i mężczyzn pochodzenia żydowskiego w armii niemieckiej,* Warszawa 2005, p. 114. [see also: *Hitler's Jewish Soldiers:The Untold Story of Nazi Racial Laws and Men of Jewish Descent in the German Military,* University Press of Kansas 2002].

annihilation of European Jews, as well as of Polish Jews. The stance taken by Hitler's Jewish collaborators resulted in Jews, who had fallen victim to the Nazi genocide, finding themselves beyond the border of Jewish solidarity.

In the decades that have passed since the end of WWII, the actions of Hitler's partakers, being deeply rooted in Jewish religion, tradition and law, were understandable only to religious Jews. For non-Jewish and Jewish historians from assimilated circles of Jews, all of whom applied the European concept apparatus in describing the events of the Holocaust, see the actions of Hitler's partakers as a straight out case of collaboration. As such, they were usually omitted in documenting these events. Therefore, should Jewish historians, as Hannah Arendt who died in 1975 had always hoped, some day decide to examine the painful: „„Aspect of the so-called "Jewish past of ours slipping away" (…) and summon the courage for honesty"", with regard to the time of the Holocaust, they will, above all, have to examine the problem of the Jew-executioners of their own nation:

- Precisely determine the full scale and reach of Jewish crimes against Jews;
- Reveal the theological-philosophical and legal foundations which lie at the basis of the Jewish tradition of sacrificing the lives of a portion of the Jews for the purpose of saving the rest of the Jewish community, as well as the unlimited rights of Jews to save themselves from imminent death (with reserving the right to sentence other Jews to death included);
- Claim outright that, during the time of the Holocaust, based on the afore mentioned foundations of Jewish theology, philosophy and tradition, Jewish crimes against Jews were sanctioned, and that after the war, the 1950 Israeli law based on these sanctions, Jewish executioners were excused and relieved of their responsibility with regard to punishment for their crimes;
- Come to terms with the problem of carrying into the future the awareness that, in our darkest hours of being tried and tested during the years of the Holocaust, dying Jews found themselves beyond the limits of Jewish solidarity;

- Come to terms with the problem of carrying into the future the awareness that, over the course of decades, in concern over preserving the good name of Jewish executioners, the truth about the lonesome Jewish victims beyond the limits of Jewish solidarity, was falsified.

Dying at the hands of the Germans in the years 1942-1945, European Jews found themselves not only beyond the limits of solidarity of other European Jews (and the 150,000 soldiers of Hitler who had actively participated in the act of genocide), but also beyond the limits of solidarity of Jews-Zionists who, during the time of WWII, resided in Palestine. In a conversation with Marek Edelman we read:

Anna Grupinska: *Listen, please, to the quote from Ben Gurion: "They didn't want to listen to us. With their own death they sabotaged the Zionist idea". And further: "The tragedy that is being experienced by European Jewry, isn't directly my problem". What do you have to say about that, Mark?*

Marek Edelman: *You know what? Ben Gurion was nothing but a small-town conman. He had absolutely no vision. There is no doubt that, for Ben Gurion, this whole situation was somehow handy, convenient. Back then they believed that the worse things are for us here, the better things are for them over there. Look, they never came here, to Poland, they didn't want to send us money. They didn't want to help us.*

Anna Grupinska: *You never received any financial help from Palestine?*

Marek Edelman: *Never. The [Polish] government in London helped a little. And Schwarzbart? The great Zionist! He wouldn't even raise a finger. Anyway, Antek [Cukierman] wrote him a letter: "We will curse you and three generations of your children". Just like it says in the Bible. And nothing! That letter, as far as I recall, was written in August of 1943 at Komitetowa 4. I'm sure it reached him.*[264]

---

264 M. Edelman, in: Grupińska A., *"Ciągle po kole"* ["Still Round the Circle: Talks with the Soldiers of the Warsaw Ghetto"], Warszawa 2005, p. 279.

If the annihilation of Polish Jews was convenient for the Jews living in Palestine, and since it is common knowledge that Jews living in countries of the free world also refused to help, then it must be concluded that, in the years 1942-1945, European Jews were dying as people for whom there simply was no place in any of the spheres of Jewish solidarity. That is, providing that Jewish solidarity as such – for reasons steeped in Jewish religion and tradition – is at all possible and had ever existed in the annals.

CHAPTER VI

BEYOND THE LIMITS
OF SOLIDARITY OF POLES

F or the sake of fairness, it must be said that the tendencies to *cover up the actual truth* for the sake of preserving the good name of the Poles that existed among Jewish historians and writers, are not so foreign among Polish historians or writers. It is, therefore, worth taking a closer look at Polish-Jewish relations during the years of the Holocaust 1942-1945 (understood, on the one hand, as objective conditions to rescuing Jews in Poland; on the other hand as the stance of the Poles with regard to the murder of the nation of Polish Jews), in order to subject it to evaluation based to the definition of guilt by Karl Jaspers. In order to fully grasp and evaluate the stance taken by Poles with regard to the annihilation of Polish Jews, it is necessary to keep in mind a few fundamental and objective truths. Above all, it is necessary to remember that in 1942, when the Germans began to undertake the annihilation of Polish Jews:

- The state of Polish-Jewish relations following the experiences of 1939-1941 which resulted from stereotypical Polish assumptions about the Jews coming to fruition (the collaboration of Polish Jews with the Germans and Soviets understood by Poles to be treason), as well as the stereotypical assumptions made by Jews with regard to Poles (mass murders of Jews at the hands of Poles in 1941, i.e., Jedwabne), was the worst of all possible things.

- The Polish State had not existed for three years, and in its elusive form, the Polish Underground State, did not have the military resources required at its disposal which would have allowed for it to save the lives of Polish Jews. With that in mind, any attempt to rescue the life of a single Jew could only have been undertaken by an individual Pole.
- **At the hands of the Germans, Poles were punished by death for rescuing Jews.**
- The Polish Jews who were locked up behind the walls of the Jewish Territorial Autonomies (the Ghettos), were completely cut off from the Poles.
- During the years 1939-1942, Polish Jews had made no attempts to communicate with the Polish Underground State, and the Polish population was seen as an undesirable element inside the Ghettos, (i.e., in Łódź); or they were merely tolerated within the framework of an exchange of goods, in terms of trade (in Warsaw and other locations).
- A prerequisite condition to saving the life of a Polish Jew was the seeking out of help among Poles by that individual.

Poles and Polish Jews entered WWII with a sizable dossier of severe economic, social and political controversies, a tradition steeped in programmed isolation by the majority of Polish Jewry as well as a long-standing, ever increasing, centuries-old series of mutually unfavorable stereotypical assumptions.

At the time of the outbreak of WWII, the average Polish Jew was convinced that:

- The Polish language with a Latin alphabet, known as the "galkhes" alphabet, the clerical alphabet, was considered to be an impure language (85% of Polish Jews considered Yiddish or Hebrew as their mother tongue);

- Poles are a version of Haman-esque anti-Semites just waiting for the opportunity to seize some loot, and occasionally even the life of a Jew;[265]
- The only personage embodying fairness, who was regal in his gestures and manner, was Marshall Józef Piłsudski. He is dead, and there is not another one like him, nor will there ever be. Therefore, it is pointless to rely on protection from the Polish authorities;
- On Polish lands, there are "Polish matters" and "Jewish matters". Between the two there never has been, nor will there ever be, a mutual interest. Therefore, let the Poles, in their usual manner, grab their swords in defense of their nation. The Jews will manage the war in their own way, just as they had managed all the other wars over the course of a two-thousand-year Diaspora.

Concurrently, the average Pole was convinced that:

- Polish Jews were Judases, infidels to the cause of an independent Poland. Therefore, rather than expect any form of assistance on their part in the fight for freedom of our country, we should expect betrayal and cooperation with the Soviet and German occupiers;
- Polish Jews, with very few exceptions, were never in solidarity with the Poles: they never picked up a weapon or fought for the freedom of our mutual land. Therefore, that will repeat itself during this war.

---

265 N. Davies, *Boże igrzysko* [God's Playground], Kraków 2003, p.739, says: *Unfortunately, the situation of the Polish Jews in the period between the two World Wars is often described without reference to context. Depicting the life in Poland in the blackest colors was in the interest of the Zionists who wanted to convince the Jews that they should leave Poland. But the Zionist point of view, which obviously could not be considered representative of the whole Jewish population, was more popular abroad than the views of any other party. In the case of the Holocaust, it is very easy to be wise after the event and suggest that the sufferings of 1918-39 were a prelude to the future tragedy.*

For the Poles, who had rebuilt their own independent statehood a mere twenty years earlier following a one-hundred-twenty-three-year-long period of occupation, the most important thing at the outbreak of the war was not to allow for a severance in the continuity of the existence of a Polish State (despite the condition of being occupied by two forces). For Polish Jews, who at the end of the XIX century, and within the first two decades of the XX century, had undergone a metamorphosis with regard to the development of national and political awareness, in 1939, the most important thing was not Poland as a state, but rather the creation of the best possible living conditions under which Polish Jews could survive the war; and within the political sphere, the creation of a series of faits accomplis with which the Poles would have to contend once the war had ended. Within the first few months of WWII, Polish-Jewish leaders had decided that both of the above mentioned goals would be reached, under the auspices of German authorities, through the realization of the idea of Jewish Autonomous Provinces that had already been formulated in 1920.

The fundamental differences in stance with regard to the invaded Polish State had already become very clearly delineated at the end of 1939. Poles undertook to build the Polish Underground State, whose structure, for obvious and understandable reasons, consisted largely of the conspiratorial army known as the Armia Krajowa (the Polish Home Army).[266] Not counting Mayor Dobrzański's (aka "Hubal's") partisans on the cusp of 1939/40, **the spring of 1943 was the definitive moment**

---

[266] The region of Lublin, whose soldiers constituted one fifth of the Home Army, is a perfect example of the temporal and numerical development of the Polish Army as well as of the improvement of the quality and equipment of the underground units. The organization that functioned under the name of *Służba Zwycięstwu Polski* (SZP) operated within the district until spring 1940. In that time it was transformed into *Związek Walki Zbrojnej* (ZWZ) and in 1942 into the Home Army (AK). The Home Army was supposed to be of a purely military character. It received from the emigrant government exclusive rights to organize conspiracy in the country and was treated as an integral part of the Polish Military Forces (Polskie Siły Zbrojne). Apart from the SZP-ZWZ-AK, within Lublin voyvodship operated a few dozen conspiracy organizations of nationwide scope, e.g. *Komenda Obrońców Polski* (KOP), *Organizacja Wojskowa* (OW), *Polska Organizacja Zbrojna* (POW), *Narodowa Organizacja Wojskowa* (NOW) and *Bataliony Chłopskie* (BCh) whose members joined the ranks of the Home Army in 1942 as a result of the integration action.

at which the strength of the Armia Krajowa had become invigorated enough to attempt to mount regular partisan campaigns against the Germans.[267]

As far as the overall Polish population was concerned, the stance that had already been taken by Polish Jews in September of 1939 during the ongoing defensive war, confirmed the stereotypical assumption of Polish Jews as the infidels of Judas. Jewish Communists considered the declaration of war against Poland by Stalin, as well as the Soviet occupation of eastern territories, as the realization of the idea for which they had been fighting all along. The fact of the matter is that the stance taken by Jewish Communists cannot be blanketed over the entirety of the Jewish population as Communists do not have a nation.

The question is not whether or not this was proper, for the masses are

---

The Home Army's structure was based on the pre-war administrative division of the voyvodship. As follows from the Home Army Main Headquarters' report from March 1944, the Lublin District numbered 755 full platoons and 73 skeletal ones (over 40,500 members). From June 1944 the forces included also the 27 Volyn Army Infantry Division with around 3,260 soldiers. As a result of a massive influx of youth, the strength of the Lublin District in the final stage of the war is estimated to be 60-70 thousand members. 80 % of them supplied the units which were designated for insurgent actions. The district of Lublin was the strongest as regards the number of soldiers. For example, the first partisan unit that started regular activity within the Lublin district was the unit of Kedyw (*Kierownictwo Dywersji,* Directorate of Sabotage). The unit had three successive commanders who were *all cichociemni* (secret special forces): Lt. Jan Poznański pseudonym 'Ewa' (killed in October 1943), Lt. Stanisław Jagielski pseudonym 'Siapek' (arrested and killed by Germans in December 1943) and Major Hieronim Dekutowski pseudonym 'Zapora' (murdered by communists in March 1949). Therefore, the first and the largest partisan unit of the Lublin region began fighting in spring 1943. [On the Polish resistance see also: *Armia Krajowa w dokumentach [The Polish Home Army in documents]*, Londyn 1970-1981, volume I-V; T. Strzembosz, *Rzeczpospolita podziemna [The Underground Poland]*, Warsaw 2000; F. Korbonski, *Fighting Warsaw: the Story of the Polish Underground State 1939-1945*, Londyn 1957.

[267] The Underground Polish Press Agency 'Biuletyn Informacyjny' from April 1, 1943 published an editorial entitled: *Akcja zbrojna? Tak - lecz ograniczona* [Military action? Yes, but limited]. The article explained the idea of the armed struggle of the Polish underground Home Army. It is worth remembering that one of the reasons why the guerilla units within the Home Army were created was the need of harboring those wanted by SS and Gestapo. The military action of the Home Army was limited not only by tactical considerations (preparation for a national rising) but also by the shortage of weapons. In fact, not every soldier could boast his own gun or revolver even in the final stages of the war.

always commanded by their own laws, Poles attributed the responsibility for the stance taken by the Jewish Communists to all Jews. To this day, legends still circulate among Poles of the warm welcome for the Soviet invaders that had been prepared by the Communists and the communizing Jewish population, as well as of this population eagerly entering every structure set up by the Soviet occupying forces.[268] A resident of a tiny eastern locality recalls the following:

In September of 1939, the Jews anxiously keep a look out for their liberators. We, Poles, are completely helpless, abandoned, as we no longer possess a Polish army, there is no police force, there is no community administration. There is no one left to protect us. Finally they arrived. They approach in tight formation the Soviets occupying the entire width of the road, infantrymen, a cavalry. We sit locked in our houses, while cheers and applause erupt on the sidewalks. It was the Jewish girls outside greeting their liberators. One of the overly excited girls barrels into the kitchen. "What's going on? Aren't you going to come out to welcome them, the Soviet army?" We remain gloomily silent. No one responds to her. "Perhaps I can pick some flowers from the garden?", as though she had had a moment of clarity in which to realize that we had no reason to celebrate. "Please help yourself," my devastated mother replied.

She hurried out. Already there were some giggling girls picking flowers from our garden. They're making small bouquets and running out into the road with them. (...) Another military unit is approaching. This time they are motorized. (...) The Jews are trying to ingratiate themselves. We are the only ones who are sad and dejected. We can taste the bitterness in our throats.

---

268 It is widely accepted that the Soviets who invaded eastern Polish lands were warmly welcomed only by Jewish communists. In fact, however, a servile welcoming of 'new' governors (including the construction of the gateways) had been the tradition of the Polish Jews for at least two hundred years. Therefore, even today one cannot tell who really welcomed the Soviets in 1939: Jewish communists (whose limited number was disproportionate to the scale of the phenomenon) or the Jewish communists together with the religious Jews (with the only difference that both groups would do it for completely different reasons). The Poles, who were not aware of such nuances in the Polish Jews' behavior, attributed it to the Jewish communists. Thus, the Poles' belief about the existence and the scope of 'żydokomuna' (Judeo-communism) had been strengthened. This issue requires independent research which may yield important findings.

"Your Poland is already gone," the Jews repeat.

In winter of 1940, Mazurek came to see my father. "Władziu, we have to help him." "Who?" "Staszewski. He's the one who worked as a railroad guard, he came here before the war." "So, he didn't get away?" "If you can imagine, he spent five months sitting up in his room (over at the Jews') and nobody even knew he existed. As long as he still had a little bit of money and some valuables, the Jews held on to him. But now, they are throwing him out. He will freeze to death or starve." "We have to help him somehow." [...]

The community now has a new administration. (...) Kaufman's son, Josek, walks around with a red armband and tells people in the community what to do. "What a scabby Kike – father gets aggravated – before the war, nobody even knew he was a closeted Communist."[269]

The above related stance that was taken by Communists, Polish Jews, with regard to the Soviet occupying forces was typical throughout the entirety of the eastern territories of Poland that had been occupied by the USSR. Moreover, the Jewish Communists residing in these Polish territories, who had found themselves under German occupation, utilized every possible means to cross over into the Soviet occupied Polish territories and actively participated in the creation of a new Soviet reality on Polish lands.

Jewish historians often overlook this chapter of shared Polish-Jewish history in silence. If they do touch upon it, however, they put forth the thesis of Professor Yisrael Gutman from Jerusalem, which claims that the behavior of Jews, which added yet another element to the existing Polish anti-Semitism, ought to be explained with the understanding that, for the Jews, the only real enemy was the Nazis. The Soviets, on the other hand, presented an opportunity for escape and salvation, for as much as this system was capable of existing in this fashion.[270]

Professor Yisrael Gutman's thesis is erroneous in part when claiming that the Soviet Union presented itself to Polish Jews as an "opportunity for escape

269 J. Zieba, *Znad Stochodu [From the Stochod River]*, Lublin 2001, p. 132-136 and 152. See also: E. Ringelblum, op. cit., p. 75, who says, for example, that: *when leaving the town, the Soviets usually took along militia forces consisting of local [Jewish] youth.*
270 Y. Gutman, *Polish and Jewish historiogrphy on the question of Polish-Jewish relations Turing World War II*, in: „The Jews in Poland. Polish-Jewish Studies", Oxford 1986, p. 178.

and salvation" from the Germans. For in 1939, neither Polish Jews, nor any other Jews, had any inkling whatsoever as to the planned German Holocaust. This thesis is correct in stating that the Soviets, who invaded the Polish State on September 17, 1939, were not immediately perceived by communizing Polish Jews to be the enemy. The Soviet Union was a deathly enemy of the Polish State. For Jewish Communists, however, for Polish Communists as well, it was a dream come true. The Soviet occupying forces on Polish lands were simply the new, desirable authorities ruling over Poland, who, as the Communists proclaimed, were going to lead all of the nationalities residing on Poland's eastern territories into a bright future. Katarzyna Meloch (Irena), who was rescued by Polish nuns, wrote this about her communist parents:

My parents were leftist people. For them, relocating to Białystok [(1939 – E.K. note) was not solely an escape from the Germans, but above all, I think, a journey towards long sought after and dreamt about ideals. With conviction, my parents participated in the Soviet order of things. This was expressed formally, but under existing conditions at the time, very tellingly, by accepting Soviet passports. My mother taught History and Latin in secondary school. This is awful, but it must be said, that my parents were at the time very much disliked by a great many Poles, perhaps even... despised.[271]

Henryk Makower, on the cusp of 1940/41, noted the following: *We would receive wonderful letters from my brother. He had relocated to a small town outside of Białystok where he became the foreman in a marmalade factory. He was doing very well for himself. He would send great care-packages: cooking fat, marmalade, coffee, cocoa and fruit spreads.*[272]

However, when speaking of the stance taken by communist Polish Jews under Soviet occupation, which ought to be called by its proper name of outright treason against Poland and Poles, it is necessary to underscore with absolute measure the remembrance of the tens of thousands of Polish Jews, as well as Poles, who have survived in Polish collective memory; a memory of the tens of thousands who, between September of 1939 and June of 1941,

[271] Relation of K. Meloch, in: Cezary Gawrys, *Turkowice – smiec i ocalenie [Turkowice – the Death and Rescue"]*, „Wiez", Year 1987, No 4, p. 25.
[272] Makower H., *Pamiętnik z getta warszawskiego [The Memoirs from Warsaw Ghetto]*, Wroclaw 1987, p. 24-25.

had filled up cattle wagon transports carrying citizens of the Polish State to Siberia and Kazakhstan for nothing less than their refusal to accept Soviet citizenship; the tens of thousands who suffered and perished along with Poles inside Soviet death camps for no reason other than they were Poles. From the train wagons of Polish Jews, it was not uncommon to hear Polish patriotic songs emerging, among which the hymn "Poland has not yet been lost..." was a song which created a unique form of solidarity between Jews and Poles.

The Warsaw Jew, Izaak Kotkowski, recalls:

We were traveling by the Soviet Union lands in a cattle car adapted for transportation of prisoners. Kazik, a young Pole from Kielce, sat next to me. Still nobody informed us where we were going. (...) When the train stopped, one of the more daring prisoners walked up to a guard: "Tell me, my friend – he asked - where are they taking us? Where are we going?" The Russian soldier looked at us and grinned broadly: "You are going to a wonderful place. You will love it! It is a well-known Russian port, Archangielsk..." (...)

Kazik had a beautiful tenor voice and when he sang Polish military songs, our eyes, red from tobacco, moistened with tears of emotion. We formed a paltry five-man chorus and sang out all sorts of songs. Full of defiance of the Soviets, we passed through Moscow singing the Piłsudski's Legion's songs as loud as we could. For us, singing was like joints: it helped us forget about hunger, thirst, dirty straw, chilly nights and overcrowded carriage.[273]

For Polish Jews and Poles being transported to Siberia, Hitler was a distant threat. Those who imposed force on them were the Soviets. For both groups, the Soviets were the deathly enemy. We cannot forget about this. Those Communist Polish Jews who had managed to subsist, for whom it was written to survive the war in "brotherly" Soviet Russia, cannot overshadow the memory of the tens of thousands of Polish citizens, Polish Jews, for whom deportation and Soviet gulags turned out to be equally as tragic in their conclusion as Hitler's crematoriums. Also, as far as they are concerned, Polish Jews, the citizens for whom a sense of Jewish-ness and Polish-ness melded together so seamlessly so as to make them loath

---

[273] I. Kotkowski, *Wyroki losu*, Lublin 1997, p. 72-76. See also: Y. Kotkowski, *The Willes of Destiny*, Texas 1991.

to betray either or choose death, the words of Mickiewicz apply: "Should I forsake them, Dear God, please forsake me…".

During WWII, Poles did not readily recall this aspect of Polish-Jewry, when they all stood on the same plank and were repressed for the sake of Poland under the Soviets during the 1939-1941 Soviet occupation. For the undisputed betrayal by Jewish Communists in 1939, in many places in the summer of 1941, Poles presented the Jewish population with a hefty bill of cruelty. Jedwabne, and many other locales in eastern Poland, became the places which, to this day, remain as not entirely documented scenes of crimes against the Jewish people. At the hands of Poles, innocent Jews perished. Nothing can justify these Polish crimes committed in 1941. For Polish-Jews, the posture taken by Poles in this instance only confirmed the popular widespread stereotype of the Pole-Haman.

Under German occupation, Polish-Jewish relations during the years 1939-1942 were no less complicated. The stance of foreigners taken by Jews expressed itself here, above all, through the claim that the war that had broken out was a Polish, not a Jewish, matter. Also, the widespread collaboration of Jews with Germans which, in at least two of the largest Jewish centers (in Warsaw and Lodz), blossomed into the construction of Jewish Autonomous Provinces, known as Ghettos, which were subject to German authorities.

At the same time, Poles who had taken the stance of citizens from the first days of the war, paid dearly. Today, very few Jewish historians of WWII are willing to remember that the ones who were first in line to bear the brunt of German repression were not Jews, but Poles. In order to come to realize the truth about the first three years of the German occupation of Poland, it will suffice to read well into Jewish sources. Emanuel Ringelblum, among other things, noted the following:

(December 1939): Lately, there have been rumors circulating about Christians being deported on trains from their native regions. 1,500 Christians from Poznań to Zamość (men) and to Szczebrzeszyn (women) (…)

29 (February, 1940): Many Poles have been taken from their apartments, from the streets, from cafes. They're saying that Christians started wearing Jewish armbands (in order to protect themselves from being arrested – E.K. note).

May 7 (1940): Young Poles between the ages of 15 and 25 are hiding out in apartments.

May 8 91940): A horrible day. In the afternoon hours, on all the streets, there were "round-ups" of Poles. They were checking the identification documents of Jews to make sure they weren't Christians. They were stopping trams and taking everybody away to the prison in Pawiak, and from there – as they are saying – they were transporting them to Prussia. Dozens of cars were headed for Dzielna Street. All the Jewish hairdressers and barbers were taken to cut the hair of those arrested Poles. They were rounding up not only the young ones, but grown-ups too, those over 40 years old. (...) During the arrests among the Polish population, people were being taken from the Gajewski's confectionary as well as from Polish neighborhoods. (...) I heard about the facts regarding Christians putting on Jewish armbands. (...) Rumors are that the Poles are wearing Jewish armbands in Warsaw and Kraków as well (in order to protect themselves against repressions). (...) Before May 3, horrible things were going on. There was a massive hunt for Poles taking place on the streets of Warsaw. Delivery trucks with armed (Germans) were zipping back and forth. The streets were empty. Cars were driving up onto the sidewalks creating panic. A few Jews were wounded. (...) In the cities and in the countryside, they're taking priests, the intelligentsia, even the directors of provincial communities.

May 9 (1940): During one of the "round-ups" of Poles, Jews with Aryan traits were instructed to speak Yiddish; this was meant to serve as evidence (that they were not Poles). (...) I heard that Germans forced their way into a church on Grzybowa Street. Despite the efforts of the priest to calm the attendees down, a terrible stampede ensued. The same thing happened days earlier in a church on Trzech Krzyży Square, where the Germans were rounding up Poles for labor.[274]

Jewish historians of WWII also rarely remember that the first people to fill up and become the symbol of genocide in the concentration camp in Oświęcim and in others built by Germans, but located on Polish lands, were also Poles. One of the first prisoners of Oświęcim, who later became an

---

[274] Ringelblum E., *"Kronika getta warszawskiego wrzesień 1939 – styczeń 1943"*, Warszawa 1983, p. 50, 98, 100, 133, 135, 138 and 139. [See also: "Notes from the Warsaw Ghetto" by Emanuel Ringelblum, paperback, Ibooks Inc., 2006].

active member of the campaign to rescue Polish Jews, Professor Władysław Bartoszewski, on the sixtieth anniversary of the liberation of Oświęcim, said this:

> *For a former prisoner of Oświęcim, this is an indescribable emotional experience and a truly overwhelming opportunity to be able to speak on the site of the largest graveyard in Europe which has no graves. This is an indescribable emotional experience, because when I as an 18-year-old Pole, in September of 1940, when I first stood in the assembly square of Auschwitz I as Schutzhaeftling nr 4427, among five and a half thousand other Poles, students, boy scouts, teachers, lawyers, doctors, priests, officers of the Polish Army, activists of various political parties and labor unions, it never occurred to me that I would survive Hitler and the Second World War; just as I never imagined that Auschwitz would become, as Auschwitz-Birkenau and Monowitz had, a place for the realization of a biological destruction of sorts of European Jews without regard for gender or age.*
>
> ***In the first 15 months of the existence of this dreadful place, we, Polish prisoners, were alone. The free world was not interested in our suffering or our deaths despite the painstaking efforts of the covert resistance organization within the camp which existed to relay information to the outside.*** *In late summer of 1941, a few dozen of thousands of prisoners-of-war of the Soviet Army were brought to Auschwitz. And it was on them and on the infirm Polish political prisoners that the effects of the deadly gas, Cyclon B, were tested in September of 1941. None of the prisoners could ever have even imagined that this was only a criminal test, a criminal preparation to execute a genocide using chemical means. And as it turned out, that is exactly what was meant to happen during those memorable years 1942-1943, 1944.*[275]

Therefore, those whose lives in occupied Poland were in the most danger during the years 1939-1942 were the Poles. As the Jewish historian, Szymon Datner, once calculated, the ratio of Poles murdered to that of

---

[275] Bartoszewski, *A wolny świat nie reagował* (And the free world did not react), the speech given on the 60th anniversary of the liberation of Auschwitz; after: 'Gazeta Wyborcza', January 28, 2005.

Jews murdered at the time was roughly 10:1. This indicates that, at the time the Germans were taking the lives of ten Poles, one Jew perished.[276] In the first three years of the war, the lives of Jews within the Jewish Autonomies (the Ghettos) were much safer on the inside than on the "Aryan" side. As Jewish sources indicate, along with the citation by Emanuel Ringelblum, in times of great danger, the more clever Poles would put on the armbands bearing the Star of David; and it was possible to avoid being rounded-up by speaking Yiddish. Concurrently, as far as Jews were concerned, the only inconveniences they were having to endure at the time was mostly economic in nature. This was conducive to the weaving of various prognoses for the future, which predicted the assumption of political constraints for Poles, and economic with regard to Polish Jews.

The state of Polish-Jewish relations under German occupation during the years 1939-1942 was lamentable. Not only was it not the result solely of Polish anti-Semitism, as it is often conveniently explained away by Jewish historians, but it was also the result of Jewish anti-Polishness. Emanuel Ringelblum wrote this:

(December 1939): **We don't want to be brotherly with Poles** *as a ravine has been dug between us that is filled with blood.*

March 30, 1940: One of the saddest symptoms is the ever-increasing hatred towards Christians. It is believed that they are the ones to blame for all the economic restrictions. (…) Today I heard that, within Polish intelligentsia circles, there is the belief that Jews have reached an agreement with the other ones [the Germans] and that that is the reason why all the mass arrests of Christians are taking place.

August 22, (1940): A little National Democratic newspaper has appeared in which they are writing: "Jews are being beaten, Poles are being killed. Jews get a few days before they are evicted, Poles in Poznan get a few hours. Jews are getting arrested, Poles are being shot. Congratulations to you (Polish Jews), your new allies".[277]

---

[276] Sz. Datner, *Las sprawiedliwych [The Forest of the Just]*, Warszawa 1968, p. 8.
[277] Ringelblum E., *"Kronika getta warszawskiego wrzesień 1939 – styczeń 1943"*, Warszawa 1983, p. 61, 118, 119 and 144. [See also: "Notes from the Warsaw Ghetto" by Emanuel Ringelblum, paperback, Ibooks Inc., 2006].

During the first three years of the war, while the Germans were focusing on murdering Poles, Polish Jews were living in relative safety behind the walls of their territorial autonomies which they had erected (the ghettos). Poles did not receive sympathy or help from Polish Jews. At the time when Poles were perishing, *Polish Jews did not want to be brotherly with Poles.* Defeated, being settled in concentration camps, being murdered and being pursued between the years 1939-1942, Poles incited a sense of hatred among Polish Jews.

For the past twenty years, as an historian, I have been dedicated to Polish-Jewish relations during the Second World War. I have not met a single Pole who can say that within the first three years of the war, he or she owes their life to a Polish Jew, despite the fact that Jews did not have the death penalty hanging over their heads were they to assist Poles. During the years 1939-1942, Poles could not rely on Polish Jews to help save their lives, even though Polish lives very often depended on Jews, especially under Soviet occupation.

For Polish-Jewish relations during WWII, an acute moment occurred in autumn of 1941, for at least two reasons. This was a time when Jewish territorial autonomies in Warsaw and Lodz, as well as in other Polish cities, had achieved a level of optimum development. On August 19, 1941, the Germans had approved the budget for the Warsaw autonomy. In Warsaw, as it was cited earlier based on the journals of Adam Czerniakow, the walls had been in place for some time *in order to protect Jews from excesses at the hands of Poles*; having been in development since September of 1940, it is certain that the plans for defense of the area of the Jewish autonomies against the Poles were already in place. The autonomy, or rather, in the words of Rumkowski, the Jewish state in Lodz with closed borders and an effective deterrent to ward off the Poles, had been dealt with earlier.

In 1942, Poles and Polish Jews were divided by everything.

The tales of the murders in Jedwabne, which serves as a symbol in this case, as Jedwabne was not the only locale in eastern Poland where Poles took their frustrations out on the Jewish population in a very cruel manner over their own sufferings under Soviet occupation from 1939 to 1941, as well as the tales of the participation of Jews in establishing a Bolshevik order to things, spread like wild fire throughout Jewish communities. Embellished and overly exaggerated, thanks to ubiquitous Jewish idle talk, the layers kept building atop an already well maintained set of pre-war Jewish stereotypes perceiving Poles as deathly enemies (the Hamans) in waiting for the opportunity to take a Jewish life.

The state of Polish-Jewish relations in spring of 1942 was perhaps the worst on record. The centuries-old stereotypes that had been constructed were, in many instances, the most important and sole source of reference regarding mutual knowledge of the other for both Jews and Poles. As Henryk Szlajfer writes: "They had already dealt with the proof of gaining a greater understanding of each other and attempting to cooperate with each other during the period between the wars, building their strength on ever increasing antagonism. Set in their mutual exit positions of 1939, strengthened by a glance at history of the war years, they came from two dramatically different points of view."[278]

In the years 1939-1941, the stereotypical "Judases", i.e. Polish Jews, saw life behind the walls, delighting in their freshly constructed autonomies and the isolation of the ghettos. Although hungry and chilly at times, they did have their free Saturdays of rest, Jewish trams, their own postal system, police force, theatres, restaurants, and in Lodz, they even had their own currency. Polish Jews on the cusp of 1941/1942 felt secure behind the walls they had erected and openly claimed: *We do not want to be brotherly with the Poles.* The stereotypical "Hamans", i.e. the Poles, were trying to outrun the German round-ups at the time, steadfastly erecting the structures of the Polish Underground State within their own hermetic circle, and in dreaming of an open battle with the Germans, they tried obtaining weapons. Quite frankly, aside from a few narrow circles of politicians, the only interest Poles had with regard to Jewish matters were strictly limited to trade.

In 1942, the Germans undertook to annihilate Polish Jews. This was the exact moment at which Polish Jews began to expect solidarity from the Poles.

---

[278] H. Szlajfer, *Polacy i Żydzi. Zderzenie stereotypow [Poles and Jews. The Crasch of the stereotypes]*, Warsaw 2003, p. 14.

That is they expected to be rescued from certain death. These expectations were perfectly natural, because where else, if not in your neighbors, does one seek support in trying times? The free world was far off in silence. In addition, Polish Jews knew that Poles, as followers of Christ and Europeans, were bound by the tradition of *solidarity among men as human beings*, and that they subscribed to the belief that *in the face of a crime, they can only save the whole or perish together*; because not unlike the French Musketeers, they are familiar with the slogan of *All for one, and one for all.*[279]

The drama of the Poles and the Jews was based mainly on the fact that, as stated by Professor Yisrael Gutman, an Israeli expert in matters of the Holocaust: *Poland was unable to save the Jews.*[280] Poland was not able to save the Polish Jews because it did not exist as a State as of autumn 1939. It did function in the illusive form of the Polish Underground State, but this form did not possess any military capabilities, nor did it have any legal or any other necessary means to facilitate the rescue of three million Polish Jews from the Holocaust. Just as it did not possess the ability to rescue three million Poles from the Germans and the Soviets. In the situation that existed in 1942, in the reality of the non-existence of Poland as an independent state, when all her territories were occupied by the Germans, and all her residents were bound by German law, the only way individual Polish Jews could have been rescued was by individual Poles.

The laws imposed on Poles and Jews at the hands of the Germans were unspeakable. On October 15, 1941, the General Governor, Hans Frank, acting on behalf of Hitler in German occupied Poland, issued a decree stating that the death penalty applies to those Jews who leave the ghettos as well as to those Poles who offer help to these Jews. This is what can be found in said decree:

---

[279] References to Christ, Christianity and the mercifulness of the Poles were the most frequent arguments regarding the nuns who rescued Jewish children. These arguments were also used by the Polish Jews regarding laypersons. See: E. Kurek, *Your Life is Worth Mine*, New York 1997.

[280] Y. Gutman, *Odwaga zbrodni, (The Courage to Crime)*, in: „Gazeta Wyborcza", Warsaw, February 10, 2001.

1. *Jews who leave their assigned neighborhoods without authorization are subject to the penalty of death. This same penalty applies to anyone who consciously offers them a place to hide.*

2. *Aiders and abettors are subject to the same punishment as the perpetrators, an attempted act shall be punished the same as a committed act. In less serious instances, one might expect severe imprisonment or imprisonment.*

3. *Sentencing shall be decided by Special Courts.*[281]

On October 15, 1941, Poland became the only country in German occupied Europe in which assisting Jews carried the highest price – death. Poles and representatives of minority groups in occupied Poland were punished by death not only for offering shelter and safe hiding to adult Jews or Jewish children escaping the ghettos, but also for any assistance provided; this included providing water to prisoners in death camps.

When the final annihilation of the ghettos started, the Germans posted announcements throughout all of Poland. Dated July 27, 1942, composed in three languages (Polish, Ukrainian, and German), the Kreishauptmann notice, in Przemysl, regarding the deportation of Jews and the death penalty for offering to aid them in any way read as follows:

To the Ukrainian and Polish population of the District of Przemysl and the City of Przemyśl.

The goal of carrying out the deportation of Jews as ordered by the SS and Polizeiführer of the District of Kraków would like to inform:

---

[281] *Dziennik rozporządzen dla Generalnego Gubernatorstwa 1941 (The Journal of Regulations for the General Government 1941)*, Nr 99, p. 595.

305

OGŁOSZENIE

Dotyczy:
przetrzymywania ukrywających się żydów.

Zachodzi potrzeba przypomnienia, że stosownie do § 3 Rozporządzenia o ograniczeniach pobytu w Gen. Gub. z dnia 15. X. 1941 roku (Dz. Rozp. dla GG. str. 595) żydzi, opuszczający dzielnicę żydowską bez zezwolenia, podlegają karze śmierci.

Według tego rozporządzenia, osobom, które takim żydom świadomie udzielają przytułku, dostarczają im jedzenia lub sprzedają artykuły żywnościowe, grozi również kara śmierci.

Niniejszym ostrzega się stanowczo ludność nieżydowską przed:

1.) udzielaniem żydom przytułku,

2.) dostarczaniem im jedzenia,

3.) sprzedawaniem im artykułów żywnościowych.

Częstochowa, dnia 24. 9. 42.

24. The German Poster in Polish, 1942.

POSTER

Concerning the Sheltering of the escaping Jews

A reminder – in accordance with paragraph 3 of the decree of October 15, 1941, on the area of Residence in General Government (Poland), page 595 of the GG Register, Jews leaving the Jewish Quarter without permission will incur the

DEATH PENALTY

According to this decree, those knowingly helping these Jews by providing shelter, supplying food, or selling them foodstuffs are also subject to the death penalty.

This is a categorical warning to the non-Jewish population against:

1. Providing shelter to Jews
2. Supplying them with Food
3. Selling them Foodstuffs

Ewa Kurek

Czestochowa, September 24, 1942.

I. On Monday, July 27, 1942, the campaign to deport Jews from the District and City of Przemysl shall be under way.

II. Any and all Ukrainians and Poles who shall attempt to interfere with the campaign of deporting Jews shall be shot.

III. Any and all Ukrainians and Poles who shall be caught in the Jewish neighborhood looting Jewish residences, shall be shot.

IV. Any and all Ukrainians and Poles who shall attempt to hide a Jew or assist them in any way, shall be shot.

V. Obtaining Jewish property for money or for free is forbidden. Those disobeying this order shall be subject to the severest of penalties.

Der Kreishauptmann Dr Heinisci[282]

A similar announcement, directed at the population of Warsaw and surrounding area, was posted in September, 1942:

Announcement

This applies to the penalty of death for offering support to Jews who have stepped outside the borders of the Jewish neighborhoods without authorization. Recently, a greater number of Jews have managed to get out of the neighborhood specifically designated for them without authorization. They are currently somewhere within the Warsaw city limits.

We would like to remind you that, in accordance with the announcement of the General Governorship dated October 15, 1941 ('VBl. GG, S. 595) which states that not only Jews shall be sentenced to death for stepping outside the borders of the Jewish neighborhood, but also any and all individuals who in any way assist them in hiding out. Please keep in mind that offering help to a Jew is not only limited to offering them food and lodging, but also to transporting them in any type of vehicle, purchasing various goods from them, etc. (…)

Director of the SS and Police for the District of Warsaw

Warschau, dated September 5, 1942.[283]

---

282 Poster in Polish, Ukrainian and German, The Archives of the Jewish Historical Institute in Warsaw, Nr 123. See also the posters Nr 147, 62a and 14.
283 Poster in Polish, Ukrainian and German, The Archives of the GKBZH in Warsaw, Portfolio 75/24.

The General Governor, Hans Franks' announcement, which was repeated in local postings, was not only the letter of the law. In summer of 1942, when the Germans officially began the annihilation of the Jewish people, when Jews were assailed by Germans and the Jewish police force and started to escape from the Jewish autonomies (ghettos), and Poles started to offer them refuge, for their brothers in humanity, for Polish Jews – Polish martyrs were the first to sacrifice their lives. Frania Aronson, who today lives in Israel, relays the following after Gawrych the gamekeeper was murdered in 1942 for harboring her:

When the war started, I was 12 years old. I lived together with my parents and siblings in Stanisławow near Minsk Mazowiecki. (...) Before the "campaign" of 1942, I was already earning money. I worked for the tailor. I met some people there, among others, the family of the gamekeeper, Gawrych from Wolka Czerniejowska. Therefore, before the final deportation from Stanisławow, I had left the town and wandered about the neighboring countryside. Mrs. Gawrych found me, was happy to see me, and she took me to her home so that I could sew clothing for her children. She wanted me to be saved. The Gawrych family were decent people. In their home, as it turned out, there was already a Jew from Warsaw being hidden, who was teaching the sons to play the violin. Mr. Gawrych had planned to eventually send me to live with his brother in the vicinity of Raszyn.

Mrs. Gawrych was a very good woman.

One day, (Polish) partisans came to the town of Stanisławow and they got some things sorted: they organized a police force and they destroyed all the communal records. The Germans arrested all the Polish police officers for allowing themselves to be made. It was on this day that Mr. Gawrych traveled to Warsaw. Before dusk, Mrs. Gawrych had asked us to chop some wood. That's when a Jewish married coupled from Stanisławow came out of the woods. They were not living at the Gawrych household. They were hiding out in the forest. They only came over for dinner. In any case, that evening, we all went inside the house, the Gawrych son started to play the violin, Mrs. Gawrych started serving dinner. Mr. Gawrych had returned from Warsaw, washed his hands and sat down at the table with the rest of us.

"You have no idea what's been going on! There are posters that all Poles who

harbor Jews shall be killed along with their entire families (by the Germans)!"
– he suddenly said.

"Mr. Gawrych, today we have no one to fear because the Germans came and arrested all the policemen from Stanisławów" – I responded.

Suddenly, a shot was fired. The Gawrych house stood just at the foot of the forest. I ran out of the house. I ran across the fields. I would fall and get up again. The Germans were shooting at me from machineguns. I ran not too far away. There was a pipe beneath the road, so I hid inside the pipe. I lay down inside of it. I could see and hear nothing. Because the Germans had set fire to the preserve, neighbors from the countryside started to gather to try to save the Gawrychs. I did not hear them approaching, but I did hear them coming back. I heard someone speaking: "Thank God that they've left with those dogs already."

The Germans came to the Gawrych home with dogs. At this time, they shot the married woman who came over from the forest to eat dinner with us. Her husband was wounded in the leg. Mr. Gawrych was arrested, and a few days later he was shot. They sent Mrs. Gawrych and her three children on their way. The Germans burned the preserve to the ground.[284]

Gawrych the gamekeeper was one of the first Poles who paid the highest price for saving Jews – he paid with his life. The story of the rescued Frania Aronson, as well as the fate of countless other Poles and Jews, including those whom it was impossible to save, but for whose salvation some unknown Pole did give up his life, leaves very little doubt that the 1941 ordinance of the German Governor-General of Poland, repeated again in 1942 by local SS chiefs and German police, was the law which was applied and was executed with full force in German occupied Poland.

It was this very ordinance which impacted most profoundly on the form and degree of help that was given to Polish Jews by the Poles. Until this truth

---

[284] Kurek E., *Your Life is Worth Mine: How Polish Nuns Saved Hundreds of Jewish Children in German-Occupied Poland, 1939-1945*, by Ewa Kurek, Hippocrene Books, NY, 1997, p. 171-177. See also: Kurek E., The documentary film: *Who Saved one Life Saved all Word*, The Polish Television canal 2, Warsaw 1998. In vain had Frania Aronson been looking for the Gawrych family for over half a century. After the screening of the film, the forester's children responded. In 1999, a moving meeting took place at the Warsaw airport. Two years later, the forester Gawrych's two sons and a daughter received the Righteous Among the Nations medal on behalf of their dead parents.

becomes widespread, and well known universally, it will be impossible to possess a current understanding of the Polish-Jewish relations that existed during the time of the Holocaust. One does not require an immense imagination to grasp the severity of the decision to assist Jews to safety. These were not family members, these were strangers in a situation in which any form of assistance, in the event of being discovered by the Germans, meant that one would have to pay with their own life and the lives of their family. This was an unbearably tremendous decision for each Pole to face. Nationality played almost no role here: only a very small number of Poles were capable of such a grand gesture. It's highly unlikely that many American, French, Irish or Japanese would be capable of such a gesture either.

Putting your life in danger along with the lives of your family members in order to rescue another human being is a decision which no one has the right to expect of another. In other words, in the event that taking some sort of action, such as saving the life of another human being is somehow connected to losing your own life, one must apply the principle of inalienable rights. In practice this constitutes that such a decision can only be made by someone whose life will be in jeopardy upon making said decision, and that the refusal of this decision can be justified in terms of both legal and moral aspects. This is why no one is put on trial for refusing to jump headlong into a whirlpool of water on a river to save another human being from drowning; the only person who can jump in to save someone from drowning is one who knows how to swim and has enough courage to risk their own life in order to save another. The nationality of the person drowning or of the person jumping in to save him, or refusing to do so, has no bearing on the matter.

The principle of inalienable rights in making a decision to save the life of a Jew, and by doing so putting one's own life and the lives of loved ones in danger, was an unwritten code among Poles during WWII. Even within the confines of female monastic circles in which nuns are bound by duty to obey their superiors, never was the participation in a campaign which was punishable by death (such as rescuing Jews or cooperating with the Polish Underground State) dictated from above. The Mother Superior always informed the nuns that any decision to participate in any such campaign was the individual decision of each nun, especially since such participation meant losing one's life, and monastic obedience did not apply in this case. Sister Maria Ena recalls this example:

All the nuns were members of the circle of interest regarding the dilemma of Jewish children. However, due to the danger involved, the whole truth was known only to the nun elders who bore the weight of absolute responsibility on their shoulders. (…) The dorms on Kazimierzowska Street in Warsaw housed 40 children, 14 of them were Jewish, along with the lady engineer, Ania K. In Wrzosów, half the foster children were Jewish.

I shall never forget Sister Wanda Garczyńska's meeting (the Mother Superior of the monastery in Warsaw – note E.K.). The year was 1942/1943. On Kazimierzowska, life is pulsating. Within this swarm there are Jews as well. Real Jews. It was clear – for harboring a Jew, the death penalty. Mother Superior was well aware that in other congregations, there had already been warnings and inspections. She is not concealing anything. Everything is out in the open. She calls all of us in. She began her meeting by reading a fragment from the Evangelia (Gospel) of St. John 15, 13-17. She had explained that she did not wish to put the home, the nuns or the congregation in danger. She knows what can be expected. She is not concerned about herself. She knows: "May you hold each other as dearly as I have held you dear." How dearly? So dearly, that He gave His life.

I lowered my head. I could not bear to look at the other nuns. We have to decide. If one single word is uttered, if we openly, truly admit that we are worried about our own skin, our own lives, the lives of so many sisters, the congregation… Should such a prudent risk be taken just to save a few Jewish girls? The decision is in our hands as to whether or not they will be sent away.

Silence. No one moves even a muscle. Barely a breath is drawn. We are ready. We shall not turn the Jewish children over. We would rather perish. All of us. The silence is deafening. We are ready.[285]

For Poles, saving the life of a Jew in Poland during the Holocaust between the years of 1942-1945 meant signing one's own death warrant.

---

285 Kurek E., *Your Life is Worth Mine: How Polish Nuns Saved Hundreds of Jewish Children in German-Occupied Poland, 1939-1945,* by Ewa Kurek, Hippocrene Books, NY, 1997, p. 48/49.

Aside from the non-existence of the Poland as a state, this is the most profound aspect of Polish-Jewish relations of that time. Meanwhile, in the sixty years that have past since the end of WWII, there exists virtually no Jewish history paper, no Jewish memoir or journal, in which one might not find the notion that Poles – most commonly known as a result of "the anti-Semitism they suckled with their mother's milk", or some such similar notions – did not effectively enough, and within far too narrow a range, save the lives of Polish Jews.[286]

The accusations that have been aimed at Poles for not saving the lives of Jews eagerly enough are accompanied by historical lies which occur mainly by concealing the fact that, in trying to save the life of a Jew, Poles were in danger of losing their own lives. This phenomenon applies not only to memoirs, journals and historical papers on the matter, but also to encyclopedic information. For example, the *Encyclopedia Judaica*, under the entry "The local population and the Holocaust" by H.S. (Jerusalem, 1972, T. VIII, p. 875) we can find the following: the risk for people willing to rescue Jews in occupied Europe varied from the death penalty in the General Governorship to the threat of being sent to concentration camps towards the end of the war in the Netherlands.

The information provided by the Encyclopedia Judaica is the truth, but at the same time an outright lie. First of all, what on Earth is the General Governorship? It is an area of Poland annexed into Germany in 1939, expanded after the outbreak of German-Soviet War in June of 1941 over a land dispute that had been under Soviet occupation 1939-1941. The name "General Governorship" was invented and used by Germans when referring to a portion of Polish land under German occupation. Therefore, the use of this Hitlerian term to refer to the territory of the Polish State some sixty years after the war had ended without including

---

[286] There is no shortage of studies and expressions that – for various psychologically complicated reasons – strive to put the blame for the extermination of the Polish Jews not on the Germans, but on the Poles. To create Polish responsibility for the extermination many different terms have been coined, e.g. 'Polish extermination camps' and 'Polish concentration camps'. The aim of these and many other terms was to persuade the people who were unaware what really happened in Europe in World War II to believe that in fact the tragedy of the extermination took place between the Jews and the Poles.

a proper explanation is culpable and offends the national sensibilities of the Poles who never identified with this invented German dual-nation creation. As for the readers who long for information pertaining to the Holocaust, they are being deprived of the truth due to a deliberate effort to conceal the fact that Poland was the only country in German occupied Europe which carried the death penalty for trying to save a Jewish life. Who, in the generations of Poles that have come since the end of the war, not to mention who among the generations of Israelis, Americans, French or British, even knows what General Governorship was?! It might just as well have been on Mars or in Alaska. It is also worth mentioning that, under the remaining entries pertaining to the Holocaust, the afore mentioned encyclopedia also omits the clear distinction that Poles were the only nation among those occupied by Hitler who were punished by death for rescuing Jews.

The information contained within the *Encyclopedia Judaica* contains outright lies. It certainly is not true that only the Poles residing within the General Governorship paid with their own lives for rescuing Jews. For saving Jews, Poles received the death penalty throughout the entirety of German occupied Poland. The ordinance of Hans Frank formally only pertained to the area of the General Governorship. In reality, the murder of Poles for providing assistance to Jews was the punishment carried out throught the entirety of occupied Poland. Evidence of this is presented in the murder of two nuns of the Niepokalanki order in Slonim. They were killed for providing refuge to a Jewish family.[287] Slonim was located in the area of the Reich Commissariat East, and was connected to the General Governorship in the administrative and legal sense simply because both administrative entities had been created by the Germans on the land belonging to Poland.

The Second World War was the direct cause of the deaths of more than 3 million Poles and close to 3 million Polish Jews. One cannot examine Polish-Jewish relations during the years of the Holocaust, especially in

---

287 See the map: Kurek E., *Your Life is Worth Mine: How Polish Nuns Saved Hundreds of Jewish Children in German-Occupied Poland, 1939-1945,* by Ewa Kurek, Hippocrene Books, NY, 1997, p. 10.

evaluating the stance taken by Poles with regard to the genocide executed on Jews, without being conscious of the fact that in Poland – the only country in occupied Europe – for aiding Jews, Poles paid the highest price: they paid with their lives and the lives of their families. In the realm of facts, this is the fundamental truth pertaining to Poland during the years 1942-1945. In concealing this fact and in accusing Poles of not providing sufficient enough aid to Polish Jews, Jewish historians are reducing historiography to levels devoid of all sense and moralistic treatise.

In mid-1942, when Germans began their mass annihilation of Polish Jews, for nearly two years, the Jewish population, locked behind the brick walls of the autonomies and ghettos, lived their own lives. Actually, not all the walls were so airtight, but nonetheless, in the best case scenario, the only group that had contact with the outside world was a small number of clerks, laborers, Jewish policemen, smugglers and certain individuals who occasionally left the ghettos for other reasons. Access to the ghettos was strictly forbidden to Poles. In some cities, Lodz for instance, Christians who were caught inside the ghettos, not only Poles, were handed over to the Germans by the Jewish police. For those captured, this meant certain death:

Noteworthy is the following instance. A woman called Edith N. arrived on transport II from Prague (January 1942 – note E.K.). In Prague, she had left behind her fiancé, a Czech (a Christian). The fiancé, in his longing for his heart's desire, performed no small feat. He embarked on a long journey on foot, and after a few weeks he had made his way over to the ghetto. He happily snuck in through the barbed wire. Once inside, he was captured by SP functionaries (Jewish police – note E.K.) who, in accordance with the ordinance pertaining to cracking down on illegal trespassing into the ghetto, were forced to deliver him to the German criminal police. The fiancée was summoned to the police station to serve as a witness. The fate that met this bold daredevil is unknown, except to say that he was not permitted to enter the ghetto. (...)

Illegal trespassing beyond the borders of the ghetto. This type of incident was recorded in the month of March. Details as follows.: On the day of March 8 (1942) at 22:00, the Jewish Police functionaries of police district II discovered a severely wounded man on Dolna Street. He had been injured by two machine-gun bullets. The wounded man was taken to hospital nr. 1 by ambulance. He died there by morning. Based on the documents recovered near the deceased, it appears he was a Pole living in the city. His name was Marian Osiecki (born in Belchatów in 1909). He was a barber by profession. He had been shot while attempting to trespass beyond the border of the ghetto.[288]

Christians were not welcomed guests both before and during the time of the Holocaust. It is true, as the author of *The Chronicle of the Łódź Ghetto* writes, that any Christian attempting to trespass beyond the borders of the ghetto had to be a *bold daredevil* and must have had a very important reason to make such a daring move. Especially since that, which the Germans were lax to notice and track down, did not escape the attention of the Jewish police obeying German orders. "The Lodz ghetto, like no other, turned out to be completely defenseless in a very critical moment. No other was as isolated or abandoned. In this isolation and abandonment lies one of the most important reasons of weakness" – is what one Jewish historian wrote.[289]

The locking up of Polish Jews inside the autonomies and ghettos, the widespread acceptance throughout their communities with regard to the result of the Jewish elite collaborating with the Germans, only deepened the isolation of Polish Jews from the Polish community that had existed for centuries in a very conspicuous manner. If we were to weigh the fact that there was not a single Jewish autonomy (ghetto) on Polish land which, between the years 1939-1942, that is during the period before the Holocaust, would have established communications and included itself within the structure of the Polish Underground State along with the fact that during WWII, there existed no political or military factions which collaborated with the Germans (as was the case in France, Lithuania, Latvia, Estonia, Bielorussia and the Ukraine), and that the Polish police (the dark-blue as they were called) had already been cast outside the walls of the ghettos at the time of their closing, then it becomes clear that the drama of the Holocaust of Polish Jews unravelled without the participation of, and outside the reach

---

[288] *Kronika getta Łodzkiego, (Chronicle of the Łódź Ghetto)*, Lodz 1965, Volume I, p. 363-364 and 429.

[289] L. Dobroszycki, *Preface* to: *"Kronika getta łódzkiego"* ["The Lodz Ghetto Diary"], Łódź 1965, p. XXIII.

of, the authorities, and more often than not, beyond the scope of what the Poles could actually see with their own eyes.

The framework of Jewish life in the years 1939-1942 was delineated in the ghettos by faith in Jewish and German authorities as well as by subjugation to the commands being issued. Once the mass deportations of Polish Jews to the death camps commenced, very little had changed in that respect. This is especially true at the end of 1942, when more than three hundred thousand Warsaw Jews had already met their demise in the gas chambers, and the real purpose of the "deportations" was no longer a secret to anyone. The obedience and credulity of the Jews continued to serve as the greatest obstacle with regard to saving their lives and their honor. The most respectable of Jewish sources can attest to this. Among these sources, the most considerable mention goes to proclamation issued by ŻOB [The Jewish Soldiers Organization of the Warsaw Ghetto – E.K.] in Warsaw on December 4, 1942 in which we read:

An uncertain tomorrow is poisoning every moment of the bitter life of a prisoner inside this Jewish gathering of Warsaw. (…) Are we going to allow ourselves to be hoodwinked by a good word from this or that Hitlerian murderer, by this or that rumor peddled by Jewish Gestapo, salesmen and infidels as well as by the credulous ones?

There is no doubt that Hitlerism set a goal for itself to get rid of all Jews. His tactics are based on deception and hypocrisy. (…) Jews! (…) Don't believe the Jewish infidels, "shop" managers, foremen. Those are your enemies. Don't let them fool you.[290]

Meanwhile, the first and most fundamental condition vital to saving the life of a Polish Jew was their rebellion expressed through incredulity and disobedience with regard to German and Jewish commands. Well documented stories of the Holocaust prove that not many Jews decided to follow these expressions of incredulity and disobedience with regard to German and Jewish commands. What dominated was a posture of faith in the wisdom of the Germans, which included authentic deportations, life beyond the current

290 Bartoszewski W, Lewinowna Z., *Ten jest z ojczyzny mojej* [*How Poles Helped the Jews, 1939-1945*], Kraków 1969, p. 42.

residential locale and a hope to remain alive. Władysław Szpilman described the atmosphere of the Warsaw Umschlagplatz in this way:

With the influx of people, it was beginning to become more and more cramped, and it was necessary to avoid groups of standing and lying people. Everybody was discussing the same thing: where are they going to take us to, and is it really for the purpose of work, like the Jewish police was trying to convince everyone. (…) One of our very good friends sat down next to Mother, her husband stood next to Father. They had been, at some point, the proprietors of a large store. There was another mutual friend, a dentist who practiced near our home on Sliska Street, standing with them. The shopkeeper had an overall positive spin on things. The dentist, on the other hand, saw things in dreary hues. He was very uptight and bitter.

- This is a disgrace which will envelop every single one of us! – he was practically shouting. – We are allowing ourselves to be led to the slaughter like a herd of sheep! (…)

Father was listening carefully. Somewhat reserved, somewhat good-natured, he smiled, shrugged his shoulders and pointed out:

- And how can you be so certain, Sir, that they will send all of us to our deaths?

The dentist smacked his palms together.

- Of course I don't know this! How would I know something like that? You think they would reveal something like that? But with ninety-percent certainty I will say that they want to eliminate all of us.

Father smiled once again, as though he had gained even more confidence after that response.

- Why don't you have a look around, Sir – he said, and with his arm he gestured grandly in a semi-circle at the crowd on Umschlagplatz as though he were presenting something – we are not heroes. We are just ordinary people and that is why we choose to take the ten-percent chance risk that we will remain alive.

The shopkeeper supported Father. And he was completely opposed to the dentist's opinion: the Germans can't possibly be so stupid as to squander so great a labor force as the Jews represent.[291]

---

[291] W. Szpilman, *Pianista [The pianist]*, Krakow 2003, p. 95-97.

It is necessary to point out the fact that the Polish-Jewish spirit described above by Władysław Szpilman with regard to facing death applies only to a very small group of assimilated Jews whose assimilation very organically predisposed them to be in the role of "rebels", that is of those who are not supposed to believe or follow German-Jewish commands, but rather search for salvation outside the walls of the ghetto. Meanwhile, the rebellion which was understood to mean absolute suspicion and doubt was not something the incredulous dentist decided to do, nor did the moderately trusting shopkeeper or father of Władysław Szpilman. They never even considered escaping to the Polish side of Warsaw.

They were not "heroes".

They were ordinary Jews.

They were dying with a ten-percent hope to live.

Rebellion lay beyond the limits of their psychological capabilities.

If this is the way assimilated Jews responded to the Holocaust, then one can only imagine that, among religious Jews, Hasidim, "heroism", which was understood to mean rebellion against Jewish and German authority, was an even rarer occurrence. Evidence of this is reflected in the scarce number of Polish Orthodox Jews who survived.

A rebellious Polish Jew who was willing to put up a fight for their own life on the "Aryan" side, that is the Polish side, stood before a whole slew of additional decisions to be made in addition to the necessity of overcoming a series of purely existential issues. Above all, they would have to overcome the deeply-seated stereotype within themselves of wariness of Poles as the anti-Semites, the Hamans lying in wait for the opportunity to take a Jewish life, and they would have to place their trust in the hands of Poles. Actually, in the fourth year of the war when the Holocaust began, no one had a better understanding of the difference between German and Polish anti-Semitism than Polish Jews. Polish anti-Semitism, according to Professor Yisrael Gutman, "never took on anti-humane or antihuman elements of racism."[292] Nonetheless, as the first years of the war clearly

---

[292] Y. Gutman, *Polish Antisemitism Between the Wars: An Overview*, in: Y. Gutman, E. Mendelsohn, J. Reinharz, Ch. Schmeruk (ed.), „The Jews of Poland Betwen two World Wars", Brandeis University Press, Hanover 1989, p. 100.

demonstrated, especially the year of 1941, it was clear that Poles were also capable of criminal acts not having anything to do with their declared Catholicism or patriotism, i.e., Jedwabne.

It is not difficult to imagine what was being said about Poles beyond the walls of the autonomies and ghettos among Hasidim and other Orthodox Jews in 1942. After all, if Marek Edelman, some forty years after the war had ended, said this in response to a question about how Jews inside the ghettos saw the world outside the walls, and whether or not this outside world was an option:

[Poles] that was the enemy. [...] That's all there was to it. An enemy in the sense that if you did venture out of here onto the other side and told them who you were, they would kill you.[293]

The fact that wariness of Poles as the enemy within Polish Jewish circles was quite prevalent is evident from notations by Adam Czerniakow stating that, in the Warsaw autonomy before the Holocaust, plans had been prepared to defend the ghetto against an attack by the Poles. In accordance with the circulating stereotype among Polish Jews, the worst Hamans amidst the Haman-esque Poles were the Catholic clergy. Marek Edelman speaks clearly and emphatically:

The Church in Poland before the war was really racist ("czarna sotnia"), (...) All the anti-Jewish pogroms came out of the churches. (...) After all, there were instances where after confession, priests would give up Jews...[294]

Indeed, as agonizingly difficult as rebellion against Jewish and German authorities was for Polish Jews, and it was linked to some very excruciating psychological maneuvers, overcoming the deeply seated stereotypes and placing trust in the hands of the nation of *Hamans* that was "controlled by" the Catholic *really racists* had to be a maneuver of immensely impossible dimensions. One thing is certain: Jewish stereotypes during the time of the Holocaust, just as various other stereotypes of different times and places, had very little to do with reality. I do not know of any anti-Jewish pogroms in the XX century that would have come from Polish churches, just as I know of

[293] M. Edelman, in: Grupińska A., *"Ciągle po kole"* ["Still Round the Circle: Talks with the Soldiers of the Warsaw Ghetto"], Warszawa 2005, p. 27.
[294] Ibidem, p. 20 and 30.

no instances of Polish Catholic priests giving up a Polish Jew to the Germans after confession. But perhaps Marek Edelman has better documentation on the matter at his disposal. In any event, all of this explains the fact that a very small percentage of Polish Jews during the time of the Holocaust had made the decision to seek help among Poles. But it is only through making such a decision that they gave Poles the opportunity to save them.

The rebellious Jew, upon discarding their faith in German and Jewish authorities as well as the negative stereotypes associated with Poles, stood at the gates of the ghetto. It then became apparent that their chances for survival depended on at least a few factors, on whose existence the Poles had absolutely no influence:

Knowledge of the Polish language. If a Polish Jew spoke Polish well, they would have a chance to hide out among Poles. If not, their chances of being rescued dropped to nil. One option was to feign being a mute. There are a few known cases of a Jewish life being saved in this manner, but for obvious reasons, this method could not be widely utilized. Meanwhile, 85% of Polish Jews did not know how to speak Polish. Given that, barely 15% of Polish Jews did have a chance of surviving the Holocaust with a good grasp of the Polish language. The fact that knowledge of the Polish language was a condition of survival is further evidenced by, among other things, the statistics regarding Jewish children that had been rescued inside convents. Among children old enough to speak, that is anyone over the age of two, there was barely one little girl who was able to be saved, as upon passing through the convent gate, she spoke only Yiddish.[295] Polish Jews not only did not know the Polish language, their isolation from the Polish world ages before the outbreak of WWII, was so hermetic that Jews did not even know Polish first names. When the head of the Warsaw Rabbinical Court, Michal Hefer, was preparing his granddaughter to leave the Warsaw ghetto, her father instructed her to take on a Polish first name. But Michal did not know any Polish first names for she had never played with any Polish children.[296]

---

[295] Kurek E., *Dzieci zydowskie w klasztorach [The Jewish Childern in the Polish Convents]*, Lublin 2001, p. 210.
[296] Kurek E., The documentary film: *Who Saved one Life Saved all Word*, The Polish Television canal 2, Warsaw 1998.

Having friends and acquaintances among Poles on whose help Jews can have relied. If Polish Jews had such social contacts, there existed a better chance that one of them would have turned out to the *bold daredevil* who would risk putting their own life in danger in order to save the life of a Jewish friend and to take care of them. If they had none, then their chances of survival dropped to nil. Lacking any knowledge of wartime realities that existed on the "Aryan" side, not possessing documents or the ability to handle oneself with the Polish "szmalcowniks"[297] in this case, placed a successful rescue more into the category of a miracle than within the realm of realistic possibilities. The centuries-old customary Jewish isolation resulted in Polish Jews having neither friends nor acquaintances among Poles at the time of the Holocaust.

External appearances. "The right" or "the wrong" looks were not relevant. Of course, those with blond hair and light eyes had an easier time of hiding out, but if a Jew were able to mask a "wrong" look with fluent Polish, a confident manner and some adequate camouflage, there was no reason to assume that the "wrong" look would create any major obstacles. After all, there is no shortage of Poles with dark hair and specifically characteristic noses.

Material means. A poor Jew who had made the decision to save his life "on the Aryan side" was subject to rely on the charity of Poles who were willing to bear the financial burden of providing refuge (i.e., renting an apartment, buying food, medication, etc...). A Jew of material means would not have to place this financial burden on the Poles providing refuge. Occasionally, they would even prove to be an additional source of income for the Pole. Due to the widespread impoverishment of the Polish population by the fourth year of the war, the financial aspect played a rather substantial role with regard to saving Jews.

Circumcision. In the case of men, it was this very element which was

---

297 SZMALCOWNIK – in Polish jargon the word „szmal" means money. The contemptous term „szmalcownik" was used during the war to describe those criminals and collaborators who demanded money from Jews in hiding or the Poles who hid them in exchange for not informing the Germans where they were. The „szmalcowniks" did not always keep their word: after receiving money, they would inform on them anyway.

ultimately the most dangerous and most telling with regards to origins and nationality.

x   x   x

The Jewish conditions dictating survival of Polish Jews in German occupied Poland boil down to the following: psychological (losing faith in German and Jewish authorities, rebellion against their commands and discarding the Pole-Haman stereotype), the social aspect (knowledge of the Polish language and possessing social contacts among Poles) and material/visible aspects (appearance, circumcision among males, and financial means).

In other words, in order for a Pole to be able to undertake the effort to save the life of a Jew, that Jew had to have abandoned his credulity and obedience with regard to German and Jewish authorities, and then, upon discarding the fear based on stereotypes, make the decision to leave the Jewish autonomy (the ghetto) in search of refuge among Poles whilst expressing a willingness to be saved. At the source of rescuing the life of another (with the exception of children whose parents make that decision), the decision must always lay with the willingness of the one being saved. The situation was no different in the case of Polish Jews facing annihilation. Because the will to be saved on the Polish side of the walls was further fortified and even more impervious as a result of the above mentioned conditions that were psychological in nature, and this required the breaking down of strong mental barriers, the "heroism", as Władysław Szpilman put it, to seek out salvation among Poles, and the expression of willingness to have one's own life saved beyond the walls of the autonomies and ghettos. Only a handful of Jews were capable of achieving this.

At the same time it is necessary to underscore, that under the conditions of WWII, it was impossible for Poles to enter beyond the walls of Jewish autonomies and ghettos in order to rescue the Jews residing there against their will. This would be tantamount to declaring war against Polish Jews (the Jewish police and the Judenrats). The results of this type of war would have been a foregone conclusion. It is important to emphasize once again:

Poles were able to save only those Polish Jews who wanted to be saved by Poles.

No one has ever counted the number of Polish Jews who were able to overcome themselves to rebel against the Jewish and German authorities, and later place their trust in Poles. It is why only mere estimates play a role here. It seems safe to assume, without being too far off the mark, that taking the step to be cautious of believing *any words, any fast ones pulled by SS thugs and Jewish infidels,* and then trusting the Polish "Hamans", which was the condition enabling Poles to save a Jewish life, was overcome by no more that 5-10% of Polish Jews, which is about 170-335 thousand individuals from throughout the entire country.

In the second half of 1942, approximately 170-335 thousand Polish Jews had left the walls of the Jewish autonomies (the ghettos) and asked Poles for help in saving their lives.

Between the years 1942-1945, institutional Poland (the Polish Underground State and the Catholic Church) as well as individual Poland (the Polish population) was confronted with the dilemma of saving the lives of Polish Jews. As far as it is possible to express in definitive and calculable categories, the results of the stance taken by the functioning institutions during WWII in German occupied Poland, it is not possible to categorize the stance taken by individual Poles, as this sort of categorization simply cannot be applied on an one-to-one basis. Poles, as individuals, were driven by various rationales, and each behaved differently. Some undertook to save Jewish lives, some refused to assist and remained indifferent, and others still turned tracking down Jews and the Poles who harbored them into a lucrative business or a source of pathological sadistic pleasure.

The Polish Underground State was the state authority of Poland during WWII and represented Poles in the international political arena (the President of the Polish State and the Government-in-Exile in Angres and London), as well as through the highest representation of the Polish Government-in-Exile, which was the Government Delegate to the Country established in December of 1940. It delegated the direction of campaigns for Poles along with moral, political and patriotic postures to be observed throughout the entirety of the German occupied country. The following underground organs were subordinate to the Government Delegate to the Country: Directorate of Civil Resistance (Kierownictwo Walki Cywilnej), the Political Consultative Committee (Polityczny Komitet Porozumiewawczy) and the Directorate of Underground Resistance (Kierownictwo Walki Podziemnej) – which was the conspiratorial Polish army known as the Home Army [Armia Krajowa – AK].[298]

Though limited in scope, the Polish Underground State possessed fairly effective means of exerting sufficient pressure on the Polish people to exact certain types of behavior from them. Above all, the Polish Underground State forbade Poles from cooperating with the occupying forces (the Germans and the Soviets), including any form of co-participation in German repressions with regard to the Jewish population. The direct result of this was that Poles, unlike other nations of occupied Europe during WWII, never created any military formations subordinate to the Germans. Nor did they create any formations that would have cooperated with the Germans in the annihilation of the Jews.[299]

In the proclamation of the Polish Underground State, which was released in "Information Bulletin" of the conspiratorial organ of the Polish underground army (The Home Army), and later reprinted in other clandestine periodicals more that a year prior to the German commencement of the annihilation of Polish Jews, this is what we read:

---

[298] Davies N., *Boże igrzysko* [*God's playground*], Kraków 2003, p. 928.

[299] T. Strzembosz, *Polskie Państwo Podziemne [The Polish Underground State]*, Warsaw 2000, 100, wrote: *During World War II, the Ukrainians, the Byelorussians and the Jews cooperated with both occupational systems. There were also incidents – not yet fully recorded or analyzed, though not marginal – of Poles serving in the Worker-Peasant's Militia. This formation was strictly connected to NKWD and, apart from the army, was a military arm of the occupant in 1939-1941. Besides, in the General Government there was the Polish Police, known also as 'the Blue Police' (called so because of the color of the uniforms and in order to avoid the adjective 'Polish'). It was created as early as 1939 and was composed partly of volunteers and partly of those intimidated and threatened. The formation was quite numerous; according to Adam Hempel, in 1942 it included 12 thousand men and took part not only in fighting common crime but also in repressive actions and in fighting conspiracy activity which was often difficult to distinguish from purely criminal offenses (e.g. murder, requisition, attacks on convoys with money and material goods etc.). At the same time, many 'Blue policemen' effectively cooperated with the The Polish Underground State, to mention for example Colonel Aleksander Reszczynski.*

March, 1941, Warsaw

Proclamation of the management of the Undderground Polish Army in Poland regarding the prohibition of appealing to the auxiliary service to requesting assistance during barrack patrol in Jewish work camps.

On March 1 of this year, the walls of the capital and Polish cities bore [the German] announcements calling for Poles with military training to enter the service of volunteer auxiliary forces to patrol the Jewish barracks.

Because:

1. Volunteer service of Poles under German command is high treason,

2. The auxiliary forces of the German police (gendarme) may be forced to commit acts which might disgrace the good name of Poles,

3. No person voluntarily entering this service has any guarantee that they will not be transported somewhere deep into Germany or some other country, which would deprive Poland of individuals with military training who will be very much needed once the battle with our occupiers intensifies,

4. Every Pole who enters the German service relieves one more German soldier to fight on the front lines against our allies, and in so doing delays our victory as well as the reconstruction of our independence,

5. The Polish Government, currently in exile, has already recommended refraining from any form of even feigned participation in anti-Jewish campaigns organized by the Germans,

6. The German enemy will take advantage of this auxiliary service in order to show the entire world that we are cooperating with them in destroying Jews, and will attempt to embarrass us internationally.

Therefore, military-organizational agencies throughout the area of the nation, acting on behalf of the Polish Government in Exile, we are calling upon all Poles to categorically refuse even the notion of being involved in the forces of the auxiliary service under the German police (gendarme).[300]

The lecture contained in the proclamation regarding the prohibition of Poles from entering German military formations designed to vanquish the Jewish minority leaves very little doubt as to the main reason why Poles

---

[300] „Biuletyn Informacyjny" ["Information Bulletin" of the Polish Underground State], March 6, 1941.

did not participate in subduing or annihilating Polish Jews. It had nothing to do with solidarity with the Jewish people, but rather it was a matter of national interest and codified expected norms of behavior with regard to propositions being offered by Poland's enemies.

There is no point in trying to conceal the fact that in March of 1941, for Poles – with the degree of distaste over the Jewish betrayal and collaboration with the Germans and Soviets still raw – the notion of revenge was far more dear to them (as the incidents in Jedwabne and other locales attest to) than feelings of solidarity with regard to Polish Jews. Despite that, Poles subjugated themselves to the directives that came down from the Polish Underground State as they pertained to the auxiliary forces created by the Germans and to the vanquish and annihilation of Polish Jews. In the Polish citizen code, there is no place for cooperation with the occupier for the patriotic and honorable.

Because the Polish Underground State refused cooperation with the occupier, in 1942, when the Germans began the annihilation of Polish Jews, not a single Polish formation took part in that disgraceful act.

The obliteration of Polish Jews was no less of a shock to Poles as it was to Jews. In May of 1941, the opening article in the "Information Bulletin" of the Polish Underground State which was dedicated to Jews, concluded with these words: "And how will the conclusion of the Jewish matter play itself out in Poland in general? What will come next? There is no answer to that question. The Germans themselves are saying that the Jewish quandary in Poland is still awaiting a permanent solution".[301]

A year later, when Germans came upon resolving "the permanent solution of the Jewish question", in the first weeks, Poles also had very little knowledge as to its character and direction. In the first issue, after the annihilation of the Warsaw ghetto began, the underground "Information Bulletin" of the Polish Underground State reported the following:

The main occurrence, which as of a week ago has been shaking up the city, is the liquidation of the Warsaw ghetto that the Germans have begun.

---

[301] „Biuletyn Informacyjny" ["Information Bulletin" of the Polish Underground State], May 23, 1941.

It is being executed with absolute Prussian barbarity. (...) On the outside, the ghetto is surrounded by thickets of dark-blue police forces as well as by a Lithuanian division. In the last couple of days, SS stations have also been added along the outside walls. Inside the actual ghetto, Ukrainian and German forces are the only ones "operating". Everyday, over 6,000 Jews are being transported out. They are being transported by trains leaving from the secondary railway platform at Stawki Street. The direction of the transport – eastward. The destination of the transport is unknown, but there is speculation that they are heading towards the Malkin and Brzesc region near the Bug River. Also, there is no information as to the fate of those being taken – nothing but the worst possible assumptions are circulating regarding that topic.

As to the method of organizing these transports, it is that evil genius of the Germans that has placed the burden on the Jewish Council [Judenrat] and the Jewish peace-keeping police. The German authorities designate only the deportation "contingent" on a daily basis. Whereas the responsibility of drawing up of proper lists, evacuating the apartments (15 minutes!), loading up the train cars, etc... is supposedly delegated to the Jews. The Ukrainian and German watchmen are designed only to oversee the processes.

The Chairman of the Jewish Council [Judenrat], Engineer Czerniakow, in the only possible respectable manner, has expressed his objections to the atrocities taking place: he has committed suicide. In his place, the Germans have assigned Wolf, a Jew serving in the Gestapo. The entire Jewish County Council [Judenrat] was one day arrested, and later dismissed from performing duties.

The deportation campaign will probably last at least several weeks.

In the course of the Jewish murders, a few Poles who had been inside the ghetto on business did perish. Among others, the renowned surgeon, dr Raszeja, professor at Poznań University, was murdered. He had been summoned to the ghetto on consultation.[302]

The Polish Government-in-Exile in London, and the entire Polish population was stricken by the information being leaked from within the walls of the ghetto. In this situation, the Directorate of Civil Resistance

---

[302] „Biuletyn Informacyjny" ["Information Bulletin" of the Polish Underground State], July 30, 1942.

of the the Polish Government-in-Exile, which had enjoyed considerable respect in occupied Poland, and which had organized and coordinated the prevalent populace resistance of the Poles, released an official protest to be published in a series of conspiratorial periodicals in September of 1942:

Declaration

Alongside the tragedy being endured by the people of Poland, decimated by the enemy, is the barbaric slaughter of Jews that has been ongoing for nearly a year now. This mass murder has no precedent anywhere in the history of the world. All other atrocities in history pale in comparison. Infants, children, youth, adults, elders, cripples, the infirm, the healthy, men, women, Catholic Jews, Mosaic Jews, for no reason other than being members of the Jewish people, are being mercilessly murdered, poisoned with gasses, buried alive, thrown to the street from their windows – before their demise, they are subject to the painful suffering of a slow agonizing death, a hellish exile, torment, brazen preying of executioners. The number of victims killed in this manner has surpassed one million and is growing with every passing day. Unable to actively prevent this from taking place, the Directorate of Civil Resistance (of the the Polish Government-in-Exile) on behalf of the entire nation of Poles, protests to the crimes being committed against the Jews. All Polish political and social groups are included in this protest. Just as in the matter of the Polish victims, the responsibility for these crimes shall fall upon the executioners and their accomplices.

The Directorate of Civil Resistance (of the the Polish Government-in-Exile)[303]

The Polish Underground State was unable to *actively prevent* the crimes being committed by Germans against Polish Jews. It is crucial to understand that this meant they did not possess the military capabilities necessary to prevent the realization of the German plan of the Holocaust. If we keep in mind that the first setback encountered by the Germans in the East near Stalingrad was in January of 1943, and the second front was

---

[303] „Biuletyn Informacyjny" ("Information Bulletin" of the Polish Underground State), September 17, 1942.

created in mid-1944, then it is not difficult to recognize that no one in the world possessed the necessary military capabilities back in 1942.

Acting in the name of accountability with regard to its Jewish citizens, the Polish Underground State did not stop at issuing its protest against the murder of Polish Jews, but rather undertook campaigns in four possible areas:

- it informed the world of the Genocide taking place in Poland at the hands of the Germans;
- it organized a rescue plan to save Jewish lives;
- it propagated pro-Jewish postures throughout the Polish population and punished those Poles who cooperated with the Germans, in any capacity, in perpetrating the crime of genocide against Polish Jews on Polish lands;
- within the realm of its capabilities, it lent support to Jews who stood up to fight against the Germans.

Accounts and messages regarding the situation affecting the Jewish population were being transmitted to the Polish Government-in-Exile in London as early as 1940. Inside the few-hundred-pages thick "black book", *The German New Order in Poland* released in early 1942, the part entitled *The Persecution of the Jews and Ghettos* was dedicated to German repressions aimed at Polish Jews. The amount of information coming into London, including accounts from Polish Underground Home Army (AK), the Polish Government Delegate to the Country, as well as wire dispatches and monographs from Jewish organizations in Poland, were all presented to the court of British public opinion on July 9, 1942 at a special press conference called by the Polish Government-in-Exile. Within a few weeks, and English-language pamphlet was issued which stated: *Stop Them Now! German Mass-Murder of Jews in Poland.* It contained reports of the annihilation of Jews that was underway.[304]

---

[304] Bartoszewski W, Lewinowna Z., *Ten jest z ojczyzny mojej* (*How Poles Helped the Jews, 1939-1945*), Kraków 1969, p. 29-32.

In the autumn of 1942, a Special Courier of the Polish Government-in-Exile, Jan Kozielewski, was dispatched to London under the name Jan Karski, who recalls the following:

Prior to leaving the country, I had received an order from the Delegate to the Country (of the Polish Government-in-Exile) to meet with two representatives of the Jewish underground who appeared on behalf of the Zionists and Association of Socialists Bund. In essence, they were appearing on behalf of all Polish Jews.

The meeting took place just outside of Warsaw. (...) The first thought that entered my mind was the realization of how hopeless their situation was. For us, the Poles, this was a war and an occupation. For them, the Jews, it was the end of the world. A death sentence had been issued on their heads for no reason than they... existed. And they supposed to not exist. They did not fear death. They were painfully aware that they had no hope of being victorious – the hope that somehow make awaiting certain death somewhat less bitter. That is how the Zionist opened the discussion.

– You Poles are lucky. Many of you are suffering, many of you are perishing, yet your nation continues to exist. After the war is over, Poland will exist. Cities shall be rebuilt, and your wounds shall heal over. From a sea of tears, pain and humiliation, this country, which was our motherland as well, shall rise again. But we, the Jews, will no longer be here. Our entire nation of people shall disappear. Hitler will lose his war against humanity, good and justice. But he will be the victor over the Jews. "Victor" isn't even the right word. He will simply murder every single last one of us. (...)

– I understand what you are feeling... As far as I am able, I will do everything in my power to obtain help. I am unable to gauge my own capabilities in this respect. I am heading to London on a mission from the Polish Underground State. I am certain that I will have the opportunity to report to the representatives of allied authorities – I tried to remain calm.

– Really? – the Zionist exclaimed with hope in his voice. – Do you think, Sir, that you will gain access to Churchill and Roosevelt?

Two days later I ventured into the Warsaw ghetto. My guide was the Bund leader (...) This was a different Warsaw. Another world. (...) After another two days I returned to the ghetto. (...) On the third day, after my recurring expedition into the Warsaw ghetto, the Bund leader organized yet another meeting.

- We want to take you to the camp in Belzec. We have a plan ready. It should work out. Do you want to go?

I agreed. We arrived in the town well after noon. My guide dismissed the driver and we traveled the rest of the way on foot to a tiny iron store just beyond the main square. It was run by a peasant who introduced himself only as Onyszko. He was in the conspiracy. He took us into the back room where a neatly folded uniform and undergarments had been laid on a chair. Next to it was a pair of tall boots. A hat was hanging on the backrest of the chair. The Ukrainian guard had refused to lend his I.D. documents. Instead, he provided the documents belonging to one of his relatives, also in service to the SS, who had disappeared without a trace. (...) After an hour had gone by, the guard who was going to escort me to the camp appeared. He spoke Polish well. (...) What I witnessed inside the camp haunts me to this day. (...)

The first person to whom I had to report (in London) was the Vice-Premier and Minister of Internal Affairs of the Polish Government-in-Exile, Stanislaw Mikolajczyk. His duties included maintaining communications with the Underground in Poland as well as providing it with financial support. Immediately afterwards I undertook to prepare my reports regarding the situation in Poland under occupation and matters pertaining to the functioning of the Underground. (...) Upon reading my reports, the Premier himself, General Władysław Sikorski, agreed to meet with me. (...) The next person to whom I was to give my report was the President of the Polish Government-in-Exile, Władysław Raczkiewicz. (...)

After a few weeks, I began a series of meetings with Alliance representatives. (...) I was very much impressed by Anthony Eden. (...) I also stood before the Committee to Investigate War Crimes, which was headed by Sir Cecil Hurst, Legal Counsel to the British Cabinet. In front of the Committee, I relayed my eye-witness account as to what I saw inside the ghetto and death camp. (...) During this time, I had contact with the political, cultural and spiritual elites of Great Britain. (...)

In early May of 1943, I was unexpectedly summoned by General Sikorski. After we exchanged greetings, he got down to brass tacks.

- You shall go to the Unites States – he said. (...)

In the United States, just as in England, I took part in dozens of exhaustive conferences, meetings, discussions and public appearances. (...) The most important meeting took place toward the end of my stay in the United States. On July 28, 1943, Ambassador Jan Ciechanowski informed me that, on this day, we are being expected at eleven o'clock in the morning by President Franklin Delano Roosevelt. (...) I also met with Supreme Court Judge Felix Frankfurter, who after listening to me said: "Do you know that I am a Jew?" I nodded. Frankfurter continued "I am unable to believe you."

In Great Britain and the United States, I informed the top people of these world powers of what I had seen. I had spoken with Jewish leaders on both continents. I talked about what I had seen with renowned authors: Herbert G. Wells and Arthur Koestler, as well as with members of the PEN Club in England and in America. They possessed talent and renown. They possessed the ability to describe this better than I ever could. Did they do this?[305]

Jan Karski and a string of equal soldiers of the Polish Underground Home Army, though putting their own lives at risk, prepared reports and disseminated information about the Holocaust throughout the world. The Polish Underground State and the Polish Government-in-Exile in London did everything within their powers to ensure that the free world learned of the German crimes being perpetrated against the Jewish population.

The Polish Underground State, through organizing within the framework of the conspiratorial structures, planned the rescue of Polish Jews escaping from the ghettos as well as organized propaganda campaigns in the underground press. In so doing, and in no uncertain terms, it expressed the model of behavior by which Poles are bound with regard to Jews being murdered as follows: providing them with necessary assistance, or, if that is not possible, exercise passive consent.

In practice this meant that if a Pole, possessing enough courage and having the capabilities to do so, ought to actively engage themselves in the rescue campaigns of the structures of the Polish Underground State;

---

[305] J. Karski, *Tajne panstwo [The Underground State]*, Warszawa 1999, p. 244, 250, 252, 253, 263, 283, 284, 286, 288-290.

if, however, they lack the courage to place their lives and the lives of their loved ones in danger, they are obliged to facilitate the ghetto escapees with passive support, which means they are not to inform Germans of hiding places, nor are they to engage in tracking down Jews in hiding. Not abiding by said recommendations of the Polish Underground State was punishable by Polish Underground Courts with the same consequences as betraying matters of national interest would be – by death. In the report prepared by the Polish Underground Home Army (AK), and dispatched to London on November 21, 1942, this is what we read:

In the period currently being reported (15.X – 15.XI, 1942), a new wave of anti-Jewish persecutions has been on the rise throughout the territory of the General Government (GG). This time, there are already repressions in place which boil down to exterminating the hitherto remaining Jewish population. (...) The extermination of the Jewish element in the GG province has been proceeding at a very fast rate. In small towns as well as in villages, German air expeditions, the SS as well as Sonderdienst (with the sporadic participation of the dark-blue police) are engaging in sweeping extermination campaigns. For example, in Lukow, several dozen have fallen victim to bloodshed, many Jews were able to escape into the forests or have found refuge in villages throughout the countryside. Approximately 5 thousand have been deported.

Persons who have remained in close contact with the Warsaw ghetto are making claims of recent transports of Jews arriving in Warsaw from France, Belgium and Holland. These transports are not very large. The fate of these Jews has not yet been made clear, but there is very little doubt that this is merely a transition point leading up to an expedition heading East, for extermination.

The incidence of Jews passing from the ghetto to the Aryan side, as indicated in the previous report, has undergone expansion and has become more focused. As of today, there are many such instances. The escapees seek material assistance, dwelling and documents. Despite the increase in probability of personal risk involved, Poles are generally eager to step up to help. Jewish escapees do not manifest extreme caution in their behavior. They move about the streets freely, visit the homes of Poles, and travel by train. Considering the recent increase in Gestapo and police activity, this current state of affairs may overburden the bank accounts and suffering to be endured by Poles. The need for assistance for these escapees requires the creation of a special funding source as well as a specific dispensation center. In addition, the funding sources which Jews still have at their disposal abroad need to be activated.[306]

The response of the government authorities of the Polish Underground State to the will of Polish Jews escaping the ghettos expressing a desire to be rescued by Poles, was the summoning to action of the Jewish Assistance Council which commenced on December 4, 1942, and was incorporated as a division of the Directorate of Civil Resistance, which made it part of one of the three pillars of the Polish Underground State.[307] The plan to create a special, clandestine institution to deal specifically with matters of assistance to Jews which would be subsidized by the authorities of the Polish Underground State came to fruition as the Office of Information and Propaganda Headquarters of the Polish Underground Home Army (AK), which had already been operational in summer of 1942.

Earlier yet, within its humble means, the campaign of assistance to ghetto escapees was run by a modestly sized social-fostering organization called the Front for the Rebirth of Poland (FOP) with Zofia Kossak at its head. The FOP efforts in assisting Jews were funded mainly by contributions collected from landowners and the intelligentsia, and Zofia Kossak's personal connections within pre-war military and monastic circles allowed her to provide her charges with "false" documents and to place women and children in convents. It was thanks to the endeavors of Zofia Kossak, that on September 27, 1942, a committee was formed, initially called the Social Assistance Committee of the Jewish Population, but for the purposes of secrecy, it operated under the codename of the Konrad Zegota Committee (ZEGOTA).

In November of 1942, a meeting of "Zegota" representatives was held, with Irena Sendlerowa and Aleksandra Dargielowa, who represented all the various agencies participating in rescue campaigns of Polish Jews. In this way, on December 4, 1942, the Polish Council for Aid to Jews (ZEGOTA)

---

[306] Archiwum ZHP (The Archive of ZHP – Warsaw), 202/XV, p. 2.
[307] Davies N., *Boże igrzysko* (*God's playground*), Kraków 2003, p. 928.

was formed, which fused all the various agencies participating in rescue campaigns for Polish Jews into one underground organization. Since it was subordinate to the Government Delegate to the Country, it gained aid and support from both the Polish Government-in-Exile in London as well as the Polish populace.[308]

Through information-propaganda campaigns sponsored by the Polish Government-in-Exile in London, through equating the value of rescuing the lives of Polish Jews with other forms of underground movements and in incorporating them into the structures of the Polish Underground State as a separate subversive entity (the Council for Aid to Jews), saving the lives of Polish Jews being murdered by the Germans became a standard state campaign of equal importance as other key campaigns of the Polish Underground State. At the same time, this sent a clear signal to the Polish population that the proper stance with regard to the annihilation of Polish Jews is that of issuing them assistance or passive support.

The Polish Underground State, within its humble means, also provided aid to those Polish Jews who opted to take up arms in their fight against the crime of genocide being perpetrated on their people. Jewish historians are quick to indict The Polish Underground State of providing insufficient military might to the handful of Jews who, in 1943, picked up arms and decided to fight, not so much for their own lives, as for an honorable death with weapons in hand. The truth of the matter is, however, that Polish Jews who had already decided in September of 1939 that the war which broke out was not a Jewish matter but rather a Polish one, took to creating their own autonomies (ghettos) – through multifaceted collaboration with the Germans and working intensely to help build the German war machine – as well as creating the most optimal conditions for survival. During the years 1939-1942, the authorities of not a single Jewish autonomy (ghetto) had attempted to establish any form of communications with the structures of the Polish Underground State.

308 M. Arczynski, W. Balcerak, *Kryptonim Zegota [The codename of Żegota]*, Warsaw 1983, p. 105; W. Bartoszewski, Z. Lewinowna, op. cit., p. 37; T. Prekerowa, *Konspiracyjna Rada Pomocy Zydom w Warszawie [The Underground General Council of Protection of Polish Jews in Warsaw]*, Warsaw 1982, p. 192, 211.

Therefore, when the time of the Holocaust came, it turned out that, aside from a Jewish Military Union (Żydowski Związek Wojskowy – ŻZW)[309] which had very few members, Polish Jews possessed none of the following: proper underground structures which would allow them to engage in a defensive battle; communications within the Polish Underground State; weapons or adequately trained personnel to use these weapons. On July 28, 1942, already during the Holocaust, the Jewish Fighting Organization (Żydowska Organizacja Bojowa – ŻOB) which in the Warsaw ghetto of half a million Jews had only one gun at its disposal.

According to Władysław Bartoszewski: "The first official communications between the Jewish underground movement in the Warsaw ghetto and the directorial cells of the Polish Underground Home Army occurred at the end of August 1942, but only a second attempt at establishing communications in September 1942 was successful." (...) The Jewish fighting organizations, had wished to establish and maintain communications with the military and civilian leaders of the Polish Underground State for the purpose of subjugating intended Jewish underground campaign, as well as for the purpose obtaining assistance from the Polish Underground Home Army with regard to weapons, ammunition and professional military training. "Jurek" (Arie Wilner) and "Mikołaj" (dr. Leon Fajner) from the Warsaw Ghetto submitted two equally worded declarations (...) addressed to the Commander-in-Chief of the Polish Underground Home Army and the Polish Government Delegate.

In response to this declaration, the commander-in-chief of the Polish Underground Home Army, General "Grot"-Rowecki, in short order issued

[309] Among the Jewish soldiers, mainly soldiers of the Polish Military, there was a small group of people who, in the first few days of the war, extablished the Jewish conspiratorial organization called „Dawn" ["Świt"]. With time, this organization morphed into the Jewish Military Union [Żydowski Związek Wojskowy - ŻZW], a conspiratorial military organization equal in its goals and activities to the Polish underground army, the Home Army [Armia Krajowa – AK]. Lieutenant Dawid Apfelbaum stood at the head of the Jewish Military Union. The soldiers of the Jewish Military Union maintained contact with the Polish Underground state and the Polish Home Army, and with an estimated 150-400-strong well armed soldiers, they fought in the Warsaw Ghetto Uprising in 1943. See also: The Judaic Lexicon [Słownik Judaistyczny], Warszawa 2003, p. 865; M. Apfelbaum, Dwa sztandary [The Two Flags], Krakow 2003.

a positive response in writing addressed to the official Jewish representative, expressing his approval of the intended activities in development within the Jewish Fighting Organization (ŻOB), as those of a paramilitary organization, recommending that they divide into "fifths" and run military training based on Home Army ideas and guidelines. The Polish Government Delegate accepted the declaration verbally in November 1942. (...)

In regard to the November order issued by General "Grot" (...), the ghetto exiles received a series of written instructions on how to handle weapons and explosives, studied methods of conducting an urban battle, became familiar with the various resources used to combat armor at close range on the spot, as well as learned how to produce typical incendiary devices, grenades among other things. (...) In general, during the winter 1942/1943 and in the first quarter of 1943, the Jewish Fighting Organization inside the Warsaw ghetto was provided with at least 70 handguns, each with two cartridges and ammunition, 500 grenades, high-explosive materials, fuses and detonators, material necessary to construct bottle bombs and hand grenades; and subsequently, in the second round, 1 hand-held machinegun, 1 light machinegun/automatic weapon, 20 handguns with cartridges and ammunition, 100 hand grenades with fasteners, and diverse materials (such as time-bombs and clock fuses) in abundant amounts. All of these various weapons were provided from the magazines of the Warsaw District Polish Home Army.[310]

In one of his interviews, Marek Edelman presents a very interesting picture regarding the Jewish Fighting Organization and evaluates the assistance the Warsaw Jews received from the Warsaw structures of the Polish Underground Home Army:

A. Grupińska: Does a complete list of the Jewish Fighting Organization (ŻOB) soldiers exist anywhere?
M. Edelman: Yes. Neustadt has it.

---

[310] Bartoszewski W, Lewinowna Z., *Ten jest z ojczyzny mojej* [*How Poles Helped the Jews, 1939-1945*], Kraków 1969, p. 25-26, 43-44 and 48-49.

A. Grupińska: Who was a member of ŻOB?

M. Edelman: Those who were in the group, in the division. (...) Those two hundred twenty members of ŻOB are the ones who fought. And aside from that, there were contacts. (...) You know, I knew those two hundred people from ŻOB. It's not that difficult to get to know two hundred people in six months. (...)

A. Grupińska: And what about connections with the Aryan side?

M. Edelman: Well sure, they existed. Up until 1941 they were pretty tight. It wasn't until later, after the walls went up, that they became rather strained. But no one from either side could ever have imagined that those half a million people in Warsaw (ghetto) would be murdered. (...)

A. Grupińska: And what about military groups?

M. Edelman: (Adam Czerniakow) wasted an opportunity. I've said this a hundred times already. He had had a lot of clout and he could have said: Gentlemen, don't let them knock you down, go fight. We were a people without a homeland. And he could have at least strengthened our passive resistance. But he did nothing. He didn't care for the underground, those little newspapers that were delivered to him. He was afraid of all that. (...) (The Poles), they didn't believe the Jews. (...) These gentlemen, (from the Polish Underground Home Arm), all they said was: – we will not give the Jews weapons because there's no telling what they might do with it, if they're going to use it. Jews just aren't cut out for shooting. (...) Go for the walls with your bare hands. Out of one hundred thousand, ten will survive. But weapons you shall not receive because we don't know if you will use them, or if it will go to waste. The truth of the matter is, they had nothing. (...) They (Poles) themselves were weak. And besides, [Poles] never trusted us. Of course they would send over some sort of directives, absolute nonsense. They didn't even give us our first weapon until after January 18. (...)

A. Grupińska: Do you believe, Sir, that the assistance provided by the Aryan side was sufficient?

M. Edelman: They [the Poles], first of all, couldn't, and second of all, didn't want to.

A. Grupińska: But you are not answering the question, Sir, you keep evading the question.

M. Edelman: What do you mean I'm not answering the question?

A. Grupińska: Because if someone cannot, then nothing can be changed, but if someone is willing, that's another story.

M. Edelman: It's difficult to answer that. It's something that cannot be measured. How much unwillingness was there, how much pilfering? It was not possible to say then, nor is it possible to say now. Those were different times. Every boy wanted to have a gun. The Poles gave us maybe five hundred guns, but we received fifty. They [the Poles] kept saying that they had given us one hundred fifty grenades, but only fifty showed up. Did they get stolen, or did something else happen to them? That cannot be clarified.[311]

A picture of the structure, training and conspiracy rules governing the Jewish Fighting Organization are filled in by the stories of Jewish soldiers. Masza Glajtman-Putermilch relays the following:

M. Glajtman-Putermilch: Shortly before the January Campaign (1943) (…) I had run into a school friend (Leja Szyfman) on the street by chance, and she said to me: -- Masza, you know, there is this new fighting organization being formed, would you be interested? I got excited immediately. (…) We went to school together. Leja had a sister, Miriam Szyfman, who was very active in the underground. Through Miriam, Leja turned to Marek Edelman. Even I eventually had a meeting with Marek Edelman. He questioned me thoroughly: -- What do you do, with whom, and why? Marek knew my mother and my sister. Both our mothers were friends from the Bund. After this whole interrogation, he said to me: -- Listen, we are putting together a new group over on Zamenhof (street), and I'd like you to be one of the organizers. He asked if I could recommend someone. He had already begun to trust me. And that's how I came to work in the organization. We looked for apartments. (…) We did find an apartment for our group at 29 Zamenhof (street). (…) There were ten of us, two girls and eight boys. We were all barracked up – we all slept in one place, we lived together. First on the agenda was learning how to handle weapons. Chaim Frymer is the one who was teaching me. (…) It must be said

311 Marek Edelman, in: Grupińska A., *"Ciągle po kole"* ["Still Round the Circle: Talks with the Soldiers of the Warsaw Ghetto"], Warszawa 2005, p. 26-27, 286, 309-310.

here that this learning was all based on theory. After all, we were not exactly allowed to actually fire the guns! (...) And so, we learned how to handle the guns and how to open the release on grenades. Our weapons were quite poor. We hand Polish grenades and our own hand-made grenades. We had a few revolvers and some Molotov cocktails.

A. Grupińska: *Do you remember any numbers, Ma'am? How many weapons were allotted to the group you were in?*

M. Glajtman-Putermilch: *Everyone, except Lea, had a revolver. That means there were nine revolvers allotted to our group. I had an FN7, a Belgian revolver, and a grenade I had made myself.*

A. Grupińska: *Did every member have a grenade?*

M. Glajtman-Putermilch: *Every single one.*

A. Grupińska: *Lea as well?*

M. Glajtman-Putermilch: *Lea did have a grenade, I think so. Because she was teamed with Adek, they both agreed that I should have the ninth revolver. At that time, there weren't many who knew how to handle weapons. There was this one (fellow) – Abram Stolak, he was from the "brushmakers'" district in Marek's territory. He knew his way around weapons. And there was also Koza – I don't know his real name – but he had a machinegun. (...) Our group was deeply underground. There were, in fact, certain Jews whom we simply could not trust.*[312]

Based on the above cited account and the fragment of Władysław Bartoszewski's monograph, a very unusual picture of Polish-Jewish relations of 1942 emerges. And even more unusual is the picture of the evaluation which, for the last sixty years, has served the worlds of both those who participated in the events of the time, that is of the actual Jewish ŻOB fighters, as well as the Jewish historians of these events. What is most shocking is the slew of accusations aimed at Poles with regard to providing an insufficient amount of arms, of not providing assistance, that before they delivered the weapons to the ghetto, *they had sent over some sort of*

---

[312] M. Glajtman-Putermilch, in: Grupińska A., *"Ciągle po kole"* ["Still Round the Circle: Talks with the Soldiers of the Warsaw Ghetto"], Warszawa 2005, p. 57-61.

directives, absolute nonsense. At the same time, based on the accounts of the actual Jewish ŻOB fighters, it is clear that without this so-called, *absolute nonsense*, not many Jewish fighters would have known how to properly use the weapons that had been provided by the Poles.

The allegations aimed at Poles of insufficient amounts of arms being provided to the ghetto are simply absurd. The decision that had been made by the Main Headquarters of the Polish Underground Home Army (AK) regarding the provision and passage of weapons into the ghetto was not an army decision. For, despite contradictions in elementary maxims of citizenship displayed in the postures taken by Polish Jews during the years 1939-1942, the sense of responsibility the Polish Underground State took with regard to the Jewish national minority, stemmed from, and was experienced to the same degree as, the sense of solidarity of one human being with regard to another. From the military stand point, Poles should not have provided any arms whatsoever to the Jews.

The Polish Home Army (AK) was an underground army which did not have massive arsenals of arms at its disposal. Its modest aggregate of weapons consisted of whatever happened to be concealed following the calamity of the 1939 Defensive War, as well as from whatever was occasionally recovered from the enemy, which posed a deadly risk to one's own life. There were three hundred fifty thousand soldiers, practically all of whom were Poles, who considered serving in its ranks as their patriotic obligation as citizens with regard to their homeland. It was created during a time when belonging to its ranks meant paying for it with your own life. There were no Jews in the ranks of the Home Army, not only because Poles did not trust them or did not welcome them in covert defenses, but because the fight for the freedom of Poland was not, as Marek Edelman phrased it, "a Jewish matter". Up until autumn 1942, Polish Jews expressed no interest whatsoever in participating in this fight. That is the truth. As the account of Masza Glajtman-Putermilch indicates, as well as the accounts of other fighters, the Jewish Fighting Organization (ZOB), in reality, was created on the cusp of 1942/43 (according to Marek Edelman, on October 15,

1942)[313], that is at the time when most Warsaw Jews had already been murdered. Its membership never exceeded more than 220 people from among the 750 Jewish insurgents.[314] It was created by amateur youth, inexperienced individuals who had never held a weapon in their hands. Thanks to their bravery, along with Polish arms, they restored the honor of Polish Jews.

In the ten-member group Masza Glajtman-Putermilch belonged to, only one member did not possess a revolver. If that is juxtaposed to the one gun in the hands of the Warsaw ghetto Jews in summer 1942, it becomes apparent that Masza's patrol was very well equipped. If we were to compare the defense capabilities of Masza Glajtman-Putermilch's division with those of an average Polish Home Army (AK) station out in the field, the Jewish division looks to have been unbelievably well outfitted. For comparison, I will recall the circumstances of the disarmament of a group of Germans by soldiers of AK during the liberation of a small town near Lublin in July 1944:

In the tiny enclave of Skrzyniec, as in most villages in the vicinity of Lublin, it was impossible to keep any secrets. For the longest time, everybody knew that the woman and her two daughters who were living at the miller's house were the wife and children of the subunit leader Mieczysław Szymanowski, pseudonym the "Vampire", from the "Zapora"partizan's division. The news of her husband being wounded near Kożuchówka, and of her bringing him back to the mill, was the biggest topic of village gossip.

During the first night he spent at his wife's side, just before sunrise, the "Vampire" was awakened by persistent rapping at his window.

– "Who's there?" his wife inquired.

– "Commander, Sir, you must get up. The Germans are coming!"– Jan Ciekot, pseudonym the „Fox", a member of the local AK station, whispered.

[313] Marek Edelman, in: Grupińska A., *"Ciągle po kole"* ["Still Round the Circle: Talks with the Soldiers of the Warsaw Ghetto"], Warszawa 2005, p. 285.
[314] I. Guterman, *Żydzi warszawscy 1939-1943 [The Jews from Warsaw 1939-1943]*, Warsaw 1993, p. 102; Marek Edelman, in: Grupińska A., *"Ciągle po kole"* ["Still Round the Circle: Talks with the Soldiers of the Warsaw Ghetto"], Warszawa 2005, p. 286; Steinlauf M. C., *Pamięć nieprzyswojona [Unassimilated memory]*, Warszawa 2001, p. 44.

The "Vampire" hopped to his feet, got dressed as quickly as he could and stepped outside the house. He was surrounded by a group of some twenty young men.

– "Commander, Sir, we know who you are. We are all soldiers of the Home Army (AK). We had been standing guard. Please look over there, the Germans are on their way. You must take command over of us" – he said in a whisper while pointing towards the field and the figures looming in the pre-dawn light.

– "How many weapons do you have?" – the "Vampire" got right to the point.

– "One machinegun and one sawed-off shotgun" – they demonstrated.

The "Vampire" was speechless. Within seconds it occurred to him that if he were to abandon these boys, they would go for the Germans without him, and the Germans would surely knock them off their feet. He would then be accused of cowardice and of being responsible for their deaths. And what's worse, he would have to carry this guilt around with him for the rest of his days. If he leads them into this confrontation, mere enthusiasm will not overcome the front-line of these, no doubt, well trained and well armed German soldiers. What to do? The boys looked into the eyes of the silent "Vampire" with expressions of longing.

"All right, then. Let's disarm them. Will you obey all of my commands?" – he asked in conclusion.

– "Yes, Sir, Commander, Sir!" – they responded in unison.

– "'Fox' and you two" – the "Vampire" pointed to the two heftier boys – "as well as that one over there with the machinegun and 'sawed-off'. Stay here with me. The rest of you go out there right now and find long, thick sticks roughly the length of a gun barrel" – he ordered them and went back inside the house to retrieve his weapons.

The fence creaked. Within moments, before the "Vampire", there stood a squadron armed with sticks.

– "You two, each of you grab a parabellum. You 'Fox', grab the tommy-gun. I'm going to hold on to my fourteen-round FN. Do you know how to use these?" – he asked handing out his own weapons.

–"Yes, Sir, Commander, Sir!" – they responded.

– *"Circle the Germans, but don't get too close. Stand at a distance from which they won't be able to tell that the sticks you guys are holding are not machineguns"* – *he instructed his baluster contingent.*

With his gun at the ready, at the head of his armed five-some, the "Vampire" took off across the field in the direction of the Germans. "Dear God, please don't let the sun come up too early... don't let the boys get too close with their sticks... don't let the Germans start shooting", he prayed in silence to the Almighty. He knew that without His protection, these might very well be the last moments of his life, and of the boys.

The Germans spotted the "Vampire". They stopped. The boys paused at a safe distance. It was starting to get light. Once their silhouettes were more visible, the "Vampire" noticed that, at the head of a dozen or so Germans, an officer was standing a few feet in front of them with pistol in hand.

It had been a while since he felt any pain from the wound sustained in his buttocks. Tensed up to his absolute limits, going eye-to-eye with the German officer, slowly, step by step, he walked straight for him. The ominous silence was interrupted only by the squooshing sound of their shoes being pulled up out of the muddied soil and the crackling of breaking beet leaves under their feet.

The "Vampire" was barely a few steps from the Germans when the German officer started to move his gun from his right hand to his left. He stood at attention and saluted. The "Vampire", quickly glanced over at the boys armed with their sticks. He took a few more steps forward, and standing directly in front of the officer, placed his weapon into his left hand and returned the salute. The German said something that sounded like a question asking, what they wanted with him.

– *"This is Poland, and no foreign soldier with arms shall pass through here"* – *the "Vampire" in his broken-German, tried to explain what was going on.*

It was decided that the Germans would lay down their weapons. In return for that, they would be granted a pass to continue on their way.

– *"Gut"* – *agreed the German officer and, much to the "Vampire's" consternation, handed him a Polish Vis (a type of pistol)*

The rest of the Germans followed in the footsteps of their leader.

When the German weapons were collected into a pile, the stick-man division that had been just standing there up until this point ran over.

"Mein Gott!" – exclaimed the German officer at the sight of the Polish boys armed with balusters and just grabbed his head in shock.

– "This is war, Sir. It has many a treacherous turn" – the "Vampire" said with a smile as he tried to express this Polish sentiment in the language of the enemy.

"My pass!" – demanded the German.

The "Vampire" obligingly reached for his notebook, tore a page out and wrote: "July 21, 1944. I have disarmed a group of Germans this morning in Skrzyniec. To anyone who shall encounter them, please assist them and make their passage to heaven a bit easier. The Vampire."

The Germans took their pass and went on their way in the direction of Chodel. In Zastawki they came upon a partisan from division "Zapora", pseudonim "Etagere". They were fed, and later hooked up with a group of German tank drivers standing at the side of the road. Armed with the weapons seized from the Germans, the soldiers of the Home Army (AK) stationed in Skrzyniec, under the leadership of the "Vampire", proceeded to liberate the towns of Bełżyce and Chodel from under German occupation.[315]

Aside from instructions on how to handle weapons, various training and providing the Jewish Fighting Organization (ZOB) with arms, from the very first day of the Uprising, the Home Army had already planned to attack the walls of the Jewish autonomy; the result of which was two Polish soldiers were killed, four were injured. In the days that followed, the Poles embarked on five more campaigns, relieving the fighting Jews. On April 27, 1943, a division of the Home Army (AK) along with groups of the Jewish Military Union (Zydowski Związek Wojskowy–ZZW) fought a heavy battle against the Germans inside the ghetto. The Poles lost three soldiers, while nearly everyone else suffered injuries. At the same time, the Polish Secret Military Printing Works, a legitimit cell subordinate to AK, created close to forty sets of documents which were passed to the fighting

---

[315] E. Kurek, *Zaporczycy 1943-1949*, Lublin 1995, p. 111-113. Photograph of the patrol of Mieczysław Szymanowski pseudonym 'Vampire' taken in the moment of the liberation of Bełżyce. The subunit is armed with captured German weapons. The photograph is published in: E. Kurek, *Zaporczycy w fotografii 1943-1963 [The Zaporczycy in Pictures]*, Lublin 2009, p. 46.

Jews with instructions on how to utilize them. (BiP–Home Army's Office of Information and Propaganda–translator's note.) [316]

The Catholic Church, not unlike the Polish Underground State, took an equally firm and clear stance with regard to the German crimes of genocide being perpetrated against Polish Jews. During WWII, it was the only countrywide structure which, due to the religious nature of the functions it performed, was able to remain above ground.

With over 35 million inhabitants within the Polish State, the mass of the Roman-Catholic Church on the eve of the outbreak of the Second World War, was able to claim nearly 23 million congregants. Five Church provinces (Gniezno-Poznań, Warsaw, Kraków, Lwów and Vilnius) constituted 21 diocese and archdiocese encompassing 458 deaneries and 5,200 parishes. There were 10,375 diocesan priests and 1,779 monks who worked within the Church, and more than 2000 seminarian candidates preparing for the priesthood. Male monasteries had at least 6,430 monks, while female monastic (convents) gatherings had more than 20,000 nuns.

Just as the circumstances of the Polish population, the circumstances of the Roman-Catholic Church in Poland cannot be juxtaposed to the circumstances of the Church in any other German occupied country. The Germans terrorized priests, monks and Polish nuns for the entire duration of the war. Although continuously being updated, the never quite completely compiled data indicates that at the hands of the Germans, a staggering number of religious personnel perished during the war: 6 Polish bishops, 1,923 diocesan priests (18.5%), 63 clergymen, 580 monks, and 289 nuns. In certain diocese, the loss of human life was as high as 50% of the pre-war population. Among all social and professional groups of the Polish population, percentage-wise, the clergy proved to be the group which suffered the greatest losses. Neither the sacral authority of the Bishop, nor the cassock or the habit was safe from persecution, concentration camps, prisons or death. Quite the contrary. Aware of its role in Poland, the Germans engaged in extraordinary efforts of persecution to weaken and curb the strength of the Church.

---

[316] Bartoszewski W, Lewinowna Z., *Ten jest z ojczyzny mojej* [*How Poles Helped the Jews, 1939-1945*], Kraków 1969, p. 52.

The main factors which illustrate the specificity of the circumstances under which the Roman-Catholic Church of Poland had to function during the years of the war, 1939-1945, were, the dismantling of hitherto existing administrative structures on the one hand, and the shattering of the pre-war hierarchy of the Church on the other. The Primate of Poland, Cardinal August Hlond, left Polish territory along with the government and, for the entire duration of the occupation, had practically no contact with the Church in Poland. Additionally, four important capitals of the episcopal principalities incorporated into the General Government (Warsaw, Tarnów, Sandomierz and Siedlce) were not staffed with ordinaries. Under these circumstances, the guidance of the Church, in the moral, not the formal sense, fell upon the Archbishop of the Kraków Metropolis, Adam Sapieha.

Deprived of the necessary substratum, an administrative structure and hierarchy, the Catholic Church in Poland found itself standing before the obligation of taking action and surviving years of battle and being terrorized with almost nonexistent administrative-hierarchal rudiments in place. Shattered, decimated, dispossessed of orders and guidelines from above, the Church of Poland did not curtail its age-old religious, national or charitable functions during the trying years of Nazi occupation. From the perspective of time, it is not possible to overestimate the significance and value of the various legal and illegal actions participated in or taken by the Catholic Church in Poland, for which, among other things, saving the lives of people in danger was an unconditional priority.

More often than not, I am confronted by Jewish historians who state that, for the entire duration of the Holocaust, the Catholic Church in Poland never issued an official statement or communiqué with regard to the matter of the Jews. One was not issued because this scrap of paper could have cost countless lives that had already been affected by the German decimation of Church hierarchies. And even so, it probably would have done nothing at all with regard to actually saving the life of a single Jew. It is highly unlikely that the Germans would have abandoned their plans of the Holocaust under the direct pressure of protests and demonstrations by the Polish clergy. The phenomenon of the Catholic Church in Poland during WWII stems from the fact that, despite operating with only its lowest rungs in place, it undertook to take unanimous action. Not only that, it did so in accordance with Christian principles even when its shattered hierarchy and territorial structure was not in any position to guide it in any specific direction or lend overt support to its actions in any way, as would have been the case during peacetime.

Forty years after the war, Marek Edelman described the Church in Poland between the years of 1918-1939 as being the *racist [czarna sotnia]*, and in addition to that, he cast the accusation that *there had been instances of priests giving up Jews after confession...* out into the world.[317] Meanwhile, Marek Edelman never set foot outside the walls of the Warsaw Jewish autonomy and was utterly clueless as to what was taking place on the "Aryan" side during the years of 1939-1943 up until the time of the Holocaust, and perhaps even longer than that, he had never personally met any members of the Polish clergy, nor did he have any inkling as to what the Catholic Church was doing. The author of this declaration never troubled himself with even attempting to understand what confession really constitutes in the Catholic religion, or how sacred its aspects of secrecy really are. Therefore, his private opinions and insinuations are certainly not deserving of any form of polemics. In this regard, the accounts of Emanuel Ringelblum are deemed to be far more trustworthy, as he often noted:

There are rumors circulating that priests are more than willing to issue Baptismal certificates to those wishing to pass for Aryans for a very small fee. They want to lessen the impact of their fate. (...) Authentic Baptismal certificates dating as far back as three generations – for money – from the Diocese of Lwów. (...) For a small fee, the Greek-Orthodox are issuing Aryan Baptismal certificates (to Jews).[318]

The first response of Polish priests (Catholic, Eastern-Orthodox and Protestant) to the enactment of the Nuremberg Laws that accompanied

---

317 M. Edelman, in: A. Grupińska, *"Ciągle po kole"* ["Still Round the Circle: Talks with the Soldiers of the Warsaw Ghetto"], Warszawa 2005, p. 20 and 30.
318 Ringelblum E., *"Kronika getta warszawskiego wrzesień 1939 – styczeń 1943"*, Warszawa 1983, p. 56, 78 and others. [See also: "Notes from the Warsaw Ghetto" by Emanuel Ringelblum, paperback, Ibooks Inc., 2006].

the German occupation of Poland was to issue Polish Jews Baptismal certificates which were the basis upon which "Aryan" documents could be obtained. For the sake of accuracy it must be admitted that, for at least the first two years of the German occupation, this was a Sisyphean task, for those Polish Jews who, with the help of Polish priests, attempted to stand up against the German racial laws and remain among Poles were given up into the hands of the Germans by the Jewish authorities.

The fact that Hasidim and representatives of other areas of Jewish orthodoxy resided inside the Jewish territorial autonomies in Poland (in the ghettos), that enlightened Jews who moved in Jewish political, academic, cultural and art circles resided there as well is quite obvious. For Jews, life in the Jewish autonomy, for a great number of reasons, represented an ideal form of Jewish life in the Diaspora as well as a realization of pre-war political aspirations. It also represented the only community of Jews which was familiar and in which they were able to function at very high levels.

The question to which I had not been able to obtain an answer over the years was why assimilated Jews were so drawn to the Warsaw Jewish autonomy as well as to other ghettos and autonomies throughout Poland in such great numbers, especially those who were Christian and had nothing in common with being Jewish other than their ancestors, or those who had obtained Baptismal certificates within the first years of the war and had the possibility of melding in on the Aryan side. I finally found an answer to that and other basic questions in the journals of Adam Czerniakow, who presents these matters in their most exhaustive form. Among the quandaries he had elaborated on in a monograph he prepared for the Germans in 1939, who had been running things in the capital for close to two weeks by now, he mentions the following topics:

14 X 1939 – Plan of the organizational structure with a personal crew: 1) Parties – organizations: 1. all of Poland. 2. Warsaw, 3. institutions; 2) Where the activists of the Jewish religious communalities are; 8) 24 – who's who? 11) **The matter of the converts.**

15 X 1939 – In the evening, prepare the materials for tomorrow's meeting with the SS.

16 X 1939 – At 5 o'clock, the material requested to be presented to the German authorities by the Jewish community.

6 XII 1939 – After lunch, the SS. **List of meches (converted Jews).**

The Germans wasted no time in taking advantage of the information about the converted Jews that had been presented to them by the Jewish authorities. Czerniakow had noted the following in his diary:

6 I 1940 – A female meches [converted Jewess] at the house in order for me to check the Jewish Municipality records for she doesn't wish to wear an armband.

4 II 1940 – A shake-up among the meches.

8 II 1940 – The matter pertaining to Baptized Jews.

10 II 1940 – **The German] authorities are demanding that the converted Jews should be considered as Jews.** *As of today, 112,620 individuals have been registered. (...) A slew of families have accused me of giving up the names of 100 (?) doctors.*

13 V 1940 – I have received list no. 2 of the Baptized ones.

29 V 1940 – In light of the wave of multiplying meches [converted Jew], this is the letter that came to the Jewish Municipality today: ... "To the Battalion of Work, c/o the Jewish Municipality, attention Mr. Goldfeil; from Aleksander Mietelnikow, residing at Żeromskiego Street 32, a declaration: Based on the work ordinances bearing the P/70 seal that I have been receiving, I have learned that the Battalion of Work considers me to be a convert. It is necessary to explain the circumstances of my being the only Jew in the neighborhood who receives these ordinances. With that said, I am declaring that I am not, nor have I ever been, a convert. In 1939 I withdrew from the Jewish Municipality as a nonsectarian. I did not withdraw from the Jewish Denominational Municipality for the purpose of seeking out faith in another, better or worse, religion, but rather as an individual who does not recognize any form of religion. Including me in the group of 'baps', which is yet another group I do not hold in highest esteem, and associating me with them in any way is a moral injustice to me. Therefore, with all due respect, I would like to request that my status and the unintended harm caused to me be corrected and updated by removing my name from the category of 'converts', and thus placing my name in the appropriate Municipality Station file. Warsaw, 29 V 1940. Aleksander Mietelnikow."

29 VII 1940 – A group of baptized ones paid me a visit at home regarding the matter of levy summonses being sent to their homes.

24 VII 1940 – I reciprocated Father Popławski a visit. He had at one time come to me regarding help for the Christians of Jewish heritage. He said that he can feel the hand of God in all this, that God had stationed him inside the ghetto, that once the war is over he shall emerge an anti-Semite, just as he had been when he arrived.

Christians of Jewish ancestry were called "meches" or "baps" by the Jews. Upon invading Poland, the Germans did not have any in-depth information regarding the Jewish population, aside from general statistical data, at their disposal. Even more so, they cannot have had any information pertaining to Christians of Jewish heritage, for Baptism, the act of accepting the Christian faith, is recorded only in Church certificates and, as it turned out, in the archives of Jewish municipalities.

Because I had over the course of several years conducted research in the Church and monastic archives, I can state with absolute certainty that the information that pertained to Jews accepting Baptism was never given to the Germans by the Catholic Church in Poland. Father Popławski was equally certain, as his declarations of anti-Semitism must be connected with the insult of being betrayed by Jewish authorities with regard to his Baptized brethren.

As can be surmised based on the cited fragments from the diary of Adam Czerniakow, the Germans came upon obtaining information about the Baptized Warsaw Jews thanks to the abject service of the Jewish authorities. Most likely this was the case in other cities as well. It is difficult to say whether it stemmed from betrayal or stupidity, but why any information at all regarding the numbers involved in terms of the Jewish populace, or its social-political-religious structures, or its Jewish religious leaders, or amassed fortunes, had been handed over to the Germans by a Jewish senator, especially that pertaining to Baptized Jews.

Senator Adam Czerniakow was very familiar with the Nuremberg Laws, just as he was aware that providing the Germans with information regarding Christians of Jewish heritage was an absolutely immoral invasion of privacy of the individuals it pertained to. Time has shown that the information provided to the Germans by the Judenrats deprived the Christian Jews of any chance of surviving the war within their own community, and in the majority of cases, of saving their lives.

The large-scale task of denouncing Christians of Jewish heritage ought to be interpreted in two ways: as fulfilling German demands that the converted Jews be treated as Jews, as well as fulfilling one of the fundamental Jewish obligations of reinstating the Jewish people who had abandoned it back into the Jewish religion and its nation. This matter was explained to me in Israel by Rabbi Dawid Kahane from Lwów, who said:

It must be said that, indeed, within the Jewish nation, every single Jew has some innate connection to the Jewish heritage. Therefore, the Jewish nation takes great care to ensure that not even a single twig falls from that Jewish tree.[319]

There does exist a possibility that the motivating factor behind the actions of Adam Czerniakow and the clerks of the Warsaw Judenrat was a desire to reinstate all of the Jewish *twigs* that had fallen off to Christianity back into the Jewish nation. Whatever the underlying Jewish motivation may have been, it must be stated that the efforts of Polish priests aiming to save Jewish lives were frustrated, for the Germans had already managed to locate the Baptized Poles of Jewish ancestry based on the lists provided them by the Judenrats on the cusp of 1939/1940; and like it or not, they were obliged to present themselves before the Jewish municipality, and later establish residence inside the ghetto.

Jewish authorities on Polish lands as well as throughout Europe behaved in the same way as they did in Warsaw. Bryan Mark Rigg writes: "The irony that the Nazis wanting to prove non-Aryan heritage to an individual serving in the Wehrmacht borders upon the fact that, more often than not, they turned to Jewish institutions for help. Jacob Jacobson, the Director of the Central Archive of German Jewry, assisted the Nazis in their racist inquiries. Based on the materials obtained from these archives, the Nazis

---

[319] Rabbi David Kahane, in: E. Kurek, *Your Life is Worth Mine: How Polish Nuns Saved Hundreds of Jewish Children in German-Occupied Poland, 1939-1945,* by Ewa Kurek, Hippocrene Books, NY, 1997, p. 213-217.

were able to prove Jewish ancestry to many an individual, including some of those serving in the armed forces."[320]

Despite denunciation on the part of Jewish authorities and Jewish archivists, Polish priests continued to issue certificates to Polish Jews throughout the entire duration of the occupation and the Holocaust. Irit Romano, who today resides in Israel, relays the following:

In 1943, I was staying at the home of a peasant who said to me:

– "The whole village is saying that you are a Jew. And so, now I shall kill you. But I won't do it myself. I will hand you over to the Germans and I will collect one kilo of sugar and two kilos of lard in exchange" – he went down the list of all the items he would receive in exchange for me.

I was not a little girl at the time, I was twelve years old. He... he was a huge man! He was probably about two meters tall. And he was so clever.

– "How can you not fear God?! You, in exchange for me will get this and that? Let's say that I am a Jew, which I'm not!" – I started shouting.

I was so scared that I was probably shouting so loud that the entire village ran out. He sat down and glared at me.

–"Everyone, have a look at him! He wants to hand me over to the Germans. Have a look! This is a human being? This is a beast not a human!" – I continued to shout.

–"Get over here. Who do you think you are?" – one of the men interrupted my tirade.

– "I am a Pole! I am not a Jew!" – I continued shouting.

– "Oh, so you're a Pole? Well then let's see. If you're a Pole, then go tomorrow and bring back your baptismal certificate."

"Very well. I shall go and bring it back to show you" – I said.

After everyone went back home, my peasant sat down and looked at me.

– "Now listen here you, goddammit. If you don't bring back a baptismal certificate tomorrow, then I will kill you" – he finally said.

---

320 B.M. Rigg, *Żydowscy żołnierze Hitlera: nieznana historia nazistowskich ustaw rasowych i mężczyzn pochodzenia żydowskiego w armii niemieckiej*, Warszawa 2005, s. 114. [see also: *Hitler's Jewish Soldiers:The Untold Story of Nazi Racial Laws and Men of Jewish Descent in the German Military*, University Press of Kansas 2002].

– *"O.K. I will go get my baptismal certificate tomorrow" – I said and the man left me alone.*

I couldn't sleep all night. I just kept thinking about my peasant and whether or not he would even let me leave the house the next day. He let me out! At first I walked slowly. But when I noticed that there was no one following me, I started to run. I just ran and ran, until suddenly I stopped. I started to question where I was running to. Then I realized that every other Pole has the last name of "Kowalczyk", and in Mazowiecki Minsk, there are probably fifty families with the last name "Kowalczyk". And so I decided to go to my hometown. (Now that I was recently in Poland, I was able to see that it really wasn't that far. But at that time, on foot, it was quite a distance.) I decided to go to my hometown. Mazowiecki Minsk is the town in which I was born. I kept walking around the main square until I spotted the church. "Every Polish child is registered with the priest when it's born, and there is a christening," I thought to myself. When exactly I thought of this, I don't know. I opened the gate and entered. And then I see that a priest is approaching.

– *"Blessed be the Name of Christ. Excuse me, Father. Everyone in the village where I live is saying that I'm a Jew. I would like to prove to them that I am not. And so, Father, I would like to ask you to give me my baptismal certificate" – I explained.*

The priest looked at me carefully.

– *"What is your last name?" – he asks.*

– *"My name is Irena Kowalczyk. I was born in Mazowiecki Minsk. Except that I don't remember whether it was in 1928 or 1929. My father's name was Władysław, and my mother's name was Zofia."*

– *"Can you repeat all of this to me" – he said once we went inside the building.*

So I repeated everything and the priest walked over to a large cabinet and started looking through the registers.

– *"Kowalczyk? There is no Kowalczyk. Listen to me, dear child. Right now I don't have the time because I'm in a hurry to get somewhere. If you come back tomorrow morning at about ten o'clock, I will give you a baptismal certificate.*

I thanked him and I left. I walked around the main square for a while and I decided to spend the night in the ruins of the ghetto. In the morning I got up, cleaned myself off, straightened out my hair and when it was about ten o'clock, I went over to the priest once again.

—"Good morning, Father. I'm back."

— "Oh good, you're here. Thank God I have found your baptismal certificate. Thank God..." – he said as he handed me my baptismal certificate.

I thanked him and left. Suddenly, I wanted to go back again and ask him whether he had given me the certificate because he knew I was a Jew, or was it some sort of coincidence that he happened to find what I had told him in the registers? But I was actually afraid to go back. I grabbed the certificate and ran back to the peasant. On the way I stopped only to have a look at what the priest had written. The certificate stated the following: "Irena Kowalczyk was born to in the village of Cudna to Zofia, unmarried."

I was already old enough to understand what the priest had done. He most definitely knew that I was a Jew. If they were to allow me to live, then that makes me a "foundling". And if a "foundling" has a baptismal certificate, then there is no way for them to be a Jew. This priest, in giving me the certificate, granted me my life. To this day I feel guilty that I did not look him up after the war to thank him. He is probably no longer living and it's too late for everything. But my dream is to at least know what his name was.

I returned to my peasant.

— "You see? Have a look! I am not a Jew!" – I said opening up the birth certificate before him.

He couldn't read, but he looked the certificate over and put it away in his coat pocket.

— "Now I'm going to the village constable to rip his head off! He was the one who said you were a Jew!" – he said as he stormed out of the house.

When he returned, he sat down and elbowed me, and started to laugh.

— "So, 'Foundling', where's your father?"

— "I know very well who my father is" – I thought as I mumbled something to my peasant.

— "'Little Foundling', knock it off" – he continued to laugh.

Suddenly, the whole village knew that I was a "Foundling". This was a wonderful thing! Because now, no one was using the word "Jew". Everybody started calling me "Foundling." The whole village had something to talk about.[321]

No one has ever counted all the congregations and monasteries in which, without receiving orders or declarations from above, Polish Jews were able to find refuge and salvation. The New York attorney, Milton Kestenberg recalls:

My father, an engineer, an architectural industrialist, had a beloved house for ages. A beautiful house on Zurawia Street in Warsaw which brought in no revenue. For years, the house had been cared for by a caretaker, a very good woman, who died shortly before the outbreak of the war. Father took me to her funeral and when he heard "Ave Maria", he started to weep.

After the war broke out, my parents found themselves in the Warsaw ghetto. Mother was deported by the Germans in one of the earliest transports, and my brother managed to smuggle my father out to the "Aryan side." He wandered aimlessly through the streets and just awaited the moment when the Germans would pick him up so that this nightmare could end.

– "Mr. Kestenberg, why don't you come with me. I shall hide you out, Sir" – he heard a woman's voice.

– "I don't know you. And you must understand that I have no more money, and you are putting your life in danger" – Father responded.

– "I'm the sister of your caretaker over on Zurawia Street. You cried at her funeral, Sir. I saw that" – the woman continued.

She was not interested in my father's money. She took him in, hid him out, and when the hide-out became too vulnerable, he was moved to another. He survived up until the Warsaw Uprising in this way. After the Uprising, along with all the other Warsaw residents, he was taken into the unknown by the Germans. Fear of the anti-conspiracy, he jumped from the train. It was there, along the railroad tracks, that guards had found him with a sprained ankle. He told them that he had been on his way to visit his priest to partake of the Sacrament of Penance. Upon being escorted to the nearest parish rectory, he was greeted by the pastor, whom he had never laid eyes on before that moment, as

---

[321] Irit Romano, in: E. Kurek, *Your Life is Worth Mine: How Polish Nuns Saved Hundreds of Jewish Children in German-Occupied Poland, 1939-1945,* by Ewa Kurek, Hippocrene Books, NY, 1997, p. 191-197.

though he were an old buddy. He was offered a roof over his head and received the best of care. The friendship between my father and this accidental pastor with a heart of gold lasted many years and was cut short only after the war due to death.[322]

The only in-depth research regarding the extent to which Jews and Jewish children were being rescued by the Catholic Church in Poland was conducted forty years after the war had ended, and it pertains mainly to female monastic congregations. Jewish children and Jewish adults were being rescued by Polish nuns in at least 200 convents. For the help provided to Polish Jews, the Germans murdered ten Polish nuns.[323] The same stance was taken by monasteries of male congregations, as well as by diocesan priests. There is no doubt that the stance taken by the Catholic Church in Poland with regard to the annihilation of Jews was unequivocal. For Polish Jews in hiding, all the parishes and monasteries represented a place where, even if Jews were not granted sanctuary, at least they knew that they would not be handed over into the hands of the Germans.

From the perspective of the Polish Underground State and the Catholic Church, between the years 1942-1945, the Polish population received clear directives and behavioral guidelines with regard to German annihilation of Jews that was taking place on Polish land during the occupation: the only righteous stance is to offer help to the Jews, or, if that is not possible due to the threat of the death penalty for assisting Jews, to maintain a stance of passive support. It is important to remember that providing assistance to Jews did not solely depend on the will of Poles. Poles were also subject to repressions at the hands of the Germans for no reason other than they were Poles. According to eyewitness accounts, this is how the annihilation of Jews took place in the village of Wereszczyn near Lublin:

I was born in Wereszczyn in 1925. Before the war, Wereszczyn was a typical village as far as its population during that time was concerned. Nearly half the residents of our village were Poles, and there was an equal number of

322 The relation of M. Kestenberg, in: E. Kurek, *Podajmy sobie ręce [Give as the hands]*, „Nowy Dziennik", New York, July 25, 1987.

323 E. Kurek, *Your Life is Worth Mine: How Polish Nuns Saved Hundreds of Jewish Children in German-Occupied Poland, 1939-1945*, by Ewa Kurek, Hippocrene Books, NY, 1997.

Ukrainians. Among them there were close to a hundred Jews. That was a lot, but at the time, Wereszczyn was that type of local business center. Weekly flea-markets drew in the neighboring population and this resulted in the village a very lively and active place. The flea-market fees alone brought in a nice profit. These days, the flea-markets take place in Urszulin, which is also a seat for municipal authorities.

In Wereszczyn, the Jews had their own synagogue and they ran about ten stores. Lejba and Ałta had a textile store; Sender sold iron; Ajzyk, Dawid and Szmaria had everything you can imagine in their shops, from kerosene to halva; the Symches traded wheat. There was also a tailor and two cobblers: Jankiel and Mordka. Other Jews leased out their orchards and managed to live off of that. Aside from all the Jewish businesses, there was one Polish shop in Wereszczyn, Stefczyk's Cashier, a dairy and cooperative.

In September of 1939, when our territories were taken over by the Soviets, certain Jews started wearing red armbands. They turned out to be Communists. In Wytyczno, which was not too far away, it even escalated into a battle between the Polish Border Defense Corps [KOP] and Soviet armies. We saw the columns of the Soviet armies. We were able to hear the battle sounds all the way from Wytyczno. People say that the Jews with red armbands served as guides for the Soviets, which is why the Soviets were successful in surrounding our boys.

The Jews in Wereszczyn spoke Jewish amongst themselves, and Polish with us. They had their own Jewish accent, but they had a pretty good grasp of the Polish language. We knew the Jewish children fairly well as we all went to school together. We had our ups and downs, but the Jewish children always kept a bit separated from us. They kept us at a distance. The Jewish girls kept to themselves, and we kept to ourselves, so there was never a really great friendship between us. But for the most part, we lived in peace with the Jews. Our mother was a seamstress, so she also had Jewish clients. Cyrla did live with my parents for a while.

When the Germans arrived, the Jews kept organizing these assemblies for all sorts of reasons for them. Aside from that, there was nothing extraordinary happening. Or at least not until the day of May 26, 1942 arrived. On that day, the boys and I had taken the cows out near Zabrodzie to graze in the morning. Suddenly, we see scattered divisions of Germans approaching from

*every possible direction, from Zabrodzie, Borysik, Andrzejów and Zastaw. It
later turned out that most of them were Vlasovists.*[324]*We immediately realized
that the German forces were headed to surround Wereszczyn, our village.*

*May 26, 1942 was our doomsday. The Germans entered our village
in the morning. Actually, only a portion of the soldiers were German, the
majority of them were Vlasovists, I think. Perhaps the Bielorussians? I don't
really know. They were even worse, though. They went house to house, left the
children behind, but shoved all the adults to the rectory. Actually, the Poles
and Ukrainians were all being shoved to go to the rectory. The Jews, on the
other hand, along with their children were being shoved separately from us,
and being directed to go behind the church, or rather all the way beyond the
cemetery. In front of the rectory they put us into groups. They lined up the
women separately, the young men separately, and the older men separately.
The Ukrainians were standing together with the Poles. They later selected every
tenth male, but then nothing was happening for a while. There were two priests
with us whom the people were begging for help. The priest put his hands in the
air. What could he have done? He was standing there along with us.*

*The Germans and the Vlasovists were waiting for somebody. All of a
sudden, a German on a motorcycle pulled up and started reading names off a
list. There were fourteen names on the list. One was a Pole by the last name of
Niewiadomski, and the other thirteen were Ukrainian names. It was then that
their leader stepped forward and informed us in Polish that they were going
to bid us farewell here because we helped the gang and that these fourteen will
be shot. The Vlasovists instructed the convicted to run into the field, and then
they shot them. They did it this way because there were German or Vlasovist
guards in the field, and they also started shooting at the convicted. One of
the convicted ran in a zigzag and managed to run half a kilometer before he
was shot down by the dragnet in the field. All of them perished. There were
suddenly tears and screams.*

---

[324] A group of predominantly Russian forces allied with Nazi Germany during WWII under
the command of a former Army general, Andrei Andreevich Vlasov, who desperately lobbied
the German high command to get aproval for the formation of an armed force that would be
exclusively under Russian control; and who collaborated with Nazi Germany during World
War II and created the Russian Liberation Army (translator note).

Aside from the ones on the list who were shot, the Germans selected one Pole, Stefan was his name. They also took the farm wagon driver, Luc, and some other male. They took them into the barn, instructed them to lie on some sacks and started to beat them with wooden batons. I saw the beaten with my own eyes. Stefan, a quiet boy, was completely covered in blood. I saw him with my own eyes. Luc was also bloody all over. A German walked up to them and shot them.

After murdering these people, the Germans selected eighteen young men and instructed them to go get shovels. When they returned, they told them to dig a ditch. The bodies of the murdered Poles and Ukrainians were thrown inside.

While the boys were digging the ditch for the murdered, the rest of the village residents, Poles and Ukrainians, were told to go to the house of the Ukrainian village constable. That's when the Vlasovists started to set the houses on fire. A German plane flew over and started dropping incendiary candles. Within moments, half of Wereszczyn was in flames.

Two days later, a German came over for some water and told us that he had burned the village and murdered the Poles and Ukrainians because they had collaborated with the partisans. In reality, this was a provocation by a Soviet prisoner-of-war in service to the Germans. Our village constable was a Ukrainian. A Soviet prisoner-of-war came to our village and said that he was going to organize a partisan movement. Perhaps he was Ukrainian, and perhaps it was easier for him to communicate with the Ukrainians than the Poles in Wereszczyn. He did not approach the Poles. And besides, I doubt that the Poles would even consider joining a Soviet partisan movement. In any event, this prisoner-of-war was supposedly putting together a partisan movement with the Ukrainians, and later on he gave up the ones who had joined the Germans. He had a gold tooth.

On the same day, during the pacification of Wereszczyn, the Germans took all our Jews behind the church and shot them all there over the old manor well. Some 200 meters from the church there was a barn. The Germans packed all the Wereszczyn Jews into the barn. Next to the barn was a large manor well. The Germans must have had some ordnance maps left over from WWI because no one in the village even knew this well existed. And they were walking as though they knew exactly where they were going. They arrived, brushed the dirt away and uncovered the well. They would take five Jews at a time and line them up over the well and murder them with machinegun series. Supposedly they threw the children in still alive and later fired shots into the well and tossed grenades inside. The Jews were murdered by the Germans. Bolek Witkowski, who lived in our village, witnessed the murder of our Jews with his own eyes. He had hidden in the loft and watched. His house stood not too far from this place. When the Germans were firing at the Jews, Bolek was in their line of fire and was wounded in the face. He did survive, and later told us what had happened.

On May 26, 1942, the Germans murdered all the Wereszczyn Jews. The only ones to survive were Maszka, and Senders two sons who had withdrawn with the Soviets to Russia back in September of 1939. Both survived. They returned to Wereszczyn after the war and sold their father's house to a Pole. They never again returned after that.[325]

The annihilation of these small enclaves of Jews was conducted by the Germans in such a fashion that the besieged Jews had absolutely no chance to escape, nor did the Poles have any opportunity to try to save them. In most instances, however, the liquidation of the ghettos located on Polish lands took place in such a way that if a Jew had decided to escape, he was able to leave the ghetto. The directives and behavioral guidelines that had been issued to the Polish population by the Polish Underground State and the Catholic Church with regard to Jews seeking rescue were unequivocal: these individuals must be helped, or at least no one can deliberately hinder their rescue. That is not to say that all Poles behaved in accordance with norms as prescribed by the Polish Underground State, or the Catholic Church.

The Poles are not a nation of saints. Each generation had, has and will continue to have, individuals among us for whom legal, national, religious and moral norms have very little value. The generation of Poles that lived during the Second World War also proved that there was no shortage of individuals who lacked basic levels of dignity and conscience, as well as utter beasts who took outright advantage of the Jewish drama by extorting

---

[325] The relations of Stanislawa Sidorowska and Henryk Harasimowicz; the collection of E. Kurek.

from Jews directly, or by shaking down the Poles hiding them out and managed to turn this into a way of life as well as into a lucrative source of income. The scale to which this phenomenon had developed ultimately required intervention on the part of the Polish Underground State. In a communiqué issued by the Directorate of Civil Resistance of the Polish Underground State in March of 1943 we read:

Blackmails and the curtailment thereof

The Directorate of Civil Resistance of The Polish Underground State advises:

The Polish population, despite itself being a victim of terror, with horror and deep sorrow looks upon the murder of the remaining Jewish population in Poland at the hands of the Germans. The DCR has voiced its protest against these crimes, which has reached the entire free world; as well as the information that Jews who have escaped the ghettos or the death camps have received such outright assistance so as to require the occupier to issue an ordinance threatening Poles with the death penalty for helping the Jews in hiding. Despite these efforts, there have been certain individuals who, deprived of honor and conscience, are being recruited from the underworld of the criminal element, and who have developed a new source of felonious income through blackmails from Poles who hide out Jews, as well as directly from Jews. The DCR advises that these instances are being recorded and that they shall be prosecuted to the fullest extent of the law, currently within existing capabilities, and certainly in the future.[326]

In Jewish historiography and journalism, the Polish context of the Holocaust is almost always woven in the concept of blackmailers [szmalcownik][327] and has risen to the position of being a symbol denoting the overall posture of Poles in general, with regard to the genocide executed on the Polish Jewish population. This is not the forum to conduct discussion regarding the scale and reach of Polish act of blackmailers. There is no point in denying that there were many among Poles who through despoiling hiding Jews and turning them in to the hands of the Germans had created a lucrative hobby for themselves during the years of the Second

---

[326] „Biuletyn Informacyjny" ("Information Bulletin" of the Polish Underground State), March 18, 1943.

[327] SZMALCOWNIK – in Polish jargon the word „szmal" means money.

World War. They were a clear and present danger to those who decided to abandon the ghetto, and to those offering protection to the escapees. They constituted a group which did not exactly function on the up-and-up, and in addition to that, they acted in direct opposition to the obligatory legal and political-moral norms that applied during WWII. It is why their activities were condemned and pursued by the Polish Underground State throughout the entire duration of the war. It is necessary to underscore that blackmail with regard to Jews in hiding was dealt with to the full extent of the law of the Polish Underground State to the same degree that treason was. In accordance with the laws of the Polish Underground State that applied during wartime, both transgressions were punishable by death:

On behalf of the Polish State!

The following posted announcements regarding the two sentences that have been issued and executed on the heads of the traitors to the national interests of Poland have been well received by the population of Warsaw. Awaiting further enunciations of this type will help clear the atmosphere. There is no doubt that we currently find ourselves at the bottom of the pile in terms of eliminating all the elements that have demoralized the war. (...)

The enunciation of the Plenipotentiary of the Polish State regarding the punishment of the accused and traitors of matters of national interest does pertain to blackmailers as well. The warning contained below as issued by the Directorate of Civil Resistance of the Polish State is proof of this. Our hope is that the words "On behalf of the Polish State!" contained in said announcements regarding sentences issued, which have been posted on city walls, have a sobering effect.[328]

Among Poles, there were individuals for whom handing other people over to die, irregardless of their nationality or practiced religion, was a source of genuine pleasure. How else can one justify the actions of Stanisław D. from Wereszczyn near Lublin, who prior to his demise, managed to turn over a Pole, Jews and Soviets to die? Witnesses to those events say the following:

After the pacification of Wereszczyn, the Germans continued to harass its

---

[328] „Prawda" [„The Truth" – The Polish Underground Bulletin], March 1943.

residents. They would drive around the village and through neighboring villages capturing people for the purpose of deporting them to Germany. Everybody was hiding wherever possible, but they still managed to capture quite a few. In 1942, in the months that followed, the Germans would set up dragnets to capture those Jews hiding out in the forest.

The dragnets for the Jews looked something like this. There was a German gendarme station in Cyców, and a Polish police station in Urszulin, that is of the dark-blue forces. The commander of the dark-blue forces in Urszulin was G. The dragnet was organized by the Germans, but the executors were the dark-blue police along with peasants. The Municipality, under orders from the Germans, ordered the village constables to dispatch the peasants from local villages and they were forced to go out and participate in the round-up. Even though I was only 15, I was also dispatched to take part in the round-up in December of 1942. Therefore, I saw all this with my own eyes.

In December of 1942, the German gendarme dispatched peasants from a few villages to participate in the round-up. They caught one Jew, and after a while I saw even two or three being executed. From among our own Wereszczyn Jews, poor Ałta and his son were hiding out in the forest. They were hiding in a stack of hay over at Podstawski's. During this dragnet, Stacho D., a peasant, ran over there with his pitchfork and chased our two Jews off. The commander of the dark-blue police in Urszulin, who was known as G., told them to take off their clothes and shoes, and later executed the both of them.

This was unusual because this very same G. was the one who drove our Jewish girl, Maszka, over to grandma Kozłowska in Urszulin. First he had a certificate made up for her in the name of Maria Kozłowska. This commander G. must have accepted money to do this. I don't know. The Germans later executed him at Lublin Castle, allegedly for collaboration with the underground. In any event, commander G. rescued our Maszka, but executed Ałta and his son. This I saw with my own eyes.

The peasant, Stacho D., who hunted down Ałta and his son, was killed during that dragnet. There was no love lost there. He was a horrible human being. Earlier, Stacho D. captured a Polish boy, Lolek Biernacki, who was running because he was being chased by the Germans. He caught him and turned him over to the Germans. A German took his revolver and executed

Lolek. He was just an innocent boy. Later he hunted down Ałta and his son in a haystack and sent them to their deaths. To top it off, during this December round-up campaign, somebody had mentioned that there were three Soviet prisoners-of-war hiding out in the forest. Stacho D. was so raring to go that he was killed while hunting the Soviets down. Because the Soviets were soldiers, they weren't about to let themselves be captured so easily. One of these soldiers was killed, but first he did manage to shoot Stacho D., who wanted to cut off their escape route. No one was mourning his loss. As for the two Soviet prisoners-of-war who made it through the dragnet, they took off to Wincencin.[329]

There was a similar campaign in the vicinity of Chodel, and based on the account of one of the local Home Army leaders, it took place as follows:

During the period of German occupation, the Jews from Chodel were given to the estate in Jezow because that's where the Liegenschaft was. Abramek Tauber worked there. He was such a clever Jew, he supplied them with something or other, he was a leader, but he stayed in touch with us. He knew when the Jews were going to be deported to the ghetto in Poniatowa, and he got away. He escaped to my place. I hid him out for over a week. But Abramek was adamant about not wanting to join Polish Underground Home Army [AK], but rather wanted me to drive him over to some Jewish group somewhere in the forest. I asked him where he wanted me to drive him to. He wanted to go to Powisle because he knew there was some Jewish group operating somewhere over there. But Powisle is rather vast, how was I to know where to even begin to look for someone over there? I finally managed to find out that somewhere in the Niedzwiady region, there was a group called "Bolek". I dropped him off in this place Niedzwiady, and Abramek later hooked up with "Bolek".

Abramek's sister's name was Ryfka. She was a beautiful girl. I used to go to elementary school with her. She was hiding out at the forest ranger's place. There was a bunker installed, and she was hiding out there. They were found out by those people from the underground Peasant Battalions [BCh], and they went over to liquidate. One of the BCh people called me over. I went over to see

---

[329] The relations of Henryk Harasimowicz; the collection of E. Kurek.

what was going on. It was a moonlit night. The Jews saw a group approaching, so they started to run. Ryfka didn't get dressed in time. She ran through the forest naked. I take a look...

– "Ryfka? Is that you?" – I'm shouting.

– "It's me" – she answers.

–"Why are you running away?"

– "I'm running away because I think we are going to die here".

– "You're not going to die. Come over here" – I said.

I took off my coat and covered her up. I saved her life. Hers and the lives of all the others who were there with Ryfka. I gave the command not to shoot and it was over. Ryfka survived the war. Her brother, Abram, also survived. [330]

These accounts draw attention to the rarely examined phenomenon of searching and capturing Jews who had found hideouts in forests between the years of 1942 and 1943. This campaign was executed by the Germans, and the participation of the peasant population was imposed. Despite that, there always existed a moment in which the posture of the Polish peasantry was the single underlying factor which weighed the lives and deaths of those in hiding. The Polish peasantry held the power of "not noticing" or "not knowing" where the Jews were hiding out in their hands, thus sparing the life of the person in hiding. They also possessed the power to notice and know, and to give the locations of hideouts up to the Germans, thus guaranteeing that every such instance resulted in the death of a Jew. What is certain is that there was no way for the Germans to hunt down all of the Jews in hideouts throughout the forests single-handedly. What is certain is that, had it not been for the eagerness of certain Polish peasants, many Jews would have walked away from the Holocaust with their lives in tact.

The act of blackmails and the crime of disclosing the locations of hideouts to Germans occupy the list of the most heinous sins committed against the murdered Polish Jews. It is not possible to run away from the responsibility of having committed these acts, there are no excuses. The only thing that remains is the matter of evaluating the scope of this

---

330 The relations of Stanislaw Wnuk, in: „Zaporczycy – Realcje" (Talks with the Soldiers of the "Zapora" partisan's division). Volumen I, Lublin 1997, p. 124.

phenomenon. It seems that the most pungent assessment with regard to this matter is that of Antek Cukierman:

Antek always had the confidence to express the most outrageous opinions. And in this way, at the Zionist conference in London which took place in 1945, immediately following the end of the war, he made the Zionists aware that "the betrayal of a hundred Jews, required one vile Pole; but the rescue of even one Jew, sometimes required as many as ten noble, brave Poles."[331]

Once again, I would like to reiterate: Poles are not a nation of saints.

The generation that lived during the time of the Holocaust did include some downright vile individuals as well as common murderers. These were individuals for whom the obligation of solidarity with regard to another human being, plain human decency, as well as the directives being issued by the Polish Underground State and the guidelines coming from the Catholic Church had as much value as the laws that apply to common criminals during peacetime. For the Poles who bear the responsibility for the deaths of Polish Jews, there is no excuse. As for the crimes they committed as Poles, they shall forever weigh on the collective conscience of the Polish nation. In the name of truth, Poles are not permitted to cover up the crimes committed by other Poles. One is also not permitted to falsify history by propagating notions such as blackmail and information on Jews in hiding were the prevalent norms among Poles, and that their only motivating factor was anti-Semitism.

Ascribing anti-Semitic sentiments to those who, whether for their own pleasure or for financial gain, surrendered Polish Jews (or for that matter Poles or Soviets) to the Germans is a monumental misunderstanding and is offensive to Polish anti-Semites. Polish anti-Semites had very little to do with the Holocaust. It is true that they were not very keen on Jews, and that they ascribed the worst of all possible characteristics to Jews, but in general, this was more of an economic-cultural-political type of anti-Semitism which never promoted the notion of taking the lives of Jews. The Jewish writer, Roma Ligocka has said the following: "I am taken

---

[331] Szczęsna J., *Ostatni Mohikanie i nowy naród (The last of the Mohicans and the new nation)*, in: 'Gazeta Wyborcza', June 28-29, 2002.

aback by what has been going on lately. History is being deliberately misrepresented and is evading its responsibility for the Holocaust. For me it is clear that the parties responsible for this crime are the Germans who perpetrated it, not some Nazis of followers of Hitler. A French journalist asked me about Polish anti-Semitism and she reminded me of the pogroms that took place in Poland. This is evidence of the absolute proportional instability. The extermination of an entire people cannot be compared to pogroms which occurred in many different places, including France."[332] With regard to self-declared [Polish] anti-Semites, Emanuel Ringelblum wrote the following during the war:

The attitude of certain National Democratic leaders as far as Jews are concerned is quite characteristic. There are more and more expressions of sorrow as a result of introducing arm patches. (...) 1,500 Jews have been taken from Włocławek. Christians in the main square (in Szczebrzeszyn) gave the Jews food, despite some of them being die-hard anti-Semites. (...) In Limanów (which is regarded to be heavily anti-Semitic),, the Franciscans behaved very well toward the 1,300 Jewish refugees (500 from Kalisz and 500 from Lublin, about 300 from Poznań). They gave them shelter inside their buildings, and helped them. They gave them a calf for slaughter and in general behaved very well toward them. (The same misfortune has befallen us all. We are equal in that respect.). (...) A National Democratic lawyer who (at one time) voted in favor of the Aryan section is now proud to be crossed off the list (of lawyers) for hiring a Jewish candidate. (...) Nowodworski[333] and other anti-Semitic lawyers are now sitting in jail because of the Jews. They were all summoned and asked for their opinion regarding the Aryan section. They all responded by saying that this does not apply during wartime.[334]

Many Polish anti-Semites had proved their solidarity with Jews during the Holocaust by exhibiting posture which put their lives, and the lives of

---

332 The relation of Roma Ligocka, in: „Wprost", Warsaw, February 6, 2005.
333 Leon Nowodworski – a lawyer, a dean of the Warsaw Bar Council, a National Democrat. At the beginning of the occupation he opposed the disbarment of Jews ordered by the German occupational authorities.
334 Ringelblum E., *"Kronika getta warszawskiego wrzesień 1939 – styczeń 1943"*, Warszawa 1983; p. 43, 50, 68, 101 and 136. [See also: "Notes from the Warsaw Ghetto" by Emmanuel Ringelblum, paperback, Ibooks Inc., 2006].

their families, in danger for saving Jewish lives. One such individual was Jan Dobraczyński, who later became a writer and politician. In the account he gave in 1984, when asked why he, an anti-Semite, had saved the lives of Jews during the war, he responded:

Why did I save them? That's simple. In the house in which I grew up, my family embraced tolerance. We did not have extensive relations with Jews. But since these encounters did occasionally take place, they were not anything out of the ordinary. Conversations took place on a wide range of topics without any animosity. I also had Jewish friends from school. One of them was even my best friend. The Jews with whom we were in contact were, how shall I say, "normal" when it came to religion. Because the Mosaic Jews steered clear of Christians, we too had very little interest in their religion. Some of their customs just seemed plain weird to us. Although I am not aware of any conflicts that were religious in nature.

Besides which, what I stated earlier, and this is no secret to anyone, I personally come from a nationalist environment. These environments are often indicted for being anti-Semitic. In reality, if we are so attached to the idea of labeling it as being anti-Semitism, then it's incumbent on us to discuss the economic anti-Semitism that was prevalent in nationalist environments. This type of anti-Semitism never had anything to do with racial-anti-Semitism, which is the type that had emerged in Hitler's Germany. Economic anti-Semitism in Polish nationalist environments stemmed from the fact that, in pre-war Poland, there was a very high, almost 12%, indicator of Jewish population. In the field of trade, there was such a high percentage of Jews that certain areas were entirely under their control. This type of economic competition would have evoked conflict sooner or later. In this sense, admittedly, I was an economic anti-Semite. But my anti-Semitism never evolved into any form of wanting to take someone's life!

Therefore, there is no contradiction between my anti-Semitism and the fact that, when it was vital, I saved the lives of Jews and Jewish children. I, therefore, above all saved them because they were children, because they were being persecuted, because their lives were in danger, because Jews were human beings... I saved every single person whose life was in danger. And the children, especially children, are especially dear to me. That is what my Catholic religion dictates. I was not expecting any reward, or even verbal recognition for that matter. If I was in a position to save the lives of hundreds of children, I did just that. That, for me, in itself is sufficient reward.[335]

It seems that the Polish Jews who perished in the Holocaust during the Second World War had a very good understanding of what Jan Dobraczyński was talking about in explaining the nuances of Polish economic anti-Semitism. For in autumn of 1940, when the character of the occupation had become quite obvious, Jews in the Warsaw ghetto shared this anecdote:

A Jew is laughing and screaming aloud in his sleep.

His wife wakes him up.

He's angered and explains that in his dream he saw slogans written on the walls: "Beat the Jews!" "Enough of the ritual slaughter!" etc.

"And why are you so joyful?"

"What? That means our guys (the Poles) had returned!"[336]

Polish anti-Semites behaved in a variety of ways. Some, through unambiguous actions, expressed their solidarity with the repressed Jewish population being murdered; the majority remained passive with regard to Jewish matters for the entire duration of the war; some did not actually participate in the annihilation of Jews, nor did they rescue them or express their sorrow, and toward the end they coined the phrase that "Hitler deserves an 'A' for liberating Poland from the Jews." Therefore, it is only through rather painstaking effort and immense good will of not being properly acquainted with historical sources that it is possible to explain all the Jewish historians who, for decades now, have attempted to equate, in terms of degree and values, Polish anti-Semitism with that of German anti-Semitism, the latter of which lead to the deaths of millions of Jews.

To the outright mockery of the suffering of their own people, they conceal the stance of contemporary German Jews, who are represented

[335] The relation of Jan Dobraczynski, in: E. Kurek, *Dzieci zydowskie w klasztorach (The Jewish Childern in the Polish Convents)*, Lublin 2001, p. 131-136.

[336] Ringelblum E., *"Kronika getta warszawskiego wrzesień 1939 – styczeń 1943"*, Warszawa 1983; p. 179. [See also: "Notes from the Warsaw Ghetto" by Emanuel Ringelblum, paperback, Ibooks Inc., 2006].

by Samuel Korn, the vice-chairman of the Central Jewish Council in Germany, who ascribes the distinct characteristic of being *subtle* to the German anti-Semite while designating the Eastern-European (implied Polish) anti-Semite with the quality of being *classic*, and thus ascribing the worst of all possible qualities to it.[337]

In judging the reactions of Poles with regard to the annihilation of Jews at the hands of the Germans between the years of 1942-1945, it is necessary to make the distinction between the postures taken by individuals and those taken by institutions. Within the realm of institutional postures, the persecuted Polish Underground State which remained in conspiracy against the Germans; in the name of the centuries-old tradition of the Polish State protecting Polish Jews; within the realm of axioms and guidelines, in addition to concrete actions (Council for Aid to Jews–Rada Pomocy Żydom-ZEGOTA) taken; all of this proved the obligation the Polish State authorities felt with regard to the fate of the Jewish national minority. The Catholic Church, in the name of Christian brotherly love, despite persecution by the Germans, showed loyalty to its postulates and rescued Jews on a scale not matched by any other country under German occupation. As for the category of postures of individuals, the reactions of specific people, regardless of the social group to which they belonged, ranged from acts of highest altruism to passivity, to betrayal, where passivity was the more dominating posture of the two.

In deliberating over the categories of postures taken by Poles with regard to the annihilation of Polish Jews, it is worth understanding what dictated and conditioned the dominating stance of passivity among Poles. From the village that had been pacified by the Germans, Wereszczyn near Lublin, Maszka is the sole survivor of the Holocaust:

Marysia Kozłowska, Miriam, is the daughter of the wealthy Jew, Ałta. We called her Maszka. Today she resides in Israel, and she erected an obelisk to commemorate the location where all the Jews of Wereszczyn had perished. She occasionally visits here(Poland). Maszka escaped the Germans with her little

---

[337] P. Jedroszczyk, *Przekraczanie czerwonej linii [The crossing of red Line]*, in: „Rzeczpospolita", April 29, 2004.

brother. She can't have been older than 9 or 10. She ran over to our house and begged my mother to hide them out. My mother told her to hide somewhere in the bushes because it was impossible to do inside the house.

– "The Germans are going from house to house! If they find you, they will kill you and us!" – she told Maszka.

The girl had blonde hair and did not resemble a Jew. She hid in the bushes. Her little brother started to cry. Not too much later, we all saw how a German took him over to the group of executed Jews. The little one perished, but Maszka managed to escape. She survived. The commander of the dark-blue police in Urszulin, his name was G., drove her over to Mrs. Kozłowska in Urszulin. She taught her prayer. Maszka asked if God won't be angry with her for praying to another God. Mrs. Kozłowska reassured her that God will not be upset because the Jewish God and the Polish God are one and the same. To this day Maszka claims that the prayer Mrs. Kozłowska had taught is what saved her life. And so, Maszka ended up with Mrs. Kozłowska. But what we had to endure after the pacification was awful. The Germans searched for Jews in every single house, they conducted inspections, and so someone, I can't remember who, drove Maszka to Załucz near the lake.[338]

The mother of the woman who relayed the above instance of a Wereszczyn resident maintained a stance of passivity with regard to the Jewish children being murdered in Wereszczyn. She empathized with them and was suffering their tragedy along with them, but she did not hide Maszka and her little brother out. A small Jewish boy was murdered. But can the mother of the woman who relayed the above instance be held responsible for the death of this little boy, or in the final analysis, was it in fact the Germans? Did she condemn him to death, or was it the Germans who murdered this little Jewish child? It is true that if the mother of the woman who relayed the above instance had agreed to hide Maszka and her little brother out in her home, there existed a chance that they both could have survived. **But if the Germans had learned that she had not maintained a stance of passivity with regard to their cruelty, then their cruelty would have been aimed directly at her home.** She had

---

[338] The relation of Stanislawa Sidorowska, the collection of E. Kurek.

a few children at home. Out of love for her own children, she opted for passivity with regard to the children of another. In this sense, Poles were not in solidarity with the perishing Polish Jews. A greater majority of Poles during the Second World War did not want to die for Polish Jews, and they did not want their children to die for Polish Jews either. In the face of Jews being murdered by Germans, Poles preferred to maintain passivity because passivity with regard to the Holocaust meant that their lives, and the lives of their children, were safe.

The dominating stance among Poles of maintaining passivity with regard to the annihilation of Polish Jews has been labeled, by Jews, as indifference, and has become the underlying factor in formulating various accusations aimed at Poles, not to mention imposing a guilty conscience on Poles. Polish Jews, including those who had survived the war in Poland, liken the Polish stance of passivity/indifference to enmity and have laid the burden of shared accountability for the annihilation of their people upon the Poles. Case in point: forty years after the war, Marek Edelman summed up the Poles living on the other side of the walls of the Jewish autonomies (ghettos) in the following way:

> *The Poles that was the enemy.*
> *Because an enemy is not only a person who kills you, but also*
> *a person who is indifferent.*
> *Not helping and killing are the same thing.*[339]

It is untrue that not helping and killing are the same thing. Marek Edelman knows better than anyone that aside from marginal instances, the greater majority of Poles had no intention of killing Jews. They maintained a stance of passivity, which he refers to as indifference, not because they desired the deaths of innocent Jews, but rather due to the German law which carried the death penalty for Poles who assisted Jews in any way.

---

[339] Marek Edelman, in: Grupińska A., *"Ciągle po kole"* ["Still Round the Circle: Talks with the Soldiers of the Warsaw Ghetto"], Warszawa 2005, p. 27.

Polish passivity was not tantamount to either condemning Jews to death, or to murdering Polish Jews.

Jews were murdered by the Germans.

This was a traumatic decision between choosing ones own life and the lives of one's family, and saving the lives of Polish Jews being murdered.

Poles did not want to be murdered by the Germans.

Every Pole during the Holocaust was very well aware that by maintaining a stance of passivity with regard to the death being assigned to Jews, they were not placing their lives or the lives of their families in danger. In a word, they possessed a chance of coming out of the war alive. If, however, they were to be unable to persevere in passivity with regard to Jewish death, if they were to extend a helping hand, there existed a very strong probability that this gesture would cost them and their families their lives at the hands of the Germans. The choices that Poles had to make under German law were cruel and traumatic: the choice between one's own life, and saving the lives of Polish Jews being murdered.

Poles were not obliged to sacrifice their own lives for the purpose of saving a Jewish life. Considering that passivity meant staying alive, and engaging in active rescue of Jews meant death, they had the right to choose passivity. No one in the world other than Jews understands better that Poles had the right to maintain a stance of passivity with regard to the death sentences that were being imposed on Jews. From the perspective of Jewish tradition, religion and law, a human (Jew) has, above all, the obligation of protecting his own life. At all costs. Even at the cost of the life of another. Evidence of this is presented in the idea within the Jewish religion of Kiddush Ha-Chaim (Sanctifying Life), and it is further verified by the Israeli law which relieves even those Jews who have murdered other Jews from responsibility providing they can justify that their crime occurred in self-defense, in the course of trying to save their own life.

The law should be applied equally to all. The same laws for Poles as exist for Jews. Being passive with regard to Jewish deaths, Poles did not murder Jews. They simply did not want to die for Jews or on behalf of Jews. As for the aspect of the individual, the decision that

had to be made by the human-Pole simply exercised their right to maintain their own life. Just as the human-Jew exercised this right during WWII.

The stance of passivity taken by Poles with regard to Polish Jews being murdered, although in accordance with Jewish law and religion, does collide with Christian ideals. The most important of these Christian ideals is brotherly love, up until and including sacrificing one's own life for another. Christianity, however, does not place the expectation of the unconditional necessity of sacrificing one's own life for another on all Christians. Christ sacrificed his life for his brethren, and his most devout followers who sacrifice their lives achieve sainthood in the Church. The symbol of the utmost Christian sacrifice of giving one's life for another during WWII is a Pole, a Franciscan, Saint Maximilian Kolbe, who willingly gave his life for another prisoner in Auschwitz.

Meanwhile, Marek Edelman, who claims that as a result of passivity/indifference Poles are responsible for Jewish deaths, says the following: *One does not sacrifice life for symbols. There is only one life.*[340] **During the time of the Holocaust, a greater majority of Poles did apply the very same presupposition that has been voiced here by Marek Edelman. They too had only one life. They did not want to sacrifice it for Jews in order to prove their conviction to symbols: the Christian ideal of brotherly love. They did not want to achieve sainthood, they wanted to live.**

Would Marek Edelman sacrifice his life for any Pole?

I can assure you, most certainly not.

For there is only one life, and it should not be sacrificed for the sake of a symbol.

Another thing that is underscored by Jewish historians and writers for the purpose of justifying their accusations aimed at Poles is that Poles did in fact possess symbols for which they sacrificed their own lives during the Second World War. They did indeed create the Polish Underground State,

---

340 Marek Edelman, in: Grupińska A., *"Ciągle po kole"* ["Still Round the Circle: Talks with the Soldiers of the Warsaw Ghetto"], Warszawa 2005, p. 28.

and the Germans imposed the death penalty on any person who entered into cooperation with them.

It is true that Poles, although not every single one, were willing to die for the freedom of their homeland. And die they did, just as they had throughout the thousand-year history of Poland. The life of a Jew did not, however, qualify within the Polish canon of ideals for which a life should be sacrificed. Saving the life of a Jew was not a fight for freedom.

"There is only one life" is what Marek Edelman has said. It is the truth and moreover:

- Every human being, Pole and Jew alike, have the inalienable right to decide whether they will sacrifice their life for the sake of a symbol or ideal, or maintain it solely for themselves.
- No one has the right to impose expectations of sacrificing one's life for the sake of a symbol or ideal on another human being.
- Giving up one's life for an ideal or symbol can only be done voluntarily.

This is why the structures of the freedom-fighting Polish Underground State were filled with throngs of volunteers. This is why Polish Jews were saved only by those Poles who were willing to put their own lives in danger, who had made the decision to do so voluntarily, and who were prepared to give up their own lives to exercise their own right to save a Jewish life.

In the sixty years that have passed since the end of the Second World War, no one has ever attempted to blame or hold accountable those Poles (and they did constitute a rather substantial majority of the Polish population) who remained passive with regard to the Poles who fought for freedom within the ranks of the Polish Underground State. Because fighting in the ranks of the Underground State was punishable by death, the choice to remain outside of the conspiratorial structures was every Pole's inalienable right. Poles had the option of joining the partisan movement or of not doing so at all. Saving the lives of Jews was also considered to be a conspiratorial act punishable by death. Therefore, Poles had the option of voluntarily putting their own lives in danger, but they also had the option of choosing not to do so.

High praise to those who did put their lives in danger and did save Jews. High praise to those who did put their lives in danger and did fight for freedom. But no one has the right to punish or indict those Poles who did not possess the courage to risk death in the name of a free homeland or saving the lives of Polish Jews. Not everyone is capable of performing such feats. Not everyone possesses enough courage to *sacrifice their life for a symbol.* Indeed, *there is only one life,* as Marek Edelman has stated.

It is therefore absurd, that in all the post-war years that have passed, Polish Jews have never once recognized their own passivity or fault with regard to the Holocaust. But rather, they have opted to pound on the chests of others in their attempt to blame those Poles who remained passive with regard to the deaths of Polish Jews in order to stay alive themselves, and to hold those Poles accountable for the deaths of Polish Jews.

In Jewish historiography, just as in any type of Jewish memoir, journal or biography, in addition to the sedulous omission of the fact pertaining to the price that Poles had to pay for saving the life of a Jew, the question that is formulated to sound like an accusation which is always woven in is why Poles did so very little in order to help the Jews. Norman Davies offers a short and concise response to this: "The question as to why Poles did so very little in order to help the Jews is just about as logical as asking why the Jews did so very little to help the Poles."[341] Władysław Bartoszewski, in response to the accusation that was presented before him at the 1988 conference in Jerusalem, that Poles did not do everything possible to save the lives of Jews during the Holocaust, said this: "Doing everything possible for the Jews during the war meant giving up one's own life for them. I am alive, so therefore I did not do everything possible in order to save Jews."[342]

The lives of Polish Jews did not qualify to be placed within the Polish canon of ideals for which a life should be sacrificed, which is precisely why Polish Jews during the time of the Holocaust between

---

[341] Davies N., *Boże igrzysko* [*God's playground*], Kraków 2003, p. 744.

[342] Professor Władysław Bartoszewski uttered these words at the panel discussion *International Conference on the History and Culture of Polish Jews* at the University of Jerusalem in February 1988. At Professor Chone Schmeruk's request, I recorded the discussion with a VHS camera and handed the tapes over to the Israeli organizers of the conference.

the years of 1942-1945 had found themselves beyond the limits of Polish solidarity.

With that said, as far as the aspect of Polish-Jewish relations during the years of the Holocaust, between the years of 1942-1954, new questions do arise:

- With regard to the afore mentioned idea which floated and propagated during WWII by Rabbi Izaak Nissenbaum and other followers Kiddush Ha-Chaim (Sanctifying Life), which dictates that Jews save their own Jewish lives at all possible costs, even at the cost of the lives of others, including participating in the murder of one's own people. In this situation, would a Jew be capable of so grand a gesture so as to sacrifice their own life for the sake of saving the life of another human being of a different nationality and religion (i.e., a Pole)?

- Do Jews, whose religious and legal laws do sanction borderline egoism with regard to the matter of maintaining a Jewish life in tact, have a moral right to indict Poles for showing them an insufficient amount of Christian mercy, even though that was understood to mean putting one's own life in danger for the sake of saving a Jewish life?

- In this case, are we not dealing with a dual morality which, on the one hand charges outsiders (Poles) with offering insufficient mortal sacrifice with regard to saving a Jewish life, but absolve their own (Jews) even in instances when other Jews were sent to their deaths in an effort to save their own life, on the other?

- With that in mind, do Jews have the right to blame Poles for being passive/indifferent and of not doing everything in their power to rescue Jews, in other words, of sacrificing a bit too few Polish existences in exchange for saving Jewish existences?

Władysław Bartoszewski reports that: "The estimates of Jewish historians with regard to the number of Jews who survived on territories of the Polish State that had been occupied by the Germans varies somewhere in the vicinity from 40-50 thousand (according to Filip Friedman), to 100-120 thousand (according to Józef Kermisz)." According to Norman Davies: "...of the 3.35 million Jews who resided in Poland in 1939, approximately 369,000 survived, about 11%. The largest group consisted of those who escaped or were incorporated into the Soviet Union. (...) During the years 1945-1946, close to 200,000 Jews crossed over from the Soviet Union to Poland. The remainder (approximately 170,000 note E.K.) survived within Poland, hiding in barns, cellars, and in attics, under false names or in the care of peasants."[343]

In order to evaluate the breadth of Jews being saved by Poles, it is crucial to be conscious of the fact that due to the stance of Polish Jews when it came to seeking out help beyond the walls of the ghettos and autonomies, the numbers of rescued Jews in Poland cannot be juxtaposed to the number of Jews living in Poland. Instead, it must be compared to the number of Polish Jews who, through abandoning their faith in German and Jewish ordinances, and later in abandoning the ghettos and trusting Poles, had undertaken to save their own lives, thus affording Poles the opportunity to save their lives. Just on principle alone, Poles were not in a position to save the lives of Polish Jews against their will.

We do not have exact numbers with regard to Jews rescued in Poland at our disposal. We will also never have the opportunity to know exactly how many Polish Jews abandoned the ghetto and sought help among Poles. However, if we were to take the rough estimates, that is the average of rescued Jews at 40-170-thousand, and the average of those seeking rescue at 170-335-thousand, then it turns out that of the 202.5-thousand Polish Jews who sought rescue among Poles, 105-thousand survived – more than half.

If an estimated simulation of this sort were to be performed using the worst case scenario possible, that of the 335-thousand Polish Jews who sought rescue among Poles, only 40-thousand survived, then it turns out that Poles had saved the lives of every tenth Polish Jew, which is 10% from

343 Bartoszewski W, Lewinowna Z., *Ten jest z ojczyzny mojej* [*How Poles Helped the Jews, 1939-1945*], Kraków 1969, p. 9; Davies N., *Boże igrzysko* [*God's playground*], Kraków 2003, p. 744. See also: F. Friedman, *Thy Brothers Keepers*, New York 1959; K. Iranek-Osmecki, He *Who Saves One Life*, New York 1971; Nechama Tec, *When Light Pierced the Darkness: Christian Rescue of Jews in Nazi-Occupied 1939-1944*, New York 1986; Richard C. Lucas, *Out of the Inferno: Poles Remember the Holocaust*, Lexington 1989.

among those seeking help. In order to achieve a more accurate estimate of the breadth of Polish rescue efforts, it would be worth fusing the above statistics with the fact that from among 250-thousand Polish Jews residing within the borders of the Jewish autonomy (the Jewish Nation), in Lodz, Chaim Rumkowski was capable of rescuing a mere 887 individuals, about 0.35% of the Jewish Nation.

According to Norman Davies, at the end of the Second World War, there were 24-million Poles living in Poland. If we take into consideration the fact that one-third of the population were children, and that as far as the rescue of Jews was concerned, the sheer nature of this endeavor implies that, with very few exceptions, only adults were able to engage in it, then it took approximately 10 Poles to be involved in the rescue of one Jew. Therefore, it turns out that roughly 400-thousand to 1.7-million Poles, out of the 16-million adults, were involved in the rescue of some 40-thousand to 169-thousand Jews. Every single one of those Poles was putting their own life, as well as the lives of their families, in danger for Polish Jews. Many among them had lost their lives for Jews.

The involvement of a greater portion of the adult Polish population in the rescue of Jews, despite the threat of losing one's life, does not carry the same weight as the statement that Poles as a nation were in solidarity with the nation of Polish Jews being murdered. Czesław Milosz dedicated his poem, "Campo di Fiori", to the merry-go-round which stood at the wall of the burning Warsaw ghetto where Poles, at the sound of merry music churning, engage in playful delight.

Let us not fear the truth.

The merry-go-round at the wall of the Warsaw ghetto did indeed go round and round. Let us, however, disregard these people who surrendered to the delights being offered at the sound of merry music churning despite the fact that just beyond the wall, just a short distance away, other people were being killed. For Jews inside the ghettos between the years of 1939-1942 hardly expressed their mourning outwardly, nor did they interrupt their concert-goings or close down theatres, or shut down restaurants or run to the Poles for help only because the Germans annihilated them in round-ups, executions and placed them in concentration camps.

The Polish merry-go-round in the poem by Czesław Miłosz serves simply as a symbol. The truth of the matter is such that, irregardless of the number of Jews rescued by Poles, the Polish "merry-go-round of chronicles of the ages" pertaining to the years of the Second World War continued to orbit its Polish path, while the Jewish "merry-go-round of chronicles of the ages" continued to orbit its Jewish path. As for the "Polish merry-go-round" and the "Jewish merry-go-round" of the last World War, there was very little room for solidarity between the two. During the time of the German genocide of Jews, Poles were preoccupied with their own matters. The wartime Polish carousel, understood to be a series of national interests which wound up in 1939 on the ruins of the Polish State, continued to rotate according to its own rules and canons. Meanwhile, inside the Jewish autonomies (the ghettos), there was a wartime Jewish national carousel in motion. There was no understanding, cooperation or communication between the two. The lack of solidarity under extreme circumstances had been consecrated by the centuries-old tradition of norms pertaining to Polish-Jewish relations.

Of course it is possible to ask the question why Poles and Jews during WWII did not simply dismiss the mutual lack of solidarity. It is possible to conjecture that this certainly would have happened even if both sides, at that time, possessed the knowledge we do today. If only they had known how all of this would end. Meanwhile, Marek Edelman, whose words it is impossible not to believe, claims the following:

In 1939, no one could have imagined that three-and-a-half-million Jews would be slaughtered in Poland. After all, up until 1939 there hadn't been any mass murders, that they would gas everyone. And once everyone had heard they were gassing people, everybody laughed and said: "What are they talking about?" But no one in their right mind, not on this [Jewish] side or that [Polish] side, ever would have thought that the 500-thousand people who lived in Warsaw would be murdered. This was not even a consideration, despite the fact that Hitler had written about it in Mein Kampf.[344]

In a word, the imaginations of Poles and Jews, up until the time of

---

344 Marek Edelman, in: Grupińska A., *"Ciągle po kole"* ["Still Round the Circle: Talks with the Soldiers of the Warsaw Ghetto"], Warszawa 2005, p. 26-27.

the Second World War, did expand far enough to reach the gas chambers or the scale of such a horrific and extensive genocide. Both peoples, who had resided alongside one another and had survived nearly a thousand years together without the necessity of any form of solidarity, assumed that things would transpire no differently than they had up until then. Meanwhile, in the third year of the war, in 1942, things turned out differently, and the Germans had decided to murder all Polish Jews, and the only people the Polish Jews could turn to were the Poles – the very same Poles with whom Jews had not been obliged to be in solidarity over the centuries. Jews had placed themselves in the face of an immense dilemma: should we seek help among those to whom we feel no sense of solidarity, and should we ask that they sacrifice their lives for us? Poles were standing in the face of an even more complex dilemma: should we demonstrate our solidarity to those who never showed their solidarity to us, and should we risk our lives for them?

Not many Polish Jews had found the "courage" to turn to Poles for help. Not many Poles found it in themselves to risk their own lives and the lives of their families in order to rescue Jews in the name of solidarity among human beings. "Those who rescued Jews," as Michael C. Steinlauf has written, "emerged from all layers of society; the one characteristic they all shared in common was, no doubt, 'individuality'. This rare characteristic allowed them not only to confront Nazi terrorism head-on, but also to go against the grain of indifference and animosity that manifested itself among a greater portion of the population. It allowed them to see Jews as human beings in need of help regardless of historical biases. It was not simply a matter of not informing against or not showing indifference to Jews, but rather it was the mere existence of such individuals that illustrated the most outstanding characteristic of Polish-Jewish relations during the time of the Holocaust."[345]

Those Poles who did rescue Polish Jews, regardless of what the final

[345] Steinlauf M. C., *Pamięć nieprzyswojona* [*Unassimilated memory*], Warszawa 2001, p. 54. See also: Nechama Tec, *When Light Pierced the Darkness: Christian Rescue of Jews in Nazi-Occupied 1939-1944*, New York 1986; Samuel P. Oliner, Pearl M. Oliner, *The Altruistic Personality*, New York 1988.

numbers indicate, do not alter the reality that: Jews during the Second World War had found themselves beyond the limits of Polish solidarity.

From among the four types of guilt with regard to the genocide of Polish Jews that have been identified by Karl Jaspers, **Poles are exempt of political guilt**, as neither the Polish Underground State or any other Polish institutional structure, nor Poles as a nation, had participated in the political decision-making process connected to the rise of Hitler, the invasion of Poland by Germany, the occupation of Polish lands or the genocide of Jews. There is no doubt, however, that Poles, and Germans, and Jews are equally culpable as far as the three remaining categories of guilt are concerned:

- **criminal guilt**: all Poles whose crimes were based upon actions objectively stated as being outside the unequivocal laws (the blackmailers; imposing death to Jews; giving up Jewish hideouts to the Germans, etc.) are subject to criminal guilt;

- **moral guilt**: all Poles who committed acts against Jews as individuals are subject to moral guilt; Poles are not excused under the umbrella of "I was just following orders" (for example, neither the dark-blue police nor the peasants participating in round-ups had any right to disclose the locations of Jewish hideouts or to murder captured Jews despite having received orders to the effect from the Germans); a crime remains a crime even if committed under an order and is subject to moral judgment;

- **metaphysical guilt**: the higher powers of God are present herewith, for there does exist a solidarity among men as human beings, on whose might every individual is subject to bear a shared responsibility for every evil and injustice.

CONCLUSION

The chief principle of the methodology of history says that if one puts new questions to old and well known sources, one may acquire new and often surprising answers. This method has proven applicable especially in the case of the World War Two Jewish sources that have been analyzed from the point of view of the Polish-Jewish relations. One of the most interesting answers has been given to the question as to what the ghettos created on Polish lands were during the Second World War politically and administratively. The question has been posed to the most reliable Jewish sources.

The Diaries written by Adam Czerniakow from September 6th 1939 to July 23rd 1942 explicitly show that the Jewish districts (especially in Warsaw and Lodz) – in historiography called the 'ghettos' – were in fact *autonomous provinces* built in 1939-1942 by the Polish Jews cooperating with the German occupants of Poland. The idea of the *autonomous provinces* had been put forward in the Constitutional Council in 1920 by deputy Grünbaum on behalf of the Jewish Deputy Assembly.

In the light of the above information, which has been confirmed by other equally trustworthy Jewish sources, the cooperation of the Jewish authorities (chairmen of the Judenrats, the Superiors of the Elders, 'kings', 'princes', mayors and their clerks, police etc.) with the Germans in the period preceding the Extermination becomes comprehensible. One can also understand the Jews' attitude to setting the borders of the *autonomies* as well as the confidence of the Jewish administration in the 'displacement' which actually meant programmatic genocide.

Having in mind that the Jewish *autonomous provinces* had been created as a result of particular political guidelines that required compromise with the Germans (and were not a form of repression towards the Polish Jewry), a number of so far incomprehensible issues concerning the extermination of the Polish Jews become more and more clear and obvious. First of all, Hanna Arendt's message saying that '…the Jewish officials who cooperated with the executors of the "Final solution" (…) cannot be considered as traitors. (…) In other words, all that the Jewish officials did, or did not do, until 1939 or even 1941, can be justified.'

Until 1941, the activity of the Jewish officials, who cannot be called traitors, can be justified by the fact that in spite of their brutality, ruthlessness and cooperation with the Germans, their lofty political aim was to build on Polish lands Jewish autonomies, which would survive the German occupation and become independent centers of Jewish life.

The year 1941, which was mentioned by Hanna Arendt, is the year when - according to Adam Czerniakow - the construction of the Jewish *autonomous provinces* in Warsaw and probably in other parts of Poland had been finished. Until that year, therefore, the actions of the Jewish functionaries could be justified by the Jewish people. Also, the suicide of Adam Czerniakow can be understood. Having realized that the policy he had been pursuing - the cooperation with the Germans and the creation of the *autonomous provinces* - had turned out to be a horrendous political mistake and that the Germans intended to murder the Jewish nation with the hands of the Jews themselves, he preferred honorable death to the role of an executioner of his own people. It seems that, over forty years ago, Hanna Arendt understood, or was very close to understanding, that the ghettos built in Poland during the Second World War were not imposed by the Germans, but were the *autonomous provinces* built by the Polish Jews with the permission of the Germans.

Thus, from the point of view of the Jews, the *autonomous provinces* that had been built on the Polish lands in 1939-1941 were not an act of treason. Rather, the *autonomous provinces* were the evidence of the political maturity of the Jewish leaders who chose for their nation an optimal form of survival of the war. It was for the first time in the last two thousand years that the Jews had constructed the foundations of the Jewish statehood which the world and - most of all Poland - would have to respect.

Information included in Adam Czerniakow's *Diaries* about the Jewish *autonomous province* in Warsaw enables us to perceive the Jewish minority in a different way than before. In 1939, the Jews proved to be an ethnic group that was fully shaped both in a national and a political sense and able to pursue an independent policy of compromise and victory. Were it not for Hitler's unforeseeable plans to kill all the European Jews, such a policy would have to be judged positively. All in all, Polish Jews managed to obtain from the Germans much more than did Ukrainians and Byelorussians despite similar cooperation.

With regard to the above remarks, Israeli historians should perhaps verify critical judgments about the attitude of the Polish Jews during the Second World War. Polish Jews were not *sabonim* (soap) but the founders of the *Jewish autonomous provinces in Poland*, which were a transitional form between the Diaspora and the State of Israel. If we consider the enormous political, social and military input of the Polish Jews rescued from the extermination in the creation of Israel in 1948, we must agree that it was possible thanks to the experiences of the Jewish autonomous self-government in Poland during 1939-1942.

However, Polish and Jewish points of view must be explicitly distinguished. The Poles have always perceived the Jews' cooperation with the Germans in 1939 and the creation of the *autonomous provinces* as treason against the Polish State. It has to be said that we Poles have a full right to such judgments. The Polish Jews were the citizens of Poland and by collaborating with the Germans in order to gain advantages for their nation they broke the basic principles of the agreement between the citizen and a democratic state.

The fact that the ghettos built on Polish lands were actually the Jewish *autonomous provinces* makes us look from a different angle at the extermination of the Polish Jews in 1942-1945 and at Jews' and Poles' collaboration with the Germans – the initiators and main executors of the genocide:

- **Poles' cooperation with the Germans was individual:** blackmailers and pursuers of the hiding Jews represented neither the Polish Underground State nor the Catholic Church; on the contrary: these institutions condemned and punished such deeds;
- **The cooperation of Polish Jews with the Germans, who intended to exterminate the Jewish nation, was institutional:** with few exceptions (e.g. Adam Czerniakow), it had been conducted with the permission and at the command of the Jewish functionaries of the *autonomous provinces* in Poland.

Institutional or individual, the Polish and Jewish cooperation with the Germans in the extermination meant the death of innocent Jews. The responsibility for this death must be equal for Poles and for Jews and must be measured according to the same criteria. What is more, the criteria should be identical to those formulated by Karl Jaspers (quoted at the beginning of the book) to be applied to the German nation. Only by treating everyone alike can historians answer the question about the quantitative, temporal and spatial responsibility of the Germans, the Poles and the Jews for the extermination of the Jewish nation. The same criteria of judgment should also apply to all other European nations that collaborated with the Germans in any way in the extermination: the French, the Italians, the Estonians, the Swiss, the Ukrainians etc. Unified research would result in a map of the deficiency of human solidarity. Such a map could be a difficult heritage for the Europeans to carry.

There is still the question of the complicated Polish-Jewish relations in 1939-1945. From the political point of view, the ways of the Poles and the Polish Jews separated in the Fall of 1939. The Poles chose the struggle against the Germans and created secret Polish Underground State. The Polish Jews chose the cooperation with the Germans and built on the Polish lands the Jewish *autonomous provinces*. There was no contact between the two forms of statehood. That was the reason why in 1942 the *autonomous provinces* remained beyond the border of solidarity of the Poles. Similarly, in 1939-1945, Polish Underground State remained beyond the border of solidarity of the Jews.

The Polish-Jewish relations became particularly significant in the years of extermination (1942-1945), when the Poles turned out to be the only ones who could rescue Polish Jews successively murdered by the Germans. However, for saving the Jews, Poles were punished with death.

The Polish-Jewish relations in the time of the extermination were extremely complicated from the psychological and moral points of view. The relativism that had been permeating the evaluation of these relations for sixty years lead to the number of misunderstandings, the most serious of which was accusing the Poles of indifference and not rescuing the Jews actively enough. That is why it is exceptionally important that we decide according to what criteria – the Christian or the Jewish ones - the attitudes of the Poles and the Jews should be judged.

Karl Jaspers defined the Christian criteria in the following way: 'Between human beings there is solidarity that makes every man share the responsibility for all evil and injustice on earth, especially for the crimes committed in his presence or that he knows about. If I do not do all I can to prevent them, I am jointly responsible.' If we apply these criteria to the Polish people, individual Poles are guilty of participation in crime and the Polish nation is responsible for *not doing all they could to prevent* the genocide. In the case of Poland, where the Germans punished with death anyone who tried to save a Jew, *doing all one could* meant giving one's life for the person rescued. Many Poles sacrificed their lives to save their brothers in humanity – Polish Jews.

However, if we apply the same, Christian, criteria to the attitudes of the Polish Jews, we must admit that not only did they not do *everything they could* to prevent the genocide, but – through political mistakes, lack of solidarity with their own nation and unconditional obedience to German orders – they did more than enough to enable the Germans to commit the cruel crime on the Jewish nation.

As far as the Jewish criteria are concerned, they are based on the Jewish tradition and religion. According to them, cooperation with the Germans in the murder of the Jewish nation and service in Nazi military forces were justifiable since the Jews enjoyed an unlimited right and duty to save their lives from immediate death (Kiddush ha-chajim), even at the cost of the lives of other people.

Applying the Jewish criteria – including *Kiddush ha-chajim* - to the attitudes of Poles, it appears that they, Poles, had no right to risk their own lives and save the lives of the Jews because such action was contradictory with the duty to rescue their own Polish lives.

In the light of the Jewish rights and tradition, the Jews certainly have no right to accuse the Poles of scarifying too few Polish people to save the Jews. On condition that in the Jewish religion and tradition the value of a human life does not depend on the nationality of a person.

Christian or Jewish, the criteria for evaluating Polish-Jewish relations in 1939-1945 prove to be extremely complicated and little known; also the research presented in my book is definitely incomplete. Nevertheless, it is certain that Polish-Jewish relations in 1939-1945 lacked simple human solidarity – from both sides.

The total lack of human solidarity in the Polish-Jewish relations in the World War Two was accompanied by the lack of the world's solidarity towards the extermination of the Polish Jews. Icchak Kacenelson said:

'And so we were murdered from Greece to Norway, and everywhere as far as Moscow – around seven million people, excluding Jewish children in the wombs, including their pregnant, would-be mothers. The world did not help them.'[346]

The words of the Jewish poet were extended sixty years later by Władysław Bartoszewski who said in Auschwitz:

'The creation of gas chambers and crematories and their efficiency are only elements of that devilish undertaking. The center of the extermination of the hated Jews had been built in Poland by a decision of Berlin (…). While Poles and Russians in Auschwitz-Birkenau were regarded by the Germans as sub-humans, the Jews from France, Belgium, Holland, Germany and Austria, Greece, Hungary, Romania, Bulgaria, the Czech Republic, Slovakia and the then Yugoslavia were for the Germans not even sub-humans but vermin. Polish underground resistance movement informed and alarmed the free world. As a

---

[346] Kacenelson I., Piesn o zamordowanym zydowskim narodzie, *[The Song about Murdered Jewish Nation]*, Warsaw 1982, p. 89.

result of the Polish emissary Jan Karski's mission, in the last quarter of 1942 the governments of Great Britain and the United States realized what was happening in Auschwitz-Birkenau. The information reached them also by other channels. Nonetheless, no country in the world reacted adequately to the weight of the problem when on December 10, 1942 the minister of Foreign Affairs of the Polish Government in London sent the United Nations a note. The note urged not only to condemn the crimes committed by the Germans and to punish the criminals but also to find means to render further massive murder impossible.[347]

The research on the Polish-Jewish relations in the Second World War and re-reading reliable Jewish historic sources display a number of so far unknown aspects of Polish and Jewish common history – from the mutual stereotypes rooted deeply in the Middle Ages to the evaluation of Polish and Jewish attitudes in the times of the Extermination. I do not consider any of these aspects as eventually settled. Still, the aim of my research will be reached as soon as it **suggests** young historians the **directions of** further **research** and inspires Poles and Jews to look in a new way at the centuries of living together on the Polish lands and at the dramatic end of the world of the Polish Jews.

In my book, I was not afraid of calling a spade a spade. I have called treason a treason, crime a crime; I did not fear to call antipolonism what was antipolonism, anti-Semitism what was anti-Semitism; the relativism of historical judgments has been called relativism. Such an open perception of problems may provoke the Polish reader to accuse me of antipolonism and the Jewish one to accuse me of anti-Semitism. It cannot be helped. Because of my respect for the Jews and for my own nation I have made no allowances for either side.

---

[347] W. Bartoszewski, *A wolny świat nie reagował (The Independent World did not React),* przemówienie wygłoszone w 60 rocznicę wyzwolenia Auschwitz (The address on the 60 anniversary of the liberation of Auschwitz); in: „Gazeta Wyborcza", Warsaw, January 28, 2005.

BIBLIOGRAPHY

I. SOURCES

1. Archival Sources

The Archives of the GKBZH in Warsaw:

Biuletyn Informacyjny 1941-1944 ("Information Bulletin" of the Polish Underground State

The Archives of the Jewish Historical Institute in Warsaw:1941-1944

Dziennik rozporządzen dla Generalnego Gubernatorstwa 1941 (The Journal of Regulations for the General Government 1941).

„Gazeta Żydowska" 1940-1942, (The Jewish Newspaper in Warsaw Ghetto 1940-1942).

„Hajnt", no. 177, October 4, 1918, p. 3; *Zasady naszego programu politycznego* "The principles of our political program"], Warszawa 1917.

Materiały w sprawie żydowskiej w Polsce ("Materials regarding the Jewish issue in Poland"), ed. I. Grünbaum, vol. I, Warszawa 1919, p. 6-7; „Hajnt", no. 198, October 27, 1918.

Organizacja Syjonistyczna w Królestwie Polskim w sprawie narodowego i politycznego uprawnienia Żydów ("The Zionist Organisation in the Kingdom of Poland regarding national and political rights of Jews"), Warszawa 1918.

Poster in Polish, Ukrainian and German, Archives of the Jewish Historical Institute in Warsaw, Nr 123. See also the posters Nr 147, 62a and 14.

Poster in Polish, Ukrainian and German, Archives of the GKBZH in Warsaw, Portfolio 75/24.

The Archives of the Polish Parliament in Warsaw:

Druki sejmowe: Sejm Ustawodawczy – Komisja Konstytucyjna 1920, ("The Polish Parlaiment Prints: The Legislative Parliament – The Polish Constitutional Committee 1920"), print No 1883.

European Parliament Resolution on Remembrance of the Holocaust, anti-Semitism and racism," January 27, 2005.

Sprawozdania stenograficzne Sejmu Ustawodawczego (Stenographic reports from the Legislative Polish Parliament), pos. 37, May 13, 1919, l. 5-6.

Sprawozdania stenograficzne Sejmu Ustawodawczego (Stenographic reports from the Legislative Polish Parliament), pos. 185, November 16, 1920, l. 37.

Sprawozdania stenograficzne Sejmu Ustawodawczego (Stenographic reports from the Legislative Sejm), pos. 185, November 16, 1920, ł. 59.

Sprawozdania stenograficzne Sejmu Ustawodawczego (Stenographic reports from the Legislative Polish Parliament), pos. 37, May 13, 1919, l. 66.

<u>The Archive of ZHP in Warsaw</u>:

„Prawda" ("The Truth" – The Polish Underground Bulletin), 1943.

2. Accounts, Memoirs and other Sources

Augustine St., *Wyznania* ("Confessions"), Kraków 2003.

Bartoszewski W., The TVN Fakty news, on September 16, 2003.

Bartoszewski W., *Warto być przyzwoitym* ("It is worthwhile being decent"), Editions Spotkania, Paris 1986.

Blatt T., *Z popiołów Sobiboru, (From the Ashes of Sobibor)*, Chelm 2002.

Cherezińska E., *Byłam sekretarką Rumkowskiego – Dzienniki Etki Daum* (I was Rumkowski's secretary. The diaries of Etka Daum"), Warsaa 2008.

Czerniakow A., *Dziennik getta warszawskiego 6.IX.1939 – 23. VII 1942*, Warsaw 1983; see also: Hilberg , "Warsaw Diary of Adam Czerniakow – Prelude to Doom", Ivan R. Dee Publisher,1998.

Czerniakow A., *Udział Żydów w odbudowie zniszczeń wojennych w Polsce* ("The Jews' participation in rebuilding the war damages in Poland"), in: "Głos Gminy Żydowskiej", Nr 10-11, Warsaw 1938.

Dobraczynski J., the relation in: E. Kurek, *Dzieci zydowskie w klasztorach (The Jewish Childern in the Polish Convents]*, Lublin 2001.

Edelman M, the relation in: Grupińska A., *"Ciągle po kole"* ("Still Round the Circle: Talks with the Soldiers of the Warsaw Ghetto"), Warszawa 2005.

Glajtman-Putermilch M., the realtion in: Grupińska A., *"Ciągle po kole"* ("Still Round the Circle: Talks with the Soldiers of the Warsaw Ghetto"), Warszawa 2005.

Grupińska A., *Ciągle po kole* ("Still Round the Circle: Talks with the Soldiers of the Warsaw Ghetto"), Warsaw 2005.

Harasimowicz H., the relation from the collection of E. Kurek.

Hurwitz L., *Pamiętnik z getta* ("The Memoirs from the Ghetto"], in: *Kronika getta lodzkiego* ("The Diary of the Lodz Ghetto"), Lodz 1965.

Kacenelson I., Piesn o zamordowanym zydowskim narodzie, *(Song of the Murdered Jewish Nation)*, Warsaw 1982.

Kahane D., the relation of the rabbi in: E. Kurek, *Your Life is Worth Mine: How Polish Nuns Saved Hundreds of Jewish Children in German-Occupied Poland, 1939-1945,* Hippocrene Books, NY, 1997, p. 213-217.

Kestenberg M., the relation in: E. Kurek, *Podajmy sobie ręce (Let us shake hands),* "Nowy Dziennik", New York, July 25, 1987.

Karski J., *Tajne panstwo* ("The Underground State"], Warszawa 1999.

Kodeks dyplomatyczny Tyniecki (The Diplomatic Code of Tyniec), Wyd. Smolka i Kętrzyński.

Kodeks Wielkopolski (The Wielkopolska Code)

Kotkowski I., *Wyroki losu,* Lublin 1997. See also: Y. Kotkowski, *The Wills of Destiny,* Texas 1991.

Kowalska I., Merżan I., *Rottenbergowie znad Buga* ("The Rottenbergs of the Bug River"), Warsaw 1989.

Kronika getta łódzkiego, ("The Lodz Ghetto Diary"), preface and notes by D.Dąbrowska and L. Dobroszycki, Lodz 1965.

Landau L. *Kronika lat wojny i okupacji* ("The Diary of the war and occupation"), Warsaw 1973.

Ligocka R., the relation in: "Wprost", Warsaw, February 6, 2005.

Lis Luba, the relation in: Kurek E., *Your Life is Worth Mine: How Polish Nuns Saved Hundreds of Jewish Children in German-Occupied Poland, 1939-1945,* by Ewa Kurek, Hippocrene Books, NY, 1997; Kurek E., The documentary film: He *Who Saved one Life Saved the World,* The Polish Television chanel 2, Warsaw 1998; Kurek E., *Dzieci zydowskie w klasztorach,* Lublin 2001.

Makower H., *Pamiętnik z getta warszawskiego* („The Memoirs from Warsaw Ghetto"), Wroclaw 1987.

Marianowicz A., *Życie surowo wzbronione* ("Life Strictly Forbidden"), Warsaw 1995.

Meloch K. [Irena], the relation in: Cezary Gawrys, *Turkowice – smierc i ocalenie (Turkowice – the Death and Rescue"), in „Wiez", Year 1987, No 4.*

Mickiewicz A., *Pan Tadeusz,* (The full title in English: "Mister Thaddeus, or the Last Foray in Lithuania: a History of the Nobility in the Years 1811 and 1812 in Twelve Books of Verse") Wrocław 1973.

Nussbaum H., *Przewodnik Judaistyczny obejmujący kurs literatury i religii* ("A Judaic guide including the course of literature and religion"), Warszawa 1893.

Olczak-Ronikier J., *W ogrodzie pamięci* („In the garden of memory"), Krakow 2002.

Polska w oczach Irlandczyków – Poland through Irish eyes, B. Wagner (ed.), Lublin 2001.

Romano I., the relation in: E. Kurek, *Your Life is Worth Mine: How Polish Nuns Saved Hundreds of Jewish Children in German-Occupied Poland, 1939-1945,* Hippocrene Books, NY, 1997, p. 191-197.

Rydel L., *Betlejem polskie ("Polish Bethlehem")*, Kraków 1983.

Sidorowska S., the relation from collection of E. Kurek.

Szpilman W., *Pianista* ("The Pianist"), Krakow 2003.

*Ścieżki pamieci ("*The path of recollection"), ed. by Jerzy Bojarski, Lublin 2002.

Weiss S., *Burzył mury milczenia (He destroyed the walls of silence)*, Israeli ambassador to Poland, in an interview with Dorota Kosierkiewicz, in: 'Echo dnia', December 22, 2003.

Ringelblum E., *Kronika getta warszawskiego wrzesień 1939 – styczeń 1943*, Warsaw 1983; see also: "Notes from the Warsaw Ghetto by Emmanuel Ringelblum", paperback, Ibooks Inc., 2006.

Sokolnicki M., Wspomnienia ("The Memoire"), quote from : Olczak-Ronikier J., *W ogrodzie pamięci* („In the garden of memory"], Krakow 2002.

Wnuk S., the relation in: "Zaporczycy – Relacje" (Talks with the Soldiers of the "Zapora" partisan's division), Volumen I, Lublin 1997.

Zięba J., *Znad Stochodu* ("From the Stochod River"), Lublin 2001.

Żeromski S., *Przedwiośnie* („Early Spring"], Warszawa 1978.

II. SCIENTIFIC DESCRIPTIONS, CRITICAL ANALYSIS, ELABORATIONS, ESSAYS

A history of Polish Jewry during the Revival of Poland, New York 1991.

Arendt H., *Eichmann w Jerozolimie*, Kraków1987; see also: Arendt H., "Eichmann in Jerusalem: A Report on the Banality of Evil", New York 1963.

Apfelbaum M., *Dwa sztandary („The Two Flags")*, Krakow 2003.

Arczynski M., W. Balcerak, *Kryptonim Zegota (The codename of Żegota)*, Warsaw 1983.

Bałaban M., *Dzieje Żydów w Galicji i w Rzeczypospolitej Krakowskiej 1772-1868* („A history of Jews of Galicia and the Republic of Kraków 1772-1868"), Warszawa 1912.

Bałaban M., *Dzieje Żydów w Krakowie i na Kazimierzu 1304-186* ("A History of Jews in Kraków and in the Kazimierz District 1304-1868"), Kraków 1912.

Bartoszewski W., *A wolny świat nie reagował [The Independent World did not React]*, przemówienie wygłoszone w 60 rocznicę wyzwolenia Auschwitz (The address on the 60 anniversary of Auschwitz liberation]; in: „Gazeta Wyborcza"), Warsaw, January 28, 2005.

Bartoszewski W., *1,859 dni Warszawy* (Warsaw's 1,859 days), Kraków 1974.

Bartoszewski W, Lewinowna Z., *Ten jest z ojczyzny mojej* (He is my of country *How Poles Helped the Jews, 1939-1945*), Kraków 1969.

Bendowska M., *Swieta i posty judaizmu*, ("The Holidays and Fasts of Jews"), in: "Kalendarz Zydowski 1984/85" (The Jewish Calendar 1984/85), Warsaw 1984.

Błoński J., *Biedni Polacy patrzą na getto* („Poor Poles Look at the Ghetto"), Kraków, 1994.

Brzezinski F., *Prawa mniejszości. Komentarz do traktatu z dn. 28 czerwca 1919 r. pomiędzy Polską a Głownemi Mocarstwami* [*The rights of minorities. A commentary on the treaty between Poland and Major Powers (June 28, 1919)*], in: 'Przegląd Dyplomatyczny', No. 5 (1920).

Burnetko K., *Getto: od azylu do Zagłady* („The Ghetto: from asylum to Extermination"), in: „Historia Żydów: trzy tysiąclecia samotności", Wydanie specjalne „Polityki", Nr 1/2008.

Davies N., *Boże igrzysko* ("God's Playground"), Kraków 2003.

Dawidowicz L., *La guerre contre les Juifs 1933-1945*, Paris 1977.

Delaruelle E., *Wpływ świętego Franciszka na religijność ludową* ("The influence of St. Francis of Assisi on folk religion"), in: "W drodze", No 10, Poznań 1976.

Dvornik N.G.M., *Franciszek z Asyżu – prorok naszych czasów* ("St. Francis of Assisi – the prophet of our times"), Warsaw 1981.

Cała A., *Wizerunek Żyda w polskiej kulturze ludowej* ("The image of a Jew in Polish popular history"), Warszawa 1992.

Chodakiewicz M.J., *Recenzje* (Reviews), in: „Glaukopis", No 7/8, Warszawa 2007.

Chojnowski A., *Koncepcje polityki narodowościowej rządów polskich w latach 1921-1939* (*Ethnic Policy Concepts of Polish Governments 1921-1939*), Wrocaw-Warsaw-Krakow 1979.

Davies N., *Boże igrzysko* („God's playground"), Krakow 2003.

Datner Sz., *Las sprawiedliwych* („The Forest of the Just"], Warszawa 1968.

Dawidsohn J., *Gminy żydowskie* („The Jewish communities"], Warszawa 1931.

Dobroszycki L., *Preface* to: *Kronika getta łódzkiego*, ("The Lodz Ghetto Diary"), Lodz 1965.

Eisenbach A., *Preface* to: *"Kronika getta warszawskiego wrzesień 1939 – styczeń 1943"* ("Notes from the Warsaw Ghetto, September 1939 - January 1043), Warsaw 1983.

Eisenbach A., *Emancypacja Zydów na ziemiach polskich 1785-1870* („Emancipation of Jews on Polish lands 1785-1870"), Warszawa 1988.

Eisner J. P., *Nadać sens śmierci* [„To Give a Sens for the Death"], in: „Wprost", Warsaw, June 8, 2003.

Eksterminacja Żydów na ziemiach polskich w okresie okupacji hitlerowskiej - zbiór dokumentów, ("Extermination of Jews under the German occupation of Poland – document collection" Jewish Historical Institute), Warszawa 1957.

Encyclopedia Judaica, Jerusalem 1972.

Encyclopedia Judaica – Das Judentum in Geschichte und Gegenwart, Berlin 1927.

Friedman F., *Thy Brothers Keeper*, New York 1959.

Fuks M., *Preface* to: *Dziennik getta warszawskiego 6.IX.1939–23. VII 1942*, ("Warsaw Diary of Adam Czerniakow – Prelude to Doom"), Warsaw 1983.

Gerson L., *Woodrow Wilson and the rebirth of Poland 1914-1920*, New Haven 1953.

Getter N., Schalla J., Z. Schipper, *Żydzi bojownicy o niepodległość Polski* ("Jewish fighters for Poland's independence), Lwów 1939.

Goldberg-Mulkiewicz O., *Postać Żyda w teatrze obrzędowym okresu Bożego Narodzenia* ("The character of a Jew in the ceremonial theater of the Christmas period"), in: „Zeszyty Naukowe Uniwersytetu Jagiellońskiego–Prace etnograficzne", Kraków 1996.

Grodziski S., *W królestwie Galicji i Lodomerii* („In the kingdom of Galicia and Lodomeria"), Kraków 1976.

Gutman Y., *Odwaga zbrodni,* ("The Courage of Crime") in: Gazeta Wyborcza, Warsaw, February 10, 2001.

Gutman Y., *Polish Antisemitism Betwen the Wars: An Overview,* in: Y. Gutman, E. Mendelsohn, J. Reinharz, Ch. Schmeruk (ed.), "The Jews of Poland Between two World Wars", Brandeis University Press, Hanover 1989.

Gutman Y., *Polish and Jewish historiography on the question of Polish-Jewish relations during World War II,* in: "The Jews in Poland. Polish-Jewish Studies", Oxford 1986.

Gutman Y,. *Zydzi warszawscy 1939-1943* ("The Jews of Warsaw 1939-1943"], Warsaw 1993.

Heck R., *Polska w dziejach politycznych Europy* („Poland in the political history of Europe"), in: 'Polska dzielnicowa i zjednoczona' (Poland fragmented and united), Warsaw 1972.

Hertz A., *Żydzi w kulturze polskiej* („Jews in Polish Culture"], Warszawa 1988.

Hoffman Z., *Berek Joselewicz,* w: Kalendarz żydowski 1984-1985 ("Berek Joselewicz", in: The Jewish Calendar 1984-1985), Warszawa 1984.

Iranek-Osmecki K., He *Who Saves One Life*, New York 1971.

Jaspers K., *Problem winy,* Warsaw 1982; see also: Jaspers K., "The Question of German Guilt" (paperback), Fordham University Press; 2 Rev. Ed. edition, January, 2001.

Jedroszczyk P., *Przekraczanie czerwonej linii (The crossing of red line),* in: „Rzeczpospolita", April 29, 2004.

Junosza K., *Cud na kirkucie – Z jednego strumienia* ("A miracle at the Jewish cementery – from one stream"), Warsaw 1960.

Katz J., *A State within a State, the History of Anti-Semitic Slogan,* in: 'Emancipation and Assimilation. Studies in Modern Jewish History', New York 1972.

Kitowicz J., *Opis obyczajów i zwyczajów za panowania Augusta III* ("The description of customs and habits in the times of August III"), Kraków 1925.

Korbonski F., *Fighting Warsaw: the Story of the Polish Underground State 1939-1945*, Londyn 1957.

Kurbis A., *Pisarze i czytelnicy* („Writers and readers"], in: „Polska dzielnicowa i zjednoczona" („Poland devided and united"), Warsaw 1972.

Kurek E., *Średniowieczny kult Dzieciątka Jezus jako inspiracja procesu dowartościowania dziecka* („The Medieval Cult of Baby Jesus as an inspiration of the process of raising the importance of a child"), in: „Summarium", Lublin 1979; see also: E. Kurek, *Średniowieczny kult Dzieciątka Jezus jako inspiracja procesu dowartościowania dziecka*, MA, Lublin 1979, Główna Biblioteka Katolickiego Uniwersytetu w Lublinie.

Kurek E., The documentary film: He *Who Saves one Life Saves all the World*, The Polish Television chanel 2, Warsaw 1998.

Kurek E., *Udział Żeńskich Zgromadzeń zakonnych w akcji ratowania dzieci żydowskich w Polsce 1939-1945 (Polish Convents and their contribution to the saving of Jewish children in Poland 1939-1945)*, in: Spotkania, 29, 1985.

Kurek E., *Your Life is Worth Mine: How Polish Nuns Saved Hundreds of Jewish Children in German-Occupied Poland, 1939-1945*, Hippocrene Books, New York, 1997.

Kurek E., *Zaporczycy w fotografii 1943-1963* („Zapora's soldiers from partisan division AK in photography 1943-1963"), Lublin 2009.

Kurek E., *Zaporczycy 1943-1949*, ("Zapora's soldiers from partisan division AK 1943-1949"), Lublin 1995.

Le Bon G., *Psychologia tłumu* („The Crowd Psychology"), Kęty 2004.

Lesik [Kurek] E., *Podajmy sobie ręce* („Let us shake hands"), in: Nowy Dziennik – Nowy Jork, June 25, 1987.

Lewański J., *Misterium* („Mystery Play"), in: „Średniowieczne gatunki dramatyczno-teatralne" („Medieval theatre genres"), Wrocław-Warszawa-Kraków 1969.

Lewański J., *Dramat staropolski* („Old Polish Drama"), Warsaw 1959.

Lucas R.C., *Out of the Inferno: Poles Remember the Holocaust*, Lexington 1989.

Mamatey V., *The United States and East Central Europe 1914-1920: a study in Wilsonian Diplomacy and Propaganda*, Princeton 1959.

Marcus J., *Social and Political History of the Jews in Poland 1919-1939*, Berlin-New York-Amsterdam 1983.

Mendelsohn E., *On modern Jewish Politics*, New York – Oxford 1993.

Mendelsohn E., *Zionism in Poland. The Formative Years, 1915-1926*, New Haven – London 1981.

Mendelsohn E., *Żydzi Europy Środkowo-Wschodniej w okresie międzywojennym* („Jews of East Central Europe in the period between the two World Wars"), Warsaw 1992.

Milchman A., Rosenberg A., *Eksperymenty w mysleniu o Holokauscie* („The Experiments in Thinking about the Holocaust"), Warsaw 2003.

Moczulski L., *Żywot z koszmarem w tle*, ("Life with a nightmare in the background"), in: „Gazeta Wyborcza", Warsaw, July 26-27, 2003.

Noaks J., *The Development of Nazi Policy towards the German-Jewish "Misschlinge" 1933-1945*, in: "Leo Baeck Yearbook", Nr 34, Year 1989.

Oliner S.P., Oliner P.M., *The Altruistic Personality*, New York 1988.

Partyka J. St., *Apokryfy w sztukach plastycznych* ("The Apocrypha in Fine Arts"), in: „Znak", No 275, Kraków 1977.

Paruch W., *Od konsolidacji państwowej do konsolidacji narodowej. Mniejszości narodowe w myśli politycznej obozu piłsudczykowskiego 1926-1939* („From state consolidation to national consolidation. Ethnic minorities in the thought of Piłsudski's followers' political camp 1926-1939"), Lublin 1997.

Powstanie II Rzeczpospolitej – Wybór dokumentów 1866-1925 („The Rise of the Polish State. The Selection of Documents 1866-1925"], ed. H. Janowska, T. Jędruszczak, Warszawa 1984.

Prekerowa T., *Konspiracyjna Rada Pomocy Zydom w Warszawie* ("The Underground General Council of Protection of Polish Jews in Warsaw"), Warsaw 1982.

Rigg B.M., *Żydowscy żołnierze Hitlera: nieznana historia nazistowskich ustaw rasowych i mężczyzn pochodzenia żydowskiego w armii niemieckiej*, Warszawa 2005. (*"Hitler's Jewish Soldiers: The Untold Story of Nazi Racial Laws and Men of Jewish Descent in the German Military"*, University Press of Kansas 2002).

Reszka P. P., Cywiński J., *Kurek: getta założyli Żydzi* [„Kurek: The ghettos were built by Jews"], in: „Gazeta Wyborcza" August 19/20, 2006.

Schipper I., *Geshikhte fun der yidisher teater-kunst un drama fun di eltste tsaytn bis 1750*, Warsaw 1923.

Schmeruk Ch., *The Esterke Story in Yiddish and Polish Literature*, Jerusalem 1985.

Sharf R., *Saints or madmen? – A meditation on Ephraim Osbry's – Response from the Holocaust*, in: "The Jewish Quarterly", London, January 1988.

Szmeruk Ch., *Majufes*, in: "The Jews in Poland" – Jagiellonian University Research Center on Jewish History and Culture in Poland, Kraków 1983.

Steinlauff M. C., *Mr Geldhab and Sambo in Peyes: images of the Jew on the Polish-Jewish Stage, 1863-1905*, in: "Polin – A Journal of Polish-Jewish Studies", Volumen IV, Year 1989.

Steinlauf M. C., *Pamięć nieprzyswojona* ("Unassimilated memory"), Warsaw 2001.

Stemplowska I., Stemplowski R., *Laicy czytają „Polin"*, w: „Śladami Polin – Studia z dziejów Żydów w Polsce (Laymen read „Polin", in: On the track of Polin – Studies in the Jewish history in Poland), Warszawa 2002.

Strzembosz T., *Rzeczpospolita podziemna* („Polish Underground State"), Warsaw 2000.

Szczęsna J., *Ostatni Mohikanie i nowy naród* ("The Last of the Mahicans and the New Nation"), in: "Gazeta Wyborcza", Warsaw, June 28/29, 2003.

Szlajfer H., *Polacy i Żydzi. Zderzenie stereotypow* ("Poles and Jews. The Crash of the stereotypes"), Warsaw 2003.

Szybieka Z., *Historia Białorusi 1795-2000* ("The History of Bielorussia"), Lublin 2002.

Tec N., *When Light Pierced the Darkness: Christian Rescue of Jews in Nazi-Occupied Poland 1939-1944*, New York 1986.

The Judaic Lexicon *(Słownik Judaistyczny)*, Warszawa 2003.

The New Standard Jewish Encyclopedia, New York 1977.

Tomaszewski J., *Mniejszości narodowe w Polsce XX wieku* („Ethnic minorities in the 20ᵗʰ century Poland"), Warsaw 1991.

Tomaszewski J., *Najnowsze dzieje Żydów w Polsce* („Modern history of Jews in Poland"), Warsaw 1993.

Tomaszewski J., *Ojczyzna nie tylko Polaków* („Not only Poles' Motherland"), Warsaw 1985.

Tomkiewiczowa A., Tomkiewicz W., *Dawna Polska w anegdocie* („Ancient Poland in anecdote"), Warszawa 1973.

Vidal-Naquet P., *Zbieram obelgi z różnych stron* („I receive insults from different sides"), in: 'Gazeta Wyborcza', 12-13 October, 2002.

Waldenberg M., *Kwestie narodowe w Europie Środkowo-Wschodniej. Dzieje. Idee.* ("Ethnic questions in East Central Europe. A history and ideas"), Warsaw 1992.

Wandycz P., *Pod zaborami: Ziemie Rzeczypospolitej w latach 1795-1918* („Under partitions: Polish lands 1795-1918"), Warsaw 1994.

Warszawski D., *Siła odrzuconych* ("The strenght of the rejected"), in: "Wprost", Warsaw, October 20, 2002.

Windakiewicz S., *Dramat liturgiczny w Polsce średniowiecznej* („Liturgical drama in medieval Poland") Kraków 1903.

Wróbel P., *Przed odzyskaniem niepodległości*, („Before regaining independence"), Warsaw 1993.

Wyrozumski J., *Kazimierz Wielki* (King Kazimierz the Great], Wroclaw 1986.

Zieleniewski L., *Zagadnienie mniejszości narodowych w Konstytucji Rzeczpospolitej* („The question of ethnic minorities in the Constitution of the Republic of Poland"), Warsaw 1935.

Żbikowski A., *Żydzi* („The Jews"), Wroclaw 1997.

Żyndul J., *Państwo w państwie? Autonomia narodowo-kulturalna w Europie Środkowo-Wschodniej w XX wieku* („A State within a State? National and cultural autonomy in East Central Europe in the 20ᵗʰ century"), Warsaw 2000.

My very special thanks for assistance given in helping
to have this book made available to all who want to know
the Polish-Jewish Relations during the years 1939-1945:

Danuta Wyszynski
Ava and Adam Bak
Paul Kochanski, Esq.
Maria Szonert-Binienda, Esq.
Irena Zapasnik, Andrew Dobranski

Ewa Kurek

THE LIST OF DONORS

American Polish Council
American Polonaise Society
Justyna and Jacek Ball
Don Banas
Maria S. Binienda
Edward Blicharski
Marion and Richard Brzozowski
Teresa Bunk
Bozena Checinska
Stefan Dekowski
Sofia Dembia
Bronislaw Dziadura
Bozenna and Richard Gilbride
Pat and John Gmerek
Anne and Julian Jurus
S.M. Kay
Patricia Kolodziejek
Al Koproski
Walter Korszun
Rev. Janusz Lipski
Wanda Lorenc
Grace Lozowski
Joseph Macielag

Augustyn Macios
Frank Milewski
Jane Mosiorowski
Kazimierz Nietupski
Polish Army Veterans Association
Irena and Leszek Puch
Maria and Kazik Rasiej
Blanka Rosenstiel
Ray Sikorski
Marek Sobczak
Stefan Szachacz
Alina Surmacka-Szczesniak
Irena Szewiola
Barbara Szydlowski
Michael Szynalski
Rev. Carl Urban
Dr. Aldona Wos
Wanda and Paul Wos and Friends
Wally West
Christine and Robert Wilson
K.C. Witchak
Jolanta Zamecka
Jan Zaufal

and many others...